D1797056

COMPARATIVE SOCIAL RESEARCH

Volume 16 • 1997

METHODOLOGICAL ISSUES IN COMPARATIVE SOCIAL SCIENCE

COMPARATIVE SOCIAL RESEARCH

METHODOLOGICAL ISSUES IN COMPARATIVE SOCIAL SCIENCE

Editors: LARS MJØSET
Department of Sociology
University of Oslo

FREDRIK ENGELSTAD
Institute for Social Research
Oslo, Norway

GRETE BROCHMANN
Institute for Social Research
Oslo, Norway

RAGNVALD KALLEBERG
Department of Sociology
University of Oslo

ARNLAUG LEIRA
Department of Sociology
University of Oslo

VOLUME 16 • 1997

 JAI PRESS INC.

Greenwich, Connecticut   *London, England*

Copyright © 1997 by JAI PRESS INC.
55 Old Post Road, No. 2
Greenwich, Connecticut 06836

JAI PRESS LTD.
38 Tavistock Street
Covent Garden
London WC2E 7PB
England

All rights reserved. No part of this publication may be reproduced, stored on a retrieval
system, or transmitted in any form or by any means, electronic, mechanical, photocopying,
recording, filming or otherwise without prior permission in writing from the publisher.

ISBN: 0-7623-0250-X

Manufactured in the United States of America

CONTENTS

LIST OF CONTRIBUTORS

Andrew Abbott	Department of Sociology University of Chicago
Dirk Berg-Schlosser	Philips Universität Marburg
Michael Braun	University of Mannheim
Gisèle De Meur	Université Libre Bruxelles
Jack A. Goldstone	Sociology Department University of California, Davis
John H. Goldthorpe	Nuffield College Oxford, England
Thomas Janoski	Sociology Department University of Kentucky
Karl Ulrich Mayer	European University Institute San Domenica di Fiesole, Italy
Christa McGill	Duke University
Walter Müller	University of Mannheim
Charles C. Ragin	Department of Sociology Northwestern University Evanston
Dietrich Rueschemeyer	Brown University
John D. Stephens	University of North Carolina Chapel Hill

Henry Teune   Department of Political Science
                                 University of Pennsylvania

Charles Tilly   Columbia University

Vanessa Tinsley   Duke University

CALL FOR PAPERS

For its next edition, *Comparative Social Research* plans thematic volumes on these topics:

- Regional Cultures (early 1997 deadline)
- Family Policies
- Academic Institutions

The editors would like to encourage potential contributors to submit papers on these themes.

Editor's address:

Comparative Social Research
Fredrik Engelstad
Institute for Social Research
Munthes gate 31, 0260 Oslo
Norway

Tel: + 47 22 55 45 10
Fax: + 47 22 43 13 85

E-mail: fen@isaf.no

INTRODUCTION:

METHODOLOGICAL ISSUES IN
COMPARATIVE SOCIAL SCIENCE

Comparative Social Research has, through the 15 volumes so far published, mainly been devoted to substantial comparative studies. Apart from a discussion and some papers in Volume 9 (1986), as well as scattered single papers in other volumes, the journal has published studies in which scholars have analysed concrete topics using comparative methods of various types, ranging from quantitative methods applied to huge cross-national data sets to in-depth case studies with strong elements of historical narrative.

In contrast, most of the present issue is devoted to a debate on methodology. The focal point of the debate is John Goldthorpe's "Current Issues in Comparative Macrosociology," first delivered as a Vilhelm Aubert memorial lecture at the University of Oslo in 1994. Finding Goldthorpe's intervention as penetrating and challenging as ever, the editors of CSR decided to invite a number of comments on his article. While Goldthorpe's title refers to macrosociology, his discussion is obviously highly relevant to political science, anthropology and other more specialized branches of social science too. The seven scholars who present comments on Goldthorpe are political scientists or sociologists. We have therefore chosen the more general title *Methodological Issues in Comparative Social Science*.

THE CONTEXT OF THE PRESENT DEBATE

Throughout the history of social science, at least since Malthus attacked Ricardo's abstract models, there has been a *dispute on methods*—what the Germans call a "Methodenstreit"—in social science. The present exchange may be seen as yet another incarnation of this struggle between scholars who go for the most abstract theories and those who prefer more *context-oriented* knowledge. But unlike many of these controversies, the present incarnation of the dispute on methods cannot be reduced to a simple theory versus facts dichotomy. All the scholars involved are committed in principle to empirical work.

In our introduction to last year's volume (CSR, Vol. 15, p. xii), we noted that in the 1970s, social science was breaking out of its "nationalist phase," returning to comparative topics, strengthened by the technical and methodological advances of the 1950s and 1960s. But comparative work was conducted within two camps. Goldthorpe's recent comparative work on social mobility exemplifies a *quantitative* approach, while the work of Theda Skocpol and others exemplifies a *qualitative* approach. A first clash between these two branches of comparativists (*British Journal of Sociology* 1994) related to an earlier methodological essay by Goldthorpe (1991). But even earlier, debates within the qualitative camp had shown some weaknesses in Skocpol's (1984) position. There was thus at least two alternative suggestions of a methodological rationale for qualitative studies. One was Charles Ragin's (1987) account of the case-oriented approach as a method in its own right, with strengths and weaknesses different from those of the mainstream, variable-oriented approach. The other was Charles Tilly's (1984) criticism of the nation-state centered approach that has marked most of the comparative work within historical sociology.

The present debate may be regarded as a follow-up to the one in *British Journal of Sociology* (1994) in the sense that Goldthorpe's intervention now directly adresses the question of whether the case-oriented approach offers specific advantages compared to the variable-oriented approach.

Goldthorpe argues that the case-oriented approach has the same problems as the variable-oriented approach. Making his case, Goldthorpe surveys much of the recent methodological discussion and also comments on substantial studies that have inspired this discussion. Among the commentators, Teune supports Goldthorpe's position, although from a somewhat more sceptical position, since most of his contribution emphasizes how hard it is to generate cumulative knowledge in social science.

The rest of the commentaries on Goldthorpe criticize his position. Several of the commentators rely on experience earned through their own substantial studies (Tilly on state formation and social movements, Rueschemeyer/ Stephens on democracy and development, Goldstone on revolutions), others draw on their earlier contributions to methodological debates (Ragin, Abbott). Goldthorpe provides a reply to these critics.

Although Goldthorpe in his reply is surprised by the lack of coherence among his critics, it would seem that Ragin, Rueschemeyer/Stephens, and Goldstone, all support a program of cooperation between case- and variable-oriented approaches, but they insist that the case-oriented approach has specific advantages. Tilly and Abbott distinguish themselves by also criticizing the distinction between case- and variable-oriented approaches. Tilly accuses both of not seeing the serious problems involved in the national-state centered approach to comparative studies, and he also links the present debate to another important contemporary debate, the debate on causal mechanisms (Hedstrøm/Swedberg 1996). Abbott, finally, implies that the case-/variable-dichotomy should be discarded in favour of a theoretical approach built around the notion of narrative explanations. While there are clear differences between Abbott and Tilly, they both seem to regard network theory as an important component in their suggested syntheses.

SOME UNRESOLVED MATTERS

No attempt will be made here to list further differences between the various contributions. Rather, in order to indicate where the debate may progress from here, we shall point out some unresolved questions in the present debate.

From Popper's (1957) defence of the ideographic/nomothetic distinction, Goldthorpe derives a strict dualism: Certain topics allow generalization, and they should be the object of sociological (or social science) research. Many other topics do not allow generalization, and so they belong to the realm of historical science. Since social science is grouped with the nomothetic natural sciences, its goal is generalization. Historical components may be included in social science explanations as initial conditions, but social scientists should not make it their goal to explain such singular events. As Goldthorpe explicitly states, this implies that quite a lot of the topics dealt with in historical sociology (e.g., revolutions) may be too specific to be allowed into social science. Historical sociologists should realize that they are simply doing comparative history.

Goldthorpe's critics reject such a slicing up of social reality into two areas, one of which social scientists are told to avoid, at least when they search for dependent variables. But it is striking that all of the critics accept the goal of generalization. Also in another crucial respect, the difference between the two groups seems not to be a principal one. Goldthorpe emphasizes the logic of inference, while his critics emphasize the importance of defining and delimiting the case(s). Goldthorpe warns his critics of the danger of endless reconceptualizations that never gets to the stage of testing, but does not really deny that reconceptualization may be a necessary part of the preparation for testing. Neither does his opponents deny the need to bring theories to the testing stage. In future debates, it would maybe be fruitful if the Popperians dealt more with the construction of cases (theory formation, typologies, etc.), while the critics dealt more with testing.

But the agreement on generalization seems even more puzzling. Behind this agreement we do in fact find different notions of theory. Within the philosophy of science, Popper's critical rationalism converges with logical positivism in the conception of theory as a body of universal laws (hypotheses). Goldthorpe supports this notion, but commenting on the criteria of a theory being applicable across time and place, he adds in brackets: "even if subject to *some* delimitation of scope" (Reply, p. 128). There is widespread agreement, namely, that social science has never produced an "empirical law" in the positivist sense: unspecified in time and place, while providing some substantial information on society. Thus, for social science, Goldthorpe requires as general laws (hypotheses) as possible. But in this way, he circumvents the question of how to establish the limits to these generalizations. It seems clear that Goldthorpe's opponents, even if they agree to Goldthorpe's idea of theory as a body of generalizations, must go for a narrower delimitation of the scope of theory in social science. But the debate below scarcely explicates different conceptions of theory.

Goldthorpe has the advantage of relying on a clearcut Popper-based philosophy of science, but runs the danger of pushing the quest for generalization so far that in fact any social science theory we have so far seen fails to meet his norm. In this respect, his remarks on his own comparative work (with Erikson) on social mobility are striking. Their discovery of stable rates of "social fluidity," he says, calls for general theory, a theory of causal processes "capable of producing temporal constancy and cross-national communality," "a theory which is precisely *not* sensitive to context" (p. 16). But he admits that they were only able to make "a very modest beginning" (p. 16), so there is still no theory "that will adequately account for" their empirical findings (note 17, p. 22).

Goldthorpe notes at one point that his critics have a "less demanding" notion of theory than himself. This may in fact prove to be the critics' advantage, as they are then at least able to relate to the existing body of more or less middle range theories that have been developed, discussed and accumulated within social science. "Less demanding" notions of theory may have some strength precisely because Goldthorpe's notion of theory may be "too demanding" for social science. Tilly, in his promotion of explanations based on causal mechanisms, is the only one to mention Merton's notion (1968) of middle range theories as a third position which social science may take, thus overcoming the ideographic/nomothetic-dualism.

The debate does bring these difficult questions out, but future debates should more thoroughly discuss the different notions of theory. Since there is agreement that social science theories cannot be fully universal, the different notions of theory may well be defined by different solutions to the problem of how social science theories are delimited.

INSTITUTIONAL SPECIFICITIES IN COMPARATIVE ANALYSIS

The debate on methodological principles is supplemented by four articles taking up methodological questions related to specific research problems. Common to all four is the focus on institutional specificities in comparative analyses: political governance, labor markets, education, and institutions for care and support in old age.

Dirk Berg-Schlosser and Gisele De Meur study the ability of democratic governments to resist fascist take-over. The empirical anaysis uses data from 18 European countries in the interwar period. The scope of the study is institutional in a strong sense: the dependent variable is the functioning of the political institutions, seen in relationship to the constellation of other relevant social institutions and patterns of social resources.

The methodological problem encountered is that of complexity. More than 18 variables will obviously be necessary for the testing of possible explanations. Surveying prospective explanatory factors, the authors end up with 63 variables of specified relevance, thus making the small N problem acute. The solution proposed to this problem is a method for compressing the information in the large amount of variables into a relatively small set of composite variables, or what the authors term "super-variables."

In this way they are able to demonstrate the significance of the total network of social institutions established before the wave of fascist movements hit Europe. In countries where democracy already was embedded in a set of interlocking social institutions, anti-democratic movements turned out to be of marginal importance. The method presented entails more than just the establishment of a list of prerequisites for democracy. Its main strength is the simultaneous treatment of complex causal processes in a set of cases which is after all of considerable size. Detailed visual inspection would hardly yield equally clear results.

Tom Janoski, Christa McGill and Vanessa Tinsley also focus on institutional problems in a historical perspective, but within a somewhat different framework. Their concern is not one type of institutional transition over a given period, but gradual changes in the functioning of institutions. Their example is the effects of labour market institutions on unemployment rates. While it is a truism that institutions change over time, most empirical analyses tend simply to treat institutions as if they were constants. Janoski et al suggest that labour market institutions be broken down into a detailed set of subinstitutions. Temporal changes in these subinstitutions are then recorded for each of the countries analyzed, and summarized in additive indexes. 18 countries are analyzed for the period 1978-1989. Controlling for the volume of private capital formation, they show that labor market institutions do matter. For obvious reasons, variation between countries comes out most strongly, but a within-country effect over time is also discernible. With longer time series the historical picture would probably have stood out more sharply, but within the limits of the present study, the results obtained are encouraging.

Measuring the effects of institutions is also the concern of Michael Braun and Walter Müller, who discuss problems of operationalizing educational attainment in comparative analyses. Their analysis differ from that of Janoski and associates, due to the nature of the institution discussed. In the case of education, one measures not the workings of the institution itself, but its outcome at the individual level. Accordingly, within the institutional frame of reference, the level of analysis shifts from macro to micro.

Braun and Müller are concerned with the problem of comparability of measurements. Using data from four countries—the United States, Germany, Hungary and Poland—the authors test different measures of education and their correlation with a set of dependent variables such as personal income, political attitudes, and cultural capital. Methodologically, the simplest measure of educational attainment is the number of years in school. On theoretical grounds, however, this measure is unsatisfactory, because it hides a large amount of heterogeneity, created above all by specificities relating to vocational training. It is thus surprising to see that for the United States, years of school attendance performs better than the other, composite measures. This should not be taken as an indication of the irrelevance of institutional factors, it should rather be seen as a characteristic of the American educational institutions, in contrast to its European counterparts.

In the final contribution, Karl Ulrich Mayer reflects on the life course as an object of comparative studies, using the transition into nursing homes for the elderly as his case. More generally, he argues that the life course is a fruitful unit of analysis in comparative studies. For this purpose, Mayer discusses and rejects existing theories trying to to explain variation among life course regimes. His solution is a combination of macro and micro factors. He sees a decisive contrast between what he calls deregulated, open market systems on the one hand, and flexibly coordinated societies on the other. This taxonomy allows for flexibility in the constellation of institutions, while at the same time it serves as a framework for anayses of individual action.

A common characteristic of these four contributions is not only their focus on the institutional aspect in comparative analysis, but also their admittance that complex methodological problems still lie ahead of us. To a large extent, the fine-grained workings of such complex phenomena as social institutions resist the simplifications that we are bound to make in comparative analyses. The prospects may seem discouraging, but there is much room ahead for further methodological development.

Fredrik Engelstad and Lars Mjøset

REFERENCES

Goldthorpe, J.H. 1991. "The Uses of History in Sociology: Reflections on Some Recent Tendencies." *British Journal of Sociology* 42:2.

British Journal of Sociology. 1994. 45:1, March; "'The uses of history in sociology': A debate," with contributions by J. M. Bryant, N. Hart, N. Mouzelis, M. Mann, and a reply by J. H. Goldthorpe.

Hedstrøm, P. and R. Swedberg. 1996. "Social Mechanisms: Their Theoretical Status and Use in Sociology." *Acta Sociologica* 39:3.

Merton, R. 1968. "On Sociological Theories of the Middle Range." In *Social Theory and Social Structure,* Enlarged ed. New York: Free Press.

Popper, K.R. 1957. *The Poverty of Historicism.* London: Routledge and Kegan Paul (1961-edition).

Ragin, C.C. 1987. *The Comparative Method.* Berkeley, CA: University of California Press.

Skocpol, T. 1984. "Emerging Agendas and Recurrent Strategies in Historical Sociology." In *Vision and Method in Historical Sociology,* edited by T. Skocpol. Cambridge: Cambridge University Press.

Tilly, C. 1984. *Big Structures, Large Processes, Huge Comparisons.* New York: Russell Sage Foundation.

CURRENT ISSUES IN COMPARATIVE MACROSOCIOLOGY:

A DEBATE ON METHODOLOGICAL ISSUES

John H. Goldthorpe

ABSTRACT

Within comparative macrosociology, quantitative or "variable oriented" and qualitative or "case-oriented" methodologies are typically counterposed. It is, however, argued that in this way the nature of key methodological problems is often obscured. Three such problems—labeled the small N, the Galton and the black-box problems—are shown to arise with both approaches, and a critique is advanced of recent claims by exponents of case-oriented work that that they dispose of special and privileged means of by-passing or overcoming these problems.

I seek in this chapter to intervene in what is in fact a rather long-standing debate within comparative macrosociology, but one which appears of late to have acquired new vigor. The contending parties in this debate are now usually characterized as exponents of quantitative, "variable-oriented" methodologies,

Comparative Social Research, Volume 16, pages 1-26.
Copyright © 1997 by JAI Press Inc.
All rights of reproduction in any form reserved.
ISBN: 0-7623-0250-X

on the one hand, and of qualitative, "case-oriented" methodologies, on the other (see e.g., Ragin 1987; Rueschemeyer 1991; Janoski and Hicks 1994). I shall, however, argue that while the issues caught up in the protracted and complex exchanges that have occurred do include ones of major importance, the form that the debate has taken has not been especially helpful in highlighting just what these issues are, nor yet in pointing to ways in which they might be more effectively addressed.

I shall develop my position as follows. To begin with, I give a brief account of the contrast, or opposition, that has been set up between variable-oriented and case-oriented approaches. I then pursue my central argument by considering three rather well-known methodological problems that are encountered in the practice of comparative macrosociology. These problems are ones that have in fact been chiefly discussed in connection with variable-oriented research. But, I aim to show, they are present to no less a degree in case-oriented studies and, contrary to what several prominent authors have maintained or implied, the latter can claim no special advantages in dealing with them. Largely on account of misconceptions in this regard, I conclude, much recent discussion has tended to obscure, and divert attention away from, questions of method that comparative macrosociology does now need to engage with more actively—in whatever style it may be carried out.[1]

VARIABLE-ORIENTED VERSUS
CASE-ORIENTED APPROACHES

The variable-oriented approach to comparative macrosociology stems from a now famous proposal made by Przeworski and Teune (1970, chap. 1; cf. Zelditch 1971, pp. 269-273): that is, that the ultimate aim of work in this field should be to replace the proper names of nations (or of states, cultures etc.) with the names of variables. Przeworski and Teune first illustrate the logic they would recommend by examples such as the following. Rates of heart attack are lower in Japan than in the United States. But, in seeking an explanation for this, we do not get far by treating the differing rates as simply "Japanese" or "American" phenomena. Rather, we have to drop proper names—or adjectives—and introduce generally applicable variables: that is, variables on which each nation can be given a comparable value. Thus, in the case in point, one such variable might be "per capita consumption of polysaturated fat."

Przeworski and Teune then of course go on to provide further illustrations of their position drawn from the social sciences; and, by the present day, one could in fact add to these entire research programs in sociology—and political science—that essentially follow the approach that they advocate. As a paradigm case here, one might take research that is aimed at explaining cross-national differences in the size and institutional form of welfare states (for reviews, see Quadagno 1987; O'Connor and Brym 1988). In such research, the names of nations are typically "replaced" by such variables as "GNP per capita," "proportion of population over age 65," "degree of trade-union centralization," "share of left-wing parties in government" etc. That is to say, these are the independent variables, by reference to which the dependent variables—cross-nationally differing aspects of welfare provision—are to be "accounted for." The relationships that actually prevail between independent and dependent variables are then investigated statistically, through various techniques of multivariate analysis.

It is, for present purposes, important to recognize what Przeworski and Teune were defining their position *against*. Most importantly, they sought to challenge the "historicist" claim that any attempt to make macrosociological comparisons must fail in principle because different national societies are *sui generis*: that is, are entities uniquely formed by their history and culture, which can be studied only, so to speak, in their own right and on their own terms.[2] In opposition to this, Przeworski and Teune point out that being "comparable" or "non-comparable" are not inherent properties of things: whether meaningful comparison is possible or not is entirely a matter of the analytic concepts that we have at our disposal. Thus, apples and oranges may appear to be non-comparable—but only until we have the concept of "fruit" (cf. Sartori 1994). At the same time, though, Przeworski and Teune do insist that *if* the historicist position is accepted, then it must indeed follow that a comparative macrosociology is ruled out. If nations can only be studied as entities in themselves that will not allow of any kind of analytic decomposition—if, in other words, nations can only be studied "holistically"—then comparisons *cannot* be undertaken. Considered as wholes, nations *are* unique, and "holistic comparison" is thus an impossibility. As Zelditch (1971, p. 278) later put the point: "There is nothing else on earth quite like the United States (or the Navaho, or the Eskimo...) taken as a whole. Therefore the rule of holism [in comparative work] yields a clear and straightforward contradiction: only incomparables are comparable."

However, if the variable-oriented approach thus developed out of a critique of holism, the case-oriented approach is usually taken to represent a revival of holism—and indeed one directed against the kind of analytic reductionism that Przeworski and Teune would favor. Thus, for example, Ragin (1991, pp. 1-2) would regard it as being the very *raison d'être* of case studies that they allow a return to holism in comparative research: that is, they allow nations, or other macrosocial units, to be considered as "meaningful wholes" rather than serving simply as the basis on which "to place boundaries around the measurement of variables."

It must, though, be noted that the holism that Ragin and others thus set against multivariate analysis is not as radical as might at first appear. Case studies are indeed regarded as the only way in which macrosocial entities can be treated in their distinctive historical contexts, in their proper detail and as each constituting, as Skocpol and Somers (1980, p. 178) put it "a complex and unique sociohistorical configuration." But this, it turns out, does not imply a historicism of a quite thoroughgoing kind, which would deny the validity of any concepts that are formed in order to transcend particular cases (cf. Skocpol 1994, pp. 328-329). It is still seen as permissible to "abstract" from different cases certain of their "features" or "attributes" which can then be compared for theoretical purposes. In other words, variables *are* identified, even if sometimes behind a verbal smokescreen. Where holism enters in is with the insistence that, in any comparison, the unity of the particular cases involved should always be preserved. What is required is that, in the process of comparison, cases should always remain identifiable as such, rather than being decomposed into variables that are then interpreted only in the course of the simultaneous analysis of the entire sample of cases under investigation.

In actually pursuing holistic comparisons in this sense, exponents of the case-oriented approach appear to have found their chief methodological inspiration in the logic of John Stuart Mill (1843/1973): specifically, in Mill's "canons," or rules, of experimental induction—the "Method of Agreement," the "Method of Difference," and so forth (see e.g., Skocpol 1979, pp. 36-37, 1984, pp. 378-381; Skocpol and Somers 1980, pp. 183-184; cf. Ragin 1987, pp. 36-42). Following Mill, it is believed, each case included in a comparative enquiry can be taken as representing the presence or absence of a given phenomenon of interest—each case, that is, can be taken as a "naturally occurring" experiment relating to this phenomenon. Inferences regarding the causation of the phenomenon can then be drawn by considering which *other* features are *concomitantly* present or absent, and by in turn applying Mill's logical rules to the resulting set of comparisons. Thus, Skocpol, in her well-known study of social revolutions (1979), seeks to explain their outcomes by comparing national cases, on the one hand, in terms of whether or not revolutionary attempts succeeded and, on the other hand, in terms of the presence or absence of what she takes as likely determining factors: that is, various features of the agrarian economy and class structure, international pressures, internal political crises and so forth.[3]

It might seem that in both multivariate and logical comparisons alike the aim is in effect to "control variation" in the making of causal inferences—so that the two approaches are not, after all, so very far apart. And, indeed, the application of Mill's methods in the comparison of cases has not infrequently been represented as itself a form of multivariate analysis (e.g. Smelser 1976, chap. 7; Skocpol and Somers 1980, pp. 182-183; Dogan 1994, p. 35). However, as other commentators have pointed out (e.g. Lieberson 1992, 1994), there is one quite fundamental difference. The various forms of multivariate analysis used in quantitative work are statistical techniques, and the propositions to which they give rise are therefore *probabilistic*: they are based on associations or correlations that need not be perfect. In contrast, the methods proposed by Mill, being logical in character, entail propositions of a *deterministic* kind: they entail relationships that are entirely invariant. As will later be seen, this is a difference that matters, and indeed to overlook it is to neglect a major development in the history of sociological analysis: that which, in the course of the nineteenth and earlier twentieth centuries, saw sociology become part of "the probabilistic revolution" (cf. Krüger, Daston, and Heidelberger 1987; Krüger, Gigerenzer and Morgan 1987).

The distinction between variable-oriented and case-oriented approaches is not then a meaningless one. It captures an important divergence in preferred styles of comparative macrosociological research and further, one may suspect, in basic assumptions about the character of social phenomena. But, I would argue, focusing on this distinction will not in itself provide the key to an understanding of the more taxing methodological problems that arise in the conduct of such research; nor are attempts at combining or synthesizing the two approaches likely to make the main contribution to overcoming these problems, since they are in fact ones that confront both approaches alike. This I argument I now seek to sustain with reference to what may be labeled as (i) the small N problem; (ii) the Galton problem; and (iii) the black-box problem.

THE SMALL N PROBLEM

The small N problem arises in that, if nations or other macrosocial entities are taken as units of analysis, the number available for study is likely to be quite limited. Where individuals are the units, populations can be sampled so as to give Ns of several hundreds or thousands; but where nations are the units, N cannot rise much above one hundred even if all available cases are taken, and is often far less. In applying techniques of multivariate analysis, serious difficulties tend therefore to be encountered in that N is not much greater than the total number of variables involved. Statistically, this means that there are too few degrees of freedom, that models become "overdetermined," that intercorrelations among independent variables cannot be adequately dealt with and that results may not be robust. Substantively, it means that *competing* explanations of the dependent variable may not be open to any decisive evaluation. Thus, it has been recently claimed (Huber, Ragin, and Stephens 1993) that, for just these reasons, the research program on the determinants of state welfare provision—in which analyses based on a maximum of *c.* 20 nations have been typical—has by now reached a virtual "impasse." Theories privileging different sets of determinants can claim similar degrees of statistical support.[4]

The small N problem is then a real and troubling one. However, what I would wish to question are suggestions to the effect that it is a problem *specific to* the variable-oriented approach to comparative macrosociology, and that the case-oriented approach in some way or other allows it to be solved or circumvented. Most explicitly, Skocpol (1979, p. 36; cf. Rueschemeyer 1991, pp. 27-28, 32-34) has maintained that application of the methods "laid out" by Mill "is distinctively appropriate for developing explanations of macro-historical phenomena" when the small N problem arises; that is, "when there are too many variables and not enough cases."[5]

This claim calls for comment in several respects. To begin with, it is unclear whether Skocpol realizes that Mill himself (1843/1974: Bk. VI, chap. 7 esp.) went to some lengths to explain that his rules of induction, being developed for use in the experimental sciences, were *not* appropriate to the study of social phenomena and that, if used, would be likely to prove inconclusive if not actually misleading. At all events, Skocpol fails to take sufficient account of certain assumptions on which Mill's methods depend but which, as various critics have followed Mill in observing (e.g. Nichols 1986; Lieberson 1992, 1994), are assumptions rarely, if at all, defensible in social research. For example, Mill's logic presupposes that, in any analysis, *all* of the relevant causal factors can be identified and included—that is, that there are no "unmeasured variables"; and further that there is no multiple (or "plural") causation, nor again any interactions among causal factors.[6]

At the same time, though, Skocpol *is* well enough aware that Mill's canons are designed to lead to causal propositions of a deterministic kind—and does not appear much disturbed by this fact (cf. also 1984, p. 378). What, therefore, her argument would appear to come down to is this: that, in circumstances where there are too few cases for the satisfactory evaluation of probabilistic theories, deterministic ones may none the less be established. However, to accept this position, it should be noted, one must be ready to believe not just that the social world is indeed subject to deterministic theory rather than being inherently probabilistic. One must *further* believe that socio-historical *data* can be obtained that are of such a quality and completeness—that are so error-free—that a probabilistic approach is not even required for the purposes of relating these data to (deterministic) theory (cf. Lieberson 1992, pp. 106-107; King, Keohane, and Verba 1994, pp. 59-60). This latter implication at least is one that, I suspect, would be found by most sociologists, on due reflection, to be far more daunting than the small N problem itself.[7]

Various attempts have been made to develop the logical analysis of relatively small numbers of cases so as to overcome some of the more obvious limitations of Mill's methods in the context of social research. Most notable in this connection is perhaps the technique of "qualitative comparative analysis" (QCA) proposed by Ragin (1987) which is based on Boolean algebra. This technique aims to alleviate the small N problem by allowing inferences to be drawn from the maximum number of comparisons that can be made, in terms of the presence or absence of attributes of interest, across the cases under analysis. And, at the same time, it does permit—indeed is primarily directed towards—the analysis of multiple causation and interaction effects. Thus, Ragin (1994b, p. 328) maintains that while a regression exercise with, say, seven independent variables and only 18 cases would be generally regarded as untrustworthy, QCA would make possible the examination of all 128 (i.e., 2^7) different combinations of the causal conditions involved: that is, would in fact enable the analyst to address a degree of causal complexity far beyond the reach of regression.

Given the nature of QCA, Ragin would then further argue, it allows the macrosociologist to combine analysis with holism in that the distinctive features of particular cases need never be lost sight of. However, while this may be so, it is still somewhat misleading for Ragin to represent QCA as being a *synthesis* of the case- and variable-oriented approaches, since, as he indeed recognizes (1994b, pp. 305-306), QCA remains, no less than Mill's methods, entirely logical and non-statistical in character. And it does therefore still share with the latter the major disadvantages of being unable to make any allowance either for "missing variables" or for error in the data used.

Moreover, with QCA these disadvantages combine with two other evident weaknesses of the technique: its requirement that all variables should be treated as merely two-valued; and its high degree of sensitivity to the way in which each case is coded on each variable. Thus, where essentially continuous variables are involved, such as "GNP per capita," "proportion of population over 65" and so forth, these must be reduced (with, of course, much loss of information) to more or less arbitrary dichotomies; and all subsequent results will then be strongly dependent on the way in which particular cases are allocated. If, on account of error in the original data, or in its treatment, even a single case happens to be placed on the "wrong" side of a dichotomy, the analysis could well have a quite different outcome to that which would have been reached in the absence of such error. In an application of QCA, it should be noted, the independent variables are simply shown to be causally relevant—or not; no assessment of the *relative strengths* of different effects or combinations of effects is, or can be, made.[8]

In sum, the fact that QCA remains a logical technique means that its results are far more exposed to major distortion, both by difficulties in the selection of independent variables (cf. Amenta and Poulson 1994) and by the occurrence of error in data, than are results derived from statistical techniques. And whether, then, QCA does actually mark any significant advance in the treatment of the small N problem—as, for example, Skocpol has recently claimed (1994, p. 309)—must remain open to very serious doubt.[9]

What, I would argue, it is above all else necessary to recognize here is that *au fond* the small N problem is not one of method at all but rather of data:

more specifically, it is a problem of *insufficient information* relative to the complexity of the macrosociological questions that we seek to address. Thus, in so far as exponents of the case-oriented approach in effect choose to restrict themselves to small Ns, they are unlikely ever to avoid the difficulties of "too many variables and not enough cases" or, as King, Keohane and Verba (1994, p. 119) put it, "more inferences than implications observed"—no matter what resorts to Millian logic, Boolean algebra or other technical devices they may attempt. Conversely, what is vital to overcoming the small N problem is in principle easy to state, albeit in practice toilsome, even where possible, to achieve: that is, simply to increase the information that we have available for analysis.

One way in which this can sometimes be achieved is by exploiting more fully the experience of those nations (or other macrosocial units) for which we do have good data sources. Thus, in comparative welfare state research various investigators (e.g. O'Connor and Brym 1988; Korpi 1989; Pampel and Williamson 1989; Huber, Ragin, and Stephens 1993; O'Connell 1994) have by now taken up the lead given by econometricians and demographers and have "pooled" data for the same set of nations for several different time-points. Observations—and degrees of freedom—are in this way increased, and appropriate checks and corrections can be introduced into analyses in order to allow for the fact that the successive "waves" of information thus acquired are not, of course, entirely new and independent (see e.g., Stimson 1985; Hicks 1994a). Such a "pooling" strategy can then be reckoned as a valuable resource for macrosociologists following a variable-oriented approach; and King, Keohane and Verba (1994, pp. 221-223) have recently suggested various analogous procedures that might profitably be followed in qualitative studies.

More important, though, for the variable- and case-oriented approaches alike, is to increase the number of units to which comparisons extend; and further (cf. Przeworski 1987) to widen their geographical and sociocultural range, so that the greater variation thus obtained in supposed causal factors can improve the chances of deciding between competing theories. This will often mean bringing Third World nations into the analysis, and problems of data quality, which must always be of central concern in comparative work, may on this account be accentuated (cf. Dogan 1994, pp. 40-41). However, the challenge thus posed should not be shirked. Two recent authors, Bradshaw and Wallace (1991, p. 166) have argued for the particular appropriateness of case studies in the Third World, since, they maintain, calls for rigorous quantitative research must be biassed against poor nations that lack adequate data or even computers. While this view is clearly well-intentioned, I would still regard it as quite wrong-headed. Either the assumption is being made that case studies are, in some mysterious way, immune to problems of the reliability and validity of data with which quantitative researchers have to struggle or else case studies are being recommended for Third World use as some kind of "inferior good." It would surely be, from all points of view, a better strategy for First World social scientists to seek to help their Third World colleagues to collect *whatever* kinds of data, and to undertake *whatever* kinds of analysis, are in fact demanded by the nature of the substantive problems that they wish to pursue.[10]

THE "GALTON" PROBLEM

The "Galton" problem is named after the nineteenth-century British polymath, Francis Galton. In 1889 Galton famously criticized a pioneering comparative analysis by the anthropologist, Edward Tylor. Tylor (1889) claimed to show complex correlations among economic and familial institutions across a wide range of societies, past and present. These correlations he then sought to explain from what we would now think of as a functionalist standpoint. Galton (1889), however, questioned the extent to which Tylor's observations were *independent* ones, and pointed out that "institutional" correlations might arise not only under the pressure of functional exigencies, or through other processes operating *within* societies; they might also be the result of processes of what we would now call cultural diffusion *among* societies.

The problem of distinguishing between processes of these two kinds has subsequently plagued cross-cultural anthropology (Naroll 1973; Hammel 1980), and it obviously arises in comparative macrosociology to no less a degree. Thus, to revert to the investigation of welfare state development, it would be rather implausible to suppose that this development has proceeded quite autonomously in each national case, and free of such external influence as might have been exerted by the examples of, say, Bismarckian social policy in the nineteenth century, or the Beveridge Plan for post-war Britain, or, more recently, the "Scandinavian Model" (cf. Therborn 1993).

Moreover, the Galton problem could be regarded as potentially more damaging at the present time than ever before. Claims that the treatment of nations as independent units of analysis has been untenable ever since the emergence of a "world system" in the seventeenth century (Hopkins 1978; Hopkins and Wallerstein 1981) or that there now exists "a highly institutionalised world polity" (Meyer 1987, p. 42) might well be thought exaggerated. But it could hardly be denied that, by the late twentieth century, the independence of "national" observations is likely to be compromised, and not merely by the acceleration and intensification of cultural diffusion but further through the quite purposive actions of a whole range of international or multinational political and economic organizations. In this way, as Przeworski (1987) has recognized, the threat is created that the small N and Galton problems run together, as we do indeed enter into a world in which $N = 1$.

Lack of independence in observations, as well as limits on their number, does then undoubtedly create serious difficulties for cross-national research. However, just as with the small N problem, what I would wish first of all to stress is that while the difficulties in question may be most *apparent* with the variable-oriented approach, they are by no means restricted to it; the case-oriented approach enjoys no special immunity.

Thus, the assumption that nations can be treated as units of analysis, unrelated to each other in time and space, is one required by the logical methods of comparison that are favored in case-oriented research no less than by statistical methods. And indeed where historical cases are involved, the Galton problem is then likely to be encountered in a particularly troublesome form. The scarcely disputable fact that situations and events occurring at one time tend to have been influenced by situations and events occurring earlier clearly breaches the assumption of the independence of cases—as built into Mill's or any other logical method—and in a way that is not easily remedied. Thus, for example, one finds that Skocpol, in her study of revolutions (1979, pp. 23-24, 39), has obviously to recognize that the course of the Chinese revolution up to 1949 was in various ways influenced by events in Russia in 1917 and subsequently. But this recognition has then to be kept quite apart from her logical analyses of the factors that determine revolutionary success, which it threatens to compromise (cf. Burawoy 1989). In other words, "analytic induction" and narrative accounts that crucially rely on temporality cannot be integrated, but have to be left to play separate, and ultimately incompatible, explanatory roles (see further Kiser and Hechter 1991, pp. 12-13; Griffin 1992, pp. 412-413; cf. also Skocpol 1994, p. 338).

Despite this, the Galton problem has in fact met with only a rather limited appreciation—and response—among exponents of case-oriented research. McMichael (1990) has proposed a solution through what he calls "incorporated comparisons," which is apparently intended to take over the insights, while avoiding the "rigidity," of a world-system perspective. But since he presents his approach as an "interpretative" one that can proceed "without recourse to formal methodological procedures or a formal theory" (1990, p. 388), it is not easy to evaluate (nor, I would have to say, to understand). Another reaction is that of Sztompka (1988) which, however, is less an attempt to grapple with the Galton problem than a capitulation to it—and one that might be seen as somewhat opportunistic. The severity of the problem in the modern world, Sztompka maintains, is such that the whole agenda of comparative macrosociology needs to be changed—towards in fact a concentration on case-studies! "Globalization" has, in Sztompka's view, already made societal homogeneity and uniformity the norm. Thus, the central aim should no longer be to establish cross-national similarities or regularities of variation, using "hard," quantitative techniques; rather, comparative work should now focus on the description and interpretation of "enclaves of uniqueness"—that is, those deviant cases that stand out against globalization—and, for this purpose, should follow a "soft," qualitative approach. Sztompka does not tell us just how such enclaves of uniqueness are to be identified in the absence of systematic comparison. But, in any event, in arguing as he does, as if an extreme version of the "convergence thesis" had in fact been realized, he takes up a position that is well beyond the empirical evidence.

In addressing the Galton problem more pertinently, there are, I would suggest, two main points that need to be recognized. First, it is not so pervasive a problem as Sztompka and others (e.g., Scheuch 1989; Allardt 1990) would have us suppose. It is perhaps most regularly encountered in the comparative study of *public policy*, and especially of economic and social policy. For the pressures directly exerted by both international organizations and internationalized economies may alone bring about a high degree of uniformity of policy among nation states—quite apart from any diffusion of values and beliefs (Schmitter 1991). At the same time, though, it is not difficult to point to other areas of comparative research in which the Galton problem is far less apparent.

Consider, for example, recent research into class inequalities in educational attainment. This has revealed that in most modern societies such inequalities display a rather remarkable persistence over time (Shavit and Blossfeld 1993); but also that variation in the detailed pattern of inequality from society to society stems largely from differences in national educational institutions, which would seem endowed with substantial autonomy. Thus, even though governments—prompted, say, by international economic competition or "world-system ideology" (cf. Ramirez and Boli 1987)—may have engaged in essentially similar programs of educational expansion and reform, the processes of social selection that are distinctive to their indigenous institutions have proved hard to eradicate (see esp. Müller and Karle 1993; Ishida, Müller, and Ridge 1995). Here, then, evidence of "globalization" or convergence is, to say the least, not conspicuous.[11]

Secondly, it should be understood that, even where clearly present, the Galton problem does not necessarily preclude comparative analysis of a systematic kind. If, in a comparative study, national observations are known not to be independent, for whatever reason, it may still be possible to proceed by incorporating the processes that create this situation as an element in the analysis. That is, in the language of the variable-oriented approach, one can seek to "model" interdependence itself—as in fact demographers and statistically-minded geographers have been doing for some time (see e.g., Berry 1970; cf. Przeworski 1987). In the context of welfare state research, a notable pioneering contribution in this regard is that of Usui (1994). In a study of state-sponsored social insurance policies in a sample of 60 nations, Usui applies techniques of event history analysis in order to investigate how the development of these policies was influenced not only by "domestic" factors but further by the establishment of the International Labor Office in 1919, and by its subsequent world-wide activities.

The further large potential of attempts at thus modelling interdependence may be brought out by reference to the recent work of Castles and others (Castles 1993), who have introduced into comparative policy research the idea of "families of nations." Instead of attention centring on nations as "unattached singles," they argue, more account should be taken of the affinities that exist among groupings of nations, as a result of shared histories and cultural traditions. Castles has in fact suggested (1993, pp. xv-xvi) that recognition of such affinities may indicate the "outer limits" of the Przeworski-Teune program of replacing the proper names of nations with the names of variables. For policy similarities and differences among nations "may be attributable as much to history and culture and their transmission and diffusion amongst nations as to the immediate impact of the economic, political and social variables that figure almost exclusively in the contemporary public policy literature." And, Castles believes, the former kinds of effect are difficult to accommodate within the "prevailing intellectual paradigm," as represented by the variable-oriented approach.

Now, as regards his substantive point on the importance of historically-formed cultural patterns that transcend national boundaries, Castles may well be right. And, as will be apparent later, I share his concern with determining just where the theoretical limits of macrosociology, in whatever style it may be conducted, must in the end be drawn. But I do not see why the variables that replace the names of nations in quantitative analyses of comparative public policy need be *only* variables thought likely to have an "immediate impact"; nor why one cannot, in principle at least, also include variables that do indeed seek to capture nations' historical affinities and the longer-term influences that derive from them. Indeed, I would argue that to attempt to do precisely this is the obvious way to explore further the idea of families of nations. In other words, there seems no reason why the insights provided by Castles and his associates should not serve as the starting point for appropriate quantitative analyses that would enable us to form more reliable judgements on what is, after all, crucially at issue: that is, the *relative importance*, in regard to policy developments and repertoires, of inter- as opposed to intra-societal, and of "historical" as opposed to "contemporary" effects.[12]

In sum, we should not be led into believing that claims regarding globalization or the existence of a world system or of families of nations necessitate some quite radical transformation of cross-national comparative macrosociology, and least of all one that would entail its restriction to case studies. In dealing with the Galton problem—where there are good grounds for supposing that it does indeed exist—the variable-oriented approach at all events has resources that are in fact only beginning to be exploited.

THE BLACK BOX PROBLEM

The black box problem, even more than the small N or Galton problems, has been linked with the variable-oriented approach (see e.g., Rueschemeyer 1991, p. 26; Abbott 1992a, pp. 54-62; Esping-Andersen 1993, p. 8). A quantitative analysis may be undertaken which is successful in "accounting for" a significant part of the variation in the phenomenon of interest—let us say, the sizes of welfare states. But such an analysis, it can be objected, still tells us rather little about just what is going on at the level of the social processes and action that underlie, as it were, the interplay of the variables that have been distinguished. We know the "inputs" to the analysis and we know the "outputs" from it; but we do not know much about why it should be that, within the black box of the statistical model that is applied, the one is transformed into the other. The problem is of course mitigated if "intervening" as well as independent variables are included in the analysis, so as to give it a more finely-grained character; and further if both independent and intervening variables are chosen on theoretical grounds, so that certain causal processes may at least be implied. None the less, it can still be maintained that the black box problem is seriously addressed only to the extent that such processes are spelt out quite explicitly, so as to provide a "causally adequate" account of the actual *generation* of the regularities that are empirically demonstrated (cf. Elster 1989, chap. 1).

The black box problem, thus understood, has been seized upon by exponents of case studies in order to make the claim that the results of quantitative analyses must in effect be *dependent upon* case studies for their interpretation. Thus, Huber, Ragin, and Stephens (1993) have argued that the problem of conflicting explanations of the growth of welfare states can only be solved through a "dialogue" between variable- and case-oriented research, and that it is case studies that must play the crucial part in identifying "actual historical causal forces." Likewise, Rueschemeyer (1991, p. 28; cf. also Rueschemeyer, Stephens, and Stephens 1992, ch. 2) has maintained, with reference to comparative research into capitalist development and democracy, that in this area the tradition of historical case studies is "far richer in theoretical argument and analysis" than is that of quantitative work. Rueschemeyer accepts that quantitative studies have established a clear positive association between capitalist development and democracy; but, he is convinced, the "key to the black box" that mediates this association will only be found in theory inspired by case studies and, especially, in "explanatory ideas grappling with historical sequences."

Again, however, I would wish to call into question the privileged status that is thus accorded to the case-oriented approach. To begin with, it should be recognized that while, just as with the small N and Galton problems, the black box problem may be most apparent in quantitative work, it does in fact arise equally with the case-oriented approach where logical methods of comparison are applied. Contrary to what Rueschemeyer suggests (1991, pp. 32-33), logical methods too can only establish empirical regularities which may, at most, point to causal relations: they do not, in themselves, provide an account of the actual *processes* involved (cf. Burawoy 1989). And if, to this end, "analytical induction" is accompanied by some narrative of historical sequences, then this, for reasons earlier noted, cannot be part of the logical method itself but only in fact a rather awkward appendage to it.

I would, furthermore, argue that the *theoretical* achievement of case studies is, in any event, a good deal less impressive than the authors cited above attempt to make out. Where the unity of cases is preserved—where cases are studied "holistically," rather than being decomposed into variables—it is indeed possible, at least in principle, to provide detailed descriptions of "what happened" in each case, and with due regard for the specific contextual features involved. But to have a narrative account of a sequence of historical events is *not* the same thing as having a theoretical account, and even if one accepts—as I would be ready to do—that a historical narrative can itself constitute a form of explanation.[13] Most crucially, perhaps, such a narrative need not extend beyond the particular instance to which it is applied, or comparative narratives beyond the set of cases compared (cf. Skocpol and Somers 1980, p. 195). In contrast, a theoretical account must have *some* claim to generality. The explanation it provides of what is going on within the black box of a statistical or of a logical analysis is not one that is simply "extracted" from the actual events involved in the instances covered by the analysis but one that is, rather, derived from a theory that could, indeed should, apply to *other* instances falling within its intended scope or domain.

It might of course be suggested—and I would find it unexceptionable—that specific narratives may serve as a valuable resource for theory development: that is, by prompting attempts to conceive of some more general ideas that would allow the accounts given in different cases to be fitted into a deductive structure of argument. In other words, detailed case studies could play a *heuristic* role in the "context of discovery," prior to the testing of any resulting theory against further, independent cases in the "context of validation." However, the distinction here involved is one that proponents of the case-oriented approach appear to find uncongenial, and that Rueschemeyer, for example (1991, pp. 32-33; cf. Rueschemeyer, Stephens, and Stephens 1992, p. 36; Skocpol 1994, p. 330), flatly rejects. The view that seems rather to be favored is that the process of theory development should be advanced by successive inductions from particular cases—so that it becomes in effect essentially *merged with* the process of theory testing. The matching of developing theory against new inductions and its modification where it is found not to hold go on as one, seamless activity.

It is, however, in just this regard that the case for case studies becomes least convincing. The crucial point is that if a theory is formed in such an essentially inductive way—without, so to speak, any deductive backbone—then it is hard to see how it can be genuinely tested at all. As it stands, such a theory does no more than recapitulate observations; and it is, moreover, difficult to know exactly how it would be properly extended beyond the particular circumstances from which it has been obtained so that an independent test might be attempted. Or, to put the matter the other way around, if a theory amounts to no more than an assemblage of inductions, the possibilities for "saving" or "patching" it in the face of contrary evidence are virtually unlimited. Generality can be claimed for so long as such a theory appears to fit the cases to which it is applied; but when it fails to fit, it can then be maintained that "causal homogeneity" no longer holds, and that a somewhat different theory is required; and, in all of this, analysts can congratulate themselves on their "sensitivity to context"![14]

However, the arbitrary delimitation of the scope of a theory—that is, a delimitation that the theory does not itself provide for—is an evident weakness. Thus, in the context of welfare state research, Korpi (1989, p. 324) has critically remarked that theories of "state autonomy," as advanced by Skocpol and others (e.g. Orlof and Skocpol 1984; Weir and Skocpol 1985) on the basis of qualitative case studies "leave ample room for flexible *ad hoc* explanation," and has urged the need for such theories to be formulated in a way that would expose them to more stringent empirical critique. And yet more prominently, the charge of arbitrariness has been levelled against Skocpol's treatment of the Iranian revolution (1982), when taken in relation to her previous analyses (1979) of the French, Russian and Chinese revolutions (Nichols 1986; Burawoy 1989; Kiser and Hechter 1991), since in the Iranian case a significant, yet seemingly quite *ad hoc*, theoretical shift is introduced: that is, popular urban demonstrations become a "functional substitute" for peasant revolts and guerrilla activity (cf. Skocpol 1994, pp. 313-314).

Finally in this connection, I would also question whether the account offered by Rueschemeyer, Stephens and Stephens of the association between capitalist development and democracy does in fact bear out their contention that case studies afford a privileged ground for the development of theory capable of overcoming the black box problem. Their account fails in this respect, I would suggest, precisely because of the degree to which the analysis of their cases leads them to hedge about their central argument on power struggles among social classes with exceptions and qualifications—relating to cross-national differences in the social construction of class interests, in the possibilities for class alliances, in the form of civil society, in the role of the state, in the impact of transnational relations, and so on (1992, pp. 269-281 esp.). Not only does the ratio of explaining to "explaining away" thus seem rather low but, further, it is notable that when these authors come to address the key issue of the "generalizability" of their theory beyond the cases they have examined (1992, p. 285)—to, say, east Asian or east-central European nations of the present day—what they have to offer is not a series of derived hypotheses that would be testable against such new cases but yet more discussion of additional factors to be considered.[15] Now it may be that the awareness that Rueschemeyer and his colleagues here display of complexity and "causal heterogeneity" is empirically warranted. But, if so, what they have provided is a demonstration of the inherent difficulty of forming a theory of the relationship between capitalist development and democracy, and not that theory itself.

For macrosociologists seeking to treat black box problems more effectively, I would then argue, case studies, whether "historical" or otherwise, have no distinctive value, and an absorption in their specificities may indeed divert attention away from what is in fact crucially required: that is, theory that is as general as it is possible to make it. As Kiser and Hechter (1991) have maintained, in a strong critique of the quality of theory in comparative historical sociology, to illuminate the black boxes represented by mere empirical regularities, we need more than just a redescription of the latter within a "theoretical (sc. conceptual) framework" which appears indefinitely modifiable as our data-base expands. Rather, theory must be sought that is general in that it permits the specification of causal processes which, if operative, would be capable of producing the regularities in question *and* would have a range of *further* implications of at least a potentially observable kind. To the extent that theory is general in this sense, it can then claim both greater explanatory power, which theory must always seek, and greater openness to empirical test, which it must never evade.[16]

I would, moreover, add that such a concern with generality in theory might help macrosociologists to see the relevance of history to their enterprise in a different—and, I believe, more appropriate—way to that which appears currently in mode among exponents of the case-oriented approach. Instead of a recourse to history being regarded as essential to the development of theory, it might be better understood as marking the *limits of* theory: that is, the point at which what is causally important in regard to certain empirical findings is recognized not in recurrent social situations and processes that might be the subject of theory but rather in contingencies, distinctive conjunctures of events or other singularities that theory cannot comprehend.

Since the foregoing is put somewhat abstractly, I may try to illustrate with reference to the (primarily quantitative) work that I have undertaken with Robert Erikson on comparative social mobility (Erikson and Goldthorpe 1992a). Perhaps the most notable finding of this work was that when intergenerational class mobility was considered net of all structural influences—or, that is, as "social fluidity"—rates and patterns showed high stability over time within nations and, further, a large measure of similarity across nations. Such a degree of *in*variance clearly underlines the need for general theory. For hypotheses on the causal processes capable of producing temporal constancy and cross-national commonality of the kind that our quantitative analyses revealed will have to be derived from a theory of considerable scope: that is, from a theory which is precisely *not* "sensitive to context"—unlike the theories of national "exceptionalism" in regard to mobility which our results called into doubt—but applicable to societal contexts widely separated over both time and space. And in this respect, I should say, Erikson and I were able to make only a very modest beginning.[17]

We also found, though, that in so far as variation in social fluidity *did* occur cross-nationally, we could not account for it, to any large extent, in terms of other generalizable attributes of societies, in the way that the Przeworski-Teune program would require. Our analyses pointed here to the far greater importance of historically formed cultural or institutional features or political circumstances which could not be expressed as variable values except in a quite artificial way. For example, *levels* of social fluidity were not highly responsive to the overall degree of educational inequality within nations, but *patterns* of fluidity did often reflect the distinctive, institutionally shaped character (cf. p. 11 above) of such inequality in particular nations, such as Germany or Japan. Or again, fluidity was affected less by the presence of a state socialist regime *per se* than by the significantly differing policies actually pursued by the Polish, Hungarian or Czechoslovak regimes on such matters as the collectivization of agriculture or the recruitment of the intelligentsia. In such instances, then, it seemed to us that the retention of proper names and adjectives in our explanatory accounts was as unavoidable as it was desirable, and that little was to be gained in seeking to bring such historically specific effects within the scope of theory of any kind.

In sum, black box problems—essentially problems of "making sense" of empirical findings—are unlikely to be alleviated by comparative macrosociologists striving in effect to transcend the distinction between theory and history. For such attempts tend to lead merely to a weakening of our understanding of theory and of historicity alike, and in turn to a blurring of crucial differences in the nature of theoretical and historical explanations. A strategy of greater long-term promise would be to continue to pursue sociological theory that amounts to more than just the elaboration of concepts and aspires to generality in the sense indicated above, but at the same time to show due modesty in accepting that, for any kind of macrosociology, and no matter how theoretically accomplished it may eventually become, "history" will always remain as a necessary residual category.[18] It may, furthermore, be a consequence of such a strategy that certain phenomena that macrosociologists have sought to study—including, perhaps, revolutions or other kinds of "regime transition"—turn out to be ones on which theory can give relatively little cognitive grasp at all. That is to say, while it may be of interest to write the comparative history of these phenomena—their history as viewed within a common conceptual framework—they appear just too few, too interdependent and too causally heterogeneous for anything of much use to be said in theoretical terms. In instances where the indications accumulate that this is indeed the case, then the course of wisdom must surely be to accept the situation with good grace. Macrosociologists will still be left with a very great deal to do, and there have not, after all, ever been any guarantees that a sociology of everything should be possible.

CONCLUSIONS

I have argued that, while a divergence can certainly be observed between variable-oriented and case-oriented approaches to comparative macrosociology, to concentrate attention on this divergence—or even on ways of overcoming it—does not provide the best focus for understanding and addressing major methodological issues that are encountered in this field. As King, Keohane and Verba have emphasized (1994, chap. 1), we may distinguish between quantitative and qualitative *styles* of research in the social sciences, but each must still strive to meet the exigencies of the same underlying "logic of inference" and contend with the problems to which this common requirement gives rise. Through an examination of three such problems, recurrent within comparative macrosociology, I have tried to show how each can, and does, occur in the context of variable-oriented and case-oriented work alike. These problems are not in fact ones on which alternatives in research styles have much bearing, but are of a more elementary, which is not to say easier, kind. Thus, the small N problem is essentially a problem of insufficient information on which to base analyses—or, that is, on which to draw in making inferences; and it can be resolved, or mitigated, only by more extensive data collection, aided by techniques for exploiting to the full the information that is at any time available. The Galton problem, where it arises, is one of observations lacking a property—independence—that we would like to assume in our analyses; and, to the extent that interdependence among our units of observation is simply a feature of the way the world is, we must deal with this situation by seeking to represent the interdependence (or, better, the processes creating it) within our analyses, so that we can not just recognize its presence but also assess its importance. And finally the black box problem is one of how we move from descriptive to causal inferences or, that is, go beyond our empirical findings and the regularities they allow us to establish to an understanding of how these regularities are generated. Here what is crucial is to construct theory in a way that maximizes both its explanatory power and its openness to test against further empirical research—and that also allows us to see as clearly as possible where the limits to theoretical explanation are reached.

In this chapter, criticism has been more often directed against case-oriented than against variable-oriented research. This is not an expression of hostility on my part to qualitative research as such, whether in macrosociology or more generally, and especially not to such research of a historical character. Rather, it reflects my view that it is proponents of the variable-oriented approach who have, at all events, better appreciated and responded to the problems I have considered, while proponents of the case-oriented approach have sometimes failed to recognize that they too need to address these problems or, as I suggested at the start, have made claims to the effect that they dispose of special and privileged means of by-passing or overcoming them. My critical comments have then been chiefly directed against such claims. I have sought to show that they do not, at least as so far presented, have any very secure basis, and that, if they are to be maintained, they will need to demonstrated far more cogently than hitherto. I would doubt if this will prove possible, since I see no reason at all to believe in such special and privileged means. The small N, Galton and black box problems pertain to quite basic issues that are likely to arise in any instance of comparative macrosociological research, whatever the style in which it is conducted. Whether investigators choose to work quantitatively or qualitatively, with variables or with cases, the inherent logic of these issues remains the same, and so too therefore will that of any solutions that may be achieved.

ACKNOWLEDGMENT

This paper is an extended and rewritten version of the Vilhelm Aubert Memorial Lecture for 1993, given at the University of Oslo. I am indebted to Anne Gauthier, Andrew Hurrell, Olli Kangas, Philip Kreager, John Stephens and Laurence Whitehead for information, advice and helpful conversation. The usual disclaimers do of course apply.

NOTES

1.   This discussion, it should be said, has often ended on an eirenic note, the complementary nature of quantitative and qualitative work and the need to "build bridges" between them being emphasized. Thus, the present paper may appear disobliging and contrary to the prevailing spirit of methodological pluralism. But it seems to me, for reasons that will become clear, that often, behind the rhetoric of pluralism, an *entente* is being proposed on terms that are in fact unduly skewed in favor of the case-oriented approach.

2.   "Historicist" is thus being used here in what one might describe as the sense of Meinecke rather than the sense of Popper.

3.   Whether or not Skocpol does in practice apply Mill's canons appropriately is a matter of some dispute. See, for example, Nichols (1986), Skocpol (1986), Ragin (1987, pp. 38-42), Burawoy (1989), Lieberson (1991). However, as will later emerge, I would see this as an issue that is overshadowed by far more serious ones.

4.   Without seeking to deny the force of the general point being made here, one could question whether the illustration suggested is in fact the most apt. A good deal of the apparent conflict in results from welfare state research would appear to be resolved once differing understandings of the dependent variable are recognized: that is whether this is taken as the amount of social welfare *expenditure* or as the extent and quality of *social rights* to welfare (cf. Korpi 1989).

5. It may be noted that while Skocpol invokes Mill directly, Rueschemeyer refers rather to Mill at one remove: that is, via Znaniecki's notion (1934) of "analytic induction," which, however, Rueschemeyer would wish to see developed beyond its reliance on the Method of Agreement alone (1991, p. 36, n. 12). It is in the present context of particular interest that Znaniecki contrasts analytic induction with "enumerative induction," based on probability theory, and asserts that, since the former is capable of providing *exhaustive* knowledge of the situation under study, the latter is rendered superfluous.

6. Mill presented his canons in Book III of *A System of Logic*, which is entitled "Of Induction." They are first formulated in chapter viii, "Of the Four Methods of Experimental Inquiry." His treatment of the "moral"—that is social—sciences is quite separate, coming in Book VI, "On the Logic of the Moral Sciences." His views on the unsuitability in this context of methods of experimental induction are found chiefly in chapter vii. For illuminating commentary, see Ryan (1970). Skocpol's discussion of the problems of applying Mill's methods is very brief (1979, pp. 36-40) and her dismissive response (1994, p. 338) to Lieberson (1992) indicates only that she has failed to grasp the force of his argument. Rueschemeyer gives no recognition to the powerful critiques that have been made of Znaniecki's analytic induction—classically, by Robinson (1951).

7. It may be found surprising that such strong "positivistic" commitments are taken up within the qualitative camp. However, I have elsewhere (1991) made the point that Skocpol and other "grand historical sociologists" are in effect compelled by their dependence on secondary works as their main empirical resource to adopt a distinctively positivistic attitude towards historiography and, specifically, the nature of historical "facts." Further, Burawoy has acutely observed that Skocpol's reliance on inductive logic likewise puts limits on the doubts that she can allow herself about just what the historical facts are. For Skocpol, he remarks (1989, p. 773), "the facts have a certain obviousness that they don't for historians," and she pays little attention to the controversies that rage over them: "She is forced into this blindness in order to get her induction machine off the ground." It may be observed that a similar penchant for inductive and deterministic accounts is to be found among exponents of case studies at a microsociological level—or at all events among those following in the "Chicago" or "symbolic interactionist" tradition. See for example, the very explicit statements, made in this regard by Becker (1992, p. 212).

8. As an illustration of the critical point here made, one may take the application of QCA reported by Kangas (1994) in the context of a comparative study of the quality of health insurance provision. Through reanalysis of the data given in Table 14.2 of his paper, it is possible to show that the result Kangas achieves—that high quality provision (as of 1950) is associated with strong Christian Democracy *and* a unified bloc of bourgeois political parties, but not with the level of working-class mobilization—turns entirely on the coding on the dependent variable in a single case: that is, that of Switzerland, which, from other evidence given in the paper and also in Kangas (1991), is in any event arguable. If this coding were to be changed (e.g. by dichotomizing "high" versus "low" quality provision in another, perhaps no less arbitrary, way), then the result of the entire analysis would become quite different. Now, in fact, all that would matter would be the strength of Christian Democracy, and the unity or fragmentation of bourgeois parties would join the level of working-class mobilization as an irrelevant factor. Kangas, I should make clear, is not unaware of the problem of QCA here demonstrated; the main purpose of his paper is to compare the results he obtains from QCA with those deriving from different analytical approaches to the same problem and data.

9. Skocpol chiefly bases her claim on the work of Wickham-Crowley (1992). However, this author's applications of QCA reveal exactly the same flaw as that noted in the instance discussed in the previous note. Thus, his analysis of causal factors in peasant support for guerrilla movements in Latin America turns crucially on certain codings which, as he himself recognizes, are highly doubtful on account of data problems. Readers who enjoy Boolean algebra can work out for themselves what would happen to Wickham-Crowley's conclusions if just a few of these problematic codings were changed: if, say, (see his Table 12-1 1992, p. 306) positive rather than

negative codes were given to Cuba (Las Villas) on factor B (agrarian disruption) and to Guatamala (Zacapa) on factor D (peasant linkage); or—yet more dramatically—if, in addition, positive codings on factor D were also given to Nicaragua (N. Central rural and Northwest towns).

10.   Lack of data quality, and especially in regard to cross-national comparability, does of course still often impose serious limitations on macrosociological studies, whatever the technical resources they may command. However, it can be said that this problem does now attract growing critical attention among those engaging in quantitative research. See, for example, in the case of research in social stratification and mobility, the issues taken up in Treiman (1975), Goldthorpe (1985), Ganzeboom, Luijkx and Treiman (1989), Erikson and Goldthorpe (1992a, chap. 2; 1992b). In some contrast, advocates of historical case studies especially would appear to resort to double standards. Thus, one finds Rueschemeyer, Stephens, and Stephens (1992, p. 26) commenting, with good reason, on the problem of "not always reliable information" in quantitative studies of capitalist development and democracy—but just one page after an encomium on the "towering achievement" of Moore (1966). Why, one wonders, do they not consider in an equally critical way the question of the reliability, or even of the very existence, of the evidence to which Moore appeals in support of his central thesis—for instance, as regards the social sources of the English Civil War ? See further Goldthorpe (1991).

11.   Even in public policy research the importance of diffusion and also of international economic or political pressure can be exaggerated. As regards the development of welfare state institutions, see, for example, Flora and Alber (1981), Garrett and Lange (1991) and Huber and Stephens (1993). For an insightful review of the recurrent problems of diffusionist theory itself, and in an area of prime application—fertility studies—see Kreager (1993). Sociological fashion as well as real world developments would seem to play a large part in current writing on "globalization." It is not long since the emphasis was rather on the "non-exportability" of institutions—for example, of those of the "Westminster model" to the new nations of the former British empire or of Soviet institutions to the satellite nations of the USSR. Recall discussion of Stalin's comments about "saddling cows."

12.   Several contributors to the collection edited by Castles do in fact make at least implicit moves in the direction suggested. See in particular Busch (1993) on differences in anti-inflation policies and Schmidt (1993) on differences in male and female workforce participation rates and their determinants.

13.   I have in mind here the various arguments that have been advanced on the possibility of historical explanation being achieved without reference to general theories through the use of narratives that show how specific events form part of "continuous series" (Oakeshott 1933), have "followability" (Gallie 1964), are "colligated" within a "continuing process" (Walsh 1974) or are otherwise "internally" rather than "externally" connected. For a valuable brief review, see Dray (1993).

14.   Again a close parallel can be noted with case studies oriented towards microsociological issues. Even a sympathetic commentator (Hammersley 1989, chaps. 7 and 8) is forced to acknowledge that problems of theory testing are acute with both "analytic induction" and with the no less inductive "grounded theory" (Glaser and Strauss 1967) to which it seems more common for case analysts working at a micro-level to appeal. It is of interest that in a recent work Ragin (1994a, p. 94) should acknowledge that "analytic induction"—of which his own QCA is in effect a systematization—is to be seen as primarily concerned with "the degree to which the image of the research subject has been refined, sharpened, and elaborated in response to both confirming and disconfirming evidence"; or, that is, with no more than *conceptualization* (cf. also Hicks 1994b).

15.   I would, as it happens, entirely agree with the *substantive* criticisms that Rueschemeyer and his colleagues make of earlier efforts at explaining the association between capitalism and democracy—that is, via "modernization" theory. But I would totally disagree that it should be seen as a fault of this, or of any other theory, that it is insufficiently grounded in prior research

or is indeed "pure conjecture" (1992, p. 29; cp. Goldthorpe 1992). Theories must be judged not by their empirical origins but by their empirical implications. And what better epitaph could a theory possibly hope for than that it was bold enough to provoke research and clear enough to be proved wrong by it?

16.   The only responses to Kiser and Hechter of which I am aware are those of Quadagno and Knapp (1992) and Skocpol (1994). However, these seem to me to concede far more than they effectively contest. That is, their authors show themselves ready to accept a much less demanding idea of theory than that of Kiser and Hechter and, in turn, the implication that comparative historical sociologists are not interested in testing theories in the way Kiser and Hechter would require.

17.   While it is surely disappointing, it should not be thought a disgrace for sociologists to admit that they have not been able to develop a theory that will adequately account for their empirical findings. This is so because one cannot expect effective theory, in the sense I intend, to be produced at will, nor by following specified procedures or guidelines—as would appear the case with "grounded theory." I do not find it accidental that it is in case-oriented, qualitative sociology that the rather absurd use of "theorise" as a *transitive* verb has become most common: that is, it can, apparently, be demanded that a topic be "theorised" in the same way as it can be demanded that the kitchen be cleaned or the shopping brought home. This confirms me in my belief that, typically, no more than (re)conceptualization is in fact involved.

18.   In other words, I would still see force in the nomothetic-idiographic distinction as applied to sociology and history, if, that is, it is understood as referring essentially to the direction of intellectual effort (and without any implication either that sociological theory must be entirely "universal" or that historiography must avoid all general concepts). Claims that comparative historical studies applying some form of "analytic induction" are capable of overcoming this distinction (e.g., Zaret 1978, p. 118; Skocpol 1979, pp. 33-37) seem to me, for reasons given above, not to be borne out on the evidence of these studies themselves. And I would take leave to doubt that the further attempt now apparently being made via "sociological narrativism" (see e.g., Griffin 1992; Quadagno and Knapp 1992) is any more likely to succeed. While one may sympathize with efforts such as those of Abbott (1992a, 1992b) to establish analogues between narrative accounts and causal explanations, there are still basic differences to be recognized among the kinds of narrative that may be deployed. For example, one may understand rational choice theory in terms of narratives—but ones which, in contrast to historical narratives, are generalized rather than specific, set in analytic rather than real time, and implicative rather than conjunctive in their structure.

REFERENCES

Abbott, A. 1992a. "What Do Cases Do? Some Notes on Activity in Sociological Analysis." Pp. 53-82 in *What is a Case?*, edited by C.C. Ragin and H.S. Becker. Cambridge: Cambridge University Press.

————. 1992b. "From Causes to Events: Notes on Narrative Positivism." *Sociological Methods and Research* 20: 428-455.

Abell, P. 1992. "Is Rational Choice Theory a Rational Choice of Theory ?" In *Rational Choice Theory: Advocacy and Critique*, edited by J.S. Coleman and T.J. Fararo. Newbury Park: Sage.

Allardt, E. 1990. "Challenges for Comparative Social Research." *Acta Sociologica* 33: 183-193.

Amenta, E., and J.D. Poulsen. 1994. "Where to Begin: A Survey of Five Approaches to Selecting Independent Variables for Qualitative Comparative Analysis." *Sociological Methods and Research* 23: 22-53.

Becker, H.S. 1992. "Cases, Causes, Conjunctures, Stories, and Imagery." Pp. 205-216 in *What is a Case?*, edited by C.C. Ragin and H.S. Becker. Cambridge: Cambridge University Press.

Berry, B.J.L. 1970. "Some Methodological Consequences of Using the Nation as a Unit of Analysis in Comparative Politics." New York: Social Science Research Council, Committee on Comparative Politics.

Bradshaw, Y., and M. Wallace. 1991. "Informing Generality and Explaining Uniqueness: The Place of Case Studies in Comparative Research." P. 154-171 in *Issues and Alternatives in Comparative Social Research*, edited by C.C. Ragin. Leiden: E.J. Brill.

Burawoy, M. 1989. "Two Methods in Search of Science: Skocpol versus Trotsky." *Theory and Society* 18: 759-805.

Busch, A. 1993. "The Politics of Price Stability: Why the German-Speaking Nations are Different." P. 35-91 in *Families of Nations: Patterns of Public Policy in Western Democracies*, edited by F.G. Castles. Aldershot: Dartmouth.

Castles, F.G. 1993. "Introduction." In *Families of Nations: Patterns of Public Policy in Western Democracies*. Aldershot: Dartmouth.

Dogan, M. 1994. "Use and Misuse of Statistics in Comparative Research." Pp. 35-71 in *Comparing Nations*, edited by M. Dogan and A. Kazancigil. Oxford: Blackwell.

Dray, W. 1993. *Philosophy of History*, 2nd ed. Englewood Cliffs, NJ: Prentice Hall

Elster, J. 1989. *Nuts and Bolts for the Social Sciences*. Cambridge: Cambridge University Press.

Erikson, R., and J.H. Goldthorpe. 1992a. *The Constant Flux: A Study of Class Mobility in Industrial Societies*. Oxford: Clarendon Press.

_____. 1992b. "The CASMIN Project and the American Dream." *European Sociological Review* 8: 283-305.

Flora, P., and J. Alber. 1981. "Modernization, Democratization, and the Development of Welfare States in Western Europe." Pp. 37-80 in *The Development of Welfare States in Europe and America*, edited by P. Flora and A.J. Heidenheimer. New Brunswick, NJ: Transaction Books.

Gallie, W.B. 1964. *Philosophy and the Historical Understanding*. London: Chatto and Windus.

Galton, F. 1889. Comment on E.B Tylor "On a Method of Investigating the Development of Institutions; Applied to Laws of Marriage and Descent." *Journal of the Royal Anthropological Institute* 18: 245-256, 261-269.

Ganzeboom, H.G.B., R. Luijkx, and D.J. Treiman. 1989. "Intergenerational Class Mobility in Comparative Perspective." *Research in Social Stratification and Mobility* 8: 3-84.

Garrett, G., and P. Lange. 1991. "Political Responses to Interdependence: What's Left for the Left?" *International Organization* 45: 539-564.

Glaser, B.G., and A.L. Strauss. 1967. *The Discovery of Grounded Theory*. Chicago: Aldine.

Goldthorpe, J.H. 1985. "On Economic Development and Social Mobility." *British Journal of Sociology* 36: 549-573.

_____. 1991. "The Uses of History in Sociology: Reflections on Some Recent Tendencies." *British Journal of Sociology* 42: 211-230.

_____. 1992. "The Theory of Industrialism and the Irish Case." Pp. 411-431 in *The Development of Industrial Society in Ireland*, edited by J.H. Goldthorpe and C.T. Whelan. Oxford: The British Academy.

Griffin, L.J. 1992. "Temporality, Events, and Explanation in Historical Sociology." *Sociological Methods and Research* 20: 403-427.

Hammel, E.A. 1980. "The Comparative Method in Anthropological Perspective." *Comparative Studies in Society and History* 22: 145-155.

Hammersley, M. 1989. *The Dilemma of Qualitative Method: Herbert Blumer and the Chicago Tradition*. London: Routledge.

Hicks, A.M. 1994a. "Introduction to Pooling." Pp. 169-188 in *The Comparative Political Economy of the Welfare State*, edited by T. Janoski and A.M. Hicks. Cambridge: Cambridge University Press.

————. 1994b. "Qualitative Comparative Analysis and Analytical Induction." *Sociological Methods and Research* 23: 86-113.

Hopkins, T.K. 1987. "World-System Analysis: Methodological Issues." Pp. 199-218 in *Change in the Capitalist World Economy*, edited by B.H. Kaplan. Beverly Hills, CA: Sage.

Hopkins, T.K., and I. Wallerstein. 1981. "Structural Transformations of the World Economy." Pp 235-286 in *Dynamics of World Development*, edited by R. Rubinson. Beverly Hills, CA: Sage.

Hough, R. 1959. *Admirals in Collision*, London: Hamish Hamilton.

Huber, E., and J.D. Stephens. 1993. "The Future of the Social Democratic Welfare State: Options in the Face of Internationalization and European Integration." International Sociological Association, Research Committee 19 Meeting, Oxford.

Huber, E., C.C. Ragin, and J.D. Stephens. 1993. "Social Democracy, Christian Democracy, Constitutional Structure and the Welfare State." *American Journal of Sociology* 99: 711-749.

Ishida, H., W. Müller, and J.M. Ridge. 1995. "Class Origin, Class Destination and Education: A Cross-national Study of Ten Industrial Nations. *American Journal of Sociology* 101.

Kangas, O. 1991. *The Politics of Social Rights: Studies on the Dimensions of Sickness Insurance in 18 OECD Countries*. Stockholm: Swedish Institute for Social Research.

Kangas, O. 1994. "The Politics of Social Security: on Regressions, Qualitative Comparisons, and Cluster Analysis." Pp. 346-364 in *The Comparative Political Economy of the Welfare State*, edited by T. Janoski and A.M. Hicks. Cambridge: Cambridge University Press.

King, G., R.O. Keohane, and S. Verba. 1994. *Designing Social Inquiry*. Princeton, NJ: Princeton University Press.

————. 1995. "The Importance of Research Design in Political Science." *American Political Science Review* 89: 475-481.

Kiser, E., and M. Hechter. 1991. "The Role of General Theory in Comparative-Historical Sociology." *American Journal of Sociology* 97: 1-30.

————. 1991. "The Role of General Theory in Comparative-Historical Sociology." *American Journal of Sociology* 97: 1-30.

Korpi, W. 1989. "Power, Politics, and State Autonomy in the Development of Social Citizenship: Social Rights During Sickness in Eighteen OECD Countries since 1930." *American Sociological Review* 54: 309-328.

Kreager, P. 1993. "Anthropological Demography and the Limits of Diffusionism." *Proceedings of the International Population Conference, Montreal* 4: 313-326.

Krüger, L., L.J. Daston, and M. Heidelberger. (Eds.). 1987. *The Probabilistic Revolution*, Vol. 1, *Ideas in History*. Cambridge, MA: MIT Press.

Krüger, L., G. Gigerenzer, and M.S. Morgan. (Eds.). 1987. *The Probabilistic Revolution*, Vol. 2, *Ideas in the Sciences*. Cambridge, MA: MIT Press.

Lieberson, S. 1987. *Making it Count: The Improvement of Social Research and Theory*. Berkeley: University of California Press.

————. 1987. *Making It Count*, 2nd ed. Berkeley: University of California Press.

————. 1992. "Small Ns and Big Conclusions: An Examination of the Reasoning in Comparative Studies based on a Small Number of Cases." Pp. 105-118 in *What is a Case?*, edited by C.C. Ragin and H.S. Becker. Cambridge: Cambridge University Press.

————. 1994. "'More on the Uneasy Case for Using Mill-Type Methods in Small-N Comparative Studies." *Social Forces* 72: 1225-1237.

Lindesmith, A. 1948. *Opiate Addiction*. Bloomington, IN: Principia.

March, J.G. 1978. "Bounded Rationality, Ambiguity, and the Engineering of Choice." *Bell Journal of Economics* 9: 587-608.

McMichael, P. 1990. "Incorporating Comparison Within a World-Historical Perspective: an Alternative Comparative Method." *American Sociological Review* 55: 385-397.

Meyer, J.W. 1987. "The World Polity and the Authority of the Nation-State." Pp. 41-70 in *Institutional Structure*, edited by G.M. Thomas, J.W. Meyer, F.O. Ramirez, and J.Boli. Newbury Park: Sage.

Mill, J.S. 1843/1973-1974. "A System of Logic Ratiocinative and Inductive." In *Collected Works of John Stuart Mill*, edited by J.M. Robson. Toronto: University of Toronto Press.

Moore, B. (1966) *Social Origins of Dictatorship and Democracy*. Boston: Beacon Press.

Müller, W., and W. Karle. 1993. "Social Selection and Educational Systems in Europe." *European Sociological Review* 9: 1:23.

Naroll, R. 1970. "Galton's Problem." Pp. 974-989 in *A Handbook of Method in Cultural Anthropology*, edited by R. Naroll and R. Cohen. New York: The Natural History Press.

Nichols, E. 1986. "Skocpol on Revolution: Comparative Analysis vs. Historical Conjuncture." *Comparative Social Research* 9: 163-186.

O'Connell, P.J. 1994. "National Variation in the Fortunes of Labor: A Pooled and Cross-sectional Analysis of the Impact of Economic Crisis in the Advanced Capitalist Nations." Pp. 218-242 in *The Comparative Political Economy of the Welfare State*, edited by T. Janoski and A.M. Hicks. Cambridge: Cambridge University Press.

O'Connor, J.S., and R.J. Brym. 1988. "Public Welfare Expenditure in OECD Countries." *British Journal of Sociology* 39: 47-68.

Oakeshott, M. 1933. *Experience and its Modes*. Cambridge: Cambridge University Press.

Pampel, F.C., and J.B. Williamson. 1989. *Age, Class, Politics, and the Welfare State*. Cambridge: Cambridge University Press.

Przeworski, A. 1987. "Methods of Cross-National Research, 1970-83: An Overview." Pp. 31-49 in *Comparative Policy Research*, edited by M. Dierkes, H.N. Weiler, and A.B. Antal. Berlin: WZB-Publications.

Przeworski, A., and H. Teune. 1970. *The Logic of Comparative Social Inquiry*. New York: Wiley.

Quadagno, J.S. 1987. "Theories of the Welfare State." *Annual Review of Sociology* 13: 109-128.

Quadagno, J.S., and S.J. Knapp. 1992. "Have Historical Sociologists Forsaken Theory?" *Sociological Methods and Research* 20: 481-507.

Ragin, C.C. 1987. *The Comparative Method*. Berkeley: University of California Press.

————. 1994a. *Constructing Social Research*. Thousand Oaks, CA: Pine Forge Press.

————. 1994b. "Introduction to Qualitative Comparative Analysis." Pp. 299-319 in *The Comparative Political Economy of the Welfare State*, edited by T. Janoski and A.M. Hicks. Cambridge: Cambridge University Press.

Ramirez, F.O. and J. Boli. 1987. "Global Patterns of Educational Institutionalization." Pp. 150-172 in *Institutional Structure*, edited by G.M. Thomas, J.W. Meyer, F.O. Ramirez, and J.Boli. Newbury Park: Sage.

Robinson, W.S. 1951. "The Logical Structure of Analytic Induction." *American Sociological Review* 16: 812-818.

Rueschemeyer, D. 1991. "Different Methods—Contradictory Results? Research on Development and Democracy." Pp. 9-38 in *Issues and Alternatives in Comparative Social Research*, edited by C.C.Ragin. Leiden: E.J. Brill.

Rueschemeyer, D., E.H. Stephens, and J.D. Stephens. 1992. *Capitalist Development and Democracy*. Cambridge: Polity Press.

Ryan, A. 1970. *The Philosophy of John Stuart Mill*. London: Macmillan.

Sartori, G. 1994. "Compare Why and How." Pp. 14-34 in *Comparing Nations*, edited by M. Dogan and A. Kazancigil. Oxford: Blackwell.

Scheuch, E.K. 1989. "Theoretical Implications of Comparative Survey Research: Why the Wheel of Cross-Cultural Methodology Keeps on being Reinvented." *International Sociology* 4: 147-167.

Schmidt, M.G. 1993. "Gendered Labour Force Participation." Pp. 179-237 in *Families of Nations: Patterns of Public Policy in Western Democracies*, edited by F.G. Castles. Aldershot: Dartmouth.

Schmitter, P.C. 1991. *Comparative Politics at the Crossroads* Madrid: Instituto Juan Mach.

Shavit, Y., and H-P. Blossfeld. (Eds.). 1993. *Persistent Inequality: Changing Educational Attainment in Thirteen Countries*. Boulder, CO: Westview Press.

Skocpol, T. 1979. *States and Social Revolutions*. Cambridge: Cambridge University Press.

————. 1982. "Rentier State and Shi'a Islam in the Iranian Revolution." *Theory and Society* 11: 265-283.

————. 1984. "Emerging Agendas and Recurrent Strategies in Historical Sociology." Pp. 356-391 in *Vision and Method in Historical Sociology*, edited by T. Skocpol. Cambridge: Cambridge University Press.

————. 1986. "Analyzing Causal Configurations in History: A Rejoinder to Nichols." *Comparative Social Research* 9: 187-194.

————. 1994. *Social Revolutions in the Modern World*. Cambridge: Cambridge University Press.

Skocpol, T., and M. Somers. 1980. "The Uses of Comparative History in Macrosocial Inquiry." *Comparative Studies in Society and History* 22: 174-97.

Smelser, N.J. 1976. *Comparative Methods in the Social Sciences*. Englewood Cliffs, NJ: Prentice-Hall.

Stimson, J.A. 1985. "Regression in Space and Time: A Statistical Essay." *American Journal of Political Science* 29: 914-947.

Sutherland, S. 1992. *Irrationality*. London: Penguin.

Sztompka, P. 1988. "Conceptual Frameworks in Comparative Inquiry: Divergent or Convergent?" *International Sociology* 3: 207-218.

Therborn, G. 1993. "Beyond the Lonely Nation-State." Pp. 329-340 in *Families of Nations: Patterns of Public Policy in Western Democracies*, edited by F.G. Castles. Aldershot: Dartmouth.

Treiman, D.J. 1975. "Problems of Concept and Measurement in the Comparative Study of Occupational Mobility." *Social Science Research* 4: 183-230.

Tylor, E.B. 1889. "On a Method of Investigating the Development of Institutions; Applied to Laws of Marriage and Descent." *Journal of the Royal Anthropological Institute* 18: 245-256, 261-269.

Usui, C. 1994. "Welfare State Development in a World System Context: Event History Analysis of First Social Insurance Legislation among 60 Countries, 1880-1960." Pp. 254-277 in *The Comparative Political Economy of the Welfare State*, edited by T. Janoski and A.M. Hicks. Cambridge: Cambridge University Press.

Walsh, W.H. 1974. "Colligatory Concepts in History." Pp. 127-144 in *The Philosophy of History*, edited by P. Gardiner. Oxford: Oxford University Press.

Wickham-Crowley, T.P. 1992. *Guerrillas and Revolution in Latin America*. Princeton, NJ: Princeton University Press.

Zaret, D. 1978. "Sociological Theory and Historical Scholarship." *The American Sociologist* 13: 114-121.

Zelditch, M. 1971. "Intelligible Comparisons." Pp. 267-307 in *Comparative Methods in Sociology*, edited by I. Vallier. Berkeley: University of California Press.

Znaniecki, F. 1934. *The Method of Sociology*. New York: Farrar and Rhinehart.

TURNING THE TABLES:

HOW CASE-ORIENTED RESEARCH CHALLENGES VARIABLE-ORIENTED RESEARCH

Charles C. Ragin

ABSTRACT

Various scholars have evaluated case-oriented comparative research from the perspective of large-N, variable-oriented research and found it lacking. In this chapter I turn the tables and evaluate large-N, quantitative research relative to the standards of case-oriented work. I focus on practical concerns addressed in case-oriented research which pose serious challenges to large-N, variable-oriented inquiry. The five practical concerns I address are: (1) the problem of constituting cases (defining and delineating the class of cases relevant to a particular investigation), (2) the problem of studying the causes of outcomes which are uniform across selected cases ("positive cases"), (3) the problem of delineating and defining negative cases which can be compared with positive cases, (4) the problem of studying multiple paths to the same outcome (multiple conjunctural causation), and (5) the problem of accounting for nonconforming cases. Case-oriented scholars use flexible analytic frames than can be modified in light of the knowledge of cases that researchers gain in the course of their research. This aspect of the case-oriented approach makes it especially well-suited for concept formation and theory development.

Comparative Social Research, Volume 16, pages 27-42.
Copyright © 1997 by JAI Press Inc.
All rights of reproduction in any form reserved.
ISBN: 0-7623-0250-X

INTRODUCTION

In this chapter I offer an extended response to John Goldthorpe's discussion of the merits of case-oriented investigation in comparative social science. Goldthorpe evaluates qualitative, case-oriented social science using the standards of quantitative, variable-oriented social science. He examines three problems that "have been chiefly discussed in connection with variable-oriented research" (Goldthorpe 1996) and argues that case-oriented researchers face these same problems and, contrary to the claims of some, have failed to solve them. The three issues he considers are (1) the problem of small Ns, (2) the problem of the nonindependence of observations, and (3) the problem of "black box" explanations.

Goldthorpe does not offer solutions to these problems. He is content simply to argue that they plague macroquantitative research and are not solved in case-oriented research. In essence, he appears to be more concerned with maintaining the preeminence of variable-oriented social science in the face of recent challenges by researchers advocating case-oriented methods than with solving problems. His tact of using the concerns of variable-oriented social science to criticize case-oriented work is not new. Others who have travelled this well-worn path include widely cited treatments such as Przeworski and Teune (1970), Lijphart (1971, 1975), Lieberson (1991, 1994), and King and associates (1994). The implicit and sometimes explicit message in these discussions is that there are fundamental "problems" with the practice of case-oriented research and that this approach somehow must be made more rigorous.

It may come as a surprise to some that variable-oriented techniques need defending. After all, those who use conventional quantitative techniques align themselves with some of the most powerful social scientists in the world today—for example, economists, who are often aped by sociologists and political scientists, and practitioners of survey research hailing from many different disciplines, professions, and settings (including the world's most powerful governments and corporations). Goldthorpe's discomfort with the various criticisms variable-oriented techniques have weathered in the last decade may stem from several sources: (1) The critiques often have come from scholars who use these techniques extensively. (2) The critiques seem to resurrect and reinforce many long-standing arguments about the limitations of conventional quantitative analysis. (3) In comparative social science, variable-oriented work does not have the orthodox status that it has in most social scientific fields. Comparative social science, for good reasons, has always maintained a vigorous case-oriented wing populated primarily by scholars whose reputations rest on their accumulated, in-depth knowledge of the history and culture of "other" times and places—that is, case-oriented knowledge.

Goldthorpe's defense of variable-oriented methods touches on many important methodological issues that certainly warrant careful consideration and debate. While I find much to disagree with in his essay, I readily accept one of its basic premises—that there is a lot to be gained from a healthy dialogue between case-oriented and variable-oriented approaches. I also agree with Goldthorpe that there is much that can be improved in the conduct of case-oriented research (see Ragin 1987, pp. 36-44; and esp. Ragin and Hein 1993). Rather than engage in tedious debates on issues that cannot be resolved to anyone's satisfaction in journal articles, I offer instead a new contribution to the dialogue between case-oriented and variable-oriented approaches. Specifically, I attempt the opposite of what Goldthorpe, Lieberson (1991, 1994), King and associates (1994) and others have attempted. Rather than evaluate case-oriented work relative to the standards of variable-oriented work, I translate some of the key concerns of case-oriented research to variable-oriented research and show the difficult methodological problems these concerns pose for the variable-oriented approach. In short, I seek to enrich the dialogue between case-oriented and variable-oriented approaches by turning the tables.[1] Along the way, I address many of the issues Goldthorpe raises and offer arguments that complement those of others engaged in this exchange (e.g., Stephens and Rueschemeyer 1996—in this volume).

My goal in this chapter is *not* to repeat familiar appeals about uniqueness, holism, experience, meaning, narrative integrity, or cultural significance—the concerns most often voiced by qualitative, case-oriented researchers in debates about methods. Nor do I waste much time repeating the claim that the goals of qualitative research differ diametrically from those of quantitative research. After all, there is no necessary wedge separating the goal of "inference"—the key concern of quantitative approaches—from the goal of "representation"—a common concern of qualitative approaches (Ragin 1994, pp. 47-52). Instead, I elucidate *practical* concerns that are at the core of case-oriented strategies. These practical concerns pose several important challenges to variable-oriented approaches. I do not claim that these difficulties throw insurmountable obstacles in the path of statistical methodology. Rather, my concern is that these practical issues are usually obscured in the process of variable-oriented research or neutralized through assumptions. My ultimate goal in raising these concerns is to make those who practice the variable-oriented approach at least more self-conscious and perhaps more rigorous as well.

By *practical concerns*, I refer to the deceptively simple mechanics of constructing social scientific representations from empirical evidence, a task common to virtually all forms of empirical social research (Ragin 1994, pp. 22-29). The features of case-oriented research I discuss here constitute only a relatively small subset of the features that pose practical difficulties for variable-oriented approaches. The concerns I address are centered in five *overlapping* domains: (1) the constitution of cases, (2) the study of uniform outcomes, (3) the definition of negative cases, (4) the analysis of multiple and conjunctural causes, and (5) the treatment of nonconforming cases.

THE CONSTITUTION OF CASES

Case-oriented researchers see cases as meaningful but complex configurations of events and structures. They treat cases as singular, whole entities purposefully selected, not as homogeneous observations drawn at random from a pool of equally plausible selections. Most case-oriented studies start with the seemingly simple idea that social phenomena in like settings (such as organizations, neighborhoods, cities, countries, regions, cultures, and so on) may parallel each other sufficiently to permit comparing and contrasting them. The clause, "may parallel each other sufficiently," is a very important part of this formulation. The qualitative researcher's specification of relevant cases at the start of an investigation is really nothing more than a working hypothesis that the cases initially selected are in fact alike enough to permit comparisons. In the course of the research, the investigator may decide otherwise and drop some cases, or even whole categories of cases, because they do not appear to belong with what seem to be the core cases. Sometimes, this process of sifting through the cases leads to an enlargement of the set of relevant cases and a commensurate broadening of the scope of the guiding concepts. For example, a researcher might surmise in the course of studying "military coups" that the relevant category could be enlarged to include all "irregular transfers of executive power."

Usually, this sifting of the cases is carried on in conjunction with concept formation and elaboration. Concepts are revised and refined as the boundary of the set of relevant cases is shifted and clarified. Important theoretical distinctions often emerge from this dialogue of ideas and evidence. Imagine, for example, that Theda Skocpol (1979) had originally included Mexico along with France, Russia, and China at the outset of her study of social revolutions. The search for commonalities across these four cases might prove too daunting. By eliminating Mexico as a case of *social* revolution in the course of the research, however, it might prove possible to increase the homogeneity within the empirical category and, at the same time, to sharpen the definition of the concept of social revolution.

This interplay of categorization and conceptualization is a key feature of qualitative research (Ragin 1994, Chap. 4). In their recent treatise on the design of qualitative research, however, King and associates (1994) strongly discourage this practice, arguing that it is not appropriate to "add a restrictive condition and then proceed as if our theory, with that qualification, has been shown to be correct." They offer the following example of their concern (1994, p. 21, original italics):

If our original theory was that modern democracies do not fight wars with one another due to their constitutional systems, it would be less permissible, having found exceptions to our "rule," to restrict the proposition to democracies with advanced social welfare systems *once it has been ascertained by inspection of the data that such a qualification would appear to make our proposition correct.*

They state subsequently (1994, p. 22, original italics) that "*we should not make it* [i.e., our theory] *more restrictive without collecting new data to test the new version of the theory.*" Unfortunately, this well-reasoned advice puts an end to most case-oriented research as it is practiced today. The reciprocal clarification of empirical categories and theoretical concepts is one of the central concerns of qualitative research. When the number of relevant cases is limited by the historical record to a mere handful, or even to several handfuls, it is simply not possible to collect a "new sample" to "test" each new theoretical clarification.

Both Goldthorpe and King and associates (1994) recommend switching to a different unit of analysis, say subnational units or time periods, to enlarge the number of "cases" relevant to an argument formulated for larger units.[2] However, most case-oriented comparative social scientists do not find this practice satisfactory. They study the cases they do because these cases are historically, politically, or culturally significant in some way. Typically, the shift to smaller units (i.e., to subnational units or to time periods) entails an unavoidable reformulation of the research question which, in turn, severely undermines the substantive value of the study. Researchers end up asking questions dictated by methods or by data availability, not by their theoretical, substantive, or historical interests. One common reformulation, for example, is to transform questions about qualitative change (i.e., historically emergent phenomena) to questions about variation in cross-sectional levels (i.e., static phenomena).

In fairness to both Goldthorpe and King and associates (1994), it is important to note that their primary concern is theory testing, not concept formation, elaboration, and refinement. Neither King and associates nor Goldthorpe would object to the common practice of using knowledge of the empirical world—however it may have been gained—to build better concepts and thus, ultimately, stronger theories. Still, it is worth pointing out that in their perspective theory testing is the primary, perhaps sole, objective of social science and researchers should organize their research efforts around this important task. It is as though Goldthorpe and King and associates and others start with the assumption that social scientists already possess well-developed, well-articulated, testable theories. Nothing could be further from the truth. In case-oriented research, the bulk of the research effort is often directed toward constituting "the cases" in the investigation and sharpening the concepts appropriate for the cases selected (see Ragin and Becker 1992).

The first practical concern can now be summarized in succinct terms: In much case-oriented research cases usually are not predetermined, nor are they "given" at the outset of an investigation. Instead, they often coalesce in the course of the research through a systematic dialogue of ideas and evidence (see McMichael 1990, especially his discussion of Polanyi). In many qualitatively oriented studies, the conclusion of this process of "casing" (Ragin 1992) may be the primary and most important finding of the investigation (see, e.g., Wieviorka 1993). Consider the serious practical problem this poses for conventional quantitative analysis: The boundary around the "sample of observations" must be relatively malleable throughout the investigation, and this boundary may not be completely fixed until the research is finished. Thus, any statistical result (say, the correlation between two variables across cases) is open to fundamental revision up until the very conclusion of the research because the cases that comprise the sample may be revised continually before that point. Quantitative analysis of the relationships among variables presupposes a fixed set of relevant observations.

THE STUDY OF UNIFORM OUTCOMES

Because the constitution and selection of cases is central to qualitative inquiry, case-oriented researchers may intentionally select cases that differ relatively little from each other with respect to the outcome under investigation. For example, a researcher might attempt to constitute the category "anti-neocolonial revolutions," both empirically and conceptually, through the reciprocal process just described. At the end of this process his or her set of cases might exclude both lesser uprisings (e.g., mere anti-neocolonial "rebellions") and mass insurrections of varying severity that were successfully repressed. In the eyes of the variable-oriented researcher, however, this investigator has committed a great folly—selecting cases that vary only slightly, if at all, on the outcome, or dependent variable.

The first and most obvious problem with this common practice—in the eyes of the variable-oriented scholar—is the simple fact that the dependent variable in this example, anti-neocolonial revolution, does not vary substantially across the cases selected for study. All cases selected display, more or less, the same outcome—anti-neocolonial revolutions. Variable-oriented researchers tend to equate "explanation" with "explaining variation." If there is no variation in the outcome, they reason, then there is nothing to explain. From the perspective of statistical analysis, therefore, the case-oriented investigation of anti-neocolonial revolutions just described may seem to lack even the possibility of analysis or research design. It appears to be an analytic dead end.

The second problem with this common case-oriented practice is known to statisticians as "selecting on the dependent variable."[3] Assume (1) that the category "anti-neocolonial revolutions" encompasses cases with the highest scores (say, 90 through 100 on a 100 point scale) of the more general variable "level of mass insurrection" and (2) that this dependent variable has a strong positive correlation with measures of foreign capital penetration, say, the proportion of fixed capital that is owned by transnational corporations. No doubt, the cases of "anti-neocolonial revolt" identified by the qualitative researcher would all have high levels of foreign capital penetration. However, within the relatively narrow range of mass insurrection that encompasses "anti-neocolonial revolution" (i.e., countries with scores over 90), there may be no apparent relationship between level of foreign capital penetration and the level of mass insurrection. Instead, the relationship between these two variables might be visible only across the entire range of variation in the dependent variable, level of mass insurrection, with scores ranging from near zero to 100. For this reason all researchers are advised, based on sound statistical arguments, to examine the entire range of variation in broadly defined dependent variables and thereby avoid this analytic sin.

From the perspective of variable-oriented analysis, therefore, not only is there little to explain when qualitative investigators "select on the dependent variable," as in the example just described, but investigators are likely as well to be misled about the impact of underlying factors—those that account for the "entire range" of variation in an outcome.

These statistically based criticisms are well reasoned. However, they are based on a very serious misunderstanding of case-oriented research. The first response to these criticisms concerns the theoretical status of the categories elaborated through case-oriented research. The fact that anti-neocolonial revolutions all have very high scores on the variable "level of mass insurrection" does not alter the possibility that anti-neocolonial revolutions are fundamentally (i.e., qualitatively) different from other forms of insurrection and therefore warrant separate analytic attention. Social scientists study the phenomena they study because these phenomena are often culturally or historically significant. The fact that some phenomena (e.g., anti-neocolonial revolutions) can be reconstrued as scores on more general variables (e.g., mass insurrection) does not negate their distinctive features or their substantive importance.

The second response to these criticisms is the simple observation that most case-oriented investigators would not be blind to the fact (in the hypothetical example) that countries with anti-neocolonial revolutions have unusually high levels of foreign capital penetration. Indeed, the very first step in the qualitative analysis of anti-neocolonial revolutions, after constituting the category and specifying the relevant cases, would be to identify the possible causal conditions they share—their commonalities. Their high levels of foreign capital penetration no doubt would be one of the very first commonalities identified. It is not a causal factor that would be overlooked because of its lack of apparent correlation with the intensity of anti-neocolonial revolutions within the relatively narrow range of outcomes selected for study.

The second practical issue, therefore, concerns the function and importance of what statisticians call *constants* in case-oriented analysis. Often the outcome (i.e., the "dependent variable") and many of the explanatory factors in a case-oriented analysis are constants—all cases have more or less the same values. In the example just presented, anti-neocolonial revolutions (the uniform outcome) occur in countries with uniformly high scores on one causal variables (foreign capital penetration) and probably with relatively uniform values on other causal variables as well (for elaboration of these ideas about constants see Griffin et al. 1996). While using constants to account for constants (i.e., the search for commonalities shared by similar instances) is common in case-oriented, qualitative work (and in everyday life), it is foreign to statistical techniques that focus exclusively on relationships among variables—that is, on causal conditions and outcomes that must vary across cases.

THE DEFINITION OF NEGATIVE CASES

The discussion so far has brought us to a debate recognizable to many as the controversy surrounding the method of analytic induction, a technique that follows John Stuart Mill's (1967) method of agreement. The method of agreement looks only at positive cases (that is, cases displaying an effect) and assesses whether or not these positive cases all agree in displaying one or more causes. The usual statistically based objection to this practice is that only two cells of a two-by-two crosstabulation (presence/absence of a cause by presence/absence of an effect) are studied and that, therefore, causal inference is impossible. After all, what if many of the negative cases (that is, cases not displaying the effect) display the same causal factors (e.g., in the example just elaborated, a high level for foreign capital penetration)?

This criticism appears sound. However, it is very important to recognize that this criticism *assumes* a pre-existing population of relevant observations, embracing both positive and negative cases, and thus ignores a central practical concern of qualitative analysis—the constitution of cases, as described above.[4] From the perspective of case-oriented qualitative analysis, the crosstabulation of causes and effects is entirely reasonable as long as these analyses are conducted *within an appropriately constituted set of cases*. For example, it would be entirely reasonable to assess whether or not the emergence of "multiple sovereignty" in anti-neocolonial revolutions is linked to the prior existence of democratic institutions. However, this analysis would be conducted only within the duly constituted category of anti-neocolonial revolutions. The statistically-based critique of analytic induction and the method of agreement ignores this essential precondition for conventional variable-oriented analysis, namely, that relevant cases must be properly constituted through a careful dialogue of ideas and evidence involving the reciprocal clarification of empirical categories and theoretical concepts.

From the perspective of case-oriented analysis, to crosstabulate the presence/ absence of causes of anti-neocolonial revolution with the presence/absence of anti-neocolonial revolution, it first would be necessary to constitute the category of relevant negative cases (for example, the category "countries with a strong possibility of anti-neocolonial revolutions"). Before doing this, of course, it would be necessary to examine actual anti-neocolonial revolutions closely and identify their common causes, using theory, substantive knowledge, and interests as guides. In other words, the investigator would have to constitute the empirical category "anti-neocolonial revolutions" and identify common causal factors (using the method of agreement or some other method appropriate for the study of uniform outcomes) before attempting to constitute the category "countries with a strong possibility of anti-neocolonial revolutions" and then proceed with conventional variable-oriented analysis of the differences between positive and negative cases (see also Griffin et al. 1996).

Thus, conventional variable-oriented analysis *assumes* the very thing that case-oriented analysis typically considers most problematic—the relevant population of cases, including both positive and negative instances. The many simple-minded critiques of the method of agreement (and analytic induction) fall apart as soon as it is recognized that the constitution of populations is a theory-laden, concept-intensive process. Further, as I have argued, the constitution of relevant "negative cases" typically rests on the careful prior constitution of "positive cases." Even once both positive and negative cases have been identified, the boundaries of the relevant population of cases may still be adjusted further in the course of case-oriented research.

THE EXAMINATION OF MULTIPLE AND CONJUNCTURAL CAUSES

After constituting and selecting relevant instances of a phenomenon like "anti-neocolonial revolutions" and, if possible, defining relevant negative cases as well, the case-oriented investigator's task is to address the causal forces behind the phenomenon, with special attention to similarities and differences across cases. Each case is examined in detail—using theoretical concepts, substantive knowledge, and interests as guides—in order to answer the question of "how" the phenomenon of interest came about in each positive case and why it did not in the negative cases—assuming they can be confidently identified. While it is standard practice for case-oriented researchers to search for constants (e.g., high levels of foreign capital penetration) across positive cases in their attempts to identify the causal forces behind an outcome (e.g., anti-neocolonial revolutions), the typical case-oriented inquiry does not assume or even anticipate causal uniformity across positive cases. On the contrary, the usual expectation is that *different* combinations of causes may produce the same outcome. That is, case-oriented researchers often pay special attention to the diverse ways a common outcome may be reached.

When examining similarities and differences across cases, case-oriented researchers usually expect evidence to be causally "lumpy." That is, they anticipate finding several major causal pathways in a given body of cross-case evidence. A typical finding is that different causes combine in different and sometimes contradictory ways to produce roughly similar outcomes in different settings. The effect of any particular causal condition depends on the presence and absence of other conditions, and several different conditions may satisfy a general causal requirement—that is, two or more different causes may be equivalent at a more abstract level. Thus, causal explanations in case-oriented research often have the form: "When conditions A, B, and C are present, X causes Y; however, if any one of these conditions (A, B, or C) is absent, and X is also absent, then Z causes Y." This argument is multiple and conjunctural in form because it cites alternate combinations of causal conditions. The hypothetical causal argument just presented essentially states that there are four combinations of conditions that result in the outcome Y. It can be formulated using Boolean algebra (see Ragin 1987) as follows:

$$Y = ABCX + ABcxZ + AbCxZ + aBCxZ$$

(Upper-case letters indicate the presence of a condition; lower-case letters indicate its absence; multiplication indicates causal conjunctures; addition indicates alternative causal pathways.)

The search for patterns of multiple conjunctural causation, a common concern of case-oriented researchers, poses serious practical problems for variable-oriented research. To investigate this type of causation with statistical techniques, it is necessary to examine high-level interactions (e.g., four-way interactions in the causal argument just described). However, these sophisticated techniques are very rarely used by variable-oriented researchers. When they are, they require at least two essential ingredients: (1) a very large number of diverse cases, and (2) an investigator willing to contend with a difficult mass of multicollinearity. These techniques are simply not feasible in investigations with small or even moderate Ns, the usual situation in comparative social science. When Ns are small to moderate, causal complexity is more apparent, more salient, and easier to identify and interpret; yet it is also much less amenable to statistical analysis.

In his essay Goldthorpe (1996) laments the inability of case-oriented methods to reveal the "relative strengths of different effects or combination of effects." However, multiple conjunctural causation, as sketched here, challenges the very idea of "relative strengths." It is not possible to assess a variable's "unique" or separate contribution to the explanation of variation in some outcome unless the model in question is a simple additive model. To isolate a single causal factor and attempt to assess its separate or "independent" impact across all cases, a common concern in multivariate statistical analysis, is difficult in research that pays close attention to causal conjunctures. When the focus is on causal conjunctures, the magnitude of any single cause's impact depends on the presence or absence of other causal conditions. The impact of X on Y in the causal statement just presented, for example, requires the co-presence of conditions A, B and C. Of course, it *is* possible in the case-oriented approach to assess which cases (or what proportion of cases) included in a study follow which causal path. Indeed, linking cases to causal pathways and assessing the relative importance of different paths should be an essential part of case-oriented comparative research.

In variable-oriented research the assessment of relative importance is conducted across all cases and involves computing partial relationships, which, in turn, are constructed from bivariate relationships. (To compute a multiple regression, for example, only a matrix of bivariate correlations, along with the means and standard deviations of all the variables, is required.) However, bivariate relationships can give false leads, even when they are partialled. Note, for example, that condition X in the Boolean equation just described must be present in some contexts and absent in others for Y to occur. A conventional statistical analysis of the bivariate relationship between X and Y might show no relationship (i.e., a Pearson's r of 0).

Simply stated, the fourth practical concern of case-oriented researchers is causal heterogeneity. Because they conduct in-depth investigations of individual cases, case-oriented researchers are able to identify complex patterns of conjunctural causation. While researchers interested only in testing general theories might find this level of detail uninteresting, in-depth study offers important insight into the diversity and complexity of social life, which, in turn, offers rich material for theoretical development and refinement.

"DETERMINISM" AND THE TREATMENT OF NONCONFORMING CASES

Because Ns tend to be relatively small in comparative research, it is possible to become familiar with every case. Also, each case selected for examination may be historically or culturally significant in some way and thus worthy of separate attention. For these reasons, case-oriented researchers often account for every case included in a study, no matter how poorly each may conform to common causal patterns. Thus, researchers hope to find causal lumps (i.e., an interpretable pattern of multiple conjunctural causation), but they also anticipate finding causal specks—cases that do not conform to any of the common causal pathways. Causal specks are usually not discarded, even though they may be inconvenient. Suppose, for example, that Iran offers the only instance of anti-neocolonial revolution with a strong religious slant. Do we simply ignore this important case? Relegate it to the error vector? Call it a fluke?

The variable-oriented critics of case-oriented work argue that accounting for every case is equivalent to trying to do the impossible—explaining "all the variation"—and that this trap should be avoided. They argue that researchers instead should stick to well-known and well-understood probabilistic models of social phenomenon. This criticism of case-oriented research has two important bases. The first is that explanations that "account for every case" are deterministic, and there is simply too much randomness in human affairs to permit deterministic explanations. (The implication is that case-oriented researchers forsake true science when they attempt to account for each case.) The second is that the effort to "explain all the variation" may lead to the inclusion of theoretically trivial causal variables or, even worse, to the embrace of theoretically incorrect causal models, understandings that take advantage of the peculiar features of a particular "sample" of cases.[5]

These arguments can be addressed with a simple example. As is well known, the typical comparative study has a paucity of cases relative to the number of variables. This feature, in fact, could be considered one of the key defining characteristics of comparative research. Consider the typical contrast: A quantitative study of voting with 3,000 voters and 15 main variables has a statistically "healthy" ratio of 200 observations per variable (200:1). A comparative study of Third World countries with violent mass protest against the International Monetary Fund, by contrast, might have about 20 cases and 30 independent variables, an "unhealthy" ratio of 2:3. Anyone who has attempted sophisticated statistical analysis of small Ns knows that with 20 cases and 30 independent variables, it is possible to construct many different prediction equations that account for 100 percent of the variation in a dependent variable (say, the longevity of the mass protest against the IMF). No special effort is required to "explain all the variation" in this hypothetical variable-oriented analysis. The researcher would not have to "take advantage" of the "sample" or of any of its "peculiar" (i.e., historically or culturally specific) features. The high level of explained variation in this hypothetical variable-oriented study is a simple artifact of the ratio of cases to explanatory factors—just as it would be in a case-oriented study of the same evidence.

No one would describe a statistical model derived in this manner *deterministic* simply because of the level of explained variance achieved (100%). A truly deterministic argument should involve explicit theorizing and explicit statements about the nature of the determinism involved. I know of no case-oriented or variable-oriented researcher who has proposed such an argument, even though it is always possible for researchers using either research strategy to explain "all the variation" in some outcome.

The more important issue here is the fact that *many different models* will perform equally well, not that it is possible to "explain all the variation." For example, suppose that with 20 cases and 30 independent variables, it is possible to derive eleven different prediction equations, each with only five predictors, that account for 80 percent of the variation in the dependent variable. Which one should the investigator choose? The key question, of course, is the *plausibility* of the explanations implied by the different equations. Faced with the possibility of achieving a very high level of explained variation with many different prediction models, the variable-oriented researcher is usually stymied. The issue of plausibility cannot be resolved by running more and more equations or by plumbing the depths of probability theory. Instead, it is usually necessary to assess the relative plausibility of equivalent prediction models by going back to the cases included in the study and trying to determine *at the case level* which model makes the most sense. In other words, having a surplus of explanatory variables—the usual situation in comparative social science—often *necessitates* case-oriented analysis.

Thus, when there are more independent variables than cases, the problem is not one of "determinism," where determinism is equated with 100 percent explained variation. This so-called determinism is a simple artifact of the ratio of independent variables to cases and has nothing to do with the researcher's arguments. On the contrary, the problem here is one of extreme *indeterminism*—the fact that there may be many different models that do equally well. The best antidote for a multiplicity of equally predictive models (indeterminism) is more knowledge of cases. All researchers should be wary of models, especially simple models, that "explain every case." They should check each case to see if the model in question offers a plausible representation of the case.

Most case-oriented investigators do not explain all their cases with a single model (even when the model incorporates multiple conjunctural causation). More typically, they confront nonconforming cases and account for them by citing factors that are outside their explanatory frameworks (a procedure endorsed by Goldthorpe). The specifics of each case are not irrelevant to social science, even when knowledge of specifics has only limited relevance to theory. Consider an example developed by King and associates (1994): Weather fluctuations intensify a flu epidemic, especially among lower strata, on election day. The Labor Party thus suffers a poor turnout and loses an election it should have won. This example is a wonderful demonstration of both randomness and of our potential for identifying the play of such forces in producing nonconforming outcomes. For those interested in what happened or in winning elections (i.e., path dependency), this bit of knowledge might be very important. For those interested in studying shifts in the link between class and party support, it may simply be an annoyance (i.e., error).

The practical issue here is that "error" is usually conceived very differently in case-oriented and variable-oriented research. In qualitative research, error is a prod: Investigators try to account for every case in their attempt to uncover patterned diversity. Cases often deviate from common patterns, but these deviations are identified and addressed. Investigators make every effort to identify the factors at work in nonconforming cases, even when these factors are outside the frameworks they bring to the research. In variable-oriented research, by contrast, the "error" that remains at the end of an investigation may embrace much more than it does in qualitative research. It includes randomness, omitted variables, poor measurement, model misspecification, and other factors, including, in some research, ignorance of the cases studied.

CONCLUSION

Case-oriented and variable-oriented researchers are joined by their common objective of constructing representations of social phenomena from evidence. They are joined as well by their use of common concepts and analytic frames to facilitate this fundamental objective. In practice, however, cross-case qualitative research, especially the variety common in the comparative study of social and political phenomena, adopts a very different approach to the work of building representations from evidence. The practical concerns sketched in this paper present a bare outline of several distinctive features of the process of case-oriented research, from the constitution of cases to the examination of uniform causes and outcomes, and from the analysis of multiple conjunctural causes to the explanation of nonconforming cases.

The case-oriented approach poses important challenges to variable-oriented research, challenges which, if answered, would make variable-oriented research more rigorous. For example, in most variable-oriented research, the sample of relevant observations is usually set at the outset of a study and is not open to reformulation or redefinition. In most variable-oriented research, the operation of causal conditions that are constant across cases is obscured. In most variable-oriented research, it is difficult to examine multiple conjunctural causation because researchers lack in-depth knowledge of cases and because their most common analytic tools cannot cope with complex causal patterns. Finally, in most variable-oriented research, ignorance of cases may find its way into the error vector of probabilistic models. Of course, the practical concerns of case-oriented research may be difficult to address in the variable-oriented approach. It is still reasonable to hope, at a minimum, for greater appreciation of the special strengths of different ways of constructing social scientific representations of social life.

ACKNOWLEDGMENT

I thank Bruce Carruthers and Larry Griffin for their many useful comments.

NOTES

1. To maximize the exchange between these two approaches, I impose a further restriction: I limit the discussion to case-oriented approaches that are explicitly concerned with patterns across multiple cases, not with the examination of a single case (see Myles and Huberman 1994). The extreme in this regard is the country specialist who might spend an entire career coming to grips with a "single case" like the fall of the Berlin Wall or the outcome of the Korean War. This researcher has "only one case" but may consider thousands of factors and conditions in his or her effort to explain the case—to "get it right." In research of this type, the goal is to piece together a whole, a single case, from the elements that constitute the case. Obviously, this research strategy cannot be made commensurable, at least not in any simple or straightforward manner, with the statistically based concern for an abundance of observations relative to explanatory variables.

2. There is great slippage in what is meant by the term "case" (Ragin and Becker 1992). Usually, Goldthorpe, King and associates (1994) and other defenders of quantitative methods in macrosocial research switch terms and speak only of "observations" and thus skirt the issue of identifying what, exactly, the case is (see also Collier 1995).

3. A parallel and more detailed illustration is offered by King and associates (1994). Unfortunately, their example does not resonate well with the substantive concerns of comparative social science. Thus, they follow the lead of Lieberson (1991), who used automobile accidents to elaborate his arguments, in presenting examples that simply do not ring true to the concerns of comparative social science.

4. Consider for example, the category "not instances of anti-neocolonial revolutions." This category is as infinite as it is vague.

5. These criticisms fail to acknowledge that the treatment of nonconforming cases is typically handled outside of the main arguments of the study. Case-oriented researchers usually try to explain why the nonconforming cases fail to conform. Sometimes nonconforming cases stimulate revisions of theories. More often, they summon arguments about specific historical factors that are outside the researcher's framework.

REFERENCES

Collier, D. 1995. "Translating Quantitative Methods for Qualitative Researchers: The Case of Selection Bias." *American Political Science Review* 89(2): 461-466.

Eckstein, H. 1969. "Case Study and Theory in Political Science." In *Handbook of Political Science, Volume 1, Political Science: Scope and Theory*, edited by Fred I. Greenstein and Nelson W. Polsby. Reading, MA: Addison-Wesley.

Goldthorpe, J. 1996. "Current Issues in Comparative Macrosociology." *Comparative Social Research*, Vol. 16. Greenwich, CT: JAI Press.

Griffin, L., C. Caplinger, K. Lively, N.L. Malcom, D. McDaniel, and C. Nelsen. 1996. "Comparative-Historical Analysis and Scientific Inference: Disfranchisement in the U.S. South as a Test Case." *Historical Methods*, forthcoming.

King, G., R.O. Keohane, and S. Verba. 1994. *Designing Social Inquiry: Scientific Inference in Qualitative Research*. Princeton, NJ: Princeton University Press.

Lieberson, S. 1991. "Small N's and Big Conclusions: An Examination of the Reasoning Based On a Small Number of Cases." *Social Forces* 70: 307-320.

_____. 1994. "More On the Uneasy Case for Using Mill-Type Methods in Small-N Comparative Studies." *Social Forces* 72: 1225-1237.

Lijphart, A. 1971. "Comparative Politics and the Comparative Method." *American Political Science Review* 65: 682-693.

_____. 1975. "The Comparable Cases Strategy in Comparative Research." *Comparative Political Studies* 8: 157-175.

McMichael, P. 1990. "Incorporating Comparison Within a World-Historical Perspective: An Alternative Comparative Method." *American Sociological Review* 55: 385-397.

Mill, J.S. 1967 [1843]. *A System of Logic: Ratiocinative and Inductive.* Toronto: University of Toronto Press.

Myles, M., and S. Huberman. 1994. *Qualitative Data Analysis, Second Edition.* Newbury Park, CA: Sage Publications.

Przeworski, A., and H. Teune. 1970. *The Logic of Comparative Social Inquiry.* New York: John Wiley.

Ragin, C.C. 1987. *The Comparative Method: Moving Beyond Qualitative and Quantitative Strategies.* Berkeley, CA: University of California Press.

_____. 1992. "Casing and the Process of Social Research." In *What Is a Case? Exploring the Foundations of Social Inquiry,* edited by C.C. Ragin and H.S. Becker. New York: Cambridge University Press.

_____. 1994. *Constructing Social Research: The Unity and Diversity of Method.* Newbury Park, CA: Pine Forge Press.

Ragin, C.C., and H.S. Becker. 1992. *What Is a Case? Exploring the Foundations of Social Inquiry.* New York: Cambridge University Press.

Ragin, C.C., and J. Hein. 1993. "The Comparative Study of Ethnicity: Methodological and Conceptual Issues." Pp. 254-272 in *Race and Ethnicity in Research Methods,* edited by John Stanfield II and Rutledge Dennis. Newbury Park: Sage Publications.

Skocpol, T. 1979. *States and Social Revolutions: A Comparative Analysis of France, Russia, and China.* New York: Cambridge University Press.

MEANS AND ENDS OF COMPARISON IN MACROSOCIOLOGY

Charles Tilly

ABSTRACT

John Stuart Mill's own warnings rule out the application of his experimental methods to social processes. Although previously popular in the social sciences, big case comparisons are properly disappearing. Social scientists should shift to the search for general causal mechanisms in multiple, never repeated, structures and processes.

Variation *in vitro* differs significantly from variation in natural history, *a fortiori* from variation in social history and macrosociology. After laying out his famous Methods of Agreement and of Differences, as well as his often-ignored Methods of Residues and of Concomitant Variation, John Stuart Mill reminded readers that his Methods applied exclusively to experimental procedures. Mill confined them, furthermore, to relatively simple phenomena entailing little interaction among causes, which meant they would not much advance understanding of living organisms. He therefore issued a stern warning:

Comparative Social Research, Volume 16, pages 43-53.
Copyright © 1997 by JAI Press Inc.
All rights of reproduction in any form reserved.
ISBN: 0-7623-0250-X

> If so little can be done by the experimental method to determine the conditions of an effect of many combined causes, in the case of medical science; still less is this method applicable to a class of phenomena more complicated than even those of physiology, the phenomena of politics and history. There, Plurality of Causes exists in almost boundless excess, and effects are, for the most part, inextricably interwoven with one another. To add to the embarrassment, most of the inquiries in political science relate to the production of effects of a most comprehensive description, such as the public wealth, public security, public morality, and the like: results likely to be affected directly or indirectly either in *plus* or in *minus* by nearly every fact which exists, or event which occurs, in human society. The vulgar notion, that the safe methods on political subjects are those of Baconian induction— that the true guide is not general reasoning, but specific experience—will one day be quoted as among the most unequivocal marks of a low state of the speculative faculties in any age in which it is accredited. Nothing can be more ludicrous than the sort of parodies on experimental reasoning which one is accustomed to meet with, not in popular discussion only, but in grave treatises, when the affairs of nations are the theme. "How," it is asked, "can an institution be bad, when the country has prospered under it?" "How can such or such causes have contributed to the prosperity of one country, when another has prospered without them?" Whoever makes use of an argument of this kind, not intending to deceive, should be sent back to learn the elements of some one of the more easy physical sciences (Mill 1887, p. 324).

Later, Mill identified the chief difficulties in applying his experimental methods to human affairs: not only the complex interaction of causes, but also the fact that his methods required *a priori* a finite, specified set of hypothetical causes. Aimed at social processes, Mill's Methods remained always, fatally vulnerable to the allegation that a hitherto-unsuspected cause was operating.

No one has much improved on Mill's own initial statement of objections to application of his four experimental methods in the explanation of social processes. Yet, as John Goldthorpe complains, twentieth century social scientists have often invoked the Method of Agreement and the Method of Differences as justifications for big case comparisons—hereafter BCC. In this invited response to Goldthorpe's analysis, I will neither recapitulate the independent critique of BCC I have presented *ad nauseam* elsewhere nor describe in any detail the alternatives to BCC I have advocated and practiced incessantly for many years; this discussion focuses on what Goldthorpe says about BCC.

Goldthorpe rightly claims that switching from "variables" to "cases" does not mitigate the problem of coherent comparison; in fact, it makes Mill's own strictures all the more applicable. If they had listened to Mill, social scientists would never have adopted BCC. Goldthorpe misses the crucial next step. Small Ns, Galton's diffusion processes, and appeal to black-box causation do bedevil many applications of BCC, but all constitute soluble secondary difficulties. Here is the primary difficulty: BCC provides a fine heuristic but a logically and ontologically flawed basis for serious explanation of social processes. Although they might not have adopted the Comtean evolutionist approach that Mill himself advocated, from the start attentive readers of John Stuart

Mill should also have rejected the program Edward Tylor styled the Comparative Method in 1889. No less a figure than Francis Galton, after all, identified the program's crippling weaknesses at its very unveiling (Hammel 1980). Yet only now, more than a century after Tylor's explication of the Method, is the program collapsing. Its charms long led social scientists to ignore its fatal vices.

As a program for investigating, writing, teaching, communicating, and job-creating, comparative-historical analysis in the BCC mode has seen very good days. Those days will soon pass. Vital, vibrant work on big structures, large processes, and huge comparisons in space-time will continue in sociology and other social sciences. Historical inquiry will thrive, but not in the mode that has come to define the field during the last scholarly generation: BCC. The lining up of civilizations, societies, cultures, wars, revolutions, and other great chunks of social experience for arguments about causes and meanings will persist as the heuristic and literary trope it has been for hundreds of years, but will shrivel as a method of systematic analysis. BCC will shrivel for several reasons: because its faulty ontological premises are finally outweighing its undoubted contributions as a means of disciplining inquiry; because the system of distinct, bounded sovereign states that long served as its implicit warrant is rapidly disintegrating; because the rise of relational, historicist, and institutional thinking in the social sciences is raising insuperable challenges to all portrayals of social life as the work of neatly-bounded, self-motivated, rule-following actors, individual or collective.

Comparison of large social chunks in search of invariant laws has marked the social sciences since their emergence as self-regarding disciplines—certainly since 1889. In different styles, Max Weber, Oswald Spengler, and Pitirim Sorokin exemplified and justified sociologists' investment in vast comparative enterprises. During the 1940s, big comparative-historical inquiries lost much of their lustre in sociology—in 1959, the American Sociological Association-sponsored volume *Sociology Today* surveyed the whole field, but offered no sustained discussion of historical or comparative analysis—only to revive handsomely with S.N. Eisenstadt, Reinhard Bendix, Stein Rokkan, Barrington Moore, Jr., and others from the late 1950s onward. That second wave is now subsiding. The sea will survive, but its chief currents already run in other directions.

In their time, historical-comparative inquiries provided splendid antidotes for unhistorical and antihistorical maladies in social science. However one disagreed with them on other grounds, such masters as Bendix, Rokkan, and Moore made evident how greatly where, when, and in what order some social process occurred mattered to *how* it occurred. They exposed the bankruptcy of the quasi-evolutionary pseudo-history in which searchers for the secrets of development lined up whole societies, generally identified by the existence of a durable state, along a single continuum from least to most advanced, then inferred the standard developmental path from that continuum—or, worse yet, from currently-observable characteristics of its most advanced members. They validated concerns about power, freedom, and human agency bequeathed to social science by Karl Marx, Max Weber, and other ancestors. They thereby motivated rich, ambitious historical and comparative examinations of human struggles.

From early on, nevertheless, postwar historical-comparative analysis followed multiple paths in addition to the comparison of civilizations, societies, cultures, and momentous events. Inspired partly by a populist hope to reconstruct history from below and partly by collaboration with historians who were trying to renew their own craft through self-conscious adoption of social-scientific procedures, students of family structure, population processes, communities, political struggle, and economic change dug deeply into historical materials without concentrating on massive case-by-case comparisons (Abbott 1994; Monkkonen 1994). Despite strident epistemological challenges from postmodern critics, such studies still thrive today (see, e.g., Hanagan 1994).

Yet the emblem of comparative-historical analysis, Big Case Comparison, is now fading. BCC is fading because of (1) ontological inadequacy, (2) disintegration of state systems, and (3) relational, historicist, and institutional thinking.

Ontological inadequacy? The presumption that distinctive, autonomous, coherent, self-sustaining civilizations, societies, cultures, and/or great events not only exist but possess their own logics *sui generis* undergirds the BCC program. Where empirically-identifiable states, organizations, networks, or connected sequences of action actually constitute the objects of study, to be sure, social scientists have ample reasons to formulate ideas concerning their regularities and to undertake systematic comparisons among them. But presuming their intelligible existence *a priori*, inferring the coherence of societies from the presence of states, or taking historically-constructed memories of events—wars, revolutions, social movements, transitions, or others—as grounds for their comparative study founds analysis on the fallacy of misplaced concreteness. Half-aware of the difficulty, many of BCC's most ardent practitioners are abandoning it for historically-grounded studies of social processes (Lloyd 1993; Smith 1991).

Disintegration of the state system? Implicitly or explicitly, the BCC program has always relied on presumptions about the division of the world into coherent nations and states, presumptions that only became prevalent with the consolidation of the European state system and its rapid seizure of world power during the nineteenth century (Thomson 1995). Whether consolidated states as the world has known them for two centuries are now losing their grip or merely adapting as the world-system changes remains hotly debated (Tilly et al. 1995). Massive flows of capital, labor, commodities, information, and technology across national boundaries and increasing prominence of such transnational structures as the European Community and GATT are surely both reducing the autonomy of most states and undermining their capacity to regulate activities within their territories. Meanwhile the expansion of communal-ethnic struggles over political power within existing states (Gurr 1994) discredits any easy equation of society or culture with state. Continuation of these trends is already attracting the attention of macroanalysts to non-national webs of social relations; it will eventually destroy the plausibility and interest of comparisons among state-defined societies (Puchala 1995; Ruggie 1993; Wendt 1994; Wendt and Barnett 1993).

Relational, historicist, and institutional thinking? As approaches in contemporary social science, we might distinguish *systems theories*, with collectivities (including that great collectivity called Society) following autonomous and compelling logics; *methodological individualism*, with its reduction of social reality to the self-motivated actions of individual actors; *phenomenological individualism*, with its parallel reduction of social reality to the consciousness of actors, individual or collective; and *relational realism*, with transactions, interactions, or social ties serving as starting-points of social analysis. The first three have run their course, while the fourth is gaining strength. In a wide variety of fields, furthermore, the idea of incessant human improvisation that lays down subsequent constraints on behavior in the form of memory, culture, institutions, and social ties contradicts any possibility of chopping social life into neatly-bounded, self-motivated, rule-following actors, individual or collective (Friedman 1995; Nelson 1995; Resnick 1996; White 1992). Macroanalysis will benefit enormously from these new ideas about social process, but not through a continuation of Big Case Comparison. In that sense, the once-dominant program of comparative-historical social science is now writing *finis*.

John Goldthorpe has in fact recently been writing anticipatory obituaries for BCC (e.g., Goldthorpe 1991). He has, however, emphasized secondary traits of our moribund friend. The situation is both worse and better than Goldthorpe claims. Worse, because social scientists including Goldthorpe have wasted a great deal of time fretting about the logic of comparing whole countries to account for similarities and differences among those countries, when for most purposes they should simply have eschewed such comparisons. Better, because social scientists have always had more effective explanatory logics available than BCC. For effective social science, like effective science of any other kind, does not concern cases or variables, but valid causal mechanisms, wherever and at whatever scale they occur.

In a limiting case—where behavior of a state or of state-circumscribed institutions is itself at issue—the state-defined country may indeed turn out to be the appropriate unit of comparison. But even there the crucial causal mechanisms will commonly operate at several different scales, and be verifiable for precisely that reason. Despite the limited scope for experiment in their inquiries, $N = 1$ has not kept geophysicists, cosmologists, paleontologists, or ecologists from doing valuable scientific work. For practical purposes, N has equaled the number of independent observations they could make of processes in action or their outcomes. Historical students of large-scale social processes similarly take advantage of multiple purchases on crucial causal mechanisms, each intervention into the historical record constituting another opportunity to be proven wrong.

On what grounds, for example, do most students of state formation believe that (a) under a wide, roughly specifiable set of historical circumstances successful warfare creates states, and (b) in those circumstances different organizations of warfare produce systematically different state structures (Porter 1994; Rasler and Thompson 1990; Starr 1994)? They believe those propositions not because of large-N statistical analyses or neat John Stuart Millian comparisons of cases but because for a large range of times, places, and situations they can construct relevant, verifiable causal stories resting on differing chains of cause-effect relations whose efficacy can be demonstrated independently of those stories. They also believe the propositions because they look robust over many kinds and scales of evidence, from statistical analyses of wars to close reconstructions of particular historical sequences.

That scholars will eventually supersede such gross, imprecise propositions with more refined, more adequate, and partly contradictory analyses does not gainsay the superiority of the search for widely applicable cause-effect relations over BCC and related searches for invariant sequences or structures. If Goldthorpe rightly stresses the impossibility of identifying such causal mechanisms by means of pure induction from case studies, he somehow fails to recognize the possibility of deducing relevant hypotheses from historically-grounded theories of the middle range (Merton 1957, p. 9).

Relevant causal situations far exceed the domain of neatly-bounded, mutually-exclusive, substantial states. States have been forming in various parts of the world for roughly sixty centuries. In most of those times and places, warmaking has dominated state formation. In a nice dialectic, the massive creation of military forces during the last two centuries has actually attenuated the impact of military activity on state structure both (a) through promoting the creation of civilian organizational infrastructure having its own autonomous weight and (b) through reliance on implicit bargains with major political actors that thereby have gained the power to steer the state toward their own interests.

Cause-effect relations linking state structure to military activity include the generalization of concentrated coercive means to non-military compulsion, the creation of centralized administrations as a by-product of extracting means for war, and bargaining with civilian populations over those means. Like the causal mechanisms to which geologists and ecologists appeal, such causal mechanisms appear in different combinations and sequences, with different weights, in concrete historical situations (Stinchcombe 1978a). No more than any geologist imagines all mountains to form as minor variants on the same model does an intelligent analyst of state structure confine the military-state relation to a single invariant pattern; like a wise geologist, she shows how widely-applicable causes concatenate into substantially different outcomes depending on initial conditions, subsequent sequences, and adjacent processes. Although all analysts can—and frequently do—aggregate these causes to a national scale, in fact they operate at many scales, from encounters between households and tax collectors to the settlements through international intervention of national rebellions and civil wars. Hence the possibility of verifying the efficacy of ostensible causes at one scale, then aggregating or disaggregating them to trace their analogs at other scales.

Do the causal mechanisms involved reduce ultimately to the rational actions of motivated individuals? Some do, most don't. More of them correspond to the complex, contingent, collective effects of social interaction dealt with by evolutionary economists, transaction-cost organization theorists, and network analysts (Baron 1984; Bowles and Gintis 1993; Granovetter 1988; Merton 1936; Nelson 1995; North 1991; Portes and Sensenbrenner 1993; Simon 1991; Stinchcombe 1978b). Warfare generates centralized administrations, for example, in part because through no one's intention the seizure of means for military action—men, horses, food, clothing, weapons, information, and money—disrupts non-military routines, creates new social connections among both rulers and ruled, alters the physical environment, produces perverse effects, and stimulates concerted popular resistance. Each of these effects calls forth remedial action on the part of authorities. Repeated, with their own unanticipated consequences and indirect effects, those remedial efforts constitute central administrations. Such a causal web certainly includes intentional action, but much of it consists of errors, unanticipated consequences, indirect effects, alterations of social networks, and influences mediated by the non-human environment.

In these regards, each state has its own distinctive concatenation of causes; the generation of central administration by land warfare operated differently (and less pervasively) in Holland than in neighboring Prussia. It does not follow, however, that the causes operated chiefly, much less exclusively, at the scale of states. Social scientists have often slipped into the fallacious assumption that if two comparable social units differ with respect to some attribute the difference between them must result from differences in other attributes of the same social units; they have relied on monad individualism writ large, a generalization to social aggregates of the idea that the cause of any individual's behavior must be some propensity, trait, or decision of that same individual (Bhargava 1992). In fact, differences among social units commonly result from locations in social networks, from environmental effects, from localized events that cumulatively affect the unit as a whole. An eternity of correlating and comparing aggregate characteristics of the units will never identify the crucial effects.

Do we need other examples? We could draw them from the historical study of citizenship, where lawful but variably-conjoined causal mechanisms at other scales than the nation clearly contributed to what we now see as entrenched national differences (Cerutti, Descimon, and Praak 1995; Cohen and Hanagan 1995; Somers 1993). We could examine gender inequality in employment, where effects of state policy and educational systems certainly appear, but the great bulk of variation depends on different concatenations of causal mechanisms—notably the fine segregation of jobs—that appear widely across the world (Bielby and Baron 1986; Blau and Kahn 1992; Charles 1992; Petersen and Morgan 1995). We could turn to genocide, infant mortality, aging, nationalism, democratization, revolution, income inequality, or racism: measurable and existentially significant international differences in all these regards exist. They result in part from events and policies at a national scale. Yet as normally practiced Big Case Comparison can do no more than discipline our thinking about these complex phenomena in preparation for genuine explanatory efforts.

It makes little difference whether we choose large-N multivariate analyses or small-N case studies. If we are to arrive at explanations, we will have to construct relevant, verifiable causal stories resting on differing chains of cause-effect relations, relations whose efficacy can be demonstrated independently of those stories. Those stories will feature strong contingency and path-dependency. Their validity will ultimately depend not on Millian experimental logic, not on deductions from covering laws, not on precise multivariate analyses, but on the demonstrated presence and robustness of the causal mechanisms they enchain.

ACKNOWLEDGMENT

I have incorporated in this paper most of my "Macrosociology Past and Future," *Newsletter of the Comparative & Historical Section*, American Sociological Association, 8 (1995), pp. 1, 3, 4, and have built on ideas laid out more extensively in "The Bourgeois Gentilshommes of Revolutionary Theory," *Contention* 2 (1993), 153-158, "To Explain Political Processes," *American Journal of Sociology* 100 (1995), 1594-1610, "Invisible Elbow," Working Paper 221, 1995, Center for Studies of Social Change, New School for Social Research, "Durable Inequality", CSSC Working Paper 224, 1995, and "Citizenship, Identity and Social History," *International Review of Social History* 40, supplement 3 (1995), 1-17. I claim to have practiced what I preach, among other places, in *The Contentious French* (Cambridge: Harvard University Press, 1986), *Coercion, Capital, and European States, 990-1990* (Oxford: Blackwell, 1990), *European Revolutions, 1492-1992* (Oxford: Blackwell, 1993), and *Popular Contention in Great Britain, 1758-1834* (Cambridge: Harvard University Press, 1995). *Big Structures, Large*

Processes, Huge Comparisons (New York: Russell Sage Foundation) made the essential points in 1985, but subsequent theorists and practitioners did not hear them; perhaps the more strident tone of this essay will catch their attention.

REFERENCES

Abbott, A. 1994. "History and Sociology: The Lost Synthesis." In *Engaging the Past. The Uses of History across the Social Sciences*, edited by Eric Monkkonen. Durham, NC: Duke University Press.

Baron, J.N. 1984. "Organizational Perspectives on Stratification." *Annual Review of Sociology* 10: 37-69.

Beramendi, J.G., R. Máiz, and X.M. Núñez (Eds.) 1994. *Nationalism in Europe, Past and Present*, Vols. 1 and 2. Santiago: Universidade de Santiago de Compostela.

Bhargava, R. 1992. *Individualism in Social Science. Forms and Limits of a Methodology*. Oxford: Clarendon Press.

Bielby, W.T. and J.N. Baron. 1986. "Men and Women at Work: Sex Segregation and Statistical Discrimination." *American Journal of Sociology* 91: 759-799.

Bjørn, C., A. Grant, and K.J. Stringer. 1994a. (Eds.). *Nations, Nationalism and Patriotism in the European Past*. Copenhagen: Academic Press.

_____. 1994b. (Eds.). *Social and Political Identities in Western History*. Copenhagen: Academic Press.

Blau, F.D., and L.M. Kahn. 1992. "The Gender Earnings Gap: Some International Evidence." Cambridge, Massachusetts: National Bureau of Economic Research Working Paper 4224.

Bowles, S., and H. Gintis. 1993. "The Revenge of Homo Economicus: Contested Exchange and the Revival of Political Economy." *Journal of Economic Perspectives* 7: 83-114.

Brubaker, R. 1993. "East European, Soviet, and Post-Soviet Nationalisms: A Framework for Analysis." *Research on Democracy and Society* 1: 353-378.

Burt, R.S., and M. Knez. 1995. "Kinds of Third-Party Effects on Trust." *Rationality and Society* 7: 255-292.

Cerutti, S., R. Descimon, and & M. Prak. 1995. (Eds.). "Cittadinanze," *Quaderni Storici* 30(89): 281-514.

Charles, M. 1992. "Cross-National Variation in Occupational Sex Segregation." *American Sociological Review* 57: 483-502.

Coase, R. 1992. "The Institutional Structure of Production." *American Economic Review* 82: 713-719.

Cohen, M., and M. Hanagan. 1995. "Politics, Industrialization and Citizenship: Unemployment Policy in England, France and the United States, 1890-1950." *International Review of Social History* 40 (supplement 3): 91-130.

Emirbayer, M., and J. Goodwin. 1994. "Network Analysis, Culture, and the Problem of Agency." *American Journal of Sociology* 99: 1411-1454.

Friedman, J. 1995. "Economic Approaches to Politics." *Critical Review* 9: 1-24.

Goldthorpe, J.H. 1991. "The Uses of History in Sociology: Reflections on Some Recent Tendencies." *British Journal of Sociology* 42: 211-230.

Goodwin, J. 1994. "Toward a New Sociology of Revolutions." *Theory and Society* 23: 731-766.

Granovetter, M. 1988. "The Sociological and Economic Approaches to Labor Markets." In *Industries, Firms, and Jobs: Sociological and Economic Approaches*, edited by George Farkas and Paula England. New York: Plenum.

Gurr, T.R. 1994. "Peoples Against States: Ethnopolitical Conflict and the Changing World System." *International Studies Quarterly* 38: 347-378.

Hammel, E. 1980. "The Comparative Method in Anthropological Perspective." *Comparative Studies in Society and History* 22: 145-155.

Hanagan, M.P. 1994. "New Perspectives on Class Formation: Culture, Reproduction, and Agency." *Social Science History* 18: 77-94.

Heilbroner, R. 1990. "Analysis and Vision in the History of Modern Economic Thought." *Journal of Economic Literature* 28: 1097-1114.

Lloyd, C. 1993. *The Structures of History.* Oxford: Blackwell.

Merton, R.K. 1936. "The Unanticipated Consequences of Purposive Social Action." *American Sociological Review* 1: 894-904.

————. 1957. *Social Theory and Social Structure,* rev. ed. New York: Free Press of Glencoe.

Merton, R.K., L. Broom, and L.S. Cottrell, Jr. (Eds.). 1959. *Sociology Today. Problems and Prospects.* New York: Basic Books.

Mill, J.S. 1887. *A System of Logic, Ratiocinative and Inductive: Being a Connected View of the Principles of Evidence and the Method of Scientific Investigation,* 8th ed. New York: Harper & Brothers.

Monkkonen, E. 1994. "Lessons of Social Science History." *Social Science History* 18: 161-168.

Nelson, R. 1995. "Recent Evolutionary Theorizing About Economic Change." *Journal of Economic Literature* 33: 48-90.

North, D.C. 1991. "Institutions." *Journal of Economic Perspectives* 5: 97-112.

Petersen, T., and L.A. Morgan. 1995. "Separate and Unequal: Occupation-Establishment Sex Segregation and the Gender Wage Gap." *American Journal of Sociology* 101: 329-365.

Petroski, H. 1992. *The Evolution of Useful Things.* New York: Knopf.

Porter, B. 1994. *War and the Rise of the State.* New York: Free Press.

Portes, A., and J. Sensenbrenner 1993. "Embeddedness and Immigration: Notes on the Social Determinants of Economic Action." *American Journal of Sociology* 98: 1320-1350.

Puchala, D.J. 1995. "The Pragmatics of International History." *Mershon International Studies Review* [supplement to *International Studies Quarterly*] 39: 1-18.

Rasler, K.A. and W.R. Thompson. 1990. *War and State Making. The Shaping of the Global Powers.* Boston: Unwin Hyman.

Resnick, M. 1996. "Beyond the Centralized Mindset." *Journal of the Learning Sciences* 5: 1-22.

Ruggie, J.G. 1993. "Territoriality and Beyond: Problematizing Modernity in International Relations." *International Organization* 47: 139-174.

Schneider, L. 1975. "Irony and Unintended Consequences" in *The Sociological Way of Looking at the World.* New York: McGraw-Hill.

Simon, H. 1991. "Organizations and Markets." *Journal of Economic Perspectives* 5: 25-44.

Smith, D. 1991. *The Rise of Historical Sociology.* Philadelphia, PA: Temple University Press.

Somers, M.R. 1993. "Citizenship and the Place of the Public Sphere: Law, Community, and Political Culture in the Transition to Democracy." *American Sociological Review* 58: 587-620.

Starr, H. 1994. "Revolution and War: Rethinking the Linkage Between Internal and External Conflict." *Political Research Quarterly* 47: 481-507.

Stinchcombe, A.L. 1978a. *Theoretical Methods in Social History.* New York: Academic Press.

————. 1978b. "Generations and Cohorts in Social Mobility: Economic Development and Social Mobility in Norway." Memorandum No. 18, Institute of Applied Social Research, Oslo.

Thomson, J.E. 1995. "State Sovereignty in International Relations: Bridging the Gap Between Theory and Empirical Research." *International Studies Quarterly* 39: 213-234.

Thomson, R. 1984. "The Eco-Technic Process and the Development of the Sewing Machine." In *Technique, Spirit and Form in the Making of the Modern Economies: Essays in Honor of William N. Parker, Supp. 3,* edited by G. Saxonhouse and G. Wright. Greenwich, CT: JAI Press.

Tilly, C. 1995. "Democracy is a Lake." In *The Social Construction of Democracy*, edited by G.R. Andrews, and H. Chapman. New York: New York University Press; Basingstoke: Macmillan.

Tilly, C. et al. 1995. "Globalization Threatens Labor's Rights," plus responses from Immanuel Wallerstein, Aristide Zolberg, Eric Hobsbawm, and Lourdes Benería, followed by Tilly reply, *International Labor and Working Class History* 47: 1-55.

Wendt, A.E. 1994. "Collective Identity Formation and the International State." *American Political Science Review* 88: 384-398.

Wendt, A. and M. Barnett. 1993. "Dependent State Formation and Third World Militarization." *Review of International Studies* 19: 321-347.

White, H. 1992. *Identity and Control. A Structural Theory of Social Action*. Princeton, NJ: Princeton University Press.

COMPARING HISTORICAL SEQUENCES—A POWERFUL TOOL FOR CAUSAL ANALYSIS

A REPLY TO JOHN GOLDTHORPE'S "CURRENT ISSUES IN COMPARATIVE MACROSOCIOLOGY"

Dietrich Rueschemeyer and John D. Stephens

ABSTRACT

John Goldthorpe is right when he identifies three major methodological problems of macrosociology—problems due to the small number of cases, problems due to the lack of full independence of the cases, and problems that arise when we move from association to causal explanation. He is wrong when he claims that comparative historical research is more plagued by these problems than cross-national quantitative research. In fact, while we advocate the integration of comparative historical and cross-national statistical analysis, we claim that comparative historical research has particular advantages in dealing with the problems identified because it focuses on historical sequence and because it can take account of varied historical contexts.

Comparative Social Research, Volume 16, pages 55-72.
Copyright © 1997 by JAI Press Inc.
All rights of reproduction in any form reserved.
ISBN: 0-7623-0250-X

John Goldthorpe discusses three central issues in comparative macro-sociology—the problem that typically only a small number of cases are available to disentangle complex causal patterns; "Galton's problem" or the question whether the cases studied are independent of each other; and the "black box" problem or the question of how to move from findings of association to causal explanation. Goldthorpe is right to consider these serious problems. He is also right to see them as problems faced by both cross-national quantitative and comparative historical research. He is wrong, however, when he claims that comparative historical research has no advantage in dealing with these issues and when he in fact seeks to turn their discussion into an argument for the superiority of the cross-national statistical approach. Both modes of analysis have their own peculiar advantages as well as difficulties.[1] Nevertheless, we claim, however, that comparative historical research has a distinctive and critical advantage in macro-sociology because it focuses on historical sequence and because it allows one to take account of varied historical contexts. When it in addition is joined to cross-national statistical research results and extended to as many cases as possible, we consider comparative historical analysis the method of choice for the study of macro-social phenomena.

Before we discuss the specific problems in greater detail, we offer a few comments on the place of historical research in macro-social analysis and on the issue of holism. We then briefly introduce the study in which we have recently collaborated and which we will use repeatedly as an instance of the research procedure we consider most appropriate.

ON THE NEED FOR HISTORICAL ANALYSIS

Navigare necesse est—the old assertion that sailing on the high seas, however risky, was necessary nevertheless can be transferred to the role of historical research in systematic social analysis. Historical research, too, is risky and fraught with problems: Historical evidence is drastically and irremediably incomplete; it is often of dubious validity; and it tends to be biased—favoring the victors rather than the losers, the lasting developments rather than the historical dead ends and detours, the rich and the educated rather than the poor and illiterate, and so forth. And yet for very cogent reasons historical research is not only useful, it is required for systematic social analysis, especially for macro-social research.

Why is historical research necessary? First, there is the fact that many social patterns, once formed, tend to persist. Many present-day conditions seem to have their roots in constellations several generations or even centuries old. Seymour Martin Lipset and Stein Rokkan came to this conclusion in their well-known analysis of voter alignments: "We simply cannot make sense of variations in current alignments without detailed data on differences in the sequence of party formation and in the character of the alternatives presented to the electorate before and after the extension of the suffrage" Lipset and Rokkan (1967, p. 2). Wherever it may be necessary to reach in this way back into history in order to understand the present, all "presentist" explanations—explanations which consider only factors in the most immediate past—become profoundly suspect.

A second argument is closely related. Many phenomena of interest—and especially macro-social phenomena—are shaped by constellations of factors rather than just one in isolation. That means often that the sequencing of major causal conditions matters. Thus, it has been argued that class formation took a different path depending on the relative timing of industrialization and the extension of the suffrage (Katznelson and Zolberg 1986) or that the character of state organization in Europe depended profoundly on whether the rationalization of rule preceded the rise of rationalized capitalist production and exchange or vice versa (Nettl 1968).

True, we do not know enough about either historical persistence and its limits or the effects of different sequence patterns to use these as *explanatory* principles; but we do know enough to consider them *heuristic* principles of the first importance, especially in macro-analyses. As such, they make historical research indispensable.

Yet, the most important argument is much more elementary. Causation is a matter of sequence. One needs diachronic evidence, evidence about historical sequences, to explore and to test ideas about causation directly. This remains true even if it is also true that simple historical narrative is not the same as causal explanation. *Post hoc* does not any more translate directly into *propter hoc* than correlation demonstrates causation. Explanation can indeed not proceed without analytic hypotheses; but causal explanation ordinarily needs hypotheses about sequence which can best be tested against evidence about sequences. And the first two arguments advanced—about historical persistence and the relative timing of causal conditions—suggest that it is advisable to look for sequences beyond the immediate past.

Goldthorpe's argument rests on a radical separation of a narrative account of "what happened," an account of a sequence of historical events, from a theoretical account.[2] True, any causal explanation (in the ordinary sense of the term) involves theoretical claims that transcend the particular historical sequence of events. But theoretically oriented historical case analysis comes closer to a causal account than a cross-sectional variable oriented research; this for two major reasons: it enables us to establish the sequence of events and it helps to establish agency. Both of these greatly facilitate the identification of causal processes or, more precisely, of potentially causal processes that may or may not match hypotheses about causal conditions and sequences.

These considerations are not new except perhaps that they are here formulated in terms that also fit cross-national quantitative research. These considerations explain why the radical neglect of historical research associated with functionalism and neo-positivism in the 1950s and 1960s appears now as a mere interlude. There was a long tradition of history-based social science, as illustrated by such names as de Tocqueville, Lorenz von Stein, Otto Hintze, and Max Weber, and this tradition has given rise during the past thirty years to a renaissance of comparative historical social science that in our judgment ranks among the major attainments of social analysis in the last generation.

ON HOLISM

Studying a given historical phenomenon in its context, studying it "as a whole," offers advantages for doing justice to historical particularity, but it may raise problems for systematic comparison. Goldthorpe's discussion turns this tension into a stark choice between a universalism in which country names are replaced by bundles of variables and a particularistic holism that makes any analysis across cases impossible. This alternative is misleading; it disregards the actual practice of comparative history. What we advocate—and practice—aims for an understanding of the case/country as a whole in order to facilitate detecting how social and historical factors combine in contingent ways to shape a given outcome.

The characteristics and factors to be examined are theoretically identified. Choosing which aspects and features to study is inevitably selective; there is no way of rendering a case as a whole in all its complexity without arbitrariness. On this we agree with Goldthorpe. We disagree with him—apparently at least—in our claim that due attention to the context of each case makes a different type of "operationalization" of concepts possible. Any operationalization involves hypotheses linking nominal concepts to indicators available for analysis. Cross-national statistical research settles on one standardized operationalization and takes inadequacies of fit, which vary across cases, into the bargain. Qualitative comparative historical research can give much closer attention to the match between evidence and theoretical conceptualization.[3]

These, then, are the major advantages we claim for historical analysis in comparative macro-sociology: it allows us to take account of historical persistencies and different constellations of major causal factors, it identifies sequences that are potentially causally relevant, it establishes agency, and it makes use of complex contextual knowledge in the operationalization of theoretical concepts. We will see that these advantages are of considerable importance for tackling the three problems under consideration.

CAPITALIST DEVELOPMENT AND DEMOCRACY

Our recent study on the impact of capitalist development on democracy (Rueschemeyer, Stephens, and Stephens 1992) will serve as a reference point for several of our arguments in what follows; it thus requires a brief introduction.

At the outset we were confronted with a conflict between two bodies of research that differed in results as well as method. Cross-national statistical research, using numerical indicators for the level of socio-economic development as well as democracy, had demonstrated again and again—with different samples, different indicators, and different research designs—fairly strong correlations between development and democracy. By contrast, comparative historical research from Max Weber to Barrington Moore and Guillermo O'Donnell, using far more complex information about the historical trajectories of only a few countries, had come to much more skeptical conclusions about the prospects of democracy in cases of late development.

It was our judgment that cross-national quantitative research had established important empirical generalizations but that its causal interpretations were problematic. Comparative historical work, on the other hand, offered the elements of a more promising theoretical framework, a framework that had also proven useful in other comparative analyses of macro-phenomena—of class formation, of state structures, of welfare policies. We decided to tackle the explanation of the relationship between development and democracy that had been established by cross-national statistical research in a new way—by comparative historical analyses on as large a scale as we could manage. We included all advanced capitalist countries, the countries of South America, and a comparison of the Spanish-speaking countries of Central America with the English-speaking islands of the Caribbean. The historical analyses were guided by a theoretical framework that, based on our interpretation of past research and theory, identified the central questions, delineated the major concepts, and developed a core of hypotheses. Starting with the proposition that democracy is a matter of power, the framework focused on three clusters of power as the major causal constellations—on the balance of class power in society, on the structure of the state and of state-society relations, and on transnational structures of power.

The individual case analyses could, and did, engender additional explanatory hypotheses; and where these hypotheses contradicted propositions included in the initial framework, they could and did lead to modifications of the initial theory. "The result," we claimed, "is , on the one hand, a set of historical cases accounted for with a coherent theory and, on the other, a set of propositions about the conditions of democracy that have been progressively modified and are consistent with the facts of the cases examined as well as with the preceding research taken into account" (Rueschemeyer, Stephens, and Stephens 1992, p. 38; also Rueschemeyer 1991, p. 34). This is a precise formulation and a modest one. We will return below to Goldthorpe's claim that our attempt to explain the relationship between development and democracy failed because our procedure allowed too much leeway for the modification of theoretical propositions in response to the analysis of consecutive cases.

After his introductory comments on holism and historicism, Goldthorpe turns to the central thesis of his essay: He contends that, contrary to the claims of its advocates, comparative historical research is not superior to quantitative cross-national research in addressing the small n problem, the Galton problem, and the black box problem. In *Capitalist Development and Democracy*, we do indeed make this claim with regard to the small n and black box problems, and we would be willing to make the same claim with regard to Galton's problem though we do not address this question in the book.

THE SMALL N PROBLEM

Goldthorpe is correct in arguing that both in quantitative variable-oriented analysis and in case-based comparative research the number of variables might exceed the number of cases, making statistical testing of competing theories impossible. In that situation, one might find a number of different explanations supported equally well by the data with no way to distinguish among them, as Huber, Ragin, and Stephens (1991) have empirically shown in the case of cross-national statistical research on the welfare state. Another example illustrates the problem in case-based comparative research: A recent collaborative research project on the breakdown of democracy in interwar Europe included more than 20 countries, all of the countries in Eastern and Western Europe, but nonetheless faced the same problem, as two of the collaborators in undertaking Ragin's Qualitative Comparative Analysis (QCA) identified over sixty characteristics which various theories had hypothesized to be related to democratic collapse (Berg-Schlosser and De Meur 1994). It is not surprising that the authors could produce a number of different, and in some cases theoretically contradictory, solutions.

In some cases, both qualitative comparative and quantitative analysis provide a criterion, essentially the same criterion, for moving beyond this point.[4] Unfortunately, this one criterion can lead to fallacious conclusions. In statistical analysis, when choosing between two or more regressions (or any other technique) of statistically equal explanatory power, the regression with the fewest variables is favored. To restate the same principle in slightly different terms, a single variable is favored over two competing variables with equal explanatory power. A similar assumption is often made in comparative analysis, an assumption which can most clearly be seen in QCA. Applying Occam's razor, it is assumed that the solution with the fewest explanatory characteristics is the best. However, this may not identify the true causal variables. To take a hypothetical example, assume that in an array of cases a characteristic Y is the dependent variable of interest and there are two different paths to this outcome, A and B. Yet if all cases having Y also have characteristic C (because A and B cause C, or Y causes C, or by pure chance), then C rather than A and B will be the preferred independent variable (characteristic) in statistical analysis or QCA.

Other than this potentially misleading criterion, there are no other criteria provided for by the logic of the comparative method or by quantitative methodology for choosing between solutions of equivalent statistical or logical power or for distinguishing spurious correlations from causal factors. Complementing the comparative method with historical analysis provides the researcher with such a tool. By uncovering agency and historical sequence, one can eliminate some potential causal variables and strengthen the case for others.

It must be admitted that our study, which compared a large number of cases on the basis of secondary historical accounts, is much better equipped to deal with the small n problem than most comparative historical studies. Indeed, it encompasses as many countries as many cross-national statistical studies, and the largest sample sizes are only twice that of ours. Comparative historical studies typically cover far fewer cases and, thus, though they gain by being able to consult with primary sources and by providing a more nuanced account of events in those cases, they sacrifice the advantage of having a larger number of cases which allows one to make fuller use of the comparative method to eliminate spurious factors. Our study combined the advantage of a substantial number of cases with the ability to study historical sequences and agency and to identify theoretical concepts in their varied contextual settings, but we had to sacrifice the use of primary sources as well as the nuanced attention to detail that characterizes the best comparative studies working on a few cases only.

Yet theory-oriented comparative historical work has yet another, more indirect way of dealing with the small n problem. The theoretical framework taps the results of earlier inquiries and thus indirectly eases the small n problem. "It is critical to fully appreciate this point because here lies one reason why the credibility of analytic induction is far greater than one could possibly justify with the few cases studied."[5]

GALTON'S PROBLEM

We agree with Goldthorpe that Galton's problem has been greatly exaggerated in the literature and that it can potentially be investigated by quantitative and comparative historical methods. However, we would contend that comparative history offers special advantages in dealing with Galton's problem as well. The reason is that historical research can trace a case over time and take full account of the way in which the characteristics that may or may not have been the result of diffusion are linked to their local context.

An example from *Capitalist Development and Democracy* will illustrate the point. In the book, we note that the correlation between democracy and British colonialism is a robust one. This statistical association has been given a diffusionist interpretation: British colonialism made a positive contribution to democratization in its colonies through the transfer of British governmental and representative institutions and the tutoring of the colonial people in the ways of British government. We did find evidence of this diffusion effect in the British settler colonies of North America and the Antipodes (p. 280); but in the West Indies, the historical record points to a different connection between British rule and democracy (Chap. VI, also see pp. 280-281). There the British colonial administration opposed suffrage extension, and only the white elites were "tutored" in the representative institutions. But, critically, we argued on the basis of the contrast with Central America, British colonialism did prevent the local plantation elites from controlling the local state and responding to the labor rebellion of the 1930s with massive repression. Against the adamant opposition of that elite, the British colonial rulers responded with concessions which allowed for the growth of the party-union complexes rooted in the black middle and working classes, which formed the backbone of the later movement for democracy and independence. Thus, the narrative histories of these cases indicate that the robust statistical relation between British colonialism and democracy is produced only in part by diffusion. The interaction of class forces, state power, and colonial policy must be brought in to fully account for the statistical result.

The two most critical advantages of comparative historical research then, the ability to study the local context of critical characteristics and the knowledge of relevant historical sequences, are very efficient tools for settling the questions raised by Galton's problem.

THE BLACK BOX PROBLEM

There is little question that neither correlations between variables nor historical sequences as such can establish causation. In both modes of research, the solution is found in theory and in the close interplay between theory and the examination of the evidence. Comparative historical research derives, here too, its advantage from its focus on historical sequences and from the close interplay between theory and varied empirical evidence in the operationalization of the critical concepts. In examining historical sequences it furthermore reveals much about agency, which is virtually inaccessible in variable oriented quantitative research; and if agency does not tell the whole story of causation, it certainly is an important part of it.

Democratization in the West Indies, just discussed in regard to Galton's Problem, also demonstrates the superiority of comparative historical analysis in "opening up the black box," that is, in moving from statements about association to statements about causality. Knowing the historical record of the Caribbean islands, knowing what the British authorities did and how various social forces pursued their interests in changing situations, we can confront these historical events with propositions about causal processes. In this way we come much closer to opening up the black box than cross-sectional statistical methods (or their qualitative counterparts) alone can ever do.

While, as Goldthorpe has pointed out elsewhere (1991), the historical "facts" underlying these narratives are based on incomplete data of varying quality, we are certainly far better off with knowledge of the historical record than simply with knowledge of a few data points or country characteristics. Moreover, most of the historical facts we rely on in our research comparison are ones which are disputed by few.

Goldthorpe correctly notes that in quantitative research, developing interpretations of the relationship would be aided by developing measures of the intervening variables, though he adds immediately that this would only mitigate, not eliminate the blackbox problem. However, it is not true that using quantitative analysis, we know what the "inputs" and "outputs" are, as Goldthorpe claims. We do not know this at all; their association could be spurious or the causal direction could be reversed and so on, as we pointed out above. For instance, in the case of quantitative research on democracy, it has been argued by various authors that democracy facilitates economic development. Consequently, without further information, we cannot even conclude that the central finding of this literature, that economic development is strongly related to democracy, can be unambiguously interpreted as demonstrating that economic development causes democratization. Interpreting quantitative measures of association requires theory and a close interaction between theory and the examination of evidence in the same way as these are required in comparative historical research. The question is which mode of research offers better access to the relevant evidence and which aids better the detailed interaction of theory and relevant evidence.

While refinements of the quantitative data may help to narrow the range of options, one must, we reassert, turn to comparative historical analysis "to open up the blackbox," to move to causal explanations. It is useful here to move from an abstract discussion to two concrete research problems, democratization and the development of the welfare state, to illustrate the potential and the limitation of refinements of data in contributing to an understanding of the phenomena in question.

In quantitative research on the development of democracy, the typical data set consists of a large number of countries (50 to 100), usually all of the countries in the world for which there are data or some large subset of it (e.g., all countries politically independent for a specified period of time, all developing countries). Generally, the data are a cross-section for some point in the post-war period.[6] The most serious problem in these data is not the "small n—too many variables, too few cases" problem, though these issues do appear when the analyst attempts to examine subgroups separately (e.g., African countries only as in one study; countries at the middle level of development which were democracies as of 1960 as in another). The key problems have rather been measurement of the independent variables due to the poor quality of the available data, questionable operationalization of variables, and exclusion of variables measuring important factors hypothesized in the literature to be related to democracy. Strength of the working class, strength of the middle class, state strength, income inequality, land distribution—these are just a few of the central concepts in the study of the social origins of democracy which are either inadequately operationalized in the cross-national statistical studies or are not measured at all. This is not due to sloppiness on the part of the scholars; indeed these studies often contain perceptive comments on the data limitations and ways to deal with them.[7] The problem is that adequate data are not available for a sufficient number of cases; nor are they ever likely to be. For example, one measure of working class strength used in comparative welfare state studies is percentage of the labor force organized, which is available for all advanced capitalist democracies from 1950 to 1989 (Visser 1991). For third world countries, this figure is available only for a scattering of countries for any point in time, and the few figures available are of questionable quality. It is very unlikely that quality data on this key variable could be collected for the present and it is unimaginable that it could be collected for time points in the past.[8]

The problem of inadequate and incomplete data, then, takes another form in the case of cross-national statistical studies but it is at least as serious as, in fact it seems more serious than, in comparative historical research. The problem of inadequate data is in many cases linked to the inattention to historical sequences because of another measurement problem. The dependent variables and independent variables are typically measured at the same cross-sectional point in time. This is often very far removed in time from the critical events in the development of democracy in a large number of cases. For instance, the critical era in most European countries was the period 1870 to 1918, yet the inferences about causal processes based on cross-national studies are being made with data from 1960 or later.

We contend that our comparative historical study gets us much closer to the relevant historical evidence. Let us take the example of working class strength and democratization. In the case of the European countries in the 1870 to 1914 period, we have good data on union organization from the early 1900s and somewhat spotty data for some countries for several decades before that. We also have figures on votes for parties of the left, which we must, however, adjust for the extent of suffrage. From historical accounts, however incomplete and spotty, we know much about how centralized union movements were, how closely they worked with the labor and socialist parties, how unified the left was and so on; all of which bears on an overall assessment of working class strength. So we are in an excellent position to state that the working class movements were much stronger in 1910 than in 1870 and in almost as strong a position to make comparative statements about in which countries these movements made the most rapid gains. If we then add information on the historical process of democratization, on what was the stance of the working class movement, who were their allies and enemies, and so forth, we are in a very good position to make statements about the effects of growing working class organization on democratization. True, these statements quite clearly involve broader theoretical assertions that transcend the cases at hand; but our evidence on historical sequences is quite precisely articulated with these theoretical assertions—contradicting them or, as was the case in this instance, confirming them.

Once we move to the Caribbean and Latin America, the "hard data" we can draw on are much spottier. However, we can make statements with which few historians disagree. For example, we do know that in both Central America and in the West Indies, plantation workers were not organized in 1930, that they rebelled in the 1930s, and that this, along with other events, led to the establishment of unions in the West Indies, but to the repression of the nascent working class movement in Central America. More precise measures would be helpful, but they are not essential to our interpretation because they are extremely unlikely to overturn our assessment of how strong the union movements were after the events of the 1930s had played themselves out. Similarly, every Latin American historian will agree that in the early post war period the Argentine working class was stronger than the Colombian which was stronger than the Salvadoran, but it would be hard to quantify just these three country assessments not to mention similar assessments for all Latin American countries we examine in the analysis. Nonetheless, our estimates of the relative strength of different movements are not arbitrary nor convenient ad hoc judgments; and they are transparently stated and open to criticism by other social scientists and historians.

Thus, while the main advantage of comparative historical analysis for opening up the black box lies in examining historical sequence, it also has the advantage that more theoretically important conceptual variables can be adequately "operationalized" and that they can be "measured" at the appropriate point in time. Given both of these advantages, it is hardly an exaggeration to say that we are in a *vastly* better position to make statements about causality from our comparative historical study than from any feasible cross-national quantitative study of democratization.

The data quality in the case of comparative welfare state research on advanced capitalist democracies is much, much better than in the case of democratization. We have reasonable and comparable measures of almost all central concepts in the literature and in most cases we have measures on an annual basis from the late 1950s on and for selected dates back to 1945.[9] Moreover, this period, that is, the post World War II period, is the period in which the social policy provisions which account for most social spending were instituted. Thus, we are measuring both the independent and dependent variables for the relevant time period. The primary problem in these data is the small n problem: the number of independent variables greatly exceeds the number of cases. Pooling cross-sections and time series data helps but does not solve the problem, because the increase in the number of cases is artificial. There is a sense in which there still are only eighteen rather than 600 cases. The fact that most of the variation explained is between the countries (about 1/2 using dummy variables for the countries) and not between the time points (about 1/5 using dummy variables for the years) makes this quite apparent. It is not surprising then that these data are plagued by multicollinearity among the independent variables to such a degree that it is not possible to enter some of them in the same equation much less sort out their relative (causal) effects. For example, union density, corporatism, and social democracy are so highly intercorrelated that it is impossible statistically to separate out their effects (and thus investigate whether union organization or corporatist bargaining arrangements are associated with social policy innovation independent of their association with social democratic governance and so on), much less move to some statement about causal relationships. Or, yet more perplexing, the aged proportion of the population is strongly correlated to social democracy ($r = $ circa 0.7) Consequently, it is rare to find that they will both have strong coefficients when dependent variables are regressed on them and other determinants of welfare state development. For instance, Huber, Ragin, and Stephens (1996) have found that, net of ten other independent variables, aged population but not social democratic governance is strongly related to the public share of total health expenditure. By contrast, social democratic governance but not aged population is strongly related to a number of other indicators of the public funding of social services. The true believer in quantitative analysis would take these results as a demonstration of differences in the underlying causal processes. We are more skeptical. Since comparative historical research by Huber and Stephens uncovered relatively few instances of successful and important aged lobbying for health care reform (the United States being an important exception), we believe that this is an instance of multiple paths to the same outcome (mainly a Scandinavian-social democratic and a British) which is spuriously correlated to aged proportion of the population in the data. Thus, even if the data quality is extremely strong as it is in the case of crossnational data on advanced industrial democracies, making causal inferences from quantitative results is a hazardous process, and historical process knowledge can make a significant contribution in deciding between different theoretical accounts.

ON INDUCTIVE THEORY BUILDING AND TESTING

Goldthorpe offers a critique of inductive theory building and testing that is distinct from the "black box" problem and thus deserves separate attention.

The strategy we have called "analytic induction"[10] begins with an explicitly formulated theoretical framework, in which questions, central concepts, and core hypotheses are clearly defined, and then proceeds to analyze a series of cases offering causal accounts of the outcomes in question. In these causal accounts of consecutive cases, new supplemental hypotheses may be developed in addition to the core theoretical propositions, and the core propositions— when contradicted—may have to be modified or rejected. The end result is a set of cases explained by a coherent theory. This theory has plausibility beyond the cases studied both because it was built initially on a critical analysis of past research and because it fits a tremendously complex and systematically analyzed body of empirical evidence from a number of historical trajectories.

Goldthorpe rejects this as a reasonable strategy. He maintains that the formulation of hypotheses must remain radically separate from their testing, that is, he insists on the classic neo-positivist distinction between the context of discovery and the context of validation. He claims that testing becomes in effect impossible if hypothesis development and hypothesis testing are intermingled. "If a theory is formed entirely inductively—without, so to speak, any deductive backbone—... it is hard to see how it can be genuinely tested at all.... if a theory amounts to no more than an assemblage of inductions, the possibilities for 'saving' or 'patching' it in the face of contrary evidence are virtually limitless" (Goldthorpe, p. 15).

To begin with, neither our analysis in *Capitalist Development and Democracy* nor, say, Skocpol's study of *States and Social Revolutions* is "entirely inductive" in character, a mere "assemblage of inductions" in Goldthorpe's sense. The theoretical frameworks that open both investigations not only direct the subsequent case analyses but clearly rule out certain historical patterns, even if they do not constitute ready-made theoretical models that are then applied to all cases. Consequently, and quite contrary to Goldthorpe's claim, these research strategies actually did not at all lend themselves to endless patching, and they ruled out other explanation attempts.

In *Capitalist Development and Democracy* we insisted at the outset that the prospects of democracy are contingent on three power clusters—relative class power, the structure of the state and state-society relations, and transnational power structures. For each of these we formulated specific hypotheses, which are not to be repeated here except for one of particular centrality: we claimed that the repeatedly established correlation between indicators of development and indicators of democracy was due to a shift in class power induced by capitalist development—a decline in the power of the landlord class and an increase in the organizational power of subordinate classes, in particular the urban working class. This we found to be supported in the vast majority of our cases. And our results starkly negate other explanations, among them (1) the thesis that it is the expansion of the middle classes that constitutes the primary link between capitalist development and democracy, or (2) the modernization hypothesis that complex societies require a flexibility of government that only democracy can offer, or (3) the claim of both classic liberal and Marxist political theory that democracy is the creation of the bourgeoisie.

Even aside from this particular, if central hypothesis, our initial theoretical propositions were by no means endlessly adjusted. In fact, even the initial formulations fit a lot of cases. A lot of the changes just nuanced the original hypotheses—for example, concerning the role of landlords in the Caribbean and Australia—or they explained details of development not anticipated in the initial theoretical framework. Others did concern more genuine deviant cases—for example, about the working class in Argentina or the fate of democracy in Grenada. It is worthwhile noting, however, that in quantitative analysis, there is no attempt whatsoever to account for such cases. Given that we dealt with fifty cases we, too, could have left the few deviant cases without an interpretation that rendered them intelligible within the broader framework. By contrast, it is certainly true that in a comparative historical analysis of three cases, failing to explain one would be rather damaging for the study's persuasiveness; and if this explanation differs substantially from the original core theory, it would indeed have an improvised, ad hoc character.

Yet if Goldthorpe is wrong in assessing how the core theoretical propositions of *Capitalist Development and Democracy* fared in our comparative historical investigations, he is not wrong when he sees in comparative historical macro-sociology a methodological strategy that deviates from textbook prescriptions of method that are inspired by the neo-positivist program and primarily oriented to quantitative research. We did not lay out a fixed and complete system of hypotheses in advance of the investigation, but developed more fully detailed explanations in response to the individual cases, we tried to explain cases that did not fit our initial expectations, and we concluded with certain, if actually quite minor, revisions of the theoretical framework. The first question, then, is whether this is a legitimate procedure or whether it in effect constitutes a method of deluding ourselves and others. A subsidiary question is whether our "deviations" are just characteristic of comparative historical work or whether they are actually quite common in macro-social investigations, quantitative or qualitative.

Scholars seeking to explain important historical trajectories usually are not completely innocent of the relevant historical evidence and of earlier attempts at explanation. Thus, it becomes quite unrealistic to demand that hypotheses developed in qualitative case analyses be tested with fresh cases about which little or nothing is known in advance. At the same time, research that is guided by a systematic theoretical framework often generates quite substantial evidence that is not known in advance. If this framework does have a core of both clear-cut orientations for the development of specific hypotheses as well as a core theory, it is simply not possible to "patch things up" forever in the face of contrary evidence.

Even if a good deal of the explanations advanced pertain either to patterns known in advance or were developed as previously unknown historical evidence became available, the overall explanation may have much greater worth than the textbook injunction against "ad hoc" explanation suggests, especially if the different explanatory propositions fit into a coherent and more or less tight theoretical framework. Arthur Stinchcombe may be right when he suggests that it is easy to find at least three different theoretical explanations for any given correlation.[11] But this faith in a cornucopia of reasons is quite misplaced when it comes to explaining with a coherent set of theoretical propositions not just a single correlation but very complex patterns of historical sequences in different national contexts. In fact, we note that Goldthorpe has come to a quite similar conclusion: "While it is surely disappointing, it should not be thought a disgrace for sociologists to admit that they have not been able to develop a theory that will adequately account for their empirical findings" (p. 29, note 17).

As to the secondary question of whether "ad hoc" theorizing is found only in case-based qualitative research, we confine ourselves to a simple apodictic assertion which readers familiar with actual research will not find difficult to accept: It is rather naive to think that a similar back and forth of data examination and theory adjustment does not go on in quantitative work. Precisely because of the textbook injunction, however, research is simply written up as if that did not happen.

Before concluding, we should briefly comment on the issue of determinist vs. probabilistic theories. A determinist position appears to be forced on us if we ever take single cases as occasion for theory revision. But here, too, we contend, Goldthorpe formulates too stark a choice. A single case may rule out a theoretical proposition even if we do not assume that history is predetermined, that whatever happened had to happen. Whether a single case has such far-reaching implications depends both on the hypothesis in question and on the evidence of the particular cases. If we had assumed for example that peasants were inherently unable to organize collectively and thus were of little import for the push toward universal suffrage and were then confronted with the actual developments in Norway, Switzerland, and the northeastern United States we would be quite ill advised not to take the massive evidence from these three countries as a rejection of our hypothesis.[12] In other cases the outcome of a certain conflict may be at odds with a given hypothesis, but the evidence may suggest that it would be problematic to see this outcome as "necessary." Since in comparative historical research a "case" is more than a single dot on a scattergram, we are with this mode of analysis in a far better position to decide whether a deviant case must be considered conclusive evidence against a given hypothesis or whether it should be considered an instance of contingent developments that are more open for variation.

CONCLUSION

Max Weber took a rather skeptical and pragmatic view of methodological discussion: "It is possible to walk without knowing the anatomy of one's legs. Only if something is not in order does this knowledge become a consideration for walking."[13] We do think that macro-sociology—of either kind—has some trouble walking, more so probably than Max Weber would have conceded; but we like the idea of giving priority to actual research over a methodological discussion based on stylized ideal assumptions.

We do maintain that comparative historical research has not only thorny problems, which it does, but also distinctive advantages. These advantages— above all its ability to consider evidence about historical sequence and agency and its capacity to identify the empirical counterparts of theoretical conceptualizations in a more complex and adequate manner—are of critical importance for all three problems under discussion.

In tackling the issues involved in the relationship between development and democracy, our comparative historical analysis struck a compromise, exchanging the opportunity of examining a very large number of cases for an almost complete reliance on secondary sources. In this, our strategy differed from other comparative historical work. Yet this choice enabled us to avoid the small n problem in its more severe form. And at the same time, the project could go substantially beyond what was possible with further quantitative research. Not only was additional data collection in the quantitative mode not likely to advance our knowledge substantially, more cross-sectional quantitative research could never have yielded the knowledge about sequence and agency that was won from comparative historical analysis and that allowed us to come closer to causal analysis.

We want to reiterate, however, that we recognize the strengths of good quantitative analysis. And we advocate a dialogue, or even a marrying, of the two. Despite the data drawbacks, the cross-national statistical studies on democracy were of great value to us. Many other comparative historical researchers ignored them much to the detriment of their own work.

NOTES

1. This has been our position all along: "Neither side has an obvious superiority in principle, and neither can be dismissed. Rather, each has made choices when confronted with a situation that did not allow obedience to all mandates of methodology—not even all the major mandates— at the same time. Each side had to pay for its peculiar strengths with equally characteristic weaknesses." Rueschemeyer (1991, p. 28); and Rueschemeyer, Stephens, and Stephens (1992, p. 32). Rueschemeyer (1991) is a revised version of an earlier draft of chapter 2 of Rueschemeyer, Stephens, and Stephens (1992). This chapter was written largely by Rueschemeyer but represents the view of all three co-authors.

2. In a footnote he accepts the idea that historical narrative itself can constitute a form of explanation. We want to make clear that this claim is not part of our position. It seems to involve a different meaning of "explanation."

3. True it has to deal with the danger of (unwittingly or intentionally) "adjusting" the operationalization to protect hypotheses from rejection; but then, all of these decisions are, in good research of this kind, laid open to scrutiny and if necessary dispute and rejection.

4. This is not to imply that the *QCA* and quantitative solutions are the same. The primary difference is that, rather than establishing associations between variables, *QCA* establishes associations between characteristics and does so in a way that leaves the links of a particular set of characteristics with a case transparent.

5. Rueschemeyer, Stephens, and Stephens (1992, pp. 37-38). Laitin (1995, p. 456) makes a similar point in his discussion of the recent King, Keohane, and Verba volume on qualitative methodology. Some studies incorporated in this indirect way may have used smaller and more numerous units of analysis, studying for instance the conditions of democratic decision making in unions and other voluntary associations. Though transferring results from the meso- to the macro-level may raise complex further questions, it is one possible way of dealing with the small n problem in macro-sociology. We did not take this route in our own research, but our theoretical framework included such references (see note 15, p. 312).

6. There are a few exceptions to this statement: Cutright and Wiley (1969) examined the relationship between development and democracy indices for 40 countries in four successive decades and established statistical associations between certain variables and constitutional change. An even closer examination of change is the event-history study by Hannan and Caroll (1981).

7. For example, see Bollen and Jackman (1985) on income distribution.

8. This can hardly be overstated. For example, in the course of writing a work on the Jamaican politics during the seventies, Stephens and Stephens (1986) attempted to collect comparative data on union organization in the West Indies, only to find that they could not even get accurate data on Jamaica where they were doing field research.

9. The dependent variable, almost always some measure of social expenditure as a percentage of GDP, was the most unsatisfactory of these measures. The most important recent innovation has been to measure social rights directly (Myles 1984; Esping-Andersen 1990) and at multiple points in time (Korpi 1989; Palme 1990; Kangas 1991). Another recent approach is to employ multiple measures of the dependent variable (Huber, Ragin, and Stephens 1993, 1996; Stephens, Huber, and Ray 1995).

10. We adopt a term coined for micro-sociology by Znaniecki two generations ago, but adapt the meaning to fit our methodological approach for current macro-sociology.

11. "A student who has difficulty thinking of at least three sensible explanations for any correlation that he is really interested in should probably choose another occupation" (Stinchcombe 1968, p. 13).

12. In fact, we considered from the beginning the hegemonic influence exercised by large landlords over peasants as the decisive factor for the limited role that peasants have played in most, but not all processes of democratization.

13. Weber (1913/1964, p. 139) as cited by Hennis (1994, p. 120).

REFERENCES

Berg-Schlosser, D., and G. de Meur. 1994. "Conditions of Democracy in Inter-War Europe: A Boolean Test of Major Hypotheses." *Comparative Politics* 26 (3): 253-79.

Bollen, K.A., and R. Jackman. 1985. "Political Democracy and the Size Distribution of Income." *American Sociological Review* 50.

Cutright, P., and J.A. Wiley. 1969. "Modernization and Political Representation: 1927-1966." *Studies in Comparative International Development*

Esping-Andersen, G. 1990. *The Three Worlds of Welfare Capitalism.* Princeton, NJ: Princeton University Press.

Goldthorpe, J.H. 1991. "The Uses of History in Sociology: Reflections on Some Recent Tendencies." *British Journal of Sociology* 42(2): 211-230.

Hannan, M.T., and G.R. Carroll. 1981. "Dynamics of Formal Political Structure: An Event-History Analysis. *American Sociological Review* 46.

Hennis, W. 1994. "The Meaning of 'Wertfreiheit': On the Background and Motives of Max Weber's 'Postulate'." *Sociological Theory* 12(2): 113-125.

Huber, E., C. Ragin, and J.D. Stephens. 1991. "Quantitative Studies of Variations among Welfare States: Towards a Resolution of the Controversy." Conference on Comparative Studies of Welfare State Development sponsored by the Research Committee on Poverty, Social Welfare, and Social Policy of the International Sociological Association; Vuoranta, August 29-September 1.

————. 1993. "Social Democracy, Christian Democracy, Constitutional Structure and the Welfare State." *American Journal of Sociology* 99(3): 711-749.

————. 1996. "Political Power and Gender in the Making of the Social Democratic Service State." Delivered at the meetings of the American Political Science Association, New York, September.

Kangas, O. 1991. *The Politics of Social Rights: Studies on the Dimensions of Sickness Insurance in OECD Countries.* Stockholm: Swedish Institute for Social Research.

Katznelson, I., and A. Zolberg. 1986. *Working-Class Formation: Nineteenth Century Patterns in Western Europe and the United States.* Princeton, NJ: Princeton University Press.

Lispet, S.M., and S. Rokkan. 1967. "Introduction." Pp. 1-64 in *Party Systems and Voter Alignments: Cross-National Perspectives*, edited by S.M.Lipset and Stein Rokkan. New York: Free Press.

Palme, J. 1990. *Pension Rights in Welfare Capitalism: The Development of Old-Age Pensions in 18 OECD Countries 1930 to 1985.* Stockholm: Swedish Institute for Social Research.

Myles, J. 1984. *Old Age in the Welfare State.* New York: Little Brown.

Nettl, J.P. 1968. "The State as a Conceptual Variable." *World Politics* 20: 559-592.

Rueschemeyer, D., E.H. Stephens, and J.D. Stephens. 1992. *Capitalist Development and Democracy.* Cambridge: Polity Press and Chicago: Chicago University Press.

Stephens, J.D., E. Huber, and L. Ray. 1995. "The Welfare State in Hard Times." Paper delivered at the conference on the "Politics and Political Economy of Contemporary Capitalism," Humboldt University and the Science Center Berlin, May.

Stinchcombe, A.L. 1968. *Constructing Social Theories.* New York: Harcourt, Brace & World.

Visser J. 1991. "Trends in Trade Union Membership." Pp. 97-134 in *OECD Employment Outlook*, July. Paris: OECD.

Weber, M. 1964. (1913). "Gutachten zur Werturteilsdiskussion im Ausschuß des Vereins für Sozialpolitik." Pp. 102-139 in *Max Weber: Werk und Person*, edited by E. Baumgarten. Tübingen: J.C.B. Mohr.

STORIES, OBSERVATIONS, SYSTEMS, THEORIES

Henry Teune

ABSTRACT

The point of departure is that comparative research is the empirical foundation of macro theories of economic, political and social systems. Today, the bedrock of such research is comparison of countries and cultures. The argument is that debates about how to conduct and analyze comparative research concern practical rather than "in principle" problems. Among those discussed are the small number of theoretically relevant cases, the complexity of social systems including their pasts, measurement of different and changing systems, and the ubiquitous question of diffusion vs. autonomous change. These are discussed as practical questions rather than issues over the nature of social inquiry. Country as the main referents in the study of complex social systems itself has to be theoretically explained as well as predicted. Recent efforts to deal with "cases" are at best research strategies in the development of macro theories, which are less likely in the future to be about countries that are systemically bounded.

Comparative Social Research, Volume 16, pages 73-83.
Copyright © 1997 by JAI Press Inc.
All rights of reproduction in any form reserved.
ISBN: 0-7623-0250-X

All theories have empirical referents—cases, instances, phenomena. The purpose of theories is to move intellectually from what is observed at any point in time to what could have been, can be, or will be observed, retrodiction and prediction. Theories state either what must be true or what might be true, deterministic and probability statements. Logical theoretical "truths" state that if empirical phenomena behave according to this particular logic, the logic of compound growth, then that phenomena will change accordingly, population will increase exponentially.

Since modern scientific thought, since Malthus, certainly since Mill, doubts have entered discourse about whether there are theories in the social realm. A question for the history of science is why such doubts come and go in the social sciences.

The debate is an old one and since the beginning of this decade has had something of a revival. It occurred in anthropology as "emics" and "etics" in the 1940s; in sociology and political science in the 1960s as area and comparative studies; in the 1970s as historical sociology; and in the 1980s as case studies.[1]

The current debates between those arguing for "cases" and those seeking general theories in sociology and political science have come a long way from the encounters of the 1940s between "area specialists" and "comparativists." Then the issue was joined as the impossibility of general knowledge without understanding the "idiom" of the particular vs. the irrelevance and instability of detailed happenings or "stories" of the particular. Today there is tolerance and openness between those emphasizing cases and those pursuing general knowledge as a difference in strategies and adaptations to special situations.

Nonetheless, fundamental principles still divide, no matter how disguised. Just as the appreciation today about the fact vs. value wars of the 1920s appears to be a compromise among the debaters, underlying their positions is the difference between the commitment to general "truth" or its denial. Those advocating cases as the prudent path to knowledge are certain the achievable is knowledge through interpretation rather than general "truth" recognizable in principle if not realizable by any particular group in any specific social or cultural setting.

Recent efforts to re-formulate the logical and empirical foundations of theoretical knowledge in the social sciences by bringing "cases back in" or devising applications of strict logics of inclusion and exclusion (Boolean algebra) are retreats from the problems of macro theoretical prediction and the messy nature of probabilities.[2] Knowing the whole system, like knowing the whole person, can be translated into estimating error in measurement or accounting for conditions under which theoretical predictions may or may not be true. Assessing systems in categories as either large or small, totalitarian or democratic, throws away information about degrees and kinds of difference that marked the 19th century advent of modern science with quantities, shades, and curves. Relationships among components within "whole systems" can be expressed in twentieth century logics of systems, bringing in the history of such interactions and its impact on current and future behavior.

The points of departure are that social science theories are not only desirable but also possible. The former is based on arguments that the greater the capacity to predict, the greater the choice. This celebrates the liberating force of knowledge. The latter stems from actual experience in developing social science theories. Some are in the behavioral part of the social sciences—from chemistry to behavior, from learning to performance. Others in the social, political, and economic domains are more difficult—from regulation of prices to supply and demand and from social differences to political conflict.

THEORIES AND COMPARISONS IN THE SOCIAL SCIENCES

By theory is meant: (a) a grammar or logic; (b) empirical terms (with referents); (c) rules of interpreting those empirical terms or measurement; and (d) when a particular case, an individual or a political system, is interpreted to have at least one of such properties defined by the empirical terms, at least one other can be derived with some probability, either of a retrodictive or predictive nature. A theory thus must have some "truth value," which is established by observing "cases." It also has to be general in that what is derived, deducted from the interpreted grammar or logic, must extend beyond what was observed in establishing or estimating the truth value in the stated relationships. Thus theoretical statements refer to no specific cases (proper names) but are open to all such cases, past, present and future.[3]

Comparisons constitute the core of the logic of all scientific theories and comparative research is their empirical underpinning. What is said to be true of something by implication at least is not true of something else. The contrived experiment in science, no matter how simple or sophisticated, involves comparisons, treatment, non-treatment, control, and whatever else. The logic of "natural experiments" or comparative research is no different, no matter how complicated practically. This is how the "truth value" of theories is established.

The core of macro theoretical comparisons in the social sciences is not only across systems over time but also among components within them. The appropriate terminology is macro and micro in sociology, political science, and economics. Individuals are influenced by the systems of which they are a part. The city impacts the voting behavior of its citizens, the region that of its cities, the country that of its regions, cities, and citizens (and visa versa). The city is the macro level in a theory of urbanization and individual values. The country is the macro level for a theory of a hierarchy of cities, although a world system of cities today is a strong theoretical contender.

Two critical questions for research on macro social theories are: is the system, a country, being studied an instance of the referents of the theories (can they have the characteristics or properties being examined or, in statistical-variable terms, are they "free to vary" on those properties) and to what extent are the properties of those systems, openness of a country to world trade and economic growth, assessed accurately for those systems, countries, asserted to be such instances?

Comparisons in the social science have received special attention because they purport to make statements about complex systems that are weakly constituted (poorly integrated), have several levels of overlapping, hierarchical relations, and change over time not only from the interaction of their components but also from the relations of the system with others. Further, social systems are readily categorized by their different levels of complexity from a dyad, to a family, to a group, association, assembly, city, country, region, and the world as a whole, each of which may require a different theory or a general one about system complexity, system change, and levels of explanation. What is required then in any social theory are specifications of instances to which it refers, systems and levels within them, as well as the history of the interaction of their components.

PROBLEMS OF COMPARISONS IN THE SOCIAL SCIENCES

If individuals in behavioral science are taken as analogous to countries in social science, which is the focus of the argument and agony in discussions of comparative research issues primarily in sociology and political science, then live individuals are fairly easily defined (although controverted in law), are highly integrated (except under pathological conditions), and are historically understood (despite the nature-nurture controversy). Countries are difficult to define, except as a curtesy of the United Nations, are poorly and variably integrated, and are only roughly understood historically or developmentally.

A major problem in social science is that it deals with fuzzy, messy, and changing systems. Fuzzy system means that any observation is potentially a part of several systems and those systems of which it is partially a part change over time. The most familiar form of this issue in cross-cultural research is Galton's problem—whether any property observed in any system is a property of that system or some other system, whether it is a "proper" property of that system or was brought or diffused into it. Did the United States invent fresh water systems for public consumption or was it an adaptation from some other country or society? The fuzzy system problem becomes more complicated in systems of partial hierarchies—the international system being one of the most controverted. Did Germany change its laws on political asylum because of whatever is Germany and its national values or because of reactions to international pressures? In both examples, the answers are "partial" or fuzzy systems, part of both. Recently, claims have been made that fuzzy logics will help address this problem. The question remains whether fuzzy logics are really fuzzy logics or fuzzy thinking about fuzzy systems.[4]

The messy system problem reflects the reality that social systems are poorly and variably integrated. The simplest interpretation of this is "noise." All systems contain noise, meaning that for all practical purposes things happen which at least appear to be non-systemic. A very expensive watch, which is highly integrated, runs-down, although this may not happen in one lifetime. Social systems have leaders who die, unanticipated riots, and other events that make a difference but cannot be easily accounted for. If Tito died earlier or later, would the recent Balkan wars have occurred? But that is only one of several things happening recorded as stories. A theoretical question is that despite all the noise are totalitarian systems "run-down" systems? The answer to that question is that it depends on whether or not randomness, defined as unaccounted or unexplained activities, like the discovery of oil, overwhelms that which can be explained. That happens from time to time, even in relatively tightly integrated social systems.

The changing nature of the components and their relations comes closest to being an inherent "logical" problem of the social sciences that challenges their status as theoretical sciences. Let us look at three types of systems theories.[5]

First, there are mechanical systems, where neither the nature of the components change nor the relationships among them. The logic or language of theories of such systems are matters of calculation, no matter how difficult. Designing mechanical systems requires equilibrium solutions.

Second, there are ecological systems where the number of components change relative to each other, but the relationships do not. The foxes always eat the rabbits and the rabbits always eat the grass. Although more complicated mathematically, there are equilibria solutions for ecological systems which, if arrived upon, can be identified as such. Mathematical biology with potential applications to the social sciences provides logics for predicting the behavior of ecological systems.

Finally, there are social systems where both the nature of the components and their relationships change. Political parties emerge and perish and the relationship of parties to nominations and elections change, often at the same time. Neither the components nor the relationships are "constants," justifying intellectual breakdown of theoretical efforts into stories.

These protypically described systems have different kinds of logical requirements. The "model" of celestial mechanics fits the first; the "model" of population ecologies, the second; the "model" of the story, the third. But a story is no theory and so we attempt a variety of approximate solutions with great tolerance for probabilities rather than being satisfied with artificial constructs of "ideal types" which were once considered theoretical successes.

PROBLEMS OF COMPARISONS IN THE SOCIAL SCIENCES

All the basic "philosophy" problems of science—the uncertainty principle, the "paradigm bias," the prejudices and politics of investigators—carry over to the social sciences, however they may be magnified. Add to those any number of special "problems"—free will, reflexive predictions (self-fulling or self-negating) and the mind, that are apparent intruders into our knowledge of the "external" social world. The social sciences are easy targets for political attacks, including those intended to destroy the credibility of any science of societies, economies, and polities whatsoever. Add to all of these practical problems of comparing complex social systems and their pasts, often etched in fragmented traces, and the social sciences are open to almost any kind of challenge in which lack of knowledge is readily transformed into a principle of what cannot be known.

A fundamental question to be addressed to any identified problem in comparing social systems is whether it is a practical or "in principle" one. Either answer or belief, however, is not sufficient justification to stop trying to develop macro-system theories, for the "proof of the pudding is in the eating." The issue is whether the social sciences have to "compromise" on the principles of scientific inquiry or whether they have to accept the best they can get, as a practical matter. This difference is not trivial, for it touches on the foundations of credibility of any social science knowledge. However one answers the question about the limits of knowing in principle, the practical answer is that it is possible to state an infinitely unlimited number of plausibly true (empirically) things about anything. The only way to limit the confounding effects of complexity is to select on the basis of criteria, which in science includes general statements that enable prediction and explanation.

The problems of "comparative" research can be de-composed into several issues: the small number of theoretically relevant or "interesting" systems; the whole being more than the sum of its parts; the compounding effects of multiple researchers and the "contexts" of their observations; and the non-systemically mediated diffusions of properties and their relationships across systems. Taken together, these issues can be made to constitute something special on a methodological agenda in the social sciences. Other formulations of these problems could expand the list. The position taken here is that these problems come from practical difficulties which are turned too readily into in principle differences between comparative research and other kinds of social science, the non-comparative nature of which is difficult to identify.

THE SMALL "N" PROBLEM

The problem of a small number of cases is an instance of a general one of insufficient observations to assess the truth value of theories. A "classic comparative" theoretical statement is that in the class of systems X, if units A are observed to have increased their property y, then they will also have increased (with some probability), their property z. The number of systems in the class X, however, is small with limited variance, even though the relationship between y and z is potentially theoretically productive or morally challenging. "Poor countries that are democratic and improve the educational level of individual females will have families that get rich faster than those in poor countries that are autocratic." This statement is cross-systems (countries), cross-level (female citizens and families), and cross-time (increases in the education of females, increases the level of wealth of families.[6]

The scientific and moral challenge in the example is that there are no, or only controverted, countries that are democratic and poor and so the generalization is accepted that only wealthy countries can be democratic. And that might be true, but we cannot know from the cases, or countries, observed. One can wait a very long time to see if such cases emerge or stretch the definition of democratic to include India or some other countries. This problem is further compounded when the variables, concepts with definitions and measures, become multiple: poor countries of medium size or large size that are democratic... What are the alternatives?

The first, short of a massive social experiment on the order of Lenin's revolution, is to "find" countries and the data. This is an alternative when countries are insufficiently studied or data unavailable or inaccessible for a particular research program.

A second is to find systems that meet the criteria of being as sufficiently autonomous politically as countries and that have sufficient variation in levels of poverty and democracy and educational opportunities for women to see whether families got or get wealthier faster than those that were or are autocratic. The units of observation, cases, or instances to "test" theories for either the first or second must be justified theoretically and empirically. In a research program on politics and economic growth, the political entities selected must have capacities to grow and variable political structures. One way to do this is to de-aggregate countries into regions and localities. Two examples are Mancur Olsen's study of the wealth of nations and his use of the Southern states in the United States and Robert Putnam's study of democracy and economic growth in the regions of Italy.[7]

A third is to seek "historical cases" which are theoretically defined. The difference between historical cases and the de-aggregation strategy is the practical one of lack of control over the acquisition of additional data. But just as the units of observation require theoretical justification, so do data and, hence, theory would give guidance in the search for data from the past. Another difference in analyzing current and past social units concerns the measurement systems based on inference from indicators taken in context. Thus the variable, capacity to mobilize militarily, may be indicated at one time in history as the effective institution of a military draft; at earlier time point, the establishment of military store houses. Establishing the validity of indicators for variables in dead systems is not fundamentally different than establishing equivalence for comparing contemporary countries with radically different political systems or cultures.

These are problems of imagination in the design and execution of research. Of course, there are data that are out of reach historically and today, perhaps forever. The acclaimed experiments of Solomon Asch on conformity and Stanley Milgram on obedience to authority were both innovative and consequential and both today are legally prohibited procedures of observation for elaboration and replication in most major research countries.[8]

THE WHOLE AND ITS PARTS

The issue of whether the whole is "more" or something different than the aggregation of its component parts remains a basic issue in the philosophy of science. The issue was debated in its extreme form in the social sciences as that of methodological individualism: whether groups or collectivities could be defined in terms of individuals and their properties, including their "relational" properties with other individuals.[9]

What constitutes the whole must include properties of the relationships among the components. These properties are inferred from the "behavior" of the components and the system. Thus a system is more or less integrated, developed, fragmented, hierarchial. These general properties of systems are established by estimating the probability of some components of systems influencing others. The probabilities can be used as defining points. A "perfectly" autocratic system is one where one individuals influences all others with certainty and without "feedback." This is the insight of the twentieth century concept of systems; it is a logic or language for expressing the boundaries of cases, estimates of "causal" relationships, and the foundations for putting together what is observed into a whole that is inferred.

The whole in the social world must include values, purposes, and perceptions that inhere in the systems. Individuals have values and so do systems, the propensity to behave in certain ways. Thus one can infer that a system is democratic from its structures, institutions, and processes. This, of course, could mean the characterization of a system as autocratic, even though the individuals within it do not intend to act autocratically.

Inferring system properties poses a number of difficulties in designing measurement systems. What is often required are elaborate measurement operations that yield index numbers used in estimates of the wealth, the quality of life, and scientific capacity of an organization or country, a popular example being the Gross National Product. Although they are often rough estimates, they are among the most used of measures of the whole to compare systems.

MEASUREMENT CONTEXTS

Observations within systems must take into account the context of the system. That is a long and unending lesson of translating languages, interpreting cultures, and understanding symbols. Again, these are practical problems, often of difficult dimensions, but, nonetheless, in principle not insurmountable.

Stories, detailed accounts by a variety of observers and interpreters, also can serve as data bases for comparing social systems. Subjective evaluations of "experts" have been used systematically in measurement. The two hundred plus years of historiography during which veracity has been used as a criterion for judging stories of the past provide at least a context for validating assessments of characteristics of systems.

There are more technical procedures for assuring that measurements within and of systems are appropriately weighted for estimating equivalence in making comparisons. Although none of these are fully satisfactory in assuring certainty, they are means by which scientific inquiry reduces error and sharpens its biases toward truth.

DIFFUSION AMONG SYSTEMS

It is difficult to know whether anything observed in any system was autonomously generated by that system or was simply copied or imported into it. Has the human gene pool spread from a single source or has it been generated in different species and then mixed among all groups. This is the great question of origins, the passionate human effort to find the constant, the base line, to evaluate what is. That may be the ultimate unknowable, but it is just as intriguing for the physical as it is for the biological and social worlds.

In a technical sense, diffusion can be addressed with the concepts of open and closed systems. There are theories of open systems, generically called ecological systems, and closed systems, theories that state all of the relevant variables for explanation and prediction and treat deviations as errors, expressed as probabilities or designated as exogenous.

In social science there are relatively strong theories of ecology by which social entities and their properties invade, populate, dominate, adapt, and decay.[10] These rely on theories of niches and neighbors and constitute a major theoretical road to human knowledge. Social niches are known to be extremely porous, prone to penetration from afar as well as near. Territory, as defining coordinates for human niches, has weakened and today any hypothesis about any social system or type of system must be judged against the competing hypothesis of the world as a total system.

CONCLUSION

Problems in comparative or cross-national research stem from difficulties in using radically different kinds of systems to evaluate or test macro theories. From a very macro perspective most of the contemporary social, economic, and political worlds do not look very different. Universities have libraries, students, faculty; hold classes, give examinations, and award degrees. Knowing any one of them in detail makes it look unique, and, indeed, it is. The combinatorial possibilities provides for everything being unique. Every individual, past, present, and future, has a unique combination of genes and, from what is being learned today, apparently a unique wiring of brain cells as a consequence of experiences, again unique in their sequences and combinations.

The very rationale for theory is to reduce what is unique to a few things that will extend our knowledge of the past, present, and future and from the immediate to the remote—to travel beyond the time and space specificity of direct experience. Stories are interesting for what they instruct humans morally, but to do even that, they must be "extended," lessons must be drawn. Theory is a grand license that provides rules for the individual and collective to know and learn a lot, however imperfectly. But even if those rules can be followed only approximately, the rules are not invalidated.

Comparative research, meaning comparing different systems in a complex structure of relationships across systems, levels within systems, and time, may be difficult. It took a long time to compare state and privately managed economies, the one punishing mistakes from risks taken, the other perhaps excessively rewarding successes from risks, to conclude that one "runs down" economies and the other grows them. It has taken a long time to figure out that large hierarchical, non-governmental organizations are less innovative than small ones. The debate on the relationship between open and closed economies and economic growth is just drawing to a close with evidence.

How much loss could have been avoided and how much gain could have been achieved if theoretical predictions based on comparative research could have provided some, even approximate, answers about real questions over which people and collectivities have a choice. The benefits foregone of closed planned economies are shortening the lives of millions and leaving millions of others miserable.

We now have a different kind of world system, a global-local system, rather than the countries which have dominated social science thinking since the late eighteenth century. This reality will make the ordinary problems of cross-national research less compelling and the attractiveness of the study of the world as a total system more challenging. If there are great problems in comparing countries, they may not be worth serious attention except as a chapter in some yet to be written history of modern social science.

NOTES

1.   The debate over "ideographic" and "nomenthetic" social science comes and goes, particularly in anthropology. Recently, the case study has been "re-discovered" in terms of general theory. See Ragin and Becker (1992).

2.   A claim to a new approach to comparative research is Ragin (1987).

3.   The structure of cross-level and cross-system theory in cross national research is presented in Przeworski and Teune (1970).

4.   Fuzzy logics became known in the 1970s with engineering applications and is attributed to Lotfi Zadeh. The instructing "example" is the traveling salesman with set destinations but unknown time required at any one. The arguments for its independent logical status are not convincing.

5.   These types of systems are discussed in Teune and Mlinar (1978). Only the third type, where the components and their relationships change, are considered social or developmental systems, that is, can change autonomously, not as a result of interactions with other systems.

6.   The relationships between experiments and "comparative research" in the context of cross level, cross system, and crosstime research designs is discussed in Teune (1975).

7.   Both books received public attention both as a result of general interest in well-publicized developments at the time, one as a pessimistic assessment of democracies as beset by sticky interests, Olsen (1982); the other as a celebration of democracy as a condition of prosperity, Putnam (1994).

8.   The Asch experiments on conformity to group pressures and those of Milgram on obeying authority, both much cited in texts and popular writing, both relied on deceiving the "subjects." Deception is now legally proscribed in experiments in the United States and ethically clouded.

9.   The principle of methodological individualism came from the more fundamental one that all concepts must be defined in terms of observables. The best known statement of this "logical positivist" position in U.S. social science is Brodbeck (1958). It was reprinted several times with commentary.

10.   The best exposition of the ecological paradigm is Boulding (1978).

REFERENCES

Boulding, K. 1978. *Ecodynamics.* Beverly Hills: CA: Sage Publications.

Brodbeck, M. 1958. "Methodological Individualism: Definition and Reduction." *Philosophy of Science* 25 (January): 1-22.

Olsen, M. 1982. *The Rise and Decline of Nations.* New Haven, CT: Yale University Press.

Przeworski, A., and H. Teune. 1970. *The Logic of Comparative Social Inquiry.* New York: Wiley.

Putnam, R. 1994. *Making Democracy Work.* Princeton, NJ: Princeton University Press.

Ragin, C.C. 1987. *The Comparative Method.* Berkeley, CA: University of California Press.

Ragin, C.C., and H.S. Becker. (Eds.). 1992. *What is a Case?* Cambridge: Cambridge University Press.

Teune, H. 1975. "Comparative Method and Experimental Designs." *Comparative Political Studies* 8 (July).

Teune, H., and Z. Mlinar. 1978. *The Developmental Logic of Social Systems.* Beverly Hills, CA: Sage Publications.

ON THE CONCEPT OF TURNING POINT

Andrew Abbott

ABSTRACT

This paper outlines the concept of turning point. Turning points are narrative concepts, referring to two points in time at once. They are not necessarily retrospective constructions, although they may be so constructed. Turning points separate extended, more routine trajectories. These trajectories are embedded in a larger structure: constrained in number and limited in extent. They are causally more comprehensible than turning points, but ultimately less important. The concept of turning points requires a processual theory of social life, in which change is eternal and stability an accidental, although common, happening. On the arguments given here, a turn to methods attending directly to turning points and trajectories seems necessary.

In his chapter in this volume, John Goldthorpe advances three claims against what he calls the "case-oriented" approach in comparative macrosociology. First, he argues that problems created by small numbers of cases are just as important for case-oriented as for variable-oriented approaches. Second, he argues that Galton's problem (the impossibility of distinguishing heterogeneity and contagion in most data: see Taibelson 1974 and Loftin and Ward 1981)

Comparative Social Research, Volume 16, pages 85-105.
Copyright © 1997 by JAI Press Inc.
All rights of reproduction in any form reserved.
ISBN: 0-7623-0250-X

arises equally in both approaches. Third, he argues that case-oriented approaches have no preferential access to the interior of the causal "black box;" where they do illuminate causal patterns they do not generalize; where they generalize, they have are no better than, and often worse than, variable-based approaches.

Goldthorpe's points are well taken. And he argues them with magnanimity (cf. Lieberson 1992). But he has chosen the easy target. The real critique of variable-based approaches comes not from case studies, but rather from approaches that characterize the social process through patterns of complex particulars. By avoiding this other critique, Goldthorpe is able to steer his discussion toward the old and familiar one of idiographic versus nomothetic, talk versus numbers.

But the variables-based approaches that Goldthorpe defends are not the only formal means of generalizing about the social process. They follow one among a number of possible generalizing strategies. They seek to understand the social process by developing linear transformations from a high-dimensional space (of "main effects" and occasionally of interactions between them) into a single dimension (the dependent variable). If this transformation provides a sufficient approximation for the dependent dimension, the independent variables are said to "causally explain" the dependent one.

Now this strategy—which is effectively one of reducing by one the dimensionality of the data space—is useful only if the data space is more or less uniformly filled. It is then necessary to have a general model that applies everywhere in the data space and that is more or less the same everywhere in that space. But much or most of the time, the data space is not uniformly filled with data. On the contrary, most of the time most possible combinations of particular values of variables either don't occur or occur very rarely. Social reality usually has very strong local association of variables; data points are clumped within data space even in the presence of low values of global association measures like Pearson correlation coefficients. (For an example and discussion, see Abbott 1990a, p. 142ff).

If most things that could happen don't happen, then we are far better off trying first to find local patterns in data and only then looking for regularities among those local patterns. Indeed, it is for this reason that cluster analysis and scaling, not regression, dominate big-money social science—market research—where the aim is to find, understand, and exploit strong local patterns. For these are methods that seek clumps and partitions of data and make no attempt to write general transformations. Put another way, clustering and scaling try to describe data by finding multivariable local regularities rather than by trying to select one data dimension for selective elimination.

Thus the real alternatives to Goldthorpe's variable-based approaches are not case-based approaches, but what I shall call, for want of a better term, pattern-based approaches. Pattern-based approaches begin by establishing local patterns among the variables before setting out to generalize. These preliminary patterns are complex particulars: clusters of cases that have roughly the same values on many variables. In variable-based approaches, we don't seek such complex particulars, but rather generalize immediately on the basis of the given variables, which are treated as substantively independent of one another (i.e., as main effects). By contrast, pattern-based approaches use the variables to define types. They then seek more general patterns across types or relating types to one another. As I noted, this procedure will be most useful when much or most of the data clusters around a few types and a considerable portion of the data space is more or less empty. (This is an empirical issue, and one easily tested by straightforward methods.) In this case, we are best off establishing local associations first.

Note that these local associations need not be cross-sectional. That is, they need not be clusters in cross-sectional data space. They could equally be patterns of successions of values of one or more variables. In the simplest sense, an auto-regressive scheme is such a pattern. In a more complex sense, any common succession of values of a variable (indeed any common succession of values of several different variables) would be such a pattern.

It is here that we arrive at "sociological narrativism," as Goldthorpe calls it. Late in his paper, Goldthorpe states that "for any kind of macrosociology,...'history' will always remain as a necessary residual category." A footnote to this remark outlines Goldthorpe's worries:

> And I would take leave to doubt that the further attempt now apparently being made [to overcome the distinction between sociology and history] via "sociological narrativism" .... is any more likely to succeed. While one may sympathise with the efforts such as those of Abbott (1992a, 1992b) to establish analogues between narrative accounts and causal explanations, there are still basic differences to be recognized among the kinds of narrative that may be deployed. For example, one may understand rational choice theory in terms of narratives—but ones which, in contrast to historical narratives, are generalised rather than specific, set in analytic rather than real time, and implicative rather than conjunctive in their structure.

I am less interested here in Goldthorpe's definitional relegation of history to the category of residuals than in his recognition that regular narrative patterns are in fact a reasonable way to generalize about the social process. That is, he concedes here the possibility of a pattern-based approach to social analysis based on temporal sequences, or, as I shall call them, "narrative patterns."[1] His last sentence calls useful attention to certain aspects of narrative patterns. We want them to be generalized (as indeed I argued in the papers to which Goldthorpe refers). We want them to take place in a temporality more flexible than clock time. (Goldthorpe's insistence on purely abstract time reduces pattern to mere succession, and we should retain the possibility of patterns involving duration.) And we want to have some sense that such narratives are "coercive" in the sense that after some point they imply a certain denouement, a certain result. (This last is my interpretation of what Goldthorpe means by "implicative rather than conjunctive in their structure.")

In this paper, I would like to take up this last issue of finality, of certainty, of implicative result. I view this finality within the broader issue of turning points in narrative patterns. Believing that after a certain point a narrative becomes coercive means believing that a turning point has been passed. We have moved out of a former pattern and onto a new trajectory. Turning points are commonly hypothesized in both quantitative and qualitative analysis in the social sciences. But we lack a sustained analysis of them. Indeed, the metaphors of "trajectory" and "turning" with which I have just conceptualized them may be completely misleading. I would like therefore to take up the logical and formal properties of the concept of turning point.

I begin with some illustrative references to literatures employing the concept of turning points. I then discuss some mathematical analogies for turning points and develop the idea of a narrative concept. This leads to a dicussion relating turning points to trajectories and developing a social structural approach to turning points. The second section of the paper considers two particular problems in the theory of turning points: that of proliferating futures and that of instantaneous change. The substantive discussion of the paper closes with a multiple contingency theory of unexpected social change.

THE CONCEPT OF TURNING POINT

In sociology, the concept of turning point is quite old (see, e.g., Hughes 1971[1950]). It has had its main application in studies of the life course. Elder's widely cited review (1985) parses the life course into "trajectories and transitions." Trajectories are interlocked and interdependent sequences of events in different areas of life. Transitions are on the one hand stages along such regular trajectories and on the other hand radical shifts. "Some events," Elder tells us, "are important turning points in life—they redirect paths" (1985, p. 35). That turning points interrupted regular patterns was a major insight of the life course literature; earlier conceptions of the life course had spoken of a regular "life cycle," a concept ultimately traceable to the Chicago School's concept of natural history (See, e.g., Park 1927. For a critical review of the life cycle concept, see O'Rand and Krecker 1990).

Although the life course literature will be my touchstone here, similar arguments are made elsewhere, for example in the criminological literature. Sampson and Laub (1993) argued that turning points played a central role in jolting delinquents into and out of trajectories that led to further criminality. But the concept of turning point is not merely a life history or even a sociological concept. In political science, turning points have been sought in studies of political realignment (Lasser 1985) and critical elections (see the long literature responding to Key 1955; e.g, Burnham 1970 and Clubb, Flanagan, and Zingale 1981). In applied economics, studies of business cycles and other economic regularities have led to widespread analysis of turning points (e.g., Chaffin and Talley 1989; Zellner, Hong, and Min 1991). In the history of science, revolution has been a central concept for decades or even centuries (see, e.g., Kuhn 1970; Cohen 1985).[2]

In developing a concept of turning point that would support these various literatures, it is easiest to begin with concepts from mathematics. Imagine a continuous single-valued function of x. A turning point is a maximum or minimum point in this function, the point at which the slope of the function changes sign. (In practice, this is the operational definition of turning point in the applied economics literature, see, e.g., Zellner et al. 1991.)

However, we would not think of two such changes in quick succession as anything more than a minor ripple in a generally monotonic trend. But if the two changes were spread out from one another, we would think of the whole curve as divided into three segments, separated by the two turning points.

This homely example, illustrated in Figure 1, captures a most important aspect of turning points. The concept of turning point is, in Arthur Danto's language, a "narrative concept."[3] That is, the concept has reference to two points in time, not one. What makes a turning point a turning point rather than a minor ripple is the passage of sufficient time "on the new course" such that it becomes clear that direction has indeed been changed.

Note that this "narrative" character of turning points emerges quite as strongly in quantitative and variable-based methods as in qualitative or case-based ones. If quantitative turning points could be identified merely with reference to the past and the immediate present, algorithms locating turning points could beat the stock market. It is precisely the "hindsight" character of turning points—their definition in terms of future as well as past and present—that forbids this.

Given this narrative quality, we can reformulate and generalize our concept of turning point to include simpler "bends" in a curve. What defines a turning point as such is the fact that the turn that takes place within it contrasts with a relative straightness outside (both before and after). Thus, as in Figure 2a, there is no need for actual change of sign. What matters is the separation of relatively smooth patterns by a turn that is by comparison abrupt. Note that we wouldn't think of an undifferentiated smooth curve (Figure 2b) as having a turning point, although it clearly involves long-term change.

The same concept of turning point emerges if we think about reality as discrete and categorical rather than as continuous and numerical. In this view, we imagine social processes as Markov processes. Imagine a simple process that jumps around between various states, with each jump being probabistically determined given the last location. For example, suppose a process takes on

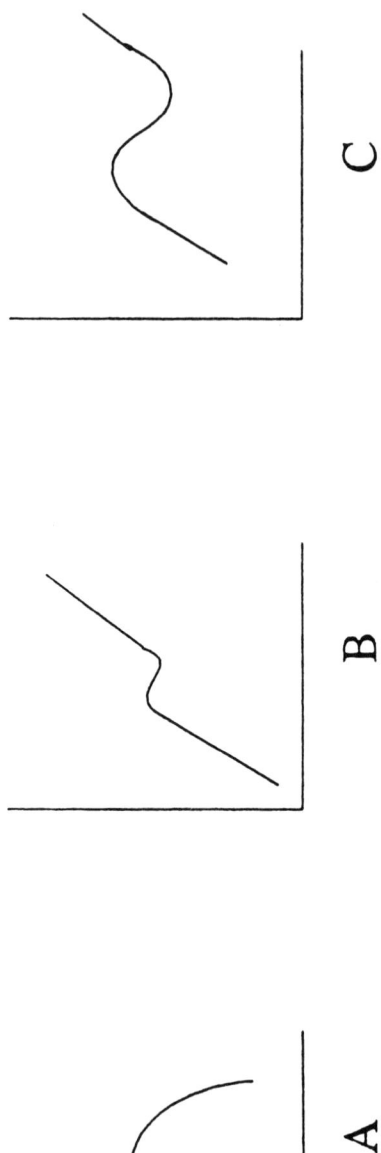

Figure 1.

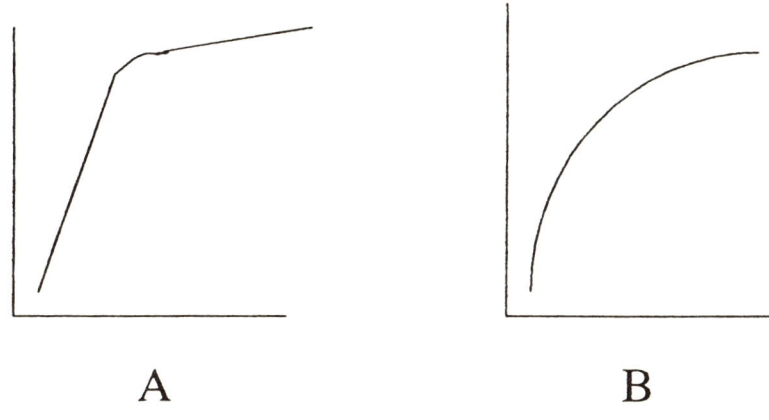

A   B

Figure 2.

values 0 and 1, such that 95 percent of the time our next step is simply to repeat the last value. This is a Markov process with the transition matrix:

		After	
		0	1
Before	0	.95	.05
	1	.05	.95

Such a process will produce long runs (median length about 15) of 0s and 1s. The turning points will be those relatively rare off-diagonal events that lead to changing the run element. Once in a while, we will get quickly repeated turning points. (In a sequence of six elements after a given start, at these probabilities, we will see two turning points only about 3% of the time.) But most of the time, turning points will be rare and clearly evident.

One can generalize this example by imagining a much larger state space with distinct clumps of states, the clumps being areas of that space within which the process wanders randomly while only occasionally jumping to another area. In this case, the Markovian transition matrix would be block-diagonal, with submatrices of substantial probabilities on the diagonal, and sparse submatrices off the diagonal.

This Markov formulation suggests that turning points are related to what Simon (1969, p. 99ff.) called "near-decomposability." By a nearly decomposable system, he meant a system whose parts could be looked at more or less independently. Similarly, a process has turning points because it has regular subprocesses between which we switch only rarely. Those rare switches are what we call turning points. In this view, turning points are a second-level matter, governing changes between different first-level regimes, which can to a certain extent be understood on their own. A long-run career can be "nearly decomposed" into these constituent trajectories.

In the continuous formulation, then, turning points involve the separation of relatively smooth and directional tracks by relatively abrupt and diversionary moments. In the discrete formulation, turning points are those rare transitions that take us between different probability regimes. These two formulations both tie directly to traditional themes in the life course literature. The smooth befores and afters are trajectories, linked by a relatively abrupt "turning point." They are stable regimes separated by unusual transitions.[4]

Although the life course literature leads us to focus on the succession of trajectories within a single case, it is important to envision the social structure implied by (or entailed in) this view of turning points. The models given so far suggest a social structure in which there are numbers of trajectories of certain kinds and the life course consists of a person's attempt to hook those trajectories up into a reasonable sequence. People's lives are typically on a steady course, but at various times external and internal shocks mean that an individual must leap to a new steady trajectory.

This view applies well to elite career paths. Once one enters, say, an elite graduate school, one enters a stable trajectory from entry courses through exams and dissertation work. Graduate school is a strongly coercive trajectory: with minor internal variation, of course, but with an enormous amount of inertia. But it is followed by a quite chaotic turning point—entry into the job market—through which a graduate student leaps onto the next more or less stable trajectory: an assistant professorhip, a research job, a postdoc, a job outside the specialty. The career constitutes a hooking up of a sequence of such inertial trajectory structures into a life course.[5]

From a theoretical point of view, what is important here is the inertial, historicist character of the trajectories. These are life episodes with a capacity for self-regeneration and self-perpetuation. Such episodes are widely programmed into our social institutions: in graduate and professional schools, in internal labor markets, and still, to a surprising extent, in institutions like marriage. Thus, from this view of turning points emerges an implicit image of the social process as comprising a number of programmed inertial trajectories, with strong constraints on their number and desirability. Indeed, one might hypothesize that at extremes of the social spectrum these constraints are quite strong. There are only so many careers available for great opera singers, and these career trajectories exist quite independently of the voices generated and discovered in a given epoch. How the trajectories are actually filled is largely an arbitrary matter of what trajectories are open and who is ready to leap when. And at the other end of the social scale, Erikson's (1966) famous account of deviance suggests that there exist similarly inertial deviant trajectories, to which some persons' prior lives must end up being attached, even if that attachment is more or less random with respect to their own prior experience.

In short, this conceptualization of turning points seems closely related to a structuralist view of social life. The focus is on constraints and vacancies, on availability and chance.

But this recognition of the social structural character of turning points should not blind us to the nature of the actors' individual experiences of them. There is for the individual actor a curious inversion of "causality" and "explanation" in the trajectory/turning point model of careers or life cycles. From the point of view of the actor moving from trajectory to trajectory, the "regular" periods of the trajectories are far less consequential and causally important than are the "random" periods of the turning points. The causally comprehensible phase seems unimportant, while the causally incomprehensible phase seems far more so. This paradox deserves elucidation.

What makes the trajectories trajectories is their inertial quality, their quality of enduring large amounts of minor variation without any appreciable change in overall direction or regime. Trajectories are trajectories precisely by virtue of what we might call their stable randomness, their causal character, in particular their comprehensibility under the image of cause implicit in regression thinking. Their inertia arises in stable, but localized, causal parameters.

Thus, trajectories might be called "master narratives" in the sense Hughes (1945) speaks of "master statuses." Just as a master status like race overrides subordinate statuses like occupation, eradicating them in a simple comparison, so a master narrative is an overarching social process that has the character of coercing processes within it, and indeed of preventing those processes from creating combinations that disrupt it. It is this coercive characteristic that makes trajectories master narratives.

By contrast, turning points are more consequential than trajectories precisely because they give rise to changes in overall direction or regime, and do so in a determinate fashion. Thus, while we may want to think of them as "abrupt" and "chaotic," and indeed we may discover them because they appear as irregularities in what has hitherto been a stable trajectory or regime, in fact they are the crucial sites of determination in the overall structure of a life course or an organizational career because they change its parameters. Thus, ironically, trajectories are the periods within which standard statistical modeling might be expected to produce good predictions of outcome, because in a sense that is the definition of a trajectory. But the turning points, precisely because they are the more causally central shifts of regime, will not be discovered by methods aiming at uncovering regimes.

The concept of turning point as so far defined can be generalized in an imoprtant way. One can loosen the assumption about the nature of the trajectories on either side of the turning point by allowing one or the other of them to be a random process, rather than a fixed trajectory. (That is, in terms of the imediately preceding discussion, one or the other of them could be a period within which standard causal models did not help us predict future outcome.) In this situation, the turning point becomes either a "focal turning point," if the move is from a relatively random trajectory to a relatively fixed and directional one, or a "randomizing turning point" if the move is from a stable trajectory to a random one.

Focal and randomizing turning points are clearly important in life course studies. With Sampson and Laub's juvenile delinquents, for example, many of crucial turning points towards "well-adjusted behavior" are focal turning points; they move individuals from random trajectories—involving occasional criminality, mixtures of employment experiences, and successions of social support and friendship networks—to stable trajectories organized around one job, one spouse, one way of life.

A number of writers have considered focal turning points whose outcomes are a function of the specific sequence or type of events within the turning point. Thus, in Thrasher's (1963, p. 56) account of the natural history of gangs, a number of forces combine to coalesce a group into a gang, which then goes through a number of turning points that have varying outcomes depending on the nature of events within them. It is thus important to add to the concepts of focal and randomizing turning points that of the contingent turning point, a turning point whose outcome is dependent on its internal event sequence.

Having characterized the standard, inter-trajectory turning point as well as the focal, randomizing, and contingent turning points, we can reflect briefly on the empirical problem of discovering turning points in social processes. In the simplest sense—where we are not concerned about the problem of "quick shifts" (Figure 1B)—an inspection of signs is sufficient. But within the broader conceptual framework sketched here, the problem is to establish some kind of moving window that can assess both the degree of "trajectoriness" in a currently ongoing trajectory and the "direction" of whatever trajectory does exist. In the broad sense discussed above, "trajectoriness" refers to some form of consistent causal regime: a constant slope, a constant set of transition probabilities, a constant set of regression coefficients. On the other hand, turning points are evidenced by chaotic internal regimes: varying internal slopes, irregular transitions, inconsistent regressions. (See Griffin and Isaac 1992 for an illustrative analysis.) A true turning point, as distinguished from a mere random episode, has the further character that the trajectories it separates either differ in direction (slope, transition probabilities, regression character) or in nature (one is "trajectory-like," the other is random).

Recall that neither the beginning nor the end of a turning point can be defined until the whole turning point has passed, since it is the arrival and establishment of a new trajectory (or a determination that randomness will endure, in the case of randomizing turning points) that defines the turning point itself. This means that turning point analysis makes sense only after the fact, when a new trajectory or system state is clearly established. It is this quality that makes the moving window strategy for identifying turning points both practicable and necessary.

PROCESS, INSTANT, AND DURATION IN TURNING POINTS

The life course literature, however, has often taken a much broader and looser view of turning points. Writers in that literature have often defined turning points as "a process." Hareven and Masaoka (1988, p. 274) write:

> All transitions are potential turning points. Under certain conditions, transitions are perceived and experienced as turning points over the life course—as processes, which continue to influence subsequent events in various forms. [...] A turning point is not an isolated event of short duration. Nor does it entail a sudden jump from one phase to another. A turning point is a process involving the alteration of life path, of [sic] a "course correction." A turning point requires, therefore, certain strategies and choices.

There are several noteworthy aspects to this definition. First, it conforms to our idea that turning points are inherently narrative events, that they are defined as having happened only by observing things that occur after them in time. For example, transitions—which in the life course literature refer to normatively defined life changes like getting married or acquiring a first job—can sometimes be defined as turning points a posteriori by flows of events that proceed out of them.

Second, this definition regards turning points as to some extent subjective. Indeed, the rest of the Hareven and Masaoka article, along with much of the life course literature, regards as turning points those particular events that are defined as such by respondents themselves, however long the hindsight involved. However, while I would not deny that rewriting one's biography is an important aspect of turning points in empirical personal experience, such retrospective interpretive work is not necessary. The work of defining a prior moment as a turning point can as easily be accomplished by a social fact (as in the slope reversal concept of the economists) as by an interpreting human consciousness.

But most important, this definition asserts that turning points "are" processes and that as such they have duration in time. The statement that turning points are processes seems to me a muddled version of the fact that turning point is a narrative concept.[6] On the other hand, the idea that turning points have duration is quite important. The discussion above indicates that a turning point is always relatively small, compared to the longer (and usually more uniform) trajectories around it. At the same time, the notion of turning point developed here presupposes that turning points in fact have extension in time. Indeed, if we follow a causal theory of the social world, of whatever sort, it seems necessary to believe in this duration. Without it, we would have to assume that the social process sometimes took on new directions instantaneously. But then, there would be no source, in some sense, for the change. It would simply arise de novo.

But this issue of instants actually arises even if we allow for turning points with finite duration. We still have to consider the delimitability of those turning points; they have to have a beginning. That beginning is either instantaneous or extended, and if extended, must have a beginning, and so forth. This Eleatic logic forces us to posit an instantaneous beginning to something (i.e., the beginning of the beginning of the beginning of a turning point) and thus leaves us unable to escape from the issue of how it is that change begins.

In empirical practice, of course, we expect the beginnings of turning points to be fuzzy. The turning point of Figure 2A, for example, would be very hard to delimit if the entire curve were endowed (realistically) with some high frequency variability. But the fuzzy character of the practical reality does not free us from requiring a philosophical account for an instantaneous change in an underlying regime. (Note that these considerations apply as well to the ends of turning points as to their beginnings.)

The life history literature's broader picture of turning point and duration thus raises the question of how turning points or beginnings of turning points may be instantaneous. A correlative problem arises when we try to think of turning points in the context of choice models of social life. In a choice model, we view the actor's experience as a perpetual branching process. The actor must first chose a or b, then, depending on that choice, a.1 versus a.2 or b.1 versus b.2. Now the choice/branching model seems to be an instant by instant model. But at the same time, the logical nature of the turning point concept—its narrative character—seems to forbid the one-step Markovian view implicit in branching models, since in the latter, choices are defined only with reference to the single moment of decision. A choice is made with respect to the expected future, but not in certain knowledge of whether or not the choice involved will prove to be a turning point.[7]

But there is as well a second difficulty here. In a choice model, individuals are constantly facing decisions; some choose one way, some choose another. In this sense, individuals' experience seems to become ever more unique, ever more specific as time passes. Lives are like dendritic systems starting from simple roots and developing along tracks that always have more possibilities downstream than upstream; choice is always in the future and involves more different things than does the dead past.

The concept of trajectories urged here seems to deny this whole proliferating model. For in its strong form, it imagines a world of socially structured and generated trajectories linked by occasional turning points: a network in time. The social process is made up of overlapping generations of trajectories linked to past and future trajectories by turning points, resulting in sequences (e.g., careers) of "trajectory a, turning point 1, trajectory b, turning point 2, trajectory c," and so on. Such a process is no more complex or open downstream than up, because there are always about the same number of trajectories under way across the whole system, and each individual is either on a trajectory or in a turning point. The issue is merely who gets hooked up to what. That is, the trajectories/turning point model discussed here is a structural, social level model, whilst the choice model assumes that there is a purely individual world, whose only "social" structure is something like a clearing market, not a constraining structure.

There are two responses to this question of branching and proliferation of possible futures. One comes from of the recollection that just as potential choices proliferate downstream, potential antecedents proliferate upstream. Individual choices may have more possible descendants with each passing generation. But any given trajectory could have been linked backward (by a turning point) to many different individual prior trajectories, and each of these, in turn, to many trajectories in the next preceding generation. There are dendritic systems going in both directions, and we care about the one or the other depending on whether we view the system from the viewpoint of individual living into the future or the trajectory that comes to have a certain occupant.

But the second response is the more important. Choice is not an isolated act, but rather one made in a context of many others' choosings. To the extent that trajectories are constrained system-wide, everyone who enters a turning point at any given time is aiming for the same limited array of trajectories. Only a network, not a proliferating system, is possible.

But apparent proliferation of futures is only the second problem raised by choice models. There remains the more important problem of instantaneous-ness, which is raised, as I noted, by turning point duration as well. The problem, again, is how it is that change begins. In particular, if turning points are the embodiment or extended process of change, how is it that they get started? This start must take place at a moment, and yet it would seem that given normal ideas about causality, an instant cannot see the production of enduring change. Similarly, since choice processes take place moment by moment, it is not clear how they can give rise to turning points, since we have defined those as necessitating reference to two points in time, not one.

A simple answer to this conundrum relegates turning points to the realm of the subjective, seeing them as post hoc interpretations of choices. This would be the view of most rational choice theorists, but it has the difficulty of failing to deal with turning points that don't arise in such immediate interpretation—turning points in stock prices and the like. Stock prices could of course be reduced to aggregates of individual choices, but changes in, say, an individual's ensemble of preferences could not. The relegation of turning points to the realm of the subjective doesn't work, even if it is clear, as I noted above, that turning points are central concepts in the subjective reinterpretation of the past.

A more effective answer addresses the problem the way Newtonian physics addresses Zeno's arrow paradox. We can't know from looking at an arrow for an instant whether it is in motion or not. But some arrows happen to be in motion while others don't; the passage of time tells us which. This answer worked well for Newton. He dealt with motion by deciding not to explain it, but rather to take it as a primal fact and find the fundamental regularities in which it is involved. ($F = ma$ says nothing whatever about causation; it is a purely descriptive statement.) But this strategy shies away from the fundamental issue of explanation; it suggests that we simply assume the existence of turning points as Newton assumed motion.

But Newton's answer to the Aristotelian question does suggest one way to approach explanation. We should assume that change is the normal state of affairs. The social world is constantly changing and reforming itself. To be sure, large parts of the social world reproduce themselves continually; much of it looks stable. But this is mere appearance. What transpires is reproduction, not endurance. The central reason for making this assumption is practical. It is possible to explain reproduction as a phenomenon sometimes produced by perpetual change; it is not possible to explain change as a phenomenon sometimes produced by perpetual stasis.

By making change our constant, we also exchange our explanada. It becomes necessary to explain reproduction, constancy, and entity-ness, rather than development and change. While I cannot give a full theory here, I shall sketch those aspects of it logically necessary to an account of turning points. (For further discussion see Abbott 1996a, 1996b).

The reproduced (or "constant") portions of the social structure are best imagined as made up of networks of relations between social actors. (They are made up of social relations between actors because, in the simplest sense, that is all there is in the social world. They are networks because the joint occurrence of such relations implies such networks.) Some of these networks of relations involve many actors, some few. Some are compact, some stringy. All are constituted by actors' actions in the present. For example, a university is produced by hundreds of people's coming daily to a set of buildings and talking and acting in certain ways. A great deal of individual variation within those activities is compatible with the endurance of the thing we call a university. That is the resilience of structure—to be impervious to large amounts of variation in teaching practices, ways of being a student, and so forth. (To discuss how this resilience is produced would take me beyond my subject here.)

That these networks of actions always take place in the present is crucial. The choice theorists and their ancestors the pragmatists are right that the past doesn't exist; it is dead and gone (Mead 1931; see also Abbott 1996b). All its influence on the present comes through its structuring of the immediate past. Social structure is continuously enacted by actors doing things with others. They may do these things for any of a variety of reasons: habit, rational calculation, irrational commitment, and so forth. All that exists in the social process, however, is the momentary totality at any moment of these actions and the interlocked patterns that they create by connecting and disconnecting multitudes of actors in myriads of relations, of hundreds of types.

Note that any single action impacts many of these networked structures at once. No action accomplishes only one thing. (To believe that was the great error of role theory, as it is of the simpler versions of rational choice.) When I write this chapter, I further my career (presumably), I connect my department to certain literatures, I identify my university with certain intellectual stances, I create rivalries with some of my colleagues, I provide employment for editors. The list is endless. These are not simply alternative emplotments. They are the real multiplicity of action. By doing many things, each action reconnects some existing structures, disconnects others, and indeed creates some structures unseen before. These "structures" should not be reified as things; they are simply the patterns of relations (networks of connections) that are likely to reappear at the next iteration of the social process.

At any given time, structures have a particular arrangement—the total network made by them. Some parts of this network are "nearly decomposable," in Simon's term, and can be seen in isolation. Others are interwoven. Given the diverse arrangements of the various networks, there must inevitably exist some peculiarly essential junctures. By "peculiarly essential junctures," I mean junctures where action might make particularly consequential bridges by making or breaking links between many networks, with the consequence of at once rearranging the overall pattern of networked structures. Structure, that is, embodies arrangements that make certain actions or events particularly consequential. For example, it made no difference that some random eighteenth century London pauper was insane. But encoded and created structures made it rather significant that King George III was subject to fits of near insanity. We can think of peculiarly essential junctures as being like arrangements of tumblers in a lock; if an action sits just right under the tumblers, it becomes the key that opens, the agent of sudden advantage or disadvantage.

As I noted, not all parts of these structures are the same and, moreover, some parts will be more or less decomposable from others. In particular, some parts are arranged in such a fashion as to be very difficult to disconnect, to prevent from reproducing. They may acquire this quality because of their extent, their redundancy, their disconnection with other structures, or a number of other reasons. In Braudel's language, these difficult, resistant parts of the network of relations are structure: long, enduring patterns. (We often call them underlying, but that implies a hierarchy that is not necessary to enduring structures; they can as well be small as large.) In terms of macropolitics, examples of such enduring structures might be modes of production or regimes of nationhood. In life course studies, they might be "personal character." That these are long-enduring means only that they are difficult to disconnect, difficult not to reproduce even if one consciously sets about stopping that reproduction. Often this will be because long-enduring structures are congeries of other shorter-enduring structures or local structures that provide reservoirs of redundancy that enable, indeed often enforce, reproduction even in the face of concerted effort. Hierarchy, that is, is often involved in reproduction. But, as I noted, it is not necessary.

However, hierarchy creates a particular version of the peculiarly essential juncture. Since all structures are continuously reenacted, it will happen from time to time that several local structures under a larger one might be simultaneously disconnected and their own reproduction prevented. This leaves an opening for action, a new juncture, that might assemble their constituent parts in a new way. If some actor takes that action, the result could be a minor turning point, the larger structure going on invulnerable. But once in a while, this minor turning point may line up with other minor turning points to create an opening in the overarching, master structure. Then we have a potential major turning point, in which a whole general regime can change if the proper action is taken. But just as all reproduction hinges on continuous action, so a potential turning point becomes actual only if the action is taken that makes it so. Many potential revolutions fail for want of attempt, just as many attempted revolutions fail for want of structural opportunity.

In summary, it is the nature of structures—partly interlocked with one another, partly hierarchical—that creates the possibility for sudden change in what seemed very stable. The heart of this suddenness is the merely apparent character of the stability in the first place. Change is the normal nature of things, but the effects of local habit and training, in the context of networked structures, mean that a substantial number of networks of social relations reproduce themselves, which makes us call them "large-scale structures." (My point is that such reproduction, and nothing else, is the defining characteristic of those structures.) But since structures always have a particular arrangement, and since that arrangement is always being reenacted in action, the possibility always exists for a pattern of actions that puts the key in the lock and makes a major turning point occur.

Thus the answer to the question of instantaneousness is that the social process is always instantaneous. Instants—the momentary steps of the dialogue of immediate past, present and immediate future—these are all that exist. The world is Markovian. But the past is encoded into the present in patterns of connection that we call structure. The production of the next moment of socal life happens from the basis provided by that structure. And the arrangements of structures always leave openings for actions, which if they fit the situation can change the longest-enduring structures quite quickly.

Only after the action has been taken that turns the key can we speak of the turning point as having occurred. It is in this dialogue of structural possibility and action that turning points are defined. Often, as in fall of the Soviet Union, it takes a long time for a system to settle back into structures once decisive action has been taken in a context of structural openness. At other times, the return to (possibly a new type of) stability is swift. But it is the necessity that potentiality be acted upon that makes turning points narrative concepts, in the sense earlier developed. Possibility must emerge before action. Possibility and action together provide the two moments necessary to the narrative structure of a turning point.

Finally, this argument implies that social structure is itself the memory of the social process. In the arrangements that we call social structure lie all the influences of the past. Of course interpretation adds a further dimension to this. Human memory contains much of the past and we act, always, on that basis of that memory. But even without it, the social process still has a memory. That memory is what we give the label of structure.[8]

CONCLUSION

This paper has established a number of aspects of turning points. Turning points are best envisioned as short, consequential shifts that redirect a process. The concept is inevitably a narrative one, for a turning point cannot be conceived without a new reality or direction being established, a judgment that requires at least two temporally separate observations. Not all sudden changes are turning points, but only those which are succeeded by a period evincing a new regime.

There is a sense in which turning points are "second-level" moments that separate more uniform trajectories within which a "first-level" regime obtains. However, there is no necessary warrant for seeing turning points as organized or connected by an underlying or overarching (depending on your choice of metaphor) process. They could be simply random, but major, disturbances intervening in a life course. An individual actor (biological or social) experiences such a life course as a sequence of trajectories linked to one another via turning points: trajectory, turning point, trajectory, turning point, and so forth.

Linked to this view of turning points is a structuralist view of the social process. That process is organized into trajectories, many of which are programmed into institutions like schools, professions, marriage, and the like.

These trajectories are often subject to various levels of constraint, ranging from pure vacancy constraint to looser class constraints. (See Abbott 1990b). Trajectories are strongly inertial, enduring substantial variation without change, because of consistent internal causal regimes.

Paradoxically, individual actors experience the causally comprehensible trajectories as less important and less consequential than the less comprehensible turning points. Indeed, there is no necessary reason for turning points to be systematic in their effects. In tightly constrained vacancy systems, for example, they will exercise a largely random effect.

Extended periods of non-trajectory experience are possible. In these, events are random or inexplicable. The turning points leading into and out of such periods are called randomizing and focal turning points respectively. We also recognize turning points whose results are determined by events within them, calling them contingent turning points.

While the concept of turning points is absolutely central to the normal process of autobiography, there is no *necessity* for interpretation for turning points to be recognized. Some turning points exist in se, without needing to be "discovered" or "invented."

Turning points have duration and extension. They take time. This follows in part from their inherently narrative character. Nonetheless, they are instantaneous in the sense that all social life is instantaneous. Allowing for the possibility of instantaneous change requires a social ontology founded on process and change, in which stability is a mere appearance. Turning points are thus best theorized as points at which the interlocked networks of relation that preserve stability come unglued and the (normal) perpetual change of social life takes over. This can happen in a variety of ways, particularly in hierarchically organized processes. A major turning point has potential to open a system the way a key has the potential to open a lock. In both cases, too, action is necessary to complete the turning.

My theory of turning points thus fits within a larger view of social structure as the encoded memory of past process. Since at any time the given structure of relations is all that exists (I ignore human memory for the moment), all influence of the past works through the shape given to those relations by the actions of the past. Memory of course provides a symbolic record of the past, which then reinterprets and reshapes it as a foundation for current action. But in the first instance, social structure is itself the memory of the social process.

Where does this leave us with respect to Goldthorpe's critique, with which I began? This chapter challenges Goldthorpe to say what a variables-based methodology would make of the social world if it were constructed in the way suggested here. (By methodology here, I mean not regression specifically, but rather the broader vision of the world implicit in it, what I have elsewhere called "general linear reality," Abbott 1988.) Within trajectories, I have argued, variable-based methods might work. Identifying those trajectories, however, is a task for pattern-based methods, not variable-based ones. And once turning points are themselves introduced into the data to be analyzed, variable-based methods become even less useful. For through turning points constraint and contingency play roles that mock the presuppositions of variable-based analysis. If the world actually has turning points and trajectories, the only way to find them is to pursue the project of narrative positivism (Abbott 1992b). Goldthorpe has little hope for this project. With due respect, I disagree.

NOTES

1. When I first began to talk about analysis of sequential social patterns, in the early 1980s, "narrative" had not yet become the fashionable word that it later would. Hence I used the word to refer to actual historical regularities as well as to narrated versions of them, specifying which meaning applied when necessary. Unfortunately, the word "narrative" has latterly become completely conflated with what the French call *discours*, the telling of a story. Throughout this paper, I use "narrative patterns" to refer to actual regularities in the social process itself and treat the entire issue of discourse and representation of such regularities as non-problematic. This is of course a draconian assumption, but one necessary for my present purposes.

2. The literature on political revolutions is so immense and familiar that I give no references. The historical antecedents of the concept of revolution are covered in Cohen's (1985, c. 4) rather wooden history of the idea of revolutions. The idea of revolutionary turning points in historical processes is ultimately a Christian one (Collingwood 1956, p. 49ff). Indeed the concept later developed for turning points in this paper—transition between relatively sharply differentiated regimes—is effectively captured by Paul's image of the turning point of incarnation separating the period of redemption from that of the Law (AV Galatians 3, pp. 23-24):

> But before faith came we were kept under the law, shut up unto the faith which should afterward be revealed. Wherefore the law was our schoolmaster, to bring us unto Christ, that we might find faith. But after that faith is come, we are no longer under such a schoolmaster.

Paul's description of turning points in the life course is similar (AV 1 Corinthians 13, pp. 11-12):

> When I was a child, I spake as a child, I understood as a child, I thought as a child. But when I became a man, I put away childish things. For now we see through a glass darkly; but then, face to face.

3. Actually, Danto discusses "narrative sentences," which he defines as that class of sentences that has reference to two points in time rather than one. I am here extending his insight to cover concepts more generally and arguing that turning point, as a concept, inherently refers to two points in time.

4. The distinction of trajectories from turning points, in practice, will be less draconian. Every trajectory has little turnings within it, just as turning points—if extended—may have little trajectories in them. This fractal interpenetration will make identification difficult. The problems of hierarchically nested processes—which give rise to this interpenetration definitionally—are considered below.

5. It should not be assumed that the ultimate elite career is one that hooks together all the perfect elite trajectories. It may very well be that a Padgett/Leifer robust action argument applies here (Padgett and Ansell 1993; Leifer 1988). The most elite individual may be that person who maintains the largest number of possible future trajectories that s/he could jump onto, just as the most powerful action is the one whose actions are the least predictable and least specifiable.

6. In the passage quoted above, as in some other life course writing, the turning point becomes so extended that it no longer is a point in any sense, but rather simply a name for the fact that a change was made over some long period, thus including the situation shown in Figure 2b as well as relatively sharp turns such as 2a. It seems best to distinguish these situations, indeed it seems that is the point of having a concept of turning point, as opposed to simply one of change or causality or succession, all of which would cover a turning point of this extremely gradual kind. For an empirical example using such a broad definition, see Pickles and Rutter (1991, e.g., p. 134).

7. One aspect of turning points not considered at length here is the aspect of irrevocability. I have simply mentioned the concept of a "point of no return" in remarking on Goldthorpe's paper. But there are a number of kinds of threshold events that could productively be viewed within a branching framework. Making the choice to know the sex of one's unborn child is an example. Once known, the fact cannot be unknown.

8. In particular, not only is there the issue of actual human memory of the past. There is also the difficulty that the past can, literally, be rewritten. It can change after the fact because of new discoveries and new interpretations. Of course this is not a change in the past for itself, then, as it affected those actors. But it is a change in the interpreted, and hence presently consequential, past.

REFERENCES

Abbott, A. 1988. "Transcending General Linear Reality." *Sociological Theory* 6: 169-186.
———. 1990a. "Conceptions of Time and Events in Social Science Methods." *Historical Methods* 23: 140-150.
———. 1990b. "Vacancy Models for Historial Data." Pp. 80-102 in *Social Mobility and Social Structure*, edited by R.L. Breiger. Cambridge: Cambridge University Press.
———. 1992a. "What Do Cases Do?" Pp. 53-82 in *What is a Case*, edited by C.C. Ragin and H.S. Becker. Cambridge: Cambridge University Press.
———. 1992b. "From Causes to Events." *Sociological Methods and Research* 20: 428-255
———. 1995. "Things of Boundaries" *Social Research* 62: 857-882.
———. 1996. "Temporality and Process in Social Life." In *Social Time and Social Change*, edited by F. Engelstad and R. Kalleberg. Norwegian University Press.
Burnham, W.D. 1970. *Critical Elections and the Mainsprings of American Politics.* New York: Norton.
Chaffin, W.W., and W.K. Talley. 1989. "Diffusion Indexes and a Statistical Test for Predicting Turning Points in Business Cycles." *International Journal of Forecasting* 5: 29-36.
Clubb, J.M., W.H. Flanagan, and N.H. Zingale. 1981. *Party Realignment.* Beverly Hills, CA: Sage.
Cohen, I.B. 1985. *Revolution in Science.* Cambridge, MA: Harvard University Press.
Collingwood, R.G. 1956. *The Idea of History.* New York: Oxford University Press.
Danto, A. 1985. *Narration and Knowledge.* New York: Columbia University Press.
Elder, G.H. (Ed.). 1985. "Perspectives on the Life Course." Pp. 23-49 in *Life Course Dynamics.* Ithaca, NY: Cornell.
Erikson, K. 1966. *Wayward Puritans.* New York: Wiley.

Griffin, L.J., and L.W. Isaac. 1992. "Recursive Regression and the Historical Use of 'Time' in Time-Series Analysis of Historical Process." *Historical Methods* 25: 166-179.

Hareven, T.K., and K. Masaoka. 1988. "Turning Points and Transitions." *Journal of Family History* 13: 271-289.

Hughes, E.C. 1945. "Dilemmas and Contradictions of Status." *American Journal of Sociology* 50: 353-359.

————. 1971. [1950]. "Cycles, Turning Points, and Careers." Pp. 124-131 in *The Sociological Eye*. Chicago: Aldine.

Kuhn, T.S. 1970. *The Structure of Scientific Revolutions*. Chicago: University of Chicago Press.

Lasser, W. 1985. "The Supreme Court in Periods of Realignment." *Journal of Politics* 47: 1174-1187.

Leifer, E. 1988. "Interaction Preludes to Role-Setting." *American Sociological Review* 53: 865-878.

LeSage, J.P. 1990. "Forecasting Turning Points in Metropolitan Employment Growth Rates using Bayesian Techniques." *Journal of Regional Science* 30: 533-548.

Lieberson, S. 1992. "Small N's and Big Conclusions." Pp. 105-118 in *What is a Case*, edited by C.C. Ragin and H.S. Becker. Cambridge: Cambridge University Press.

Loftin, C., and S.K. Ward. 1981. "Spatial Autocorrelation Models for Galton's Problem." *Behavior Science Research* 1: 105-140.

Mead, G.H. 1931. *The Philosophy of the Present*. Chicago: University of Chicago Press.

O'Rand, A.M., and M.L. Krecker. 1990. "Concepts of the Life Cycle." *Annual Review of Sociology* 16: 241-262.

Padgett, J.F., and C.K. Ansell. 1993. "Robust Action and the Rise of the Medici, 1400-1434." *American Journal of Sociology* 98: 1259-1319.

Park, R.E. 1927. "Introduction" Pp. xv-xix in *The Natural History of Revolution*, by L. Edwards. Chicago: University of Chicago Press.

Pickles, A. and M. Rutter. 1991. "Statistical and Conceptual Models of 'Turning Points' in Developmental Processes." Pp. 133-165 in *Problems and Methods in Longitudinal Research*, edited by D. Magnusson, L.R. Bergman, G. Rudinger, and B. Torestad. Cambridge: Cambridge University Press.

Sampson, R.J., and J.H. Laub. 1993. *Crime in the Making*. Cambridge: Harvard.

Simon, H.A. 1969. *The Sciences of the Artificial*. Cambridge: MIT Press.

Taibelson, M.H. 1974. "Distinguishing Between Heterogeneity and Randomness in Stochastic Models." *American Sociological Review* 39: 8877-8880.

Thrasher, F.M. 1963. [1927]. *The Gang*. Chicago: University of Chicago Press.

Zellner, A., C. Hong, and C-k. Min. 1991. "Forecasting Turning Points in International Growth Rates Using Bayesian Exponentially Weighted Autoregression, Time-varying Parameter, and Pooling Techniques." *Journal of Econometrics* 49: 275-304.

METHODOLOGICAL ISSUES IN COMPARATIVE MACROSOCIOLOGY

Jack A. Goldstone

ABSTRACT

John Goldthorpe and other critics of small-N comparative case studies have severely faulted this methodology for relying on canons of logic from John Stuart Mill that are inappropriate for the social sciences. Goldthorpe is correct that Mill's logic *is* inappropriate for social inquiry. However, the comparative method of small-N case studies is not based on Mill's cannons. Both critics and supporters of small-N studies err when making their case on those grounds. Comparative case study methods are a combination of deductive and inductive reasoning more comparable to detective work than true experiments. In conditions where true experiments cannot be undertaken, this detective method has certain advantages over standard statistical analysis.

Professor John Goldthorpe has, in his usual masterful way, identified several key problems in the search for causal explanations of macrosociological phenomena. Moreover, he sides with critics of case-study methods such as Stanley Lieberson (1991, 1994), in arguing that case-study methods have no

Comparative Social Research, Volume 16, pages 107-120.
Copyright © 1997 by JAI Press Inc.
All rights of reproduction in any form reserved.
ISBN: 0-7623-0250-X

special utility in solving these problems, and further that case-study methods seem to be based on Millian principles (determinism, completeness) that are inappropriate for sociological issues.

I fully endorse the position of both Goldthorpe and Lieberson that Millian logic is wholly inapplicable to macrosociology, and scholars who claim that such logic is useful (Skocpol 1979; Savolainen 1994) either misunderstand Mill, or are mistaken in discussing their own techniques. However, I would claim that the logic of small-N studies or comparative case studies is *not* Millian, nor indeed primarily inductive. Thus the criticisms leveled at case-study methods are based on misrepresentation of those methods by both their advocates and their critics.

The true logic of comparative case-studies is a combination of deductive and inductive reasoning, more like that of a criminal detective or insurance adjuster than like that of an experimental scientist. It is aimed at providing explanations for particular cases, or groups of similar cases, rather than at providing general hypotheses that apply uniformly to *all* cases in a suspected case-universe. Although increasingly general hypotheses may be suggested, tested, and modified through expanding the range of cases, this is an incremental process that may or may not occur as part of the research program of a particular field in comparative macrosociology.

I shall argue that this logic of case-study analysis is wholly compatible with the probabilistic nature of social events. Moreover, because it necessarily combines internal with external analysis (Janowski 1991) through a procedure I call "process-tracing" (Goldstone 1991), it *is* better than variable-based approaches at dealing with what Goldthorpe calls the "black box problem." In addition, because variable-based methods both assume the uniform action of variables across cases (or at least that only lower-level interactions are present), and tend to be far more inductive (although not wholly or necessarily so) than case-studies, I shall argue they have weaknesses for macro-social studies that case-study methods generally avoid.

MISUNDERSTANDING MILL

It is remarkable that, despite substantial criticism of whether practitioners of small-N macrosociology actually use Mill's method at all (Nichols 1986; Burawoy 1989), arguments regarding the virtues of comparative case-study methods still focus on Millian logic (Skocpol 1986; Lieberson 1991, 1994; Savolainen 1994, Goldthorpe 1994). Let me be perfectly clear—Mill's methods *cannot* be used and *are not* used by comparative case-study analyses.

Lieberson (1991) is quite right in pointing out that Mill's methods require cases to be identical in *all* respects except one, or to differ in *all* respects except one. Such complete and precise specification can only be obtained in true experimental designs where either through randomization, matching, or complete control of the independent variables such configurations can be obtained. Mill himself argued clearly that his logic of comparison was intended for interpreting true controlled experiments, which were being undertaken in the natural sciences, and *not* to be used in social inquiry.

For example, when a corn field is divided into two otherwise identical parts, receiving identical weather and planted with identical seeds and only fertilizer is varied, Mill's logic can be used to determine that differences in yields result from the differences in fertilizing.

As an aside, I should point out that Mill's logic is not limited to strictly deterministic results, nor to cases where there are no interactions, and Lieberson and Goldthorpe are mistaken in this regard. In the cornfield experiment just described, the observed difference in yields is not wholly determined by the input of fertilizer. If the experiment is run in a year in which frost kills the crops, the difference will be zero; if the experiment is run in a year of low rainfall, the effect of the fertilizer will be modest as drought will be the main factor limiting yields; if the experiment is run in a year with plentiful rainfall, the difference in yields will be huge.

Thus if the identical experiment is run over many years, the results will suggest a high probability that yields are higher where fertilizer input is higher, and an average or expected value for the yield increase can be computed. But this result will not be deterministic in the sense that one can predict in any given year exactly what the difference in yields will be. What Mill's logic produces is the conclusion that in these otherwise identically matched fields, *if* any difference in yields appears, *then* that difference will be wholly due to differences in the one factor (fertilizer) that has varied between them. Mill's logic does not depend on, nor imply, that the difference in yields will always be the same or even always appear.

But to return to the main point: no comparison of real-world macrosocial cases can ever hope to be, even abstractly, a "true" experiment with cases that are identical except for a single independent variable that differs among cases. Thus Mill's logic cannot be applied in macrosociology.

It is therefore extremely unfortunate that one of the most masterful practitioners of case-study methods, Theda Skocpol, has identified her methods as Millian, or inspired by Millian logic. In fact, in many obvious ways, her methods depart sharply from Mill's canon.

Her cases of social revolution—France, Russia, and China—*differ among themselves on several independent variables.* Skocpol's main independent variables are international pressure, elites with leverage against the state, and autonomous peasant village organization. The first two weaken the state; the last provides the organizational framework for popular uprisings when the state weakens. But look closely at the cases: *only* in France are all three conditions present. In Russia in 1917, elites had no significant leverage against the state.

Overwhelming defeat by Germany in World War I was sufficient to fatally weaken the state, without opposition from entrenched elites. China in 1911-1949 did face international pressures and opposition from powerful elites. But peasants had *no* autonomous village organization; they remained under local gentry control in most areas until the Chinese communists took power in those areas. In other words, communist party organization of the peasantry (a factor that appears in no other case) substituted for autonomous village organization. So Skocpol is in fact not even making any claim that identical causal factors are present in all her cases of social revolution: France has three of the key factors present; Russia had only two; and China had only two (and not the same two as Russia). If Skocpol thinks she is employing Millian logic, she is either misrepresenting her own method, or misunderstanding Mill.

Moreover, not only do Skocpol's positive cases not show uniformity, this is even more true of her negative cases. Mill's logic requires that a clear difference in the dependent variable be associated with differences in the independent variables. But how do Skocpol's negative cases differ from her positive ones? Her negative cases are in fact all revolutions, albeit not social revolutions. The English Revolution of 1640 and the Japanese Meiji Restoration of 1868 both had political crises and a change of regime, but autonomous popular mobilization did not play a major role. The German Revolutions of 1848 had a political crisis and autonomous popular mobilization, but not a change of regime. Skocpol is thus comparing social revolutions, which combined a political crisis, regime change, and autonomous popular mobilization, with events that had at least two (and not always the same two) but not three of those components.

But this is an odd comparison. For while it is perfectly valid to ask what factors separated these three major social revolutions (France, Russia, and China) from lesser crises or revolutions, mightn't one also want to know what factors separated these episodes of revolution from times and places where no political crises or revolutions occurred at all? If there was no causal story in Skocpol's work (which fortunately there is) but only Mill's logic at work, we would be left to conclude that even *if* Skocpol's three causal factors were uniformly present in social revolutions, that only tells us which factors separate greater from lesser revolutions; the comparative logic alone tells us *nothing* about what separates revolutionary crises from periods of non-crisis, or in other words, nothing about what causes revolutions at all.

Further misunderstanding of Mill's logic appears in Savolainen's (1994) defense of Skocpol and the application of Mill's methods to social science. Savolainen's main argument is a concession that Mill's methods cannot be used in discovery or proof of general propositions, but *can* be used to eliminate certain hypotheses. This relies on the erroneous assertion that "No factor can explain an outcome satisfactorily that is not common to all occurrences of that outcome" (p. 1218). Therefore, if a factor appears in only one case (such as the role of the communist party in China in mobilizing the peasantry against the state), it cannot be a general explanatory factor, and can be "eliminated" from general causal propositions. Although one can see the intuitive appeal of this proposition, it is simply wrong. In real social life, different factors *can* be functional substitutes.

Savolainen (p. 1220) gives the following table as an example of this mode of argument:

Table 1. Fallacious Millian Reasoning

	Factors Present	Phenomenon Observed	Causal Factor
Case 1	C1, C2, C3	Yes	
			C1
Case 2	C1, C4, C5	Yes	

Savolainen claims that since *only* C1 is present in both cases, *only* C1 can be the cause of the phenomenon; C2, C3, C4 and C5 can be ruled out as primary causes. Yet this reasoning is fallacious. C1 could be the primary cause. But C1 could also be wholly irrelevant, with either the combination of C2 and C3, or that of C4 and C5, being sufficient to cause the effect. Or C1 might be necessary, but not sufficient, being effective only in the presence of the above combinations of C2 and C3, or of C4 and C5. This tabular array of causes neither fits Mill's model of reasoning, nor provides any logical deduction of causation. It is a misguided and misleading attempt to apply Millian-type logic.

Skocpol's own work betrays this model. Let us say that the cases are Russia and China, and C1, C2, and C3 are international pressure on the state, autonomous peasant village organization, and the presence of the Russian Orthodox Church, respectively. Let C4 be Communist Party organization of the peasantry against the state, and C5 be opposition to the state from an entrenched elite. According to Skocpol, the cause of social revolution in Russia was *the combination* of C1 and C2, while the cause of social revolution in China was *the combination* of C1, C4, and C5. C1 was present and necessary in both cases, C2 and C4 were functionally equivalent, while C3 was irrelevant and C5 was necessary in one case due to the "moderate" level of C1. The "causal factor" in the last column therefore should *not* be merely "C1," but the more complex (and totally non-Millian) "*either* (high C1) + C2 *or* (moderate C1) + C4 + C5."

In short, Savolainen is wrong—Mill's method cannot be applied to macrosociology. As the above example of Skocpol's causal reasoning demonstrates, what Skocpol has actually done in practice, despite her allusions to Mill's method, is something quite different. Thus critiques of Skocpol's work, or small-N studies generally, that focus on the problems with Millian logic miss the point. But this leaves the question: what is Skocpol's method, or the comparative case-study method more generally? How does it provide non-Millian, complex, alternative causal configurations for events, which is what Skocpol in fact provides?

THE TRUE LOGIC OF COMPARATIVE CASE-STUDIES

Goldthorpe (1994, p. 16) claims that "'History' [in the sense of unique or contingent events] is for macrosociology a necessary residual category." By this I believe he means that if we invoke in our explanations factors that because they are unique or contingent cannot play a general causal role across different cases, we have stopped doing anything like scientific, generalizing, sociological work. I must disagree strongly, for this statement shows how much the critics of comparative case studies misunderstand this method. "History" in this sense is at the heart of comparative case-study methods; and this no more renders them unscientific or unrelated to general causation than does the invocation of contingent or unique events (such as the initial separation of continental land-masses, or the random development of a bipedal, binocular, language-using hominid) render evolutionary biology an unscientific field of study.

The key to comparative case-studies in macrosociology is *the unravelling of historical narratives*. I have called this procedure "process-tracing." What it means is the decomposition of a complex narrative into stages, episodes, or events which can be connected by causal sequences that are simpler and easier to explain than the narrative as a whole. The explanation of these particular stages, episodes, or events is mainly deductive, although some inductive reasoning may be employed, depending on the existing state of theory and knowledge.

For example, in her study of social revolutions, what Skocpol actually does is unpack the narratives of those revolutions, claiming that there were several key events that contributed to the final character of these sequences. First, the state was rendered incapable of suppressing popular uprisings. This could come about either by overwhelming external pressure (massive defeat as in Russia in 1917) or by a combination of moderate international pressures and actions by elites who had leverage against the state and who opposed the state's efforts to respond to those pressures (as in France in 1789 where elites opposed the government's efforts to reform by raising taxes as excessive, or in China in 1911 where elites opposed the government's efforts at reform as inadequate).

Second, a large mass of the population had to be mobilized to take advantage of the state's weakness and act to overturn institutions of local control. This could not occur where local landlords were the controlling focus of rural peasant organizations (as in England before 1640, in China prior to the 1940s, and in east-Elbian Germany in 1848). However, it could occur either where peasant villages had autonomous organizations for self-administration (as in France and Russia), or where non-landlord based peasant organization developed (as in rural China in areas under Communist control).

These elements are selected largely by deductive reasoning: states that are firmly in control and able to repress popular uprisings will not be the site of social revolutions; ergo a weakening of the state must be a condition for social revolution to occur. In addition, popular mobilization for revolutionary actions will not occur if people cannot organize except through the leadership of those who will seek to prevent mobilization against landlords or the state. Thus if local landlords control rural peasant organization, no social revolution can follow state weakness, although other kinds of crises (political revolutions or reform movements) could occur. Social revolutions therefore require *both* some conditions that produce state weakness *and* some conditions that conduce to revolutionary mass mobilization.

Once these elements are deductively selected, the empirical task is one of demonstrating that the actual narratives of revolutionary (and contrasting non-revolutionary) cases conform to the deductive arguments. In fact, the empirical conditions that function to confirm the deductive links *can be* unique and/ or contingent. For example, the rural development of the Communist party in China was (up to 1949) a unique event, which was entirely contingent on Mao's escape to the mountains from Shanghai after the Kuomintang's attempt to eliminate the CCP and his consequent improvisation of a "peasant strategy" of communist revolution that was hitherto unknown. But what matters for the comparative case-study is that this unique and contingent event can be plausibly shown to have created a situation in which the landlord control of rural peasant organization was undone, prior to and in a way that facilitated the social revolution of 1949 in China.

How are these deductive elements chosen from the complex tapestry of events? That is part of the logic of discovery and theory-generation, which remains a psychological mystery. It is partly inductive, as scholars like Skocpol are struck by the similarities among peasant revolutions, and try to narrow those similarities down to a few key elements in the narratives. It is partly deductive, as abstractions of functional elements are proposed that tie together unique and contingent elements in logically compelling ways. It is therefore more like the solution of a crime or the assessment of causes of an accident than like seeking a general uniform effect of particular variables. The experienced detective will draw on her experience with similar cases in making judgements about which factors pertain to this particular case (inductive insights); but the causal reasoning proposed to explain a crime or accident will be a linking of particular facts involved in this case with general principles regarding how opportunities, motivations, and circumstances conduce to particular actions (deductive reasoning).

CASE-STUDIES VS. VARIABLE-BASED STUDIES

I mention the seeking of causes of an accident, because Lieberson (1991) used precisely this example to discredit small-N case studies. He gave the data shown in Table 2 on two automobile incidents, both involving a drunk driver running a stop light, but only one of which result in an accident. Lieberson noted that Mill's logic would perversely set aside both drunkeness and running the light as causal factors (because these factors appear in both the accident and non-accident cases), and highlight "car enters at right" as the accident's sole cause. Thus the small-N case analysis would give misleading results.

But comparative case-studies do not use Millian logic. How would a scholar using that method actually proceed? First, she would become familiar with the narrative of the two cases: In the first, a drunk driver ran a red light and hit a car entering from the right. In the second, a drunk driver ran a red light, but had no accident since there was no one in the intersection. Second, he would use deductive logic and general knowledge to identify the crucial causal element in these narratives: in this case, the fact that a car entered from the right was necessary for an accident, but we know from general knowledge that that happens all the time. What is crucial in these cases is that the car entered from the right *at the same time that a driver too drunk to see or react to the red light came from the left.* Thus the comparative case-study analyst would, in real life, not foolishly conclude that the car entering from the right was "the" cause of the accident. He or she would say it was *the combination* of the drunk driver running the light at the same time the other vehicle entered the intersection that caused that accident.

In other words, just as an insurance adjuster would try to get all the details in order, make use of his general knowledge of traffic to make deductions, and combine them with the specific contingent details (the driver entering from the right) in order to construct a convincing explanation of what happened in the first case, so too a competent comparative macrosociologist would *not* rely on Millian logic but use a similar mix of narrative reconstruction, deductive reasoning, and attention to contingent details to construct a convincing macrosociological explanation.

Interestingly, this example also shows that increasing N and using a variable-based approach might be wholly ineffective. Let us say that the number of cases is not two, but two thousand: one thousand like case one and one

Table 2. Factors Present in an Accident

Accident	Drunk Driver	Car Enters at Right	Speeding	Runs a Red Light
Yes	Yes	Yes	No	Yes
No	Yes	No	No	Yes

thousand like case two. In other words, about half of drunk drivers are lucky and don't hit anyone when they hit a red light; the other half do (this seems reasonable unless you assume that drunk drivers are systematically more likely to drive at times of high traffic than of low). Statistical analysis of these two thousand cases would also reveal *nothing* about the causes of accidents. Both drunk driving and running a red light would be wholly uncorrelated with accidents; "car entering from the right" would be highly correlated.

So, *unless the analyst has a deeper understanding of driving and the effects of drinking*, which might lead him to frame his statistical hypothesis as a test of the interaction effect of causes one and two and four, statistical analysis of a large-N sample will give misleading or perverse results.

What this example illustrates is that it is not the size of N, nor the difference between statistical and non-statistical analysis, that guards against misleading or perverse conclusions. What matters is the skill and insight that guides the framing of the hypothesis. Here, we return to what Goldthorpe calls the "black box" problem. Let us try to imagine that the nature of traffic and the process of driving were a black box to us, so that the terms "drunk driving," "car entering from the right," "speeding," and "runs a light" were just so many categorical variables that called up no picture, no hypothesis of their interaction. Let us say we could measure the presence or absence of these categorical variables, and were going to seek inductively for their impact on accidents by doing a large-N statistical analysis. If the data were distributed as shown in Lieberson's table above, this method would yield nonsense.

Let us contrast this supposition with the idea that a person who has a modest knowledge of driving, of the effects of alcohol intake and speeding on vehicle control, and of traffic laws, were to study a half-dozen or even two accidents, again with the same data pattern. What are the odds that this analyst is likely to make the same mistake of deciding that the data tell us that drinking and running a light are irrelevant? Isn't the case study approach as outlined above, beginning with a narrative reconstruction and reasonable deductions from known theory and general knowledge, more likely to protect the analyst from those errors?

The situation in many complex macrosociological phenomena is actually rather similar to this absurd example. In many cases (such as the study of revolutions, or democratization) the processes involved are so complex that it may seem simpler to treat those processes as a "black box," and search inductively for correlations of variations in the dependent variable with variations in a wide range of independent variables across many cases. But unless the processes have a certain pattern—few or only low-level interactions, significant differences in the distribution of variable levels across cases, few severe outliers driving relationships, no biases of misspecification in the inductive model being tested—the results may be misleading or perverse.

For example, Rueschemeyer, Stephens, and Stephens (1992) grant that there is a well-established cross-sectional correlation between the level of capitalist development in a country and the level of democracy in that country. Yet in examining case-histories of democratization, they find a great deal of variation, and little consistency, in the *temporal* pattern of changes in development and in democracy. They argue that the cross-sectional correlation, although accurate, is causally spurious, and that it is not the level of development *per se* but the strength of the working class (which is somewhat positively correlated with levels of development) that is the key causal factor. *Process-tracing* through a dozen or so case studies allowed Rueschemeyer and associates to penetrate the paradox of conflicting cross-sectional and temporal patterns, and identify the underlying causal factor in democratization (Rueschemeyer 1991).

Just as one can argue that Millian methods are badly suited to social phenomena, because of the latter's complexity and the functional equivalence of different causes, one can also argue that large-N inductive statistical methods are poorly suited to social phenomena, because social phenomena tend to (1) show high levels of multiple interactions; (2) show a key role for unique or contingent events; (3) show significant outliers due to such events; and (4) be very difficult to specify without omitted-variable bias. For these reasons, large-N cross-national studies of such important phenomenon as the origins of wars and the origins of revolutions, despite extensive support for such research, have provided relatively meager returns (Gurr 1980).

I do not wish to be as harsh on such large-N methods as Lieberson and Goldthorpe are on small-N methods. In practice, skilled handlers of large-N statistical methods avoid these problems, frame their hypotheses with insight and skill, and have provided many valuable results. But I would argue that the insight and skill of framing hypotheses—often derived from deductive reasoning—is more important than any special virtues of large-N statistical methods in achieving such results.

PROBABILITY AND DETERMINISM IN MACROSOCIOLOGY

One last point needs discussion. How do the small-N methods, even if compared to those of the accident investigator, handle the probabilistic nature of social phenomena? Why can anyone have confidence in Skocpol's assertions that, for example, the weakening of the state and the organization of the Chinese peasantry by the Communist party *had to bring about*, rather than merely rendered likely, a social revolution in China?

I believe the answer is that macrosociologists, although reluctant to admit it, carry with them a hidden satchel of psychological assumptions (albeit not necessarily rational choice assumptions, as some scholars [Friedman and Hechter 1988; Kiser and Hechter 1991; Abell 1992] suggest). Their observed arguments go something like this: "Macrosocial condition A leads to macrosocial condition B." For example, the weakness of the state leads to a condition of vulnerability to popular uprisings. If A, then B; hardly a probabilistic statement. But behind the observed determinism lies something rather different.

All macrosociologists know that societies do not act as wholes, but are composed of people who are the only real actors. Thus their statements about macrosocial conditions are really a shorthand for saying "Under conditions I describe as A, people will likely react in a way that produces condition B." The probability is therefore "hidden" in the unspoken words "people will likely react in a way that produces" the dependent macrosocial variable.

It doesn't really matter what is the psychology involved—whether the analyst believes in some form of rational choice, or collective irrationality in the presence of stimulus, or cultural determinism. What does matter is that the analyst has some probabilistic notion of individual psychology that says "Under conditions X, it is likely that people will do Y." In that case, the near determinism of macro-events follows.

For example, even if under condition A most individuals are equally likely or unlikely to do Y, *but* if nearly fifty percent of the people pursue action Y that will constitute or produce condition B (e.g., if nearly 50% of the people choose to engage in violent anti-state actions, that constitutes a rebellion or revolutionary situation), then if we are dealing with thousands, or even millions, of individuals, A is likely to produce B with almost 100 percent certainty. We may be unsure about how any given individual will react, and with small groups (up to a few dozen or so) we cannot have such certainty about macro-outcomes because stochastic variations will be large. But if we have a pool of thousands, or millions, it really doesn't matter much what particular individuals do; the standard deviation of the expected group outcome (which is proportional to the inverse of the square root of the number of individuals involved [Mosteller, Rourke and Thomas 1970, p. 293]) will be miniscule.

Thus in a period of stability, we may say conditions A_1 of a strong state and rising incomes create a situation in which the probability of individuals choosing revolutionary actions is extremely low: below .1 percent. But in a period of crisis and deprivation, we may say conditions A_2 prevail, in which the probability of individuals choosing revolutionary actions rises to 50 percent. At the micro-level, we have gone from a situation in which individual behavior is highly predictable (99.9% chance of no revolutionary action by any given individual) to one in which individual behavior is wholly unpredictable (individuals may engage or not engage in revolutionary action with equal probability). But at the *macro*-level, in a population of one million, we have gone from a situation (A_1) in which there is a virtual certainty of no revolution/ or rebellion to another situation (A_2) in which there is a virtual certainty that 500,000 people (with a 99% error band of plus or minus 1,500 people) will engage in revolutionary action, creating at the macro level a rebellion or revolution.

Of course, macrosociologists will be sensitive to conditions that increase the likelihood that people will choose to act on their grievances; thus the presence of village organizations, or communist mobilization of the peasantry, play an important role in theories of revolution. The main point, however, remains: regarding macro-social events, in which large numbers of people are involved, it is not at all necessary for there to be determinism at the micro-level in order to make macro-sociological statements with a high degree of accuracy.

The mistake that Goldthorpe and Lieberson make in criticizing historical sociology for being wrongly deterministic in light of the probabilistic nature of social phenomena is to overlook the effects of large numbers in *compositional* (i.e. macrosocial) phenomena. Lieberson suggests that a revolution is like a car accident; under certain conditions it will occur with probability P. But it is profoundly untrue to think of society as a single actor, responding with unitary probability P to certain conditions. Rather, macrosocial phenomena are constituted by the actions of many actors, whether choosing to follow a leader, vote a certain way, or take certain actions. If those thousands or millions of actors are *each* responding to given conditions with probability P of a certain act, then the *expected value for the proportion of individuals who will commit that act is P*, within very small limits.[1]

If we are looking to an old master in sociology for the principles that lie behind macrosocial analysis, it is not J.S. Mill, but Emile Durkheim (the Durkheim [1951] of *Suicide*) who first laid out this logic—namely, that *macro*social phenomena may be highly determinate even if the individual acts that constitute such phenomena are not, due to the stable behavior of mean outcomes with large numbers.

I have shown elsewhere (Goldstone 1994) that making certain assumptions about individual rationality, identification with groups, and solidarity, one can deduce certain macrosociological patterns observed in revolutions: the need for cross-class coalitions for successful revolutions, the role of networks in recruitment to revolutionary actions, and the existence of two patterns of revolution (Huntington's "Western" and "Eastern" types) depending on whether the solidary groups are longstanding and based on traditional patronage ties or whether new solidary groups need to be developed after modernization has weakened traditional ties. Thus relationships first discovered through macro-social analysis can be shown to be intimately related to, even derivable from, individual rational calculus.

But the choice of individual motivations is less important than the general principle: one can allow quite a bit of probabilistic behavior at the individual level, and still produce near-determinism at the macro-level. This situation is not unlike that in physics. In modern physics, macro-phenomena *are* considered practically deterministic; what is new is that even such isolated events as the bouncing of a single ball off a table is considered a *macro-phenomenon*. But at the level of individual atoms, molecules, and elementary particles, statistical and quantum effects render all statements about their behavior probabilistic. It thus makes no sense at all to ask whether, in physics, events are probabilistic or deterministic. At certain scales they are one; at other scales they are the other. A similar process, I believe, operates in amalgamating individual actions into the long-term processes displayed by whole societies.

It is this deterministic character of *macro*social processes that make it possible to utilize small-N methods—either deductively-based comparative case studies or Charles Ragin's (1987) Boolean techniques—"to uncover patterns of invariance and constant association" (Ragin 1987, p. 51) in macrosocial phenomena across cases.

CONCLUSION

In sum, critics of the use of Millian methods in macrosociology are right. Defenders of Millian methods in macrosociology are wrong. It is a good thing that macrosociologists using comparative case studies in fact don't use anything like Millian methods, or their game would be up.

The combination of narrative investigation, deductive reasoning, incorporation of contingent events, and construction of macro-social explanations of specific events (or groups of events) that I call "process-tracing" is the actual method of small-N comparative case studies. This method is free of the Millian fallacies, has some advantages over purely inductive statistical studies with regard to avoiding "black box" problems, and is fully consistent with a probabilistic approach to individual behavior. Many of the greatest achievements of macro-sociological scholarship have come from the comparative case study method (Moore 1966; Tilly 1990; Skocpol 1979; Reuschmeyer, Stephens, and Stephens 1992). They do not stand on flimsy methodological foundations, but on a stronger combination of skill and insight in framing and testing hypotheses than many large-N statistical studies.

NOTE

1. This assumes that each individual's decision is wholly independent, an assumption that is strictly speaking not the case. However, even if there are only a few thousand independent actors (i.e, villages, elite-led groups, neighborhoods), each of which sways the actions of thousands of individuals, the principle still holds that macro-social events are not simply holistic "events," but are chains of actions by individuals and groups whose composite effect produces macro-sociological phenomena.

REFERENCES

Abell, P. 1992. "Is Rational Choice Theory a Rational Choice of Theory?" In *Rational Choice Theory: Advocacy and Critique*, edited by J.S. Coleman and T.J. Fararo. Newbury Park: Sage Publications.

Burawoy, M. 1989. "Two Methods in Search of Social Science: Skocpol vs. Trotsky." *Theory and Society* 18: 759-805.

Durkheim, E. 1951. *Suicide*. Trans. by J.A. Spaulding and G. Simpson. New York: Free Press.

Friedman, D. and Hechter, M. 1988. "The Contribution of Rational Choice Theory to Macrosociological Research." *Sociological Theory* 6: 201-218.

Goldstone, J.A. 1991. *Revolution and Rebellion in the Early Modern World*. Berkeley and Los Angeles: University of California Press.

_____. 1994. "Is Revolution Individually Rational?" *Rationality and Society*: 139-166.

Goldthorpe, J.H. 1994. *Current Issues in Comparative Macrosociology*. ISO Rapport Nr. 6. Oslo: Department of Sociology, University of Oslo.

Gurr, T.R. (Ed). 1980. *Handbook of Political Conflict*. New York: Free Press.

Janowski, T. 1991. "Synthetic Strategies in Comparative Sociological Research: Methods and Problems of Internal and External Analysis." In *Issues and Alternatives in Comparative Social Research*, edited by C.C. Ragin. Leiden: E.J. Brill.

Kiser, E., and M. Hechter. 1991. "The Role of General Theory in Comparative Historical Sociology. *American Journal of Sociology* 97: 1-30.

Lieberson, S. 1991. "Small Ns and Big Conclusions: An Examination of the Reasoning in Comparative Studies Based on a Small Number of N's." *Social Forces* 70: 307-320.

_____. 1994. "More on the Uneasy Case for Using Mill-Type Methods in Small-N Comparative Studies." *Social Forces* 72: 1225-1237.

Moore, B. 1966. *Social Origins of Dictatorship and Democracy*. Boston: Beacon Press.

Mosteller, F., R.E.K. Rourke, and G.B. Thomas. 1970. *Probability with Statistical Applications*. Reading, MA: Addison Wesley.

Nichols, E. 1986. "Skocpol and Revolution: Comparative Analysis vs. Historical Conjuncture." *Comparative Social Research* 9: 163-186.

Ragin, C.C. 1987. *The Comparative Method*. Berkeley: University of California Press.

Rueschemeyer, D. 1991. "Different Methods—Contradictory Results? Research on Development and Democracy." In *Issues and Alternatives in Comparative Social Research*, edited by C.C. Ragin. Leiden: E.J. Brill.

Rueschemeyer, D., E.H. Stephens, and J.D. Stephens. 1992. *Capitalist Development and Democracy*. Cambridge: Polity Press.

Savolainen, J. 1994. "The Rationality of Drawing Big Conclusions Based on Small Samples: In Defense of Mill's Methods." *Social Forces* 72: 1217-1224.

Skocpol, T. 1979. *States and Social Revolutions*. Cambridge: Cambridge University Press.

Tilly, C. 1990. *Coercion, Capital, and European States, AD 990-1990*. Cambridge, MA: Basil Blackwell.

CURRENT ISSUES IN COMPARATIVE MACROSOCIOLOGY:

A RESPONSE TO THE COMMENTARIES

John H. Goldthorpe

ABSTRACT

In this response, issues that recur in the six commentaries on my original paper are dealt with under three heads: quantitative and qualitative research; theory development and theory testing; and theory and history.

I am sincerely grateful to those who have taken the time and trouble to contribute to the foregoing symposium. In the space available for this response, I cannot hope to deal with all of the issues that the six commentaries raise, nor to tailor an adequate reply to each separately. I shall, rather, concentrate on a number of issues that recur and that can, I believe, be usefully treated under three main heads, as follows.

Comparative Social Research, Volume 16, pages 121-132.
Copyright © 1997 by JAI Press Inc.
All rights of reproduction in any form reserved.
ISBN: 0-7623-0250-X

QUANTITATIVE AND QUALITATIVE RESEARCH

Where commentators have engaged in debate with me, they have in the main very fairly represented those of my arguments with which they wish to disagree. However, one respect in which I feel in some danger of being misunderstood is that of my stance on the question of quantitative versus qualitative research. I did indeed signal that my paper was, in part at least, motivated by dissatisfaction with a bland and rather mindless advocacy of "methodological pluralism"; and I also acknowledged that, in the paper, my critical remarks were mainly directed against qualitative (or case-oriented) rather than quantitative (or variable-oriented) studies. But at the same time I sought to emphasize that my primary concern was to uphold the idea of "one logic of inference," to which the methodologies of quantitative and qualitative research must *alike* be subject; and that, in turn, my criticisms of the latter centred on claims of "special and privileged means" that could, apparently, escape this logic—in particular in dealing with the three central problems of comparative macrosociology that I identified.

I can, perhaps, clarify matters further by observing that Ragin, and also Abbott and Goldstone, associate my paper with recent interventions by Lieberson (1992, 1994), and that Ragin further points to the connection with the work of King and associates (1994). I have to say that I am very content to be placed in this company, and for two reasons: first, because I much admire the authors in question and did of course draw directly upon their contributions; but second, because, elsewhere, Lieberson (1987) and King (1986) have shown themselves to be very ready to criticize what they see as inadequate or dubious procedures in *quantitative* as well as qualitative analysis.[1] And in this regard, too, I would like to think that I can lay claim to an affinity with them.

Thus, I have no difficulty whatever in agreeing with Rueschemeyer and Stephens that quantitative researchers are often far too casual about problems of data quality. In my own field of social stratification and mobility research I have maintained this line of criticism (Goldthorpe 1985; Erikson and Goldthorpe 1992a, 1992b) to the point, I suspect, of causing no little irritation to those colleagues who would wish to get on with what, for them, is the real business of modeling the data.[2] Further, I would fully share in the "scepticism" expressed by Rueschemeyer and Stephens, and reinforced by Ragin, over whether the results of quantitative analyses can in themselves be sufficient to demonstrate causal processes. Indeed, I have sought directly to challenge (1996a, 1996b) those quantitative sociologists who believe that they can establish their independence of theory in this regard—as, say, through the use of causal path or other forms of structural equation modelling. To repeat the point I made in introducing the "black box" problem, theory is quite essential if the causal processes that are thought to generate empirically observed social regularities are to be represented in an explicit, systematic, and thus in turn empirically testable, way.

However, even though my enthusiasm for quantitative research is, thus, far from unqualified, I would still wish to take the opportunity of this response to dispute several assumptions and assertions made by commentators in criticizing such research—and on the grounds, chiefly, that these appear to be a decade or two out-of-date.

To begin with, Rueschemeyer and Stephens (this volume, pp. 57-58) would seem to suppose that comparative macrosociological studies of a variable-oriented kind are *typically* based on *cross-sectional* data only—so that well-known problems of establishing the reality, or direction, of postulated causal effects inevitably arise. This supposition may hold in the case of the body of research on democratization to which Rueschemeyer and Stephens specifically refer—although even here they acknowledge at least one notable exception (i.e., Hannan and Carroll 1981). But it does not hold more generally. By now, a wide range of macrosociological problems can be, and are, addressed on the basis of cross-national data-sets that are also of a *longitudinal* character (see further Goldthorpe 1996b). In other words, historical case studies are *not* the only means through which a "diachronic" perspective can be achieved. And in this connection I may also record my unrelieved puzzlement over Rueschemeyer and Stephens' claim (p. 65) that where historical data capable of quantification are not to be had, a "different"—special and privileged?—type of operationalization can still be drawn on by exponents of case studies which will overcome the data shortage and put them in "a *vastly* better position" to treat issues of causality.

Again, Rueschemeyer and Stephens, and likewise Ragin, Goldstone and Abbott, all at various points write as if the analytical techniques of quantitative macrosociology were essentially confined to versions of standard linear regression. But this is no longer a realistic view. Thus, where longitudinal data are available, relating to any series of transitions made by individuals, or other "higher order" units of analysis, from one discrete state to another, techniques of event history analysis are now regularly applied. In this way, the testing of theoretically derived hypotheses regarding the causal processes at work can be undertaken far more powerfully than before (see esp. Blossfeld and Rohwer 1995) and also with the possibility in comparative work, as I noted in my paper (cf. Usui 1994), of making due allowance for the "Galton problem." At the same time, event history analysis can directly contribute to the more empirical task identified by Abbott of tracing out "patterns of succession" as, say, in the form of "natural histories," life-courses or careers.[3]

Further, in many areas of quantitative macrosociology regression analysis has from the 1970s onwards been strongly complemented, if not in fact superseded, by loglinear modeling and related techniques. Apart from allowing sociologists to work very effectively with categorical data, such techniques are directly relevant to the problems of possibly complex interaction among variables that Ragin and Goldstone would see as threatening to subvert quantitative analysis. And in loglinear modelling exercises it would—quite contrary to what these authors suggest—be not at all unusual, but rather characteristic, for multiway interactions to be considered or for hypotheses to be framed so that they depend upon tests for interaction effects.[4] Ragin, rightly, observes that such procedures demand large Ns; but this, I would maintain (cf. Teune, p. 83), is simply the price that one has to pay if causal complexity is to be successfully unravelled.[5]

This brings me to the last issue that I wish to take up in this section: that is, the use of logical, as opposed to statistical, methods in data analysis. For these methods have been represented as the preferred alternative in case-oriented historical sociology, where N will in fact be small.

On this issue, I note that the commentaries reveal a wide range of positions. As regards Mill's logical methods, Tilly quotes, with approval, the crucial passage from Mill himself in which he makes it abundantly clear that these methods should not be followed in the study of human societies. But Rueschemeyer and Stephens still insist on a role for "analytic induction," which would seem to rest simply on a subset of Mill's canons. In turn, Goldstone, while fully accepting that Mill's methods are not applicable in macrosociology, goes on to argue that they have not in fact been so applied (even by authors such as Skocpol who thought that this is just what they were doing), but then concludes by endorsing Ragin's QCA, which, as Ragin himself would presumably acknowledge, is in direct line of descent from—in effect a Boolean development of—Mill's logic. Teune, however, is obviously unimpressed by QCA and, it may be added, Rueschemeyer and Stephens also have reservations.

That such divergent views should prevail among these eminent authors must, I think, be telling us something: at very least, that any codification of appropriate analytical techniques in historical macrosociology is still far from achievement. For my own part, I find nothing in the commentaries that would lead me to modify my previous objections to logical methods, even in their most advanced form of QCA. Whatever the arguments that may go on about the assumption of determinism, the requirements of error-free data and binary variables and so forth, the ultimate issue has to be that of actual performance. Goldstone (p. 123) quotes Ragin (1987, p. 51) to the effect that QCA uncovers "patterns of invariance and constant association." But I would directly contest this claim, and on the grounds that, as illustrated in my paper (ns. 8 and 9), results from QCA appear to be inherently unstable. Adding a single new case to an analysis or even changing just one or two codings of cases already included is always likely to make the Boolean solution "flip," and perhaps quite wildly so. In other words, any "patterns of invariance and constant association" apparently revealed are in fact themselves liable to prove highly variable and inconstant.[6]

THEORY DEVELOPMENT AND THEORY TESTING

There is, I think, a consensus among all concerned that theory is necessary to the causal explanation of observed social regularities—or at very least that such explanation cannot be simply "cranked out" of data analysis, whether this is quantitative or qualitative in character. However, certain commentators are clearly at odds with me on the question of just how theory and data analysis should relate to each other.

Thus, Ragin argues that, in the same way as King and associates, I attach a too exclusive importance to theory testing and fail to see that case-oriented research differs crucially from variable-oriented research in that, in the former, a central concern of the investigator's engagement with the data is concept formation and theory development. In fact, most of what Ragin has to say in this regard, and in particular about the practice of "casing"—of determining conceptually what shall constitute relevant ("positive" or "negative") cases for the enquiry in hand—I find in itself quite unexceptionable. I would only point out that, contrary to what Ragin seems to suppose, in quantitative studies, too, researchers have often to make difficult, but crucial, decisions about just what shall, and shall not, count as a case. What constitutes, say, a suicide, a friendship relation, or a labour union is not self-evident. And if Ragin would reply that this work ought then to be done with greater care and sensitivity than is often apparent, I would again be not much inclined to quarrel.

However, it seems to me to be selling case-oriented research very short to say, as Ragin does (p. 32), that the outcome of the process of "casing" may *itself* be "the primary and most important finding of the investigation." And indeed he later appears to have second thoughts and states that (p. 35), following on "casing," the investigator's next task is "to address the causal forces" that operate to create regularities, of variation or constancy, within the population of cases that has been established. But even this—the stage of theory development—cannot be the end of the story, as Ragin is, I believe, also aware. Once a theory has been developed, the pressures of intellectual curiosity and integrity alike do indeed make it difficult to avoid some attempt at then assessing its validity.

It is at this juncture, though, that my position and that taken up by Ragin, and also by Rueschemeyer and Stephens, come into sharpest conflict. I would believe that, in principle, theory development and theory testing have to be recognized as two separate activities, and that—however difficult it may be in practice—we should always *try* to be clear about when we are engaging in the one or the other. But for Ragin and Rueschemeyer and Stephens, the distinction is of no great consequence. Thus, where particular cases do not conform to theoretical expectations, Ragin would be prepared to impose appropriate restrictive conditions on the theory or, alternatively, to return to "casing" and make the necessary "adjustments" to the population of cases under study; and Rueschemeyer and Stephens would for their part readily introduce additional hypotheses, including, perhaps, ones not derived from the initial theory or even in contradiction with it and requiring its modification.

I should here make it clear that I would not myself wish simply to rule out the possibility of the revision of a theory in the light of its confrontation with empirical evidence. The important point is, though, that where this is done, it should be regarded, not as any kind of advance but, initially at least, as a *setback*, and as one that will be overcome only in so far as the revision that is made proves to be of value in further cases apart from that which occasioned it. And if a whole series of "one-off" modifications to a theory should turn out to be necessary, this ought then to be taken as a strong indication that the theory is quite radically flawed and would best be abandoned altogether.

I cannot find that in their commentaries either Ragin or Rueschemeyer and Stephens say anything that meets the arguments that I previously set out against the conflation of theory development and testing: that is, arguments to the effect that, on the one hand, this conflation makes it difficult to see how any serious testing can be carried out at all and, on the other hand, calls into question the *quality* of theory that is being produced (cf. Kiser and Hechter 1991; also Kiser and Levi 1996). Can this theory be anything more than just a recapitulation of what has thus far been empirically observed—without the potential that good theory should possess of, to follow Teune (p. 75), extending beyond cases that happen already to have been considered to the entire population of cases, past, present and future, to which it is addressed?

It is, of course, difficult to dissent in any general way from what Ragin and Rueschemeyer and Stephens claim about the value of the interplay—the reciprocal influencing—of theory and research. But one can none the less still ask how, from the standpoint they adopt, they can tell just when this interplay has degenerated into a mere inductivist ad hoccery.[7] Or, to put the question another way: why should they not be ready *at some point or other*—after giving all the attention they might wish to "developmental" problems of "casing," concept formation and so forth—then to set out a series of specific hypotheses derived from the theory they would favour that are open to test against data other than those involved in their formulation and, thus, with the potential to challenge the underlying theory in a radical way?

One possible reply to this question lies in Rueschemeyer and Stephens' (p. 68) argument (cf. also Ragin, p. 31) that it is "quite unrealistic" to demand, at least in case-oriented research, that hypotheses be set against "fresh cases about which little or nothing is known in advance," since scholars are unlikely to be entirely innocent of such further cases and of previous treatments of them. However, while in some purely historical studies a difficulty might in this respect conceivably arise, the situation is different wherever relevant cases are not, by definition, restricted to the past—as, for example, with the very topic that concerns Rueschemeyer and Stephens of the relationship between economic development and democracy. Here, the (largely unanticipated) course of events in central and eastern Europe post 1989 surely provided them with an outstanding opportunity to undertake a systematic testing of the applicability of the theory that they had developed with reference to other regions and periods. And I still fail to see why they did not carry out such an exercise, and present their results from it, *before* considering whether the next step should be to refine aspects of their theory, to explicitly limit its scope or, perhaps, to start on the task of theory development *de novo*.

THEORY AND HISTORY

As well as some commentators differing from me on the foregoing issues (despite agreement that causal explanations must be dependent on theory) further dissension arises—and here also among the commentators themselves—on questions of a yet more basic kind which, for want of a better formulation, I will simply describe as having to do with the nature and limits of theory. It might seem to be common ground that the theory we need should, as I myself put it (p. 16), "permit the specification of causal processes" which, if operative, would be capable of reproducing observed regularities of interest. Tilly uses almost identical language and Rueschemeyer and Stephens emphasize the need for theory that yields hypotheses about processes in the sense of sequences, since "causation is a matter of sequence" (p. 57). In turn, Goldstone represents the main theoretical task of macrosociology as being that of "process-tracing," while Aobott is centrally concerned with the analysis of "narrative patterns"— understood as actual social processes rather than as discourse about them— and their "turning points." However, once the commentaries are read with any degree of care, it is clear enough that this similarity of expression conceals often widely divergent views at the level of substance.

To begin with, there are differences that reflect commitments to rival traditions of sociological theory, or conflicting assessments of which of these, to use Tilly's words, "have run their course" and which are "gaining strength." In my paper I indicate my own position in this respect, which is that central to sociological explanation must be a *theory of action* of some kind; and I have elsewhere argued further (Goldthorpe 1996a, 1996c) that it is, *pace* Tilly, a version of rational choice—or, as I would prefer to say—rational action theory, suitably adapted to sociology, that now holds out greatest promise. But these are clearly matters too large and complex to be usefully pursued here. Rather, I wish to focus on certain issues concerning the general relationship between theory and history.

In this connection, I come chiefly into conflict with Rueschemeyer and Stephens and with Goldstone and perhaps also with Abbott, though I remain uncertain about this.[8] I would hold (following Popper) that propositions or arguments can be *either* historical *or* theoretical, but not both at the same time; and, in turn, that while there is some similarity of form between narrative and theoretical explanation (we speak readily enough of "causal narratives"), *historical* narrative cannot in itself constitute such explanation: or, as Teune (p. 77) more bluntly puts it, "a story is no theory." However, Rueschemeyer and Stephens, along with Goldstone, would evidently believe that it is in historical narratives that the key to explanation, in macrosociology at least, is to be found.

The chief criticism that I would then direct against these authors' position can be simply put. I do not find in what they write any clear indication of just how they envisage the move being made from the specificity of time and place that is inherent in historical narrative (cf. Stone 1979) to the applicability across time and place that is required of theory (even if subject to *some* delimitation of scope). To be sure, they show an awareness of this problem. Rueschemeyer and Stephens acknowledge (p. 57) that any causal explanation must involve "theoretical claims that transcend the particular historical sequence of events"; and Goldstone accepts (p. 113) that, at some stage, historical narratives have to be shown to "conform to…deductive [*sc.* theoretical?] arguments." In other words, if causal explanations are to be produced, it is at all events seen that something has to be added to or combined with historical narrative *per se*. And what in fact I believe this is for these authors—what serves as their tacit solution to their problem—is theory, and indeed some kind of theory of action, *but* theory which remains of only an *implicit* kind.[9]

To clarify my criticism here, and at the same time to try to make it more constructive, I might draw attention to one recent proposal for the advancement of "sociological narrativism" that would seem of particular relevance. Kiser (1996), following on his papers with Hechter (1991) and with Levi (1996) that were previously cited, has sought to show that the concerns of narrativists to give full weight to agency, temporality and events in explanatory accounts of social processes would be better served if, in place of implicit theory, they were to make explicit use of a relatively well-developed theory of action—that is rational choice theory. The argument of Kiser's paper, I might then add, parallels one which I have myself put forward (1996a) in suggesting that the work of *quantitative* sociologists would be much enhanced if *they* became more ready to resort openly to such theory instead of merely "interpreting" their findings through implicit action theory and often, thus, in what is a quite unsystematic and *ad hoc* fashion (cf. Abbott 1992).

In the present context, I should make clear, it is on the need for theory, over and above historical narrative—just as over and above data analysis— that I wish to insist: causality is a property of theoretical statements, and can no more be directly observed in the historical record than it can in statistical results. Whether it is in fact rational choice theory that is best suited to meet this need, rather than, say, Tilly's "relational realism" or some other contender, can be left as a matter for debate elsewhere.

The sharp distinction that I would draw between theory and history has a further implication. While historical narrative can never serve as a substitute for theory in sociological explanation, it is, conversely, the case that such explanation will always be limited by "history." That is to say, there will always be social phenomena—and not just events or complexes of events but also particular structural or cultural features of societies—of which a historical account, rather than one in terms of sociological theory, will have to be given.

In my paper, I make this point by claiming that history must remain as a necessary "residual category" for macrosociology. Goldstone takes issue with this claim but, unfortunately, gets the point of it the wrong way around.[10] I do *not* wish to argue, as Goldstone (p. 112) supposes, that "unique or contingent" phenomena can play no part *as explanatory factors* in sociology— or, if so, only at cost of undermining its "scientific" credentials. In fact, I argue quite the contrary (p. 17), and I note how in my research (with Erikson) on comparative social mobility such phenomena were often found to be crucial in explaining cross-national variation, so that the Przeworski-Teune program of "replacing the names of nations with the names of variables" could not be carried through. Where I see "unique or contingent" phenomena as falling outside the scope of sociology is not as explanatory factors but rather as *explananda*. Thus, it is on this basis, in part, that I express some scepticism about the viability of a macrosociology—as distinct from a comparative history—of revolutions or other "regime transitions." That is to say, I suspect that such events will prove to have too little in common with each other to allow any great theoretical purchase on their understanding be obtained.

To pursue my point further here, I can take advantage of the example introduced by Ragin of an election surprisingly lost by a left-wing party because weather fluctuations intensified a flu epidemic which chiefly affected working-class turn-out. According to Ragin, case-oriented electoral researchers would not allow this case to be treated merely as an "outlier." If it did not conform to general expectations, as, say, under a theory of the determinants of the level of left voting among the working class, this deviance would not be put down, as in variable-oriented work, to random or "non-systematic" effects beyond sociological concern and thus be simply included in the "error" vector. Rather, it would serve as a "prod" to the researchers to get at the *full* story—at *all* the "causal specks" involved in this particular case, and including those which may have *"only limited relevance to theory"* (Ragin, pp. 38, 39, 40; my emphasis).

Now attempting to give such an account of the election result, could, in my view, be warranted if this result were itself to be taken as a factor in the explanation of the outcomes of subsequent elections, following, say, as Ragin suggests, some theory invoking "path dependence." But this would then seem to be simply the equivalent of what I would regard as treating history—that is, the history of just what happened in this election—as a residual category for sociology: as a theoretically unexplained explainer. For if, on the other hand, the aim were in fact to give an explanation of the deviant election outcome itself *from the standpoint of sociological theory*, this would not be very successful, and reference to meteorological or epidemiological processes could not of course contribute anything to this endeavour. Simply adding on to an explanation further "causal specks" that have "only limited"—if indeed any—relevance to the theory that informs the explanation, so that each case is thus accommodated, as it were, on its own terms, seems to me a procedure that can have very little social scientific appeal.

In sum, historical accounts can be as comprehensive in the range of factors they take in as is necessary to deal with the particular cases they address— and can, in this sense, be pursued deterministically. But theoretical accounts, such as, I assume, we are seeking in sociology, must be selective so as to relate to factors that are generally, though by no means exclusively, at work across the population of cases to which they are intended—probabilistically—to apply. To argue thus does not entail any invidious ranking, one way or the other, so far as history and sociology are concerned. But it does imply recognition that, while they need not of course be pursued in isolation from each other, they are still different kinds of intellectual enterprise. And, I would believe, they will in fact be best pursued where this difference is kept clearly in mind.

NOTES

1. Thus, the point made by Ragin that often in sociology what we wish to explain are constants, whereas statistical analysis is oriented towards explaining variance, is in fact one that Lieberson has previously made, and elaborated on, in a very cogent way (1987, pp. 102-107).

2. I do, however, think that Rueschemeyer and Stephens are unwarrantedly pessimistic about what can be done to improve data quality, at least in contemporary research. Consider, for example, the achievements of members of the CEPS/INSEAD team at Luxembourg in regard to data on comparative income distributions (e.g., Atkinson, Rainwater and Smeeding 1995) and the further work now in train there on labour force data.

3. Perhaps modesty forbids Abbott from noting that in this regard he has himself initiated a significant alternative approach by introducing sociologists to techniques of "optimal matching." For an application of these techniques that envisages their eventual linking to more formal statistical modeling, see Halpin and Chan (1996).

4. For example, in comparative social mobility research the well-known "FJH hypothesis" (Featherman, Jones, and Hauser 1975) is represented, and thus tested, via a model that proposes no three-way interaction among class of origin, class of destination and nation; and more elaborate tests can be made, involving possible three- and four-way interactions, if the further variables of birth cohort or period are introduced (Erikson and Goldthorpe 1992, chap. 3). Again in electoral sociology the hypothesis of class dealignment in party support can be represented by a model that envisages an interaction of a particular kind between class, vote and election (Evans, Heath, and Payne 1995; Hout, Brooks, and Manza 1996).

5. Thus, when Ragin and Rueschemeyer and Stephens point out that often in small N quantitative studies a variety of statistical models with different theoretical implications can each explain a large part of the variation of interest, I would of course agree that this is a major problem:

indeed precisely that which I discuss in my paper in regard to comparative welfare state research. Where, however, I differ from these authors is in seeing no alternative solution to that of increasing, in some way or other, the amount of information that is available for analysis—and not just "more knowledge of cases" but also "knowledge of more cases."

6. It can of course happen that the results of a quantitative analyses prove sensitive to the inclusion or exclusion of "outlying" cases. But this is a problem that can be identified and addressed, whereas, if I understand Ragin correctly, the very concept of an outlier is foreign to QCA.

7. Rueschemeyer and Stephens, at least, appear sensitive to the thrust of this question, and are thus (p. 70) led into a *tu quoque* argument: quantitative researchers also engage in theorizing of an *ad hoc* kind. I would certainly agree (see further above, p. 129) but this does not of course dispose of the issue I raise.

8. My difficulty in regard to Abbott and his "narrative positivism" centers on whether he sees the construction of narratives (in his sense) as a purely empirical task, that is, as a matter of establishing regularities in trajectories, transitions, turning points and other "clusterings" of events in time, which are then to be explained; or whether he does in fact regard the construction of narratives as in itself amounting to theoretical explanation and, if so, exactly how.

9. This seems to me to be particularly well shown up in Goldstone's case (p. 116) with his reference to the "hidden satchel of psychological assumptions" that macrosociologists "although reluctant to admit it, carry with them" and that provide the underpinnings for their accounts of action, individual or collective. In this connection I might add that I entirely agree with what Goldstone says about action being far more amenable to prediction and theoretical explanation at the aggregate than at the individual level—I exploit much the same argument myself (1996a) in defending rational action theory against charges of unrealism. However, contrary to what Goldstone here suggests, the criticism that Lieberson and I make of the determinism of historical macrosociology relates to quite other issues: that is, ones concerning the bases, ontological and epistemological, of the assumption that every case considered can be provided with a complete explanation.

10. Abbott also appears to misread me here in equating the idea of history as a residual category for sociology with that of history as the "category of residuals"! In arguing as I do, I am in no way concerned with "relegating" or otherwise disparaging history but, rather, with emphasizing that sociology has its limits.

REFERENCES

Abbott, A. 1992. "What do Cases do? Some Notes on Activity in Sociological Analysis." Pp. 53-82 in *What is a Case?* edited by C.C. Ragin and H. Becker. Cambridge: Cambridge University Press.

Atkinson, A.B., L. Rainwater, and T. Smeeding. 1995. "Income Distribution in Advanced Economies: Evidence from the Luxembourg Income Study (LIS)." LIS Working Paper 120.

Blossfeld, H.-P., and G. Rohwer. 1995. *Techniques of Event History Modelling: New Approaches to Causal Analysis*. Hillsdale, NJ: Erlbaum.

Erikson, R. and J.H. Goldthorpe. 1992a. *The Constant Flux: A Study of Class Mobility in Industrial Societies*. Oxford: Clarendon Press.

Erikson, R., and J.H. Goldthorpe. 1992b. "The CASMIN Project and the American Dream." *European Sociological Review* 8: 283-305.

Evans, G., A.F. Heath, and C. Payne. 1995. "Modelling the Class/Party Relationship in Britain, 1964-92." *Journal of the Royal Statistical Society*, Series A, 158, Part 3: 563-574.

Featherman, D.L., F.L. Jones, and R.M. Hauser. 1975. "Assumptions of Social Mobility Research in the US: The Case of Occupational Status." *Social Science Research* 4: 329-360.

132JOHN H. GOLDTHORPE

Goldthorpe, J.H. 1985. "On Economic Development and Social Mobility." *British Journal of Sociology* 36: 549-573.

————. 1996a. "The Quantitative Analysis of Large-Scale Data-Sets and Rational Action Theory: For a Collaborative Alliance." *European Sociological Review*, 12.

————. 1996b. "The Integration of Sociological Research and Theory: Grounds for Optimism at the End of the Twentieth Century." ICS International Conference, University of Groningen, June.

————. 1996c. "Rational Action Theory for Sociology." Nuffield College, Oxford.

Halpin, B., and T.W. Chan. 1996. "Class Careers as Sequences: An Optimal Matching Analysis of Work-Life Histories." ESRC Research Centre on Micro-social Change, University of Essex, Working Paper 96-5.

Hannan, M.T., and G.R. Carroll. 1981. "Dynamics of Formal Political Structure: An Event History Analysis." *American Sociological Review* 46: 19-35.

Hout, M., C. Brooks, and J. Manza. 1996. "The Democratic Class Struggle in the United States, 1948-1992." *American Sociological Review* 61.

King, G. 1986. "How Not to Lie with Statistics: Avoiding Common Mistakes in Quantitative Political Science." *American Journal of Political Science* 30: 666-687.

King, G., R.O. Keohane, and S. Verba. 1994. *Designing Social Inquiry*. Princeton, NJ: Princeton University Press.

Kiser, E. 1996. "The Revival of Narrative in Historical Sociology: What Rational Choice Theory Can Contribute." Department of Sociology, University of Washington.

Kiser, E., M. Hechter. 1991. "The Role of General Theory in Comparative-Historical Sociology." *American Journal of Sociology* 97: 1-30.

Kiser, E., and M. Levi. 1996. "Using Counterfactuals in Historical Analysis: Theories of Revolution." In *Counterfactual Thought Experiments in World Politics*, edited by P. Tetlock and A. Belkin. Princeton, NJ: Princeton University Press.

Lieberson, S. 1987. *Making It Count*, 2nd ed. Berkeley: University of California Press.

————. 1992. "Small Ns and Big Conclusions: An Examination of the Reasoning in Comparative Studies based on a Small Number of Cases." Pp. 105-118 in *What is a Case?* edited by C.C. Ragin and H.S. Becker. Cambridge: Cambridge University Press.

————. 1994. "More on the Uneasy Case for using Mill-Type Methods in Small-N Comparative Studies." *Social Forces* 72: 307-320.

Ragin, C.C. 1987. *The Comparative Method*. Berkeley: University of California Press.

Stone, L. 1979. "The Revival of Narrative: Reflections on a New Old History." *Past and Present* 85: 3-24.

Usui, C. 1994. "Welfare State Development in a World System Context: Event History Analysis of First Social Insurance Legislation among 60 Countries, 1880-1960." Pp. 254-277 in *The Comparative Political Economy of the Welfare State*, edited by T. Janoski and A.M. Hicks. Cambridge: Cambridge University Press.

REDUCTION OF COMPLEXITY FOR A SMALL-N ANALYSIS:

A STEPWISE MULTI-METHODOLOGICAL APPROACH

Dirk Berg-Schlosser and Gisèle De Meur

ABSTRACT

Macro-comparative studies are often faced with the "many variables—small N"-dilemma. One way of attacking this problem on the variables side is the systematic reduction of complexity of the cases considered. This procedure is elaborated here by starting from a comprehensive system model which is then "filled" with theoretically derived and historically informed variables. This complexity is then reduced step by step with the help of outcome-oriented quantitative and qualitative techniques such as "Discriminant Analysis" and "Qualitative Comparative Analysis." These techniques are shown to supplement each other in a meaningful way. In this manner, eight encompassing "super-variables" are constructed which retain much of the original information. The example used is drawn from a larger research project on the conditions of authoritarianism and democracy in inter-war Europe. The project's substantive findings can also be seen to point to some of the more important tenets of empirical democratic theory.

Comparative Social Research, Volume 16, pages 133-162.
Copyright © 1997 by JAI Press Inc.
All rights of reproduction in any form reserved.
ISBN: 0-7623-0250-X

INTRODUCTION

Comparative analysis at the "macro"-level of social or political systems usually refers to entire societies or nation-states. These, in themselves, are highly complex and, even on a world-wide scale, relatively few in number. The middle ground between single case configurational studies (which are the major domain of historians) and statistical procedures covering a large universe of cases (which, in the behavioral sciences, are usually available only at the "micro" level of individuals) is the realm of the comparative method in the narrower sense of the term. This field is, however, characterized by an abundance of variables, because we do not have any clear-cut relationships between causes and effects as is often the case in the social sciences. The resulting "many variables—small N" situation suffers from a tendency of "over-determination" when the proportion of variables and cases becomes unfavourable (Przeworski and Teune 1970, p. 23; López 1992). Basically, this problem can be attacked in three different ways (see also Lijphart 1971, 1975; Collier 1993).

First, the number of cases can be increased across space and/or time. At the "macro"-level of entire political systems, however, we quickly reach practical limits. The present world of 180 or so United Nations member-states is still too small to draw a meaningful and sufficiently large "random sample." Such a sample, though, is required for many procedures in terms of an assumed "normal distribution" of cases in order to be able to make probabilistic inferences. Moreover, for many kinds of analysis random sampling and the subsequent statistical procedures are not meaningful, because other qualitatively determined criteria of selection, guided by substantive and theoretical concerns, have to be employed. In contrast to cases selected at random and treating each unit more or less interchangeably, in smaller N situations each case has to be considered for its own sake and cannot be neglected. The tendency, however, to consider lesser known cases as relatively insignificant "outliers" has led to the superficiality of many macro-quantitative studies (Ragin 1987).

Second, cases can be chosen according to specific research designs. By means of a systematic matching of cases, the "most similar" ones can be selected whereby a great number of variables can be held constant or controlled for in a "quasi-experimental" design. In addition, a relatively small number of variables can be depicted which might account for the observed differences in outcome (dependent variable). Similarly, "most different" cases with identical outcomes can be selected in order to establish a series of more universal factors across these cases which might possibly explain the outcome. In both instances, the number of cases analyzed and the number of remaining variables can be brought into proportions which are still manageable and meaningful. (For an attempt to operationalize such procedures see De Meur and Berg-Schlosser 1994; Berg-Schlosser and De Meur 1996).

Third, the problem can be attacked from the variables side by attempting to reduce the complexity of the observed cases without losing too much of the relevant information. In a recent article, Amenta and Poulsen (1994) have discussed five ways to cope with the problem of variable selection. They did so in the context of "Qualitative Comparative Analysis" (QCA), a relatively new comparative technique (see also Ragin 1987, 1994). For reasons of the existing software, but also because of the inherent complexity of the underlying application of Boolean algebra, this technique is presently confined to an analysis of 10 variables at a time. But even without these technical limitations, the problems they consider are of a more general nature given the state of the art in comparative politics and some parts of the social sciences in general. Amenta and Poulsen (1994) summarize the various approaches as follows:

1. a comprehensive approach, relying on all extant theories, hypotheses, and explanations;
2. a "perspectives" approach, supplying a mixed bag of variables derived from the main theoretical perspectives in an empirical literature;
3. a "significance" approach, employing measures with significant coefficients or effects in inferential statistical analyses; and
4. a "second look" approach, adding selected statistically insignificant measures to significant ones in an analysis to see if the rejected factors have complex effects on the outcome (p. 25).

After discussing the specific emphasis, but also deficiencies of each approach they develop what they call a "conjunctural theory" approach where the selection of variables is based on "theories that are conjunctural or combinatorial in construction and predict multiple causal combinations for one outcome" (p. 29). However, as they themselves realize, "this method is not often employed or likely to be because most theories are not conjunctural in construction" (p. 51).

For most practical purposes, we are thus left with their initial uneasiness about the other ways they discuss and little more to build on. For this reason, we propose a "mixed" approach which takes care of the major arguments raised in this debate but which, it seems to us, is more pertinent for most similar research situations. We will, first, present the more general theoretical background for our chosen example and a system framework from which the major categories and variables have been derived. We will then suggest specific steps for reducing in a systematic manner the complexity of both the model and the large number of variables derived from it without losing essential information with regard to the respective outcomes. This will be done, on the one hand, with the help of some statistical procedures and, on the other, by considering certain combinatorial analyses. We contend that it can be shown that both approaches meaningfully supplement each other making up, to some extent, for their respective deficiencies. The results of both operations will be combined in a further step in order to construct a limited number of more encompassing "super-variables" which retain much of the original information. A concluding section will summarize the results and assess the specific merits and limitations of this approach as compared with those of possible alternative procedures.

All this will be done in an exemplary manner for the cases, period and problems considered. Further applications of this kind will, of course, have to be adjusted according to the specific circumstances. Although the necessity to reduce complexity has often been discussed, this idea has so far only rarely been put into practice in a more explicit and operationalized manner. In providing this example, we wish to illustrate step by step how this approach can be meaningfully employed and indicate the methodological problems and considerations which accompany such an enterprise. Our substantive results have been supplemented by other findings indicating their "robustness" (Berg-Schlosser and De Meur 1996), but even by themselves they may be regarded as a contribution to general empirical democratic theory.

THE THEORETICAL BACKGROUND
AND SYSTEM FRAMEWORK

The inter-war period in Europe was chosen for this purpose because it provides a fascinating intellectual laboratory for comparative political research. Under largely similar social and economic conditions, some parliamentary democracies survived the world economic crisis of the early 1930s while others turned to more authoritarian forms of rule and, in particular, to certain variants of fascism. Whereas some individual cases, such as Germany, have been relatively well studied and the relevant historical source material has become generally available, there are still relatively few works which deal with this period in a comparative manner. Some only consider fascist outcomes (such as Nolte 1966; Laqueur 1979; Mosse 1979) or analyze the social roots of fascism in a larger number of countries in greater detail (Woolf 1968; Larsen et al. 1980). Others examine the breakdown of democratic regimes in general (most importantly Linz and Stepan 1978). As important as these contributions are, most of them consist methodologically of compilations of single case studies and do not attempt to analyze systematically the specific factors to which the eventual survival of a larger number of regimes may be attributed. Thus, it is not so much the question "Who were the Fascists?" (Larsen et al. 1980) which interests us here, but rather *why* fascist or authoritarian regimes came into being in some cases and why they did *not* in others.

The small number studies of a broader comparative nature which deal with this period tend to focus either on particular aspects of policy responses on the part of certain regimes (e.g., Gourevitch 1986; Weir and Skocpol 1985) or on potential single factors (e.g., Zimmermann and Saalfeld 1989). Thus far, the results of such analyses have been largely negative. More sophisticated attempts (such as Lipset 1983; Luebbert 1987; Stephens 1989) have, at best, provided interesting hypotheses. When these hypotheses were tested systematically across a greater number of cases (including several smaller countries which often tend to be overlooked), however, it turned out that no single hypothesis actually applied to all of the cases considered (Berg-Schlosser and De Meur 1994). Most of them were either too narrow in scope, as, for example, Ferdinand Hermens' arguments concerning the detrimental effects of proportional electoral systems (Hermens 1941), or they were of a too vague and sweeping nature, as was the case with Robert Dahl's list of general conditions favouring polyarchy (Dahl 1971, pp. 202-207). The best score (10 out of 16) was obtained by Seymour M. Lipset's (1960, 1993) comparatively general "modernization" thesis. This was largely confirmed in the negative for the Southern and Eastern European cases but was contradicted, for example, by an important modernized breakdown case (Germany) and also did not apply to less developed democratic survivors (such as Finland or Ireland).

This points to the necessity of going beyond the analysis of a few relatively simple factors and of taking a more encompassing view of the possible range of variables involved in order to account for the entire variance observed. This may not result in a single "universalizing" explanation, as Charles Tilly (1984, p. 80 ff) puts it, but rather in a "variation-finding" pattern which characterizes the observed cases according to those specific elements which may be held accountable for the respective outcomes. An historically-oriented, comparative analysis of political systems at the macro-level, such as ours, involves, in Tilly's terms, "big structures, large processes, and huge comparisons." This awesome task can only be (tentatively) tackled if its various aspects and procedures are broken down in a systematic and theoretically guided manner so as to make the individual bits and pieces more manageable and intellectually digestible. Even if the dependent variable, that is the breakdown or survival of democratic regimes in a period of severe economic and political crisis, can be clearly defined, the range of potential independent variables affecting the eventual outcome remains enormous. Thus, even though the final *explanation* should remain as parsimonious as possible, the *framework* to begin with must be comprehensive. To this end, we employ a formal "systems" framework which is "filled" at each stage with a conceptually-derived but historically-informed set of variables.

The cases dealt with are Austria (AU), Belgium (BE), Czechoslovakia (CZ), Estonia (ES), Finland, (FI), France (FR), Germany (GE), Greece (GR), Hungary (HU), Ireland (IR), Italy (IT), the Netherlands (NL), Poland (PL), Portugal (PO), Romania (RO), Spain (SP), Sweden (SW) and the United Kingdom (UK). We thus consider all major cases in which a "breakdown" of democratic systems took place together with the various individual patterns of breakdown, and all major "survivors" including many of the smaller countries. The number of cases could have been slightly increased so as to include, for example, all the Baltic and Scandinavian states. This, however, would not have been of much help in solving the overall "small N"-dilemma. In addition, we encountered several practical restrictions resulting from the limited availability of relevant data for a certain number of cases.

The cases are thus selected because of their relatively high degree of homogeneity in time and space, being "most similar" in Przeworski and Teune's (1970) sense. They share many common regional, historical, socio-economic and political-cultural characteristics. All cases can initially be designated as parliamentary democracies, some of them relatively well established, others more recent, and some existing more in form than in substance. The time period under consideration is clearly demarcated by common events, the two world wars which significantly altered both the internal and external political landscapes and set them apart from earlier and later developments. Nevertheless, the outcomes are very distinct leading to the survival of democratic regimes in some cases or a fascist or authoritarian breakdown in others. The criteria of selection are thus qualitatively determined and not by sheer numbers.

The broad commonalities of these cases now have to be made more explicit, again following Przeworski's and Teune's admonition that "the role of comparative research in the process of theory-building and theory-testing consists of replacing proper names of social systems by the relevant variables" (1970, p. 30). This is done with the help of a comprehensive system framework and some major theoretical and conceptual considerations in this regard. The complexity of this model will then be systematically reduced by extracting some key factors. The results reveal some of the underlying patterns contributing to the respective outcome.

Our simplified system framework has been developed on the basis of well-known studies by Deutsch (1963), Easton (1965), Almond and Powell (1978) and others. However, it is used here solely in a pre-theoretical, classificatory sense in order to locate different elements and possible interactions more closely without necessarily implying distinct causal relationships (such as the effectiveness of certain links and feedbacks or the stability of the system as such). A preliminary outline of the framework is provided in Figure 1.

With the help of this framework, it is possible to distinguish and locate the general social system, the intermediary structures on the input side, the central political system and the output structures together with the respective international environment. Furthermore, with regard to each sub-system, we can distinguish an "objective" dimension consisting of its internal structures, institutions and similar aspects of a more durable and "tangible" nature, and a "subjective" dimension reflecting the respective perceptions and actual behaviour of the individuals and groups concerned. (For a fuller exposition

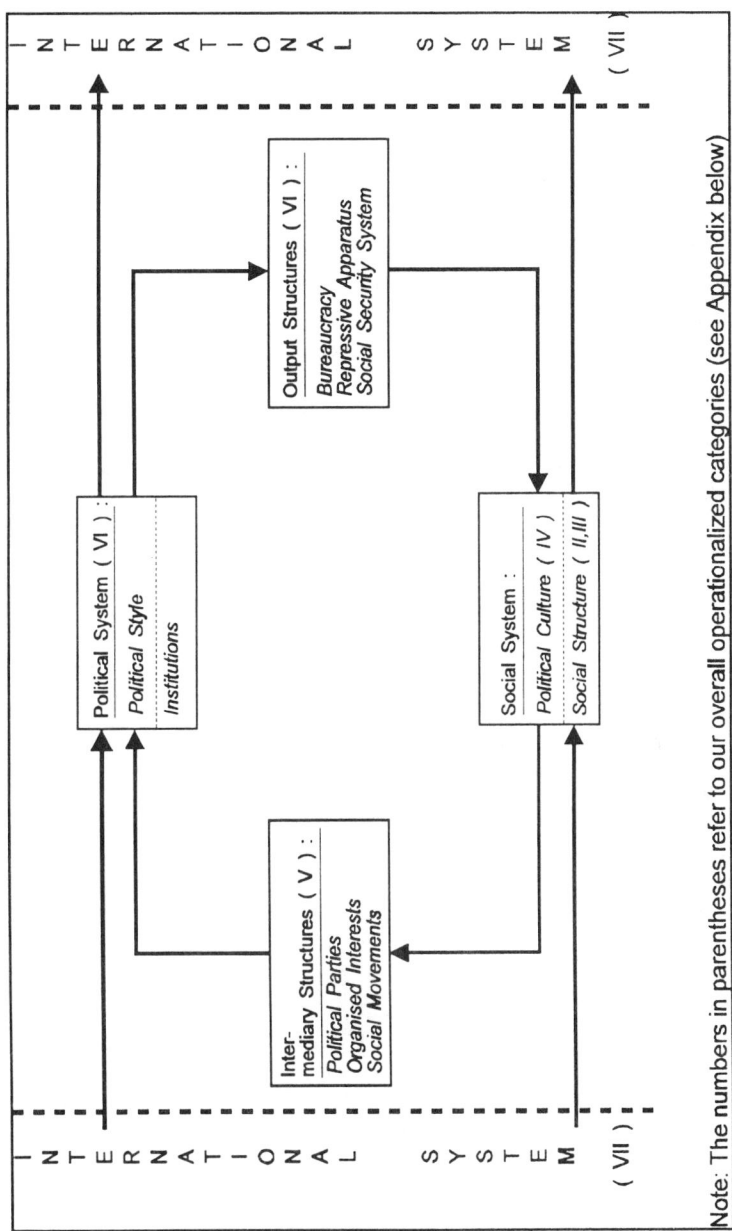

Figure 1. Simplified System Model

Note: The numbers in parentheses refer to our overall operationalized categories (see Appendix below)

139

of a model of this type see Berg-Schlosser and Siegler 1990 and, more specifically for our present concerns, Berg-Schlosser 1992).

Based on this framework and further specific conceptual and historical considerations, we selected seven major categories and a certain number of characteristic variables within each category with which to conduct our analysis. In so doing, we attempted to be as parsimonious as possible without losing sight of the overall dimensions and their complexity.

The first category (I), the overall geopolitical and historical background, draws its main substance from Rokkan's "Conceptual Map of Europe" (1975). Here, particular consideration was given to the seaward-corebelt-landward and reformation-non-reformation dimensions, the overall size of the population and the timing of both the formation of the state and the establishment of a democratic political system.

The second category (II) deals with general economic conditions and includes both their level of development and the basic class structure of the societies concerned. Among the indicators selected for this category are the levels of the national product per capita, urbanisation, literacy, industrialisation (for such "pre-requisites" of democracy see, for example, Lipset 1960) and data pertaining to the main social classes (for theses aspects cf., e.g., Moore 1996; Stephens 1989; Rueschemeyer et al. 1992 or, in a somewhat different vein, Vanhanen 1984). In the latter context, the rural structure (i.e., a significant share of landlords and a rural proletariat vs. a dominance of family farms), the extent of the middle classes and the size of the industrial labour force (coinciding with the indicator for the level of industrialization) are of particular importance.

The third category (III) is concerned with the particular ethnic, linguistic, religious and regional composition of each case together with the possible existence of overarching structures which bridge the gap between such cleavages (e.g., a pattern of "verzuiling," see Lijphart 1977). The second and the third categories thus cover the major social structural dimensions which figure in the bottom square ("social system") of the overall systems model.

The fourth category (IV) summarizes those aspects of political culture which are most relevant to our concerns. These include the overall ("national") identity of the society in question, the existence of strong cultural sub-milieus which characterize the "community system," attributes such as the extent of secularization, egalitarianism, tolerance and the acceptance of violence in the "socio-cultural" sphere, a number of more directly political orientations such as the level of political interest and information, political participation, the dominant patterns of conflict resolution (competitive or consensual) and decision-making (authoritarian or participatory), the extent of "parochial" and "subject" orientations (according to Almond and Verba's 1963, definition) and the resulting degree of overall democratic legitimacy (see also Berg-Schlosser and Rytlewski 1993).

The fifth category (V) groups together significant features of the system of intermediary structures. These include the strength of major interest groups (rural, commercial, employers, trade unions), the existence of important social movements, militias or anti-system parties, the overall fragmentation of the party system and the incidence of clientelistic or corporatist forms of interest mediation (for such aspects see also Linz 1980; Luebbert 1987, 1991).

The sixth category (VI) deals with specific features of the central political system. Among these are the general political system type, the electoral system (proportional or majoritarian), the stability of governments, the strength of the bureaucracy and the repressive apparatus, the social security system, the political role of the military and, as an important normative criterion, the guarantee and observance of civil rights and political liberties (cf., e.g., Hermens 1941; Huntington 1964; Gastil 1979ff; Sani and Sartori 1983; Karvonen 1993).

Finally, the seventh category (VII) treats the external environment and includes such factors as economic and political interactions, the degree of integration into the world market, economic dependence, cultural influences and specific historical conditions (e.g., the consequences of World War I and the possession of colonies; see, e.g., Rosecrance 1986).

Taken together, we arrive at a total of 63 variables for all 7 categories. The complete list of variables together with their respective operationalisations is provided in the appendix. Such a list can, of course, be further modified to include the peculiarities of other cases and historical factors or more specific theoretical concerns. On the whole, however, we contend that it covers relatively well both the specificities and the generalities of the cases observed in a "disciplined configurative approach" (see Verba 1967). Altogether, to take up Amenta and Poulsen's terminology once again, we thus start from a "comprehensive" approach in which the major theoretical "perspectives" have been incorporated.

The resulting data sets have been compiled in both a complete format (which retains as much information as possible for the more differentiated variables such as GNP per capita, percentages of literacy and urbanization) and a dichotomized format (absent-present, high-low, etc.) for all variables. The latter is required for such procedures as "Qualitative Comparative Analysis" (QCA). The thresholds chosen for each variable depended on their nature and the actual distribution among our cases. Some "qualitative" variables were dichotomized anyhow or had some "natural" cutting points allowing for the creation of "dummy" variables. As far as some judgemental considerations were involved (concerning, for example, some "weak" or "strong" political cultural traditions), these were based on the assessments of our respective country experts. Some of the continuous variables were dichotomized according to relevant thresholds indicated in the literature (as, e.g., for Rae's F concerning the fragmentation of the party system) or depending on some more generally accepted orders of magnitude such as the size of the population or current definitions of the rate of urbanization. Other continuous variables were dichotomized according to their mean or, if the distribution was very skewed, their median value. The final thresholds chosen for each variable are indicated in the appendix below. They can, of course, be changed, if this seems necessary for some other purposes.

From this still relatively large universe of variables we now have to select those which may turn out to be most relevant for our overall theoretical concerns. In this regard, we have to consider both relationships among a certain number of potentially explanatory variables and those towards the outcome. In this way, some variables may be combined or reconstructed indicating their common "*property space*" (for this notion see also Barton 1955; Lijphart 1971). Others may be retained or eliminated according to certain selective criteria. Both aspects can be treated by statistical procedures or by combinatorial methods. We thus pursue both what Amenta and Poulsen call "significance" and "combinatorial" or "conjunctural" approaches. It is our *contention* that several ways of selection related to both quantitative and qualitative methods can be shown to supplement each other meaningfully not only with regard to the required reduction of complexity, but also in the final substantive analysis. At the same time, not only certain "universalizing" but also certain more specific "conjunctural" or "variation-finding" aspects may be discovered.

STATISTICAL PROCEDURES

One frequently used method of assessing relationships between variables and establishing common property space is factor analysis. This method, however, resembles a general exploratory "fishing expedition" in that it is highly unspecific and not directly related to any particular outcome. Moreover, in our project, the relationship of the number of variables to the number of cases (63 to 18) remained extremely unfavorable for such a simple comprehensive procedure. We therefore decided to examine step by step a larger variety of possible techniques. We finally retained the two following procedures:

Our first step consisted in inspecting all of the variables which showed a relatively strong bivariate correlation with the outcome, that is the survival or breakdown of a democratic regime (using $p < 0.05$ as a threshold value). In all, 21 variables turned out to be highly correlated when their Boolean expressions were used. When more finely graded measures were employed— for example those available for some of the economic data—20 variables showed strong correlations (see Table 2). This procedure, however, did not yet consider the relationships which existed among the different variables.

In order to accomplish this, we turned in a further step to "Discriminant Analysis." Discriminant Analysis groups variables which are related to either outcome around the respective poles of a single axis. We employed this procedure category by category to retain in the beginning the dimensions of the original theoretical framework and, moreover, not to treat too many variables at one time. Keeping the usual default values set by SPSS, and utilizing Wilks' lambda in a stepwise procedure for each category, we arrived at a total of 16 variables using the binary data and 17 using the more finely graded data.

Statistical procedures such as these remain, however, at the "universalizing" level considering the entire distribution of cases and do not take account of any specific "conjunctural" patterns among them. At best, as indeed Discriminant Analysis does, some deviant cases not fitting in the overall picture can be identified. Furthermore, all such statistics are based on a number of restrictive assumptions such as the linearity of relationships, the additivity of explanatory variables, the orthogonality of selected factors and the like, but which may not always be justified, particularly in small N situations.

To change our focus now to more "case-oriented" and conjunctural patterns we employed a number of combinatorial procedures which are not based on such limiting assumptions (see also Ragin 1994). In this way "multiple" or "conjunctural" relationships may be discovered which lead to a more distinct process of "variation-finding" among the cases considered. Multiple causation (or "chemical causation" in Mill's terms) refers to the simultaneous presence of several factors, which only in this combination lead to a particular outcome: c_1 *and* c_2 result in o_1 or, in Boolean terms: $c_1 c_2 \rightarrow o_1$. Conjunctural causation may occur when different factors, including differing sequences over time, lead to the same result: c_3 *or* c_4 result in o_2; in Boolean terms, this is $c_3 + c_4 \rightarrow o_2$. Both patterns can also be combined. Such a conceptualization of possible causal patterns within a more comprehensive analysis is certainly a more complex but, in our view, also more realistic way of approaching the question at hand.

COMBINATORIAL PROCEDURES

Given its specific nature, this step in our analysis could only be conducted with dichotomized data. Although this implied a certain loss of information for some variables, the loss could be compensated for by the efficiency of using Boolean algebra in reducing complexity. A first and relatively simple step, which also could have been done "by hand," was to identify those variables which did not show any variation with either outcome. These were variables, for example, which had values of 0 for all breakdown cases. This produced a series of "constants" which consistently exhibited 1 or 0 for either outcome. More differentiated patterns, however, could not be assessed in this way.

As a second step we, therefore, employed QCA[2]. It computes the "prime implicants" for the considered variables by using certain "simplifying

Table 1.   "Truth Table," Category 3

ETHNLING	RELIG	REGION	OVERVERZ	OUTCOME	QCA Characteristic	Cases
1	0	1	1	1	1	BE
0	1	1	1	1	1	NL
1	1	1	1	1	1	CZ
0	1	1	0	0	0	ge
1	0	1	0	0	0	sp
1	1	1	0	0	0	pl
0	0	0	0	1	C	SW, IR
0	0	0	0	0		hu, es
1	0	0	0	1	C	FI
1	0	0	0	0		ro
0	0	1	0	1	C	FR, UK
0	0	1	0	0		au, it, pr, g

assumptions." Here, the "beauties" of Boolean methods for the analysis of an exponentially growing number of possible combinations in a multi-dimensional space can be brought to fruition (for a detailed discussion see Ragin 1987, another application can be found in Berg-Schlosser and DeMeur 1994). Because QCA cannot handle more than 10 independent variables at one time, we proceeded once again category by category. QCA being a fairly recent procedure in the social sciences and because it is not yet very widely known, we will describe the steps employed and the choices made in some more detail here. The results usually are, given its "combinatorial" nature, somewhat more complex.

For didactic reasons, we begin with category 3, describing the social composition of our cases, for which we had retained the lowest number of variables, that is, four altogether concerning the presence or absence of ethno-linguistic, religious or regional cleavages and the possibility of some overarching "consociational" arrangements. The complete information concerning this category is contained in the above "truth table."

For the sake of convenience, we use upper case letters for our survivor and lower case letters for our breakdown cases. A similar convention is employed in the formulas calculated by QCA where the presence of a variable is rendered in upper case and its absence in lower case letters (see also below).

On the basis of this truth table QCA can calculate the minimal formulas which describe a certain outcome (1 or 0), that is in our case the survival or breakdown of 18 European democracies in the inter-war period. In addition, it lists those combinations which are identical for certain cases but had different outcomes ("contradictions" = C). Over and above the actual cases analyzed it can also take account of "logical remainder cases" (R), that is combinations which are logically possible but which happen not to be covered by any one of our empirical cases. The number of such "logical remainders" increases exponentially with the number of variables considered. For example, for the possible actual maximum of 10 variables for our QCA analysis $2^{10} = 1024$ logical combinations are possible, of which, of course, only a few are covered by our empirical cases. The inclusion of the "logical remainders" allows, however, very often for a much more simplified formula which emerges from QCA. For this reason in what follows the "remainders" will always be considered for arriving at the minimal formulas.

The reductive power of this procedure can also be illustrated graphically for the relatively low number of variables we are employing at this point. The distribution of our cases for the four "social composition" variables of *category 3* can be listed as in Figure 2.

In Figure 2 the $2^4 = 16$ zones for the possible combinations of four variables considered here are indicated, the arrows pointing to the positive (1) direction of each variable. In addition, the cases described by each constellation of variables are listed in the respective zone together with the corresponding QCA characteristic (1,0 or C). The remaining zones concerning "logical remainder cases" not covered by the countries analyzed here are marked with "R." As becomes apparent from this illustration, all the non-contradictory breakdown cases (originally covered by 3 zones marked "0"), the 3 contradictory zones marked "C," and 2 "remainder" zones ("R") can be described by the much simplified expression " oververz," that is the absence of overarching structures bridging social cleavages on the left hand side of this figure. Similarly, the three survivor zones ("1") together with the other "remainders" ("R") can be expressed by the single term "*OVERVERZ*."

What can be visualized in this way is actually computed by QCA, even for much more complex constellations. For this category QCA calculates first the "prime implicants" covering the zones 1 or 0. From these the following minimal formulas are deducted:

Survivors (1): *OVERVERZ* (covering the cases *BE, NL* and *CZ*)

Breakdowns (0):   *ETHNLING · REGION · oververz (covering sp, pl)*
                              + RELIG · oververz (ge, pl)

The breakdown formula can be shortened to: *oververz · (ETHNLING · REGION + RELIG)*

(The + here, in Boolean algebra, stands for a logical "or" and the · for a logical "and").

This means that among the non-contradictory constellations either strong social cleavages coincided with the breakdowns or these were overcome by some overarching structures for the survivors.

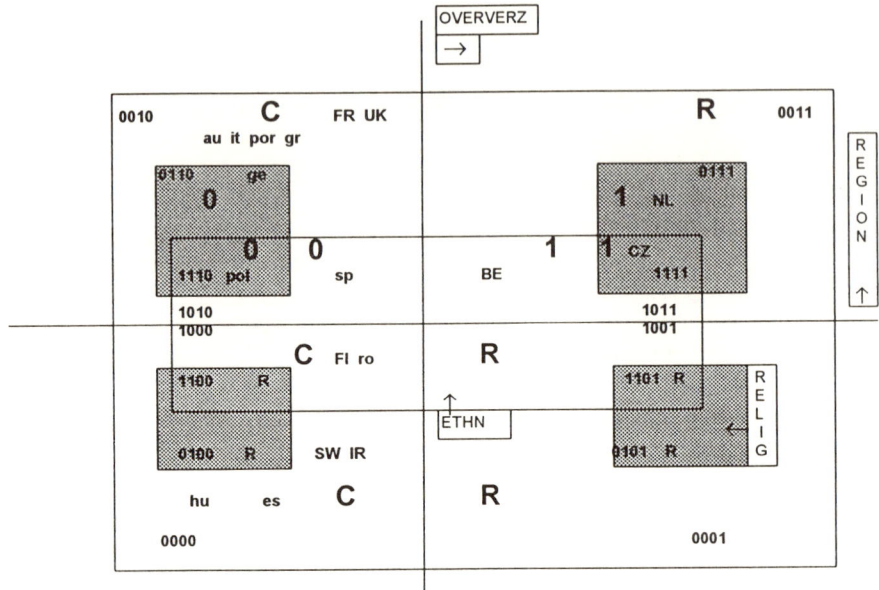

Figure 2.   Graphical Illustration for Four Variables (Category 3)

If we include the (rather numerous) contradictions (*C*) with the survivors (1) or the breakdowns (0) the following formulas emerge:

1, C: OVERVERZ (*B, NL, CZ*) + region (*SW, IR, FI, hu, es, ro*)
        + *ethnling · relig* (*SW, IR, FR, UK, hu, es, au, it, pr, gr*)

0, C: * oververz* (*SW, IR, FI, FR; UK, hu, es, ro, au, it, pr, gr, ge, sp, pl*)

This means, in effect, that either the existence of some overarching structures or the absence of some strong social cleavages (including the contradictory cases) coincides with the survivors or that the absence of overarching structures characterizes all the breakdowns (again including the contradictions). Thus, as in the graphic illustration above, the formulas for the zones 1, *R* and *O, C, R* produced the most simplified results, identifiying a single variable. This will be taken into consideration for our final selection (see section below).

We now proceed, after this more elaborate example on the basis of four explanatory variables, with the other categories in their original order. Among the 10 variables of *category 1* characterizing the more general geo-political and historical background the following formulas emerged:

Survivors (1):

(a) *PREWARDEM* (*SW, BE, NL, FR, UK*) + *earlstat* · *corebelt*
    · *landward* (*IR*)

(b) *PREWARDEM* (*SW, BE, NL, FR, UK*) + earlstat · population
    · landward (*IR, BE*)

(c) *PREWARDEM* (*SW, BE, NL, FR, UK*) + *earlstat* · *SEAWARD* (*IR*)

This means, that in fact three minimal formulas emerged. The substantive choice among them has to be made by the theoretically guided and historically informed researcher. For the sake of convenience, these three formulas can also be synthesized to:

$$PREWARDEM + earlstat \cdot \left\{ \begin{array}{l} corebelt \cdot landward \\ population \cdot landward \\ SEAWARD \end{array} \right\}$$

Breakdowns (0): *nonref* · *reform* 1(*gr*) + *EARLSTAT* · *prewardem* (*pr, sp*)

$$+ POPULATION \cdot \left\{ \begin{array}{l} prewardem\ (ge,\ it,\ sp,\ pl) \\ earlstat\ (ge,\ it,\ pl) \\ seaward\ (ge,\ it,\ pl) \end{array} \right\}$$

The existence of democracy prior to World War I thus accounted for five of the survivors, only Ireland, expressed by three different terms, constituted a rather special case. Similarly, the absence of pre-war democracy, in combination with some other characteristics, described five of our breakdown cases.

Again, some contradictory constellations, concerning *FI*/*es* and *CZ*/*au, hu, ro,* could also be observed. If these were included with the respective outcomes, we obtained the formulas:

1, *C: PREWARDEM* (*SW, BE, NL, FR, UK*)
    + *population* · *NONREF* · *earlstat* (*BVE, IR, CZ, au, hu, ro*)

$$+ REFORM \cdot \left\{ \begin{array}{l} nonref\ (SW,\ UK,\ FI,\ es) \\ corebelt\ (SW,\ UK,\ FI,\ es) \\ population\ (SW,\ NL,\ FI,\ es) \\ LANDWARD\ (SW,\ FI,\ es) \end{array} \right\}$$

0, *C: prewardem* · (*seaward* (*ge, it, gr, pl, es, au, hu, ro, FI, CZ*)
    + *EARLSTAT* (*pr, sp*))

In the latter case thus a certain simplification could be obtained. For this reason, it is important to consider each time whether the contradictions, which can be included either among the survivors or the breakdowns, lead to a simplification of the zones considered. All in all, the absence or presence of democracy before the war turned out to be by far the most important single determinant accounting for most of the survivor and, in some combination, for all of the breakdown cases. This was, therefore, retained for our final selection (see below).

For the 8 variables of *category 2* concerning the socio-economic structure and the overall level of socio-economic development as expressed by several indicators, QCA again identified certain dominant characteristics for the survivors and breakdowns. Here, it turned out that it was not a single overriding factor which could be retained, as in the previous two examples, but particular combinations of variables, which proved to be of interest.

QCA produced the following formula for the survivor cases:

$$
agrprol \cdot \left\{ \begin{array}{l} NATPROD\,(BE,\ NL,\ FR,\ CZ,\ UK) \\ URBAN\,(BE,\ NL,\ FR,\ CZ,\ UK) \\ INDLAB\,(BE,\ NL,\ FR,\ CZ,\ UK) \\ MIDDLE\,(BE,\ NL,\ FR,\ CZ,\ UK) \end{array} \right\}
$$

$$
+\ landlord \cdot \left\{ \begin{array}{l} NATPROD\,(SW,\ BE,\ NL,\ FR,\ CZ) \\ MIDDLE\,(SW,\ BE,\ NL,\ FR,\ CZ) \end{array} \right\}
$$

The breakdowns were rendered by:

$$
literacy\,(it,\ ro,\ pr,\ sp,\ gr)\ +\ LANDLORD
$$
$$
\cdot\ \left\{ \begin{array}{l} FAMFARMS\,(au,\ ge,\ hu,\ ro,\ sp) \\ AGRPROL\,(au,\ it,\ hu,\ ge,\ ro,\ pr,\ sp) \end{array} \right\}
$$

This means that democracy survived either in the absence of a strong agricultural proletariat or a large landholding class together with some factors each time indicating a higher level of socio-economic development. The almost exact reverse was true for the breakdowns. These were expressed by the simultaneous presence of a strong landholding class and a large agrarian proletariat or a low level of literacy.

There remained two contradicory constellations concerning IR/es and FI/pl. When these were included each time this produced the formulas:

1, *C: LITERACY · agrprol* (*BE, NL, FR, CZ, UK, IR, es*)

$$+ landlord \cdot \left\{ \begin{array}{l} LITERACY (SW, BE, NL, FR, CZ, FI, IR, es, pl) \\ AGRPROL (SW, IR, es) \end{array} \right\}$$

$$0, C: LANDLORD \cdot \left\{ \begin{array}{l} AGRPROL (au, ge, it, hu, ro, pr, sp) \\ FAMFARMS (au, ge, hu, ro, sp) \end{array} \right\}$$

$$+ \left\{ \begin{array}{l} middle (au, it, hu, ro, pr, gr, pl, es, FI, IR) \\ natprod (it, hu, ro, pr, sp, gr, pl, es, FI, IR) \end{array} \right\}$$

The previous formulas thus were not simplified much further and our substantive result remained essentially the same. Thus, both rural social structures and level of socio-economic development will be considered in our final choice.

For *category 4*, concerning the respective political cultural traditions, there was an additional obstacle to circumvent for the application of QCA: This category contains 14 variables, but the presently available software allows only for treating a maximum of 10 explanatory variables at a time. Instead of examining all possible 14! / (10! · 4!) = 1001 combinations which each take several hours of calculation we adopted a different strategy. We first inspected the correlations of all variables with the outcome and retained seven which had significant values (see Table 2). These were *EGALITAR, PAROCHIAL, DEMLEGITIM, TOLERANCE, AUTH/PART, SECULAR, SUBJECT*.

In addition, in a first run, we added three more which seemed to have some bearing on democratic traditions, namely *POLITPART, STATISM* and *CONSENS*:

QCA produced for this first set the following formulas:

$$1: \left\{ \begin{array}{l} EGALITAR (SW, FI, BE, NL, IR) + TOLERANCE (SW, BE, NL, FR, CZ, IR, UK) \\ TOLERANCE (SW, FI, BE, NL, IR) + AUTH/PART (SW, FI, BE, NL, FR, UK, CZ) \\ AUTH/PART (SW, FI, BE, NL, IR) + EGALITAR (SW, FI, BE, NL, FR, UK, CZ) \end{array} \right\}$$

0:   *egalitar · auth / part* (au, ge, it, hu, ro, pr, es, sp, gr, pl)
   + *tolerance · egalitar* (au, ge, it, hu, ro, pr, es, sp, gr, pl)
   + *auth / part · tolerance* (au, ge, it, hu, ro, pr, es, sp, gr, pl)

This means that the presence of two of the three variables *EGALITAR, TOLERANCE* and *AUTH/PART*, in all combinations, accounted for all of the survivors whereas the opposite was true for all of the breakdowns. This was a very strong and unequivocal result without any contradictory cases.

In a second run, we therefore decided to retain these three variables and added the remaining four (*NATIDENT, SUBMILIEU, VIOLACC* and *POLINFORM*). Furthermore, we retained, because of theoretical considerations, the variables characterizing Almond and Verba's (1963) three major sub-types of political culture (*POLITPART, PAROCHIAL* and *SUBJECT*). These 10 variables produced results which were absolutely identical with our first run (see above). We felt thus assured of these results and did not attempt any further variations.

Category 5, which covers "intermediate structures" such as strong interest groups, forms of interest mediation, the nature of the party system, social movements and the like, revealed some more ambiguous information. The shortest possible formulas for the survivors were rather straightforward:

$$1: \quad INTUNIONS \cdot antisysp\,(SW,\ BE,\ NL,\ FR,\ UK,\ IR)$$

$$+\,intunions \cdot INTEMPLOYER \cdot \left\{ \begin{array}{l} PARTFRAG\,(FI,\ CZ) \\ ANTISYSP\,(FI,\ CZ) \end{array} \right\}$$

This means that, except for the also otherwise somewhat special cases *FI* and *CZ*, democracy survived in all of our cases where trade unions were strong and anti-system parties weak. There were no contradictions either.

For the breakdown cases, however, no such clearcut pattern emerged. Altogether, there were 12 different prime implicants covering a few cases each which could not be summarized further. This result shows that QCA does not always come up with highly simplified solutions, but if this is the case it demonstrates at least the complexity of the "real world" across all the cases treated.

The *sixth category* deals with institutional aspects of the central political system. Here, again, a quite clear-cut pattern emerged. There were no contradictions. The survivors were covered by the formula:

$$military \cdot (socialsec\,(SW,\ FI,\ BE,\ NL,\ FR,\ IR)$$
$$+\,STABGOVERN\,(UK,\ CZ,\ IR))$$

The breakdowns were listed as:

$$MILITARY\,(au,\ ge,\ it,\ hu,\ po,\ pr,\ sp,\ gr,\ pl) + stabgovern$$
$$\cdot\,SOCIALSEC\,(ge,\ ro,\ es,\ pl)$$

Thus, in both instances the presence or absence of a political involvement of the military played a rucial role in the vast majority of cases (15 out of 18).

The *seventh category*, finally, treats external factors such as the victory in World War I, the level of world market integration, economic dependence, cultural and ideological influences or the possession of colonies. Here, again, we were confronted with the situation that we had more variables (11) than could be dealt with at once. In several trial runs of QCA in different combinations we always obtained very complicated formulas both for survivors and breakdowns and there still remained some contradictions. In view of this great heterogeneity we decided not to consider the variables of this category any more.

CONSTRUCTION OF "SUPER-VARIABLES"

In view of this comprehensive but still somewhat mixed information we tried to make some sense of the respective results. We inspected all variables marked by the various methods (as indicated in Table 2) and attempted to link them to some of the current theoretical propositions in the relevant literature mentioned before.

Again, we proceeded, at first, category by category. As far as the more general "Rokkanian" background conditions of the first category were concerned, only the existence or non-existence of democracy before World War I consistently emerged, across all the methods employed, as a variable relevant to the outcome. We thus decided to retain it in its existing form ($P =$ "$PREWARDEM$").

In the second category, the "developmental" and "social structural" factors could be clearly distinguished. Among the latter, the existence of a pattern of large-scale landholding and a large rural proletariat was particularly evident. The presence of both factors was combined into the single variable "feudalism" ($F = LANDLORD$ and $AGRPROL$) in line with Moore's or Stephens' arguments. The five relevant variables relating to the level of socio-economic development (GNP per capita, urbanisation, literacy, industrialization and a large urban middle class) could be grouped into a single "economic development" factor ($E = f_1 (NATPRODCAP, URBANIZATI, LITERACY, INDLAB, MIDDLE)$) in support of Lipset's and Vanhanen's ideas with the help of a *confirmatory* factor analysis based on the differentiated expression of these variables. This confirmed their unidimensionality loading on the same factor. This procedure, in contrast to the "fishing expedition" cited above, thus was conducted within a much more limited range of variables.

In the third category, either the absence of major ethnic, religious or regional cleavages or—if one of these was present—the existence of some overarching arrangements in Lijphart's sense proved to be relevant. These elements were combined into a single variable for "social heterogeneity" ($H = (ETHNLING$ or $RELIG$ or $REGION)$ and no $OVERVERZ$) which designates the existence of some sort of cleavage without the presence of any overarching structures.

With regard to the fourth category ("political culture"), three variables relating to more general democratic orientations (or their opposites) in Almond's and Verba's sense consistently emerged across all the methods

Table 2. Reduction of Variables—Synopsis of Results

Procedures:	Correlations (p < 0.05)		Discriminant Analysis by Category		Constants by Outcome	OCA by category
Variables	Binary	Integer or %	Binary	Integer or %	Binary	Binary
1. General Background						
POPULATION						
SEAWARD						
COREBELT						
LANDWARD						
NONREF						
REFORM						
EARLSTAT						
PREWARDEM	x	x	x	x	x	x
2. Socio-economic conditions						
NATPRODCAP	x	x	x	x		x
URBANIZATI	x	x	x	x		x
LITERACY	x	x			x	x
LANDLORD	x	x	x	x		x
FAMFARMS						
AGRPROL	x	x				x
INDLAB						x
MIDDLE	x	x				x
3. Social composition						
ETHNLIN						
RELIG						
REGION						
OVERVERZUI	x	x	x	x	x	x
4. Political-cultural traditions						
NATIDENTIT				x		
SUBMILIEUS						
VIOLACC						
EGALITAR	x	x	x	x	x	x
POLINFORM				x		
POLITIPART						
STATISM						
PAROCHIAL	x	x				
DEMLEGITIM	x	x				
CONSENS/CONFL			x	x		
TOLERANCE	x	x	x	x	x	x
AUTH/PART	x	x	x	x	x	x
SECULAR	x					
SUBJECT	x	x			x	

(continued)

Table 2. (Continued)

Procedures:	Correlations (p < 0.05)		Discriminant Analysis by Category		Constants by Outcome	OCA by category
Variables	Binary	Integer or %	Binary	Integer or %	Binary	Binary
5. Intermediate structures						
INTRURAL						
INTCOMMERC						
INTUNIONS						x
INTEMPLOYER						
CLIENTELISM						
MOVEMENTS						
MILITIAS						x
PARTFRAG						
ANTISYSP	x	x	x			x
CORPORATISM						
6. Central political system						
POLITTYPE						
ELECTSYSPR						
STABGOVERN						
ROLEBUREUA						
MILITARY	x	x	x	x	x	x
SOCIALSEC						
CIVRIGHT	x	x	x	x	x	
POLRIGHT	x	x	x	x	x	
7. External factors						
WW1WINNER			x	x		
WORLDMIN	x	x	x	x		
MILITEX						
ECONDEPEND						
CULTANGLO	x	x	x	x	x	
CULTGERM						
CULTROMAN						
CULTSLAVIC						
IDEOLCATH						
IDEOLMARX						
COLONIES						
Sum: 63	21	20	16	17	11	15

employed. These can be combined to a single super-variable "democratic political culture" ($D = EGALITAR$ and $TOLERANCE$) or ($EGALITAR$ and $AUTH/PART$) or ($TOLERANCE$ and $AUTH/PART$)).

As far as intermediate structures (category 5) were concerned the resulting pattern remained rather diverse. Only the variable ANTISYSP, as discussed by Linz for example, was highlighted by all the methods. When we inspected some other correlations with this variable, it turned out that, in conformity with Linz' concept, it loaded on the same factor as *MOVEMENTS* and *MILITIAS*. The reconstructed variable "political unrest" ($U = f_2 (ANTISYSP,$ *MOVEMENTS, MILITIAS*) with a somewhat enlarged property space was, therefore, retained.

Among the variables characterising different aspects of the central political system (category 6), only the political role of the military ($M = MILITARY$), as emphasized by Huntington for example, and the observance of civil and political rights in Gastil's sense ($R = CIVRIGHT$ and *POLRIGHT*) proved to be worth retaining. The seventh category, finally, not having shown any kind of more consistent factor (*CULTANGLO* the only one showing up more often only applies to three positive cases anyhow) was dropped altogether.

Factors similar to ours have also been listed by Dahl (1989), although in a more enumerative and not yet operationalized form. There he stated that "a country is very likely to develop and sustain the institutions of polyarchy

1. if the means of violent coercion are dispersed or neutralized;
2. if it possesses a "modern and dynamic pluralist" society;
3. if it is culturally homogeneous, or, if it is heterogeneous, is not segmented into strong and distinctive subcultures, or, if it is so segmented, its leaders have succeeded in creating a consociational arrangement for managing subcultural conflicts;
4. if it possesses a political culture and beliefs, particularly among political activists, that support the institutions of polyarchy;
5. and if it is not subject to intervention by a foreign power hostile to polyarchy" (1989, p. 264).

As is readily apparent, points 1-4 of this list correspond quite closely to our "super-variables" no. 2-5 and 7 covering our categories 2 to 6 (see Figure 3 below). Only the more specific "regional-historical" aspect of category 1 is omitted here: Similarly, Dahl's point 5 (concerning our category 7) did not apply for the cases and the period analyzed (but did occur, of course, in 1938 in Czechoslovakia!). In this way, we think, our "super-variables" not only fulfill Lijphart's demand of reducing the number of variables, but also his criterion of "using stronger theory" (Collier 1993, p. 109).

One problem concerning the joint utilization of these variables *across* our categories still has to be addressed. As has been mentioned before, systematic comparative analysis such as that undertaken here is not only capable of arriving at broad correlational relationships of one or several variables across all cases ("concomitant variation" in J.S. Mill's terms),thus providing a "universalizing" explanation (in Charles Tilly's sense), but also of identifying "multiple" and "conjunctural" patterns. If we now consider the impact of those variables which were retained or reconstructed *across* our seven categories, we find that some more multiple and/or conjunctural patterns may have been overlooked. This is because, given the small-N dilemma, we had to proceed category by category without taking note of possible interactions across them. Once again, there is no easy solution to this problem. If, however, our procedures have succeeded in retaining most of the infomation contained within the increased property space of our remaining variables, such multiple or conjunctural patterns should become apparent in the course of further joint utilization (this, indeed, has been the case in further applications of these "super-variables" in our project, see for example Berg-Schlosser 1994, 1995).

CONCLUSIONS

The preceding analysis has demonstrated a particular manner in which the general dilemma of "many variables—small N" in comparative political research can be treated. Starting from a system model with seven general categories (including particular sub-systems) and specific variables which are conceptually derived and empirically founded, we proceeded by reducing this complexity in a systematic, outcome-related manner with the help of both statistical and combinatorial methods. This resulted in the extraction and, in part, reconstruction of eight most relevant "super-variables" of a more comprehensive character. Thus, even for our limited universe of originally very complex cases, the "many variables—small N" dilemma was able to be reduced to manageable proportions without losing essential information.

In a substantive sense, if we look at our results case by case and attempt to compile them in a more coherent manner, an interesting pattern is revealed. This is presented in the "Analytic Map of Europe" (Figure 3) which is based on the factors which favoured or prejudiced the survival of democracy in each case. On the left-hand side of the map, we find the most clear-cut examples of democratic survival: the Netherlands, the United Kingdom, Sweden and Belgium. On the right-hand side, the clearly unfavourable patterns characteristic of the Romanian, Spanish, Polish and Italian cases are listed. The most interesting cases are those in the middle (for example Finland as survivor, Estonia and Germany as breakdown cases) since they do not readily correspond to some of the more commonly held tenets of empirical democratic theory. The specific conditions which led to the respective outcome in each of these cases, including the particular impact of the crisis and the reactions of the most important social groups and actors, could, on this basis, be analyzed elsewhere (see Berg-Schlosser 1994). In this way, then, more "structure-oriented" and more "actor-oriented" types of analysis can be meaningfully combined if the respective "opportunity set" (for the use of the term see Elster 1989, p. 13ff) can be defined more closely.

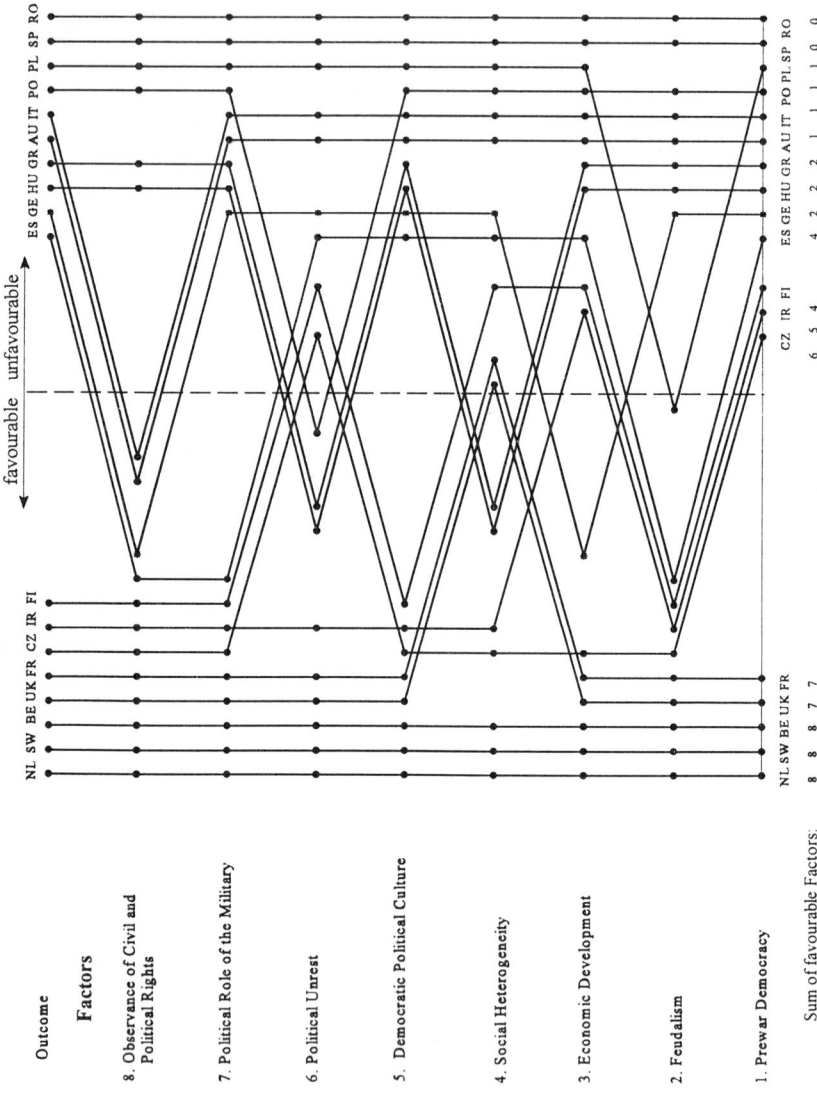

Figure 3. "Analytical Map of Europe"

156

In this way, not only general and "universalizing," but also more specific "variation-finding" results could be obtained. Some of the original hypotheses tested concerning the level of economic development, the role of feudalism, the involvement of the military, a democratic political culture, and so forth which, taken by themselves, usually "over-determine" this kind of analysis, could thus be reduced and applied to their more specific domains. "Better theory" (Collier 1993) not only guided the use of the specific procedures employed and the process of reconstructing of the variables, but also proved itself to be an important possible result of such an analysis.

Beyond the particular example analyzed, we contend that a similar approach can be adapted to quite a number of macro problems in small N situations. The systems framework which has been employed here is based on more general "structural-functional" and "system theoretical" considerations as developed in the works of Almond, Deutsch and Easton, for example. The specific emphasis on a particular aspect or sub-system can vary, of course, and the more or less detailed selection of variables for a particular category has to be guided by the specific research interest and the theoretical concepts developed in this regard. But to consider interactions across sub-systems and possible overall feedback mechanisms certainly is a more general feature of similar "macro"-research. This is also demonstrated, for example, by the emphasis on overall system linkages and respective "cycles" in an area like "policy analysis" which has an original focus quite different from our own (see also Heidenheimer and Heclo 1983; Windhoff-Héritier 1987).

In this field and others the state of theory also is such that we often have a number of relatively sweeping propositions on the one hand, the applicability of which to particular cases has rarely been tested, or very detailed case studies with a very limited theoretical impact on the other. In this regard, too, systematic small N comparisons such as ours can help to establish the "range" of any particular theory much more precisely in space and time.

Similarly, the parallel utilization of statistical and combinatorial procedures can help to overcome the respective limitations and more specific assumptions of each of them. The small N field thus becomes an area of investigation with a specific relevance and methodology which borrows, to some extent, from some other areas, but which also has to be developed independently and for its own sake. In this way, the comparative method proper, which has a potentially enormous area of application in macro-political and macro-social research can be disentangled from techniques which mostly have been developed with large number of cases and a much more limited problem area in mind.

For these reasons, the more thorough investigation of a smaller number of cases certainly need not be inferior to large-scale quantitative studies. As David Collier put it, "...the idea that small-N analysis is (only) a step towards studies based on more sophisticated statistical analysis is ... unconvincing or irrelevant" (Collier 1991, p. 24).

APPENDIX: DEFINITION OF VARIABLES
(BOOLEAN VERSION)

0: *"no," "low," "weak," "below threshold"* and so forth (indicated in brackets)
1: *"yes," "high," "strong," "above threshold"* and so forth

1. General Background

POPULATION	population (20 million)
SEAWARD	seaward periphery
COREBELT	core belt
LANDWARD	landward periphery
NONREF	non-reformed or counter-reformation
REFORM	reformation
EARLYSTATE	early state-building (before 1800)
PREWARDEM	consolidated pre-WWI democracy

2. Socio-economic conditions

NATPRODCAP	national product/cap. (200 US-$)
URBANIZATI	urbanization (50%; population in towns with more than 20.000 inhabitants)
LITERACY	literacy (75%)
LANDLORD	significant share of landownership by landlords (100 ha)
FAMFARMS	family farmers (50% of agrarian population)
AGRPROL	agrarian proletariat (20% of agrarian population)
INDLAB	industrial labour force (30% of labour force)
MIDDLE	old and new middle classes

3. Social composition

ETHNLINGCL	ethno-linguistic cleavage(s)
RELIGCL	religious cleavage(s)
REGIONALCL	regional cleavage(s)
OVERVERZUI	overarching structures ("verzuiling")

4. Political-cultural traditions

NATIDENTIT	national identity
SUBMILIEUS	sub-milieus (class, religion, regional, or ethnic; at least one of these "strong")
VIOLACC	acceptance of violence
EGALITAR	egalitarianism
POLINFORM	political information
POLITIPART	political particpation
STATISM	statism

PAROCHIAL	parochialism
DEMLEGITIM	democratic legitimacy
CONSENS/CONFL	dominant pattern of conflict resolution (0 conflictual/1 consensual)
TOLERANCE	social and political tolerance
AUTH/PART	authoritarian / participatory style of decision making
SECULAR	secularization
SUBJECT	subject orientation

5. Intermediate structures

INTRURAL	rural interest groups
INTCOMMERC	commercial interest groups
INTUNIONS	trade unions
INTEMPLOYE	employers' organizations
CLIENTELISM	clientelism
MOVEMENTS	social movements of more recent orign
MILITIAS	armed militias
PARTFRAG	fragmentation of party system (Rae's F 0.8)
ANTISYSP	share of votes of right and left antisystem parties (15%)
CORPORATISM	corporatism

6. Central political system

POLITTYPE	political system (constitutional monarchy / republic)
ELECTSYSPR	electoral system (majoritarian / proportional)
STABGOVERN	stability of governments
ROLEBUREUA	political role of bureaucracy
MILITARY01	political role of military
SOCIALSEC	social security system
CIVRIGHT	Index of civil rights (0 if score 3 and above)
POLRIGHT	Index of political rights (0 if score 3 and above)

7. External factors

WW1WINNER	winner of WWI
WORLDMIN	world market integration (proportion of exports of national product; mean of all countries)
MILITEX	military expenditures (mean of all countries)
ECONDEPEND	economic dependence (manufactured goods' proportion of foreign trade; mean of all countries)
CULTANGLO	cultural links: Anglo-Saxon
CULTGERM	cultural links: Germanic
CULTROMAN	cultural links: Romanic
CULTSLAVIC	cultural links: Slavic

IDEOLCATH   ideological links: Catholicism
IDEOLMARX   ideological links: Marxism
COLONIES   colonies

NOTES

1. The provision of data by our friends and colleagues Frank Aarebrot (for the Netherlands), Folko Arends and Gerhard Kümmel (Germany), Walter Bernecker (Spain), John Bradley (Czechoslovakia), Antonio Costa Pinto (Portugal), Gisèle De Meur (Belgium), Michel Dobry (France), Stephen Fischer-Galati (Romania), Tom Garvin (Ireland), Peter Gerlich and David Campbell (Austria), Jerzy Holzer (Poland), Gabriella Ilonszki (Hungary), Lauri Karvonen (Finland), Ulf Lindström (Sweden), Jeremy Mitchell (United Kingdom), Marco Tarchi (Italy), Toomas Varrak (Estonia) and Allan Zink (Greece) is gratefully acknowledged.

2. Throughout this paper we utilized both versions 2.02 and 3.0 of QCA to verify our results. Whereas the latter is much more convenient to handle, it does not always arrive at the shortest possible solution for the Quine-Mc Cluskey algorithm and does not always provide all the possible solutions, in particular for analyses with a large number of variables. We, therefore, in addition inspected "by hand" the printouts of the "prime implicant charts" provided by version 2.02, in order to cover all possible solutions.

REFERENCES

Almond, G.A., and G.B. Powell. 1978. *Comparative Politics–System, Process, and Polity*. Boston: Little, Brown.

Almond, G.A., and S. Verba. 1963. *The Civic Culture. Political Attitudes and Democracy in five Western Nations*. Princeton, NJ: Princeton University Press.

Amenta, E., and J.D. Poulsen. 1994. "Where to Begin: A Survey of Five Approaches to Selecting Independent Variables for Qualitative Comparative Analysis." *Sociological Methods and Research* 23: 22-53.

Barton, A.H. 1955. "The Concept of Property Space in Social Research." Pp. 45-50, in *The Language of Social Research*, edited by P.F. Lazarsfeld and M. Rosenberg. Glencoe, IL: Free Press.

Berg-Schlosser, D., and G. De Meur. 1994. "Conditions of Democracy in Inter-War Europe. A Boolean Test of Major Hypotheses." *Comparative Politics* 26: 253-279.

_____. 1996. "Conditions of Authoritarianism, Fascism and Democracy in Inter-War Europe—Systematic Matching and Contrasting of Cases for "Small N" Analysis." *Comparative Political Studies* 29: 423-468.

Berg-Schlosser, D., and R. Siegler. 1990. *Political Stability and Development*. Boulder, CO: Lynne Rienner.

Berg-Schlosser, D., and R. Rytlewski. (Eds.). 1993. *Political Culture in Germany*. London: Macmillan.

Berg-Schlosser, D. 1992. "Conditions of Democracy in Inter-war Europe—A Data Set for Comparative Analysis." Paper presented at the Workshop on "Integrating the European Database: Facilitating Comparative European Research" of the European Consortium for Political Research at Limerick, Ireland.

Berg-Schlosser, D. 1994. "Crisis, Compromise, Collapse: Social and Political Reactions to the Great Depression in Europe." Paper presented at the Congress of the International Political Science Association, Berlin, August 21-25.

Berg-Schlosser, D. 1995. "Das Scheitern der Weimarer Republik—Bedingungen der Demokratie im europäischen Vergleich." *Historical Social Research* 20: 3-30.

Collier, D. 1991. "New Perspectives on the Comparative Method." Pp. 7-31 in *Comparative Political Dynamics*, edited by D.A. Rustow and K.P. Erickson. New York: Harper.

———. 1993. "The Comparative Method." Pp. 105-119, in *Political Science: the State of the Discipline II*, edited by A.W. Finifter. Washington, DC: American Political Science Association.

Dahl, R.A. 1971. *Polyarchy–Participation and Opposition*. New Haven, CT: Yale University Press.

———. 1989. *Democracy and its Critics*. New Haven, CT: Yale University Press.

De Meur, G., and D. Berg-Schlosser. 1994. "Comparing Political Systems—Establishing Similarities and Dissimilarities." *European Journal for Political Research* 26: 193-219.

Deutsch, K.W. 1963. *The Nerves of Government*. New York: The Free Press.

Easton, D. 1965. *A Systems Analysis of Political Life*. Chicago: University of Chicago Press.

Elster, J. 1989. *Nuts and Bolts for the Social Sciences*. Cambridge: Cambridge University Press.

Gastil, R.D. 1979. *Freedom in the World*. New York: Random House.

Gourevitch, P.A. 1986. *Politics in Hard Times: Comparative Response to International Crisis*. Ithaca, NY: Cornell University Press.

Heidenheimer, A., H. Heclo, and C.T. Adams. 1983. *Comparative Public Policy*. New York: St. Martin's Press.

Hermens, F.A. 1941. *Democracy or Anarchy?–A Study of Proportional Representation*. Notre Dame IN: University of Notre Dame Press.

Huntington, S.P. 1964. *The Soldier and the State*. Cambridge, MA: Harvard University Press.

Karvonen, L. 1993. *Fragmentation and Consensus. Political Organization and the Interwar Crisis in Europe*. Boulder, CO: Social Science Monograhps.

Laqueur, W. 1976. *Fascism–A Reader's Guide*. London.

Larsen, S.U., B. Hagtvet, and J-P. Myklebust. (Eds.). 1980. *Who were the Fascists?* Bergen: Universitets Forlaget.

Lijphart, A. 1971. "Comparative Politics and the Comparative Method." *American Political Science Review* 65: 682-693.

———. 1975. "The Comparable Cases Strategy in Comparative Research." *Comparative Political Studies*: 157-175.

———. 1977. *Democracy in Plural Societies*. New Haven, CT: Yale University Press.

Linz, J.J. 1975. "Totalitarian and Authoritarian Regimes." Pp. 175-411 in *Handbook of Political Science Volume 3: Macropolitical Theory*, edited by F.J. Greenstein and N.W. Polsby. Reading, MA: Addison-Wesley.

———. 1980. "Political Space and Fascism as a Late-Comer." Pp. 153-189 in *Who were the Fascists?* edited by S.U. Larsen, B. Hagtvet and J.-P. Myklebust. Bergen: Universitets Forlaget.

Linz, J.J., and A. Stepan 1978. *The Breakdown of Democratic Regimes*. Baltimore, MD: Johns Hopkins University Press.

Lipset, S.M. 1960. *Political Man–The Social Bases of Politics*. New York: Doubleday.

———. 1983. "Radicalism or Reformism—The Sources of Working Class Politics." *American Political Science Review* 77: 1-18.

Lipset, S.M., K.-R. Seong, and J.C. Torres. 1993. "A Comparative Analysis of the Social Requisites of Democracy." *International Social Science Journal* 136 (May): 155-175.

López, J.J. 1992. "Theory Choice in Comparative Social Inquiry." *Polity* XXV(2): 267-282.

Luebbert, G.M. 1987. "Social Foundations of Political Order in Interwar Europe." *World Politics* 39: 449-478.

———. 1991. *Liberalism, Fascism, or Social Democracy. Social Classes and the Political Origins of Regimes in Interwar Europe*. Oxford: Oxford University Press.

Mill, J.S. 1843. *A System of Logic*. Quoted from the eighth edition 1904. New York.

Moore, B. Jr. 1966. *Social Origins of Dictatorship and Democracy*. Boston: Beacon Press.
Mosse, G.L. (Ed.). 1979. *International Fascism, New Thoughts and New Approaches*. London, Beverly Hills: Sage.
Nolte, E. 1966. *Die faschistischen Bewegungen*. München: dtv.
Przeworski, A., and H. Teune 1970. *The Logic of Comparative Social Inquiry*. New York: Wiley.
Ragin, C.C. 1987. *The Comparative Method*. Berkeley: University of California Press.
————. 1994. "Introduction to Qualitative Comparative Analysis." Pp. 299-319 in *The Comparative Political Economy of Welfare States*, edited by T. Janoski and A. Hicks. New York: Cambridge University Press,.
Rokkan, S. 1975. "Dimensions of State Formation and Nation-Building." Pp. 562-600 in *The Formation of National States in Western Europe*, edited by C. Tilly. Princeton, NJ: Princeton University Press.
Rosecrance, R. 1986. *The Rise of the Trading State*. New York: Basic Books.
Rueschemeyer, D., E.H. Stephens, and J.D. Stephens. 1992. *Capitalist Development and Demcoracy*. Cambridge: Polity Press.
Sani, G., and G. Sartori. 1983. "Polarization, Fragmentation and Competition in Western Democracies." Pp. 307-340 in *Western European Party Systems: Continuity and Change*, edited by H. Daalder and P. Mair. London: Sage.
Skocpol, T. (Ed.). 1984. *Vision and Method in Historical Sociology*. Cambridge: Cambridge University Press.
Stephens, J.D. 1989. "Democratic Transition and Breakdown in Western Europe 1870-1939, A Test of the Moore Thesis." *American Journal of Sociology* 94: 1019-1077.
Tilly, C. 1984. *Big Structures, Large Processes, Huge Comparisons*. New York: Russell Sage Foundation.
Vanhanen, T. 1984. *The Emergence of Democracy*. Helsinki: Societas Scientiarum Fennica.
Varrak, T. n.d. "The Collapse of Democracy in Inter-War Estonia." In *Democracy in Europe 1919-1939, Vol I*, edited by D. Berg-Schlosser and J. Mitchell. Basingstoke: Macmillan.
Verba, S. 1967. "Some Dilemmas in Comparative Research." *World Politics* 20: 111-127.
Weir, M., and T. Skocpol. 1985. "State Structures and the Possibilities for 'Keynesian Responses' to the Great Depression in Sweden, Britain, and the United States." Pp. 107-163 in *Bringing the State Back In*, edited by P. Evans, D. Rueschemeyer and T. Skocpol. New York: Cambridge University Press.
Windhoff-Héritier, A. 1987. *Policy-Analyse*. Frankfurt, New York: Campus.
Woolf, S.J. (Ed.). 1968. *The Nature of Fascism*. London: Weidenfeld and Nicholson.
Zimmermann, E., and T. Saalfeld. 1989. "Economic and Political Reactions to the World Economic Crisis of the 1930s in Six European Countries." *International Studies Quarterly*: 305-334.

MEASUREMENT OF EDUCATION IN COMPARATIVE RESEARCH

Michael Braun and Walter Müller

ABSTRACT

This chapter discusses the difficulty in arriving at truly comparable measures of education, the main source of which is identified as being grounded in actual differences in the educational systems of different countries. In order to develop theoretically based guidelines for measurement, the concept of education is clarified by discussing the multi-faceted consequences of education. Based on these theoretical deliberations, frequently used approaches to education are evaluated including number of years of schooling, educational scoring and typologies such as the ISCED and CASMIN classifications. In the empirical section similarities and differences of various measures of education with regard to their respective explanatory power for a broad array of dependent variables are analyzed. These dependent variables are directly derived from the theoretical discussion of the various consequences of education. As data from four countries is used it is possible to distinguish between country-specific characteristics and more general trends. On the basis of both the theoretical considerations and the empirical analyses, the desirability of a most detailed measurement of education in emphasized, especially with regard to the inclusion of formal qualifications in the form of categories in surveys and subsequent analyses. If possible,

Comparative Social Research, Volume 16, pages 163-201.
Copyright © 1997 by JAI Press Inc.
All rights of reproduction in any form reserved.
ISBN: 0-7623-0250-X

additional information on vocational training and on the type of school (public vs. private) should also be collected. As years of schooling is measured quite differently in individual countries any comparison might be ambiguous. In addition, from the countries investigated only in the United States did this variable emerge as a better measure than formal qualifications.

Education is a very widely used concept within the sphere of the social sciences. And yet this concept is rather poorly understood, perhaps precisely *because* its use is so conventional and self-evident. In population surveys education is generally included as one of the so-called "background variables" without much concern as to why and how it should be measured. It is a variable for all purposes, and therefore—at best—researchers stick to more or less established standards concerning the way this variable is conventionally measured in a given national context.

Frequently, comparative research provides both the incentive and the necessity to make some basic reflections on what seems to be evident in the national context. Even though systematic international comparisons have become increasingly important in recent years, the problems connected with the development of an international comparative scale of education have rarely been made the explicit focus of research. This is all the more puzzling, given the fact that precisely in international comparisons the researcher is usually not able to make use of his/her own surveys, and is instead dependent upon secondary data. With such data, the parameters of data collection cannot be controlled by the data user. The analyst using secondary data is dependent on those decisions taken by the primary researcher or—as is often the case with education—on some nationally established conventions. The latter may differ from country to country in terms of the underlying theoretical conceptions as well as in terms of the concrete ways to operationalize the concepts. Even in the studies of the International Social Survey Program (ISSP, see Braun 1994; Davis and Jowell 1990) measurements of education adopted for individual countries differ considerably.

In this chapter we discuss some of the methodological problems—in theory and research practice—of the measurement of education in comparative research. We begin with a brief outline of the specific problems of measurement of education in comparative research. We then focus on clarifying the concept of education by discussing the multi-faceted consequences—both direct and indirect—of education. Based on these theoretical deliberations we evaluate different approaches in the literature in measuring education for comparative purposes including number of years of schooling, educational scoring and typologies such as the ISCED and the CASMIN classifications. The remainder of the chapter is an empirical exercise in the study of the consequences of different measures of education in comparative research. Using data from the

United States, East and West Germany, Poland and Hungary we study, for a broad array of dependent variables, the extent to which different educational measures lead to different conclusions concerning the explanatory power of education in comparative research. From this we finally derive several recommendations for a better treatment of education in data collection which may then improve its comparability in comparative studies.

PROBLEMS OF MEASUREMENT OF EDUCATION IN COMPARATIVE RESEARCH

The construction of instruments for comparative measurement of education turns out, in fact, to be very difficult since educational systems that differ systematically in reality have to be mapped upon measurement instruments that—according to conventional wisdom—should at least be functionally equivalent (Przeworski and Teune 1970). The difficulties of measuring education in comparative research thus mainly result from the fact that the reality to be measured is different. Societies differ to a large extent with respect to the institutions through which they provide and certify education. Indeed, large differences already existed in the previous century among nations in the process of developing mass education and of building a system of higher education (Archer 1979; Ringer 1979; Boli, Meyer, and Ramirez 1985). In the course of this century these systems have undergone various reforms at different points in time. From an attempt to describe the early developments of the educational systems in several European countries and their transformations (König, Lüttinger and Müller 1988), one can reach the conclusion that current educational systems probably differ among nations more than ever. Although participation in secondary and tertiary education expanded in this century in all developed nations and particularly in the latter half, the expansion occurred in different institutions at different times and at a different pace.

The differences in educational systems and the resulting problems of international comparison in this area can best be illustrated with a few examples. Contemporary educational systems have arisen through long historical development driven by diverse social forces. For example, since the French Revolution conflicts about education in France pitted the Church against the centralized State. The enormous importance of (largely parochial) private schools (alongside public schools) has been the result of this historical conflict. France is also characterized by a high degree of standardization and strict, bureaucratic direction in her educational system, stemming from the country's traditional centralization. In Germany, on the other hand, private schools have played only a subordinate role and federal diversity and decentralized features of the educational system came to dominate. What is also distinctive for Germany is the dual system of occupational training which grew out of elements of the feudal heritage. This system is found in only a very few countries, but has wide-ranging consequences for the process of occupational placement (Haller et al. 1985; König and Müller 1986).

Systematic institutional differences can be found in many of the more specific features of the organization of education such as:

- the degree of actual openness of the respective educational institutions, for example, by tuition requirements
- the division of secondary schooling into different school types
- the age at which selection for secondary school types typically takes place and in the different selection criteria employed
- the organization and internal differentiation of the field of higher (i.e., tertiary or post-secondary) education and in its admission criteria
- the importance of private and elite schools and universities and in the variation of the quality and the public recognition of different educational institutions
- the degree of integration of general education and vocational training; in the organization and frequency of further systematic education after entry into the labor market and so on.

In developing comparative measures of education to be used in population surveys the additional difficulty arises that even within one society different age cohorts have experienced schooling in educational institutions that differ from each other because of the relatively frequent educational reforms in the course of this century. The construction of comparative measures of education is thus a major task that cannot be accomplished in a single paper.

The question as to the way in which education should be conceptualized and measured in comparative research is generally perceived to be of such difficulty that researchers frequently end up with a kind of minimal solution. In order to achieve comparability, at least in a broad sense, the researchers adopt one of the following two solutions. Either they opt for a measure that considers only one single dimension of education which seems to be relatively easy to measure in similar ways in different countries. A prominent example of such a measure is years of schooling or some other indicator of duration of educational experience. The second solution often adopted is agreement on a small set of rather broadly defined educational categories. The more detailed national classification systems are collapsed into a much broader measure. Usually this strategy implies making cuts at such levels of education where similarity or functional equivalence appears possible to establish and thus neglecting national details and peculiarities. In both cases Jules Peschar's concerns may be well taken: "That which is considered 'interference' and is correspondingly done away with, actually represents the most important aspect of research, namely, its national elements" (Peschar 1984, p. 15). Ultimately, classifications like these lead to the homogenization of social reality and the leveling of nationally distinctive characteristics.

THEORETICAL PERSPECTIVES AS GUIDELINES TO MEASURE EDUCATION

In order to define the problem on a more theoretical level we have to clarify the concept of education and reflect on what is generally intended to be measured when we measure education. It is probably not possible to find a generally acceptable definition of education, but we may approach the problem by pointing to the crucial elements the researcher probably intends to capture through measuring education. Here two aspects are straightforward. The first relates to the more or less *direct* effects of education, that is, what pupils and students learn. The second concerns consequences of education that are more *indirect* or are *mediated* by other social experiences.

As schools teach various subjects, education can be supposed to have different immediate effects depending on the kind of curricula followed by the students:

- Education provides students with *general basic skills* such as reading, writing, arithmetic and general cognitive skills like understanding information, reasoning on logical grounds and information processing.
- Education provides students with more *specific instrumental skills* such as accounting, using a computer, learning foreign languages or the specific techniques of a craft.
- Education provides *knowledge* of different kinds (about facts—or what is taken as a fact—theories, interpretations, for example, in history, geography, politics, physics).
- Education includes *socialization* in values, norms and social behavior more or less accepted in a given society or in a subculture of a given society. Socialization occurs openly through specific subjects at schools, but even more important are probably the latent processes of socialization through the hidden curriculum (Fend et al. 1976; Bowles and Gintis 1976; Bourdieu and Passeron 1970).

Among the *mediated* consequences of education at least the following two should be mentioned and distinguished:

- Education may have consequences not because of the knowledge, the qualifications, the values and behavior patterns per se that are induced in the individuals who acquire education, but because of the *social meaning* attached to the acquisition of education in different societal contexts. This aspect has been most discussed with reference to the *certificates* and *credentials* provided by educational institutions (Weber 1956; Collins 1979; Arrow 1973; Spilerman and Lunde 1991). Certificates and credentials testify the acquisition of particular sets of skills and knowledge. Sociologically, most interesting is the socially recognized value that credentials may have in some contexts and which is more or less independent of the actual knowledge and skills of the possessors of the credentials (Collins 1979). The credentials may be linked to specific rights, legitimate claims, exclusive privileges or preferential treatments. In modern societies this aspect is crucial in particular for the occupational career, for the earning opportunities and herewith for setting the material constraints for one's *Lebensführung* (life style).

The relationship between the credentials and the characteristics which individuals gain through the acquisition of education is difficult to establish. For example, different knowledge could produce the same credentials, and comparable knowledge could result in different credentials. Such variation in the significance of a given body of knowledge for credentials may be particularly pertinent in comparisons across societies. Credentials may also have effects for different reasons: for instance because the underlying (i.e., learned) knowledge is indeed more or less indispensable for a given job or because credentials are considered a sign of productivity or efficiency (Arrow 1973; Thurow 1976), or because they are regarded as an indicator of extra-functional qualities such as obedience, discipline, social contacts or social skills (Dahrendorf 1956).

- As Hyman, Wright and Reed (1975) in particular have sensibly discussed, mediated effects of education can be expected in yet another sense. Variation in levels of education are connected with variations in other life experiences. Those experiences may be indistinguishably confounded with effects of education. For example, education is related to specific intellectual and cultural activities that provide new learning experiences such as reading books or selecting information from different kinds of printed material and other mass media. Different occupational careers resulting from different levels and kinds of education are associated with different opportunities and challenges to improve one's skills and knowledge. From studies of social networks or assortative mating we know that education is also linked with one's integration into distinctive communication networks: "the more educated tend to move in a different milieu from the less educated. In general, their personal contacts are likely to be with individuals who are better informed and more influential" (Inglehart 1979, p. 347).

In methodological language, this aspect concerns the omitted variable problem. Mediated effects of education will occur precisely because education is correlated with many different social phenomena. Such correlates can be responsible for spuriousness[1] or causal intervention, or both. In theory, effects of this kind can be accounted for by statistical controls but in practice this will be difficult in the case of education, first because of the large number of potential correlates and, second because the correlation with education may be so strong that a serious problem of multicollinearity exists.

We have drawn attention to the various dimensions and components of education in order to increase the awareness of several basic problems in the measurement of education in general, and for comparative research in particular. For different substantive areas in which education is used as an explanatory variable different dimensions of education may be crucial. For the study of occupational careers or the study of economic returns to education, the certificate obtained and the level of specific instrumental skills achieved are probably most important. For the explanation of values, socialization experiences in schools might be more relevant and, in the study of political competence, general basic skills that help people to understand political processes.

Generally, most of the basic dimensions cannot be measured directly—at least not in a population survey in which education is not the focal topic but is used rather as a background variable. It would be much too costly to test the knowledge persons have and it would be impossible to find out whether their knowledge, skills and abilities have been acquired through formal education or otherwise. The most appropriate proxies are the length of educational experience, the institutions at which education has been received, the kind of curricula and examinations individuals have successfully taken, and the credentials they have received.

APPROACHES FOR MEASURING EDUCATION IN COMPARATIVE RESEARCH

In the following we discuss some of the more prominent attempts to measure education in comparative research. For each of them we try to characterize its theoretical foundation, its operationalization principles and its potential strengths and weaknesses.

Number of Years of Schooling

One of the most straightforward attempts of measuring education is based upon the length of educational experience (e.g., Blau and Duncan 1967). It assumes that the longer someone is exposed to education, the more skills and knowledge he or she can acquire, and the more he or she is socialized, direct or indirectly. It is often regarded as an advantage that the concept seems to have a clear interpretation and that it also has properties that are practical in statistical analysis. Though the operational procedures to measure the number of school years vary somewhat, they all are relatively simple in principle. Since the concept involves straightforward counting, in theory the technical aspects do not present particularly difficult problems for comparative measurement, although there may be some definitional difficulties concerning the kinds of schooling that should be included (for example, kindergarten or forms of pre-school).

The meaningfulness of this approach evidently depends on whether all kinds of skills and knowledge are of similar value and whether there is an intrinsic relationship between inputs in educational effort and outputs in terms of skills and knowledge or in terms of the publicly recognized value of education. From this the number of years of schooling as an indicator of education appears to be most adequate when more or less all students follow the same kind of curriculum at relatively similar educational institutions. In other words: the adequacy of the years of schooling-approach depends on the degree of institutional homogeneity of the educational system. It is consistent with this that the approach has been mainly used in the context of the American school system which exhibits a relatively low degree of institutional differentiation (Wanner 1986). However, considering the quite substantial differences in the quality of schooling at private or public schools (Coleman and Hoffer 1987) and the high variation in the standing of colleges and universities, one may have some doubts regarding the utility of this indicator even for the United States.[2] The underlying assumption is even less valid for European systems of education. Institutionally they are so widely differentiated that the simple counting of school years will inevitably appear as a very poor indicator of education obtained. The same number of years of schooling can vary greatly as a predictor of occupational opportunities, for example, depending upon which educational path is involved. For occupational opportunities as a dependent variable, this is especially true concerning the division separating educational paths oriented towards general education and those more strongly oriented towards specific vocational qualifications. Thus, with increasing differentiation between educational systems, the indicator "years of schooling" loses information value (cf. Rubinson 1986, p. 524).

Institutional differences among countries may affect the social significance that is attached to years of educational participation that do not conclude with an examination. In the United States, for example, a few years at college level are regarded as a significant improvement over just a high school diploma and will thus be rewarded in the labor market. On the contrary, a number of years of university training in Germany ending in failure in the final degree is regarded somewhat as a disadvantage showing a lack of perseverance on the part of the student. This is partly due to the fact that post-secondary education has been packed with exams for a large proportion of the courses taken in America, but not in Germany (although this might increasingly be the case in the future).

An additional complication is introduced by different methods which are actually used for measuring years of schooling. The American General Social Survey asks for the highest grade achieved, for example in high school. Thus, someone who passed the high school diploma would report exactly 12 years, while a German who passed the *Abitur* or a Frenchman who obtained the baccalauréat may answer the question aiming at the length of schooling by the exact number of years it took that person to obtain the examination. Contrary to intuition, a less diligent student who had to repeat classes will obtain a higher score than his brighter counterpart.

The information value of "years of schooling" is thus limited even within one country because of the heterogeneous kind and quality of education that individuals with the same number of school years may have experienced.[3] This is even more the case if the measure is used in comparative research. The same number of school years has a different meaning in countries that differ to a considerable extent in the number of years that are generally used for obtaining a roughly comparable level of education. The more countries differ for instance in the pattern of combining study and work, the more dubious becomes a straightforward indicator of the number of years of schooling for comparative research.

Scoring Education

By scoring education we understand procedures in which educational scores are generated through scaling in such a way that the correlation between the scaled educational information and a given criterion (dependent variable, such as income) is maximized, for example by means of techniques of regression analysis (Treiman and Terell 1975) or by means of log-linear models (Smith and Garnier 1986). The theoretical rationale underlying such procedures can be found in the following deliberation: Given that, in comparative research in particular, it appears impossible to measure education in a comparable way per se, a pragmatic solution is to obtain the "best possible" measure of education for each single country and then maximize the predictive power of education in each country. Basically, this is a sensible way to go if, first, we can be assured that the original measures of education to begin with are indeed the most exhaustive measures for the countries to be compared and, second, if indeed we are mainly interested in the predictive power of education for a given dependent variable. As resulting information the procedure provides scale values for each original educational category which, under the chosen functional form, maximize the correlation between this educational scale and the criterion variable. These scores can be used to judge the "value" of the original educational categories with respect to the criterion.

Although optimal scoring seems to be an attractive procedure in order to overcome the problem of comparing the incomparable, one also has to consider serious drawbacks. First, one must indeed assume that the original national measurements exhaust the potential explanatory power of education to the same extent. In addition, the comparability problem is switched from education to the criterion variable. This variable must be measured in strictly comparable ways. Depending on the scaling procedure used, the scores derived for education may also depend on the distribution of the criterion variable. If these conditions are not met, it is generally impossible to know whether differences or similarities in results derive from real differences, differences in measurement, or both.

Second, since the scoring depends on the criterion, it is very likely that the scores vary with the criterion. Even measurement in different samples using the same criterion may produce different scores. Had a study like Political Action (Barnes, Kaase et al. 1979) in which education is used as a predictor for various different dependent variables opted for this procedure, the authors may have found different educational scores for each dependent variable—possibly in all of the countries studied. The perspective of an endless relativism becomes even more of a nightmare if we consider the fact that educational scores will depend on the population subgroups that we study and that they also will vary with the educational distributions which continuously change in time (e.g., there may be age-education interaction).

A different scaling approach has been proposed by Sorensen (1983). On the basis of certain assumptions, educational scores are generated from a hierarchic educational distribution. A related possibility is the quintile approach. Education is scaled according to the relative position in the hierarchy of the educational continuum. These approaches are most appropriate with theoretical problems in which education is conceived as a positional good. Here, apart from the problem of developing an unequivocal hierarchy, the characteristic dividing lines (certificates) are ignored. In other words, the actual existing differentiation of the educational system always corresponds only approximately to this proportional division into segments.

In order to avoid the problems related to using years of schooling and educational scoring as measurement devices a number of educational typologies have been proposed to which we will now turn.

Educational Typologies

Educational typologies have a hybrid character and it is therefore particularly difficult to describe the precise theoretical concepts underlying them. They basically attempt to define comparable educational categories which combine several dimensions within one categorical schema, for example a combination of length of schooling, general or vocational orientation of education and credentials obtained. The underlying assumption is that with a small number of such categories the crucial differences among various educational outcomes can be grasped while many details of the educational course can be neglected. The attractiveness of these schemata is that the differences between categories can be intuitively perceived such as the difference between a traditional university education and a higher education at a technical college or polytechnic institute.

The ISCED-classification

An example of an educational typology that has been constructed for comparative research is the "International Standard Classification of Education" (ISCED) developed by UNESCO. It is the most widely used standard in comparative publications of international statistical agencies. Many of the published internationally "comparable" statistical data on education sensibly attempt to adopt this standard. For instance, since 1970 the Statistical Office of the European Union has used this scale in its publications of educational statistics concerning its member countries. To some extent the conventions adopted in the construction of the ISCED classification for the European countries has been motivated by concerns about equivalence of credentials and educational titles in the labor market in European countries.[4]

The ISCED classification scheme is intended to serve different purposes in statistical reporting (for instance, in the construction of indicators measuring school attendance rates or for indicators measuring the level of education completed). The idea behind the ISCED scheme is that statistics for all these purposes should be based on the same principles. This may be difficult to achieve. Basically, the ISCED scheme is divided into four levels, and its rudimentary structure is to be interpreted hierarchically. Level 0 comprises pre-school instruction. Level 1 corresponds to compulsory education and includes elementary schools and the junior levels of comprehensive schools. The second level is divided into two stages ("cycles"). The first stage corresponds to the lower part of secondary schooling up to an intermediate level or up to the end of compulsory education. The second stage may lead to the certificate required for entry into university, but it includes also many other kinds of secondary education beyond compulsory schooling. Besides academically-oriented high schools, this includes the higher levels of comprehensive schools and different types of vocational-oriented schools such as technical high schools, vocational technical schools (e.g., the German *Berufsgrundbildungsjahr*), and also vocational apprenticeships in some countries. The third level includes the various schools of higher professional education: polytechnics, technical colleges, schools of the health system, art academies or institutes, teacher training colleges and universities. The subdivisions made here can be grasped from the brief description in the next paragraph. For some purposes additional subdivisions are made, for instance the distinction between general education and vocational-oriented education or between full-time and part-time education.

A recent version of the ISCED scheme which presents the different subdivisions of the levels described above is the following (OECD 1995, p. 211):

ISCED 0   Education preceding the first level (pre-primary)
ISCED 1   Education at the first level (primary)
ISCED 2   Education at the lower secondary level
ISCED 3   Education at the upper secondary level
ISCED 5   Education at the tertiary level, first stage, of the type that leads to an award not equivalent to a first university degree
ISCED 6   Education at the tertiary level, first stage, of the type that leads to first university degree or equivalent
ISCED 7   Education at the tertiary level, second stage, of the type that leads to a post-graduate university degree or equivalent
ISCED 9   Education not definable by level.

A criterion that seems to have a considerable weight in the allocation of specific educational courses to the categories of the ISCED scale is the place in the sequence of educational steps. The decision about the level of education that people have attained is then made on the basis of the highest certificate obtained in this series of steps. This procedure may be adequate for countries with a relatively low track differentiation in secondary education. But it produces serious problems in countries with a strong differentiation of tracks. The most serious problems of misrepresenting educational differentiation occur if no distinctions are made between general, academically oriented courses of education and those which are more vocational oriented.[5] One of the guiding ideas which led to the development of the CASMIN classification was precisely to take this distinction into proper account and which is a feature of non-negligible importance in many educational systems (see e.g., Müller, Shavit and Ucem 1996 for a comparative study of its relevance for labor market outcomes of education).

The CASMIN Classification

Another example of a comparative educational typology is the CASMIN educational classification (Müller et al. 1989; Müller and Karle 1993). This

Table 1.   CASMIN Educational Classification

1a	Inadequately completed elementary education.
1b	Completed (compulsory) elementary education.
1c	(Compulsory) elementary education and basic vocational qualification.
2a	Secondary, intermediate vocational qualification.
2b	Secondary, intermediate general qualification.
2c	Full secondary, maturity level certificate.
3a	Higher education—lower-level tertiary certificate
3b	Higher education—upper-level tertiary certificate.

classification has been constructed in view of its use for studying the links of education with processes of social mobility in European societies. In the elaboration of this comparative schema the aim was the establishment of functional equivalence in relation to the substantive context. The different educational levels should—to the greatest extent possible—optimally reflect both the typical, class-specific educational barriers in the educational system and those differentiations that represent significant signals in the labor market. Given this context of application for the educational scale, emphasis was put on *certificates* attained. The educational classification contains eight basic categories based upon two primary classificatory criteria: (1) the differentiation of a hierarchy of levels of general education and (2) the differentiation between "general" and "vocational-oriented" education. The categories distinguished are summarized in Table 1.

General education.   In terms of general education, the schema distinguishes three main levels which relate to the length of educational experience, the required intellectual capacity and the value of the educational certificate achieved: *elementary* (*1*), *secondary* (*2*) and *tertiary* (*3*). Within these three levels, further differentiations are made which we discuss in connection with each level.

Elementary education is understood in a way that should capture the "social minimum" of education in a given society at a given point in historical time; the minimal educational level that every citizen is expected to reach. It can generally be obtained without selective examinations by following the least demanding courses of education up until the legally fixed age of compulsory schooling.[6] Persons who drop out from school before reaching this goal are assigned to the category of *inadequate completion of elementary education* (*1a*), while those who leave the educational system at the least demanding end point of compulsory education are coded as *completed elementary education* (*1b*).

On the *secondary* level we distinguish between intermediate and full secondary certificates. *Full secondary certificates* (*2c*) consist of the successful passing of those exams that mark the completion of secondary schooling (e.g., the *Abitur*, Maturity, Baccalauréat, and A-level exams). *Intermediate secondary education (2a, 2b)* relates to certificates between elementary and full secondary education. In making the distinction between elementary and intermediate education, which in some cases is not clear-cut, essentially all those courses and certificates that clearly go beyond the elementary level are ascribed to the intermediate level, be it through education in selective schools, or the length of education that clearly goes beyond the compulsory years of education, or be it that exams were passed which are clearly above the elementary level.[7]

Tertiary education relates to certificates and diplomas from the tertiary sector of education. Access to respective courses of study generally (although not always) presupposes that the candidates have obtained a full secondary education. The classification distinguishes between lower-level and upper-level tertiary degrees. The *lower-level tertiary degrees (3a)* are as a rule characterized by a shorter length of study and a stronger practical orientation (e.g., a technical college diploma, a teachers' college diploma and comparable certificates). The category of *upper level tertiary degrees (3b)* presupposes the successful completion (with examination) of a traditional, academically-oriented university education.

Vocational training.   Besides general education, practically all educational systems provide courses that are vocationally oriented and intend to impart knowledge and more practical skills for specific occupations. In particular in view of the utility of one's education in the labor market, it is indispensable to take into account the acquisition of respective qualifications. In some cases it turns out to be rather difficult to map vocational training in a cross-national comparative way into a scale of education, because general and vocational education are in part linked in very different ways in different countries.[8]

In the CASMIN classification, vocational training primarily comes into play at the elementary and intermediate levels of education. At the elementary educational level, the classification assigns to the category *elementary education and basic vocational qualification (1c)* those persons who have participated beyond compulsory schooling in additional occupational training at a basic level. At the intermediate educational level, the division between general education and vocational training is sometimes ambiguous due to the variety of ways in which elements of general education and vocational training are linked. Nevertheless, on the intermediate level the classification also distinguishes between two types: *Intermediate vocational schooling (2a)* which includes all those types of school programs in which either general intermediate schooling is supplemented by additional vocational training, or in which a course of study was completed going clearly beyond elementary education but consisting of largely practical, vocational components. *General intermediate schooling (2b)*, on the other hand, consists of an education that is exclusively or essentially of a general educative character.

The Political-Action Classification

The Political-Action Study (see Barnes, Kaase et al. 1979) was not primarily directed towards making educational information from different countries comparable or to a comparison of the effects of education in different countries. However, in the way of comparing political action across nations these scholars developed two kinds of regrouping of educational categories, a five-category and a three-category scale. Both educational classifications used in the Political-Action Study are less detailed than the CASMIN-schema. Using the three-category Political-Action scale as a measure with a minimum degree of differentiation can show how much information we lose by using increasingly unrefined measures of education.

EMPIRICAL ILLUSTRATION OF THE CONSEQUENCES OF USING DIFFERENT MEASURES OF EDUCATION

In this chapter, we cannot possibly test all of the propositions made above. What we can do, however, is to present some evidence for some of the hypotheses. For this purpose, it seems worthwhile to pursue three kinds of analysis.

The first aims at gauging the extent to which different concepts of education contribute to explaining a variety of different domains. The concepts of education we are going to compare are:

1. educational categories in the most detailed form available for a given country,
2. years of schooling (used as a quantitative variable),
3. the CASMIN regrouping of the original educational categories and
4. the three-category regrouping of the original educational categories used in the Political-Action Study.

The second aim is to test whether the differences in the patterns of association found for the various measures of education vary across countries. Here our interest is not so much in the differing predictive power of education in the countries studied, but in the similarity of the consequences of various measures of education in different societal contexts. This is crucial in distinguishing between those differences in the various measures of education which are general and those which are possibly country-specific.

The third aim is to draw closer attention, at least for two countries (the U.S. and West-Germany), to the form of the relationship between measures of education and the dependent variables. This should provide information concerning the question as to whether the influence is of a continuous form, for example the dependent variable changes by a constant amount for each additional year of schooling, or whether the change in the dependent variable is related to the passing of (more or less) formal examinations and whether obtaining different credentials has similar effects.

The variables we try to explain by the different measures of education are selected in order to represent various dimensions for which education can be assumed to be a theoretically interesting predictor variable. They are directly derived from the above discussion of the different direct and indirect effects of education. The measures of *cultural capital* (if available) relate to the *knowledge*-component of education.[9] *Gender-role ideology* and two kinds of *attitudes towards social inequality* (motivational function of inequality and power explanation of inequality) refer to the *socialization* component of education. *Political interest* can be understood as an indicator for individual *competence* in political affairs for which education can be conceived as an important resource. Personal *income* and *prestige* finally relate to the *instrumental* value of education in the status attainment process. The different measures capture almost the entire range of both direct and mediated consequences of education. We hypothesize that the educational variables account very differently for each of these and, more specifically, that the variance of variables such as prestige and cultural capital which are intrinsically related to the process of education will be much better explained by education than the variance of the attitudinal variables. This is due to the fact that while the socialization component of education might be very important, education is but one agent of socialization.

Selection of Countries

In this chapter we use data from four countries: the United States, Germany, Poland and Hungary. In addition, Germany is divided in former West and East Germany. This selection of countries was pursued with the intention of including a broad span of different educational systems in different societal contexts. One important distinguishing factor is the degree of institutional differentiation of the educational system. A second distinction is between capitalist societies and former socialist societies. We would have liked to include a larger number of countries, at least two countries in each of the cells of the 2×2 tables that can be constructed from these criteria. This would have enhanced our ability to separate national idiosyncrasies from general substantial results regarding the effects of different measures of education. But nearly always the problem of finding comparable data (see the description below) restricted our possibilities to some degree of realizing the most desirable design.

The United States and West Germany are central to our purpose. The United States has a comprehensive system of secondary education which is scarcely segmented into segregated tracks and has only limited vocational components. At the same time the concept of years of schooling is very popular in the United States and promises to bear good results. West Germany's educational system on the other hand has a high degree of horizontal institutional segmentation with three rather different tracks of education. In contrast to the United States, Germany has a separate system of vocational training which is strongly institutionalized and has direct links to an occupationally segmented labor market. In this system the type of education and credentials should play a more important role than the number of years in education. As two former socialist countries Poland and Hungary are interesting because of the strong element of manpower planning in the provision of education that is less present in the two more market-oriented Western societies. The inclusion of East Germany allows us to direct attention to the systemic (socialist versus non-socialist) aspect while holding constant national culture and language, at least to some degree.

Variables and Measures of Education

As stated previously, we will compare four different ways of measuring education. The most basic one is simply to use the *educational categories in the most detailed form* available for a given country. We will take this full set of educational information as our main point of reference and examine how the different other measures relate to this baseline. These categories will be entered as a set of dummy variables into the analyses. In a special variant of this measure we will also include comprehensive information on vocational training where available. Therefore we will have two baselines: educational dummies without vocational training and educational dummies including vocational training.

Years of schooling, our second variant of educational measure, is unfortunately not measured in a strictly comparable way in the different countries. For example, the German surveys employ questions such as "How many years did you attend school? Please include university education, but exclude vocational training." However, in the United States, where the concept of years of schooling has held so much sway, the question is more sophisticated, aiming at the highest grade the respondent has obtained in a given kind of school (i.e., High School, Junior College, College). Thus, the American question is less vulnerable by imprecise interviewing or misunderstandings which, as in the German case, might lead to the exclusion of university education or the inclusion of vocational training.[10] Moreover, the German measure assigns a higher than adequate number of years to those respondents who needed more time than usual to obtain a given grade or degree. The Hungarian measure is equivalent to the American, while the Polish measure derives the number of years of schooling from the certificates obtained.

The *CASMIN-* and the *Political Action*-regrouping of the original educational categories will be used in the way they have been described above and following the documentation in the Appendix.

What can we expect from these different measures of education concerning their potential to explain the variance of the dependent variables selected for analysis? It is very unlikely that the measures of education based on any form of regrouping of degrees (i.e., the CASMIN and Political-Action measures) could possibly exceed in explanatory power the measure that preserves the full information. They could, at best, explain a similar amount more parsimoniously. The CASMIN measure may, however, fare better than the educational dummies without vocational training in those countries where there exists an extended vocational training and when information on such training is available, because the CASMIN measure also takes this information into account.

However, the relative explanatory power of years of schooling and any of the concepts based on credentials is not clear *a priori*. Not even in those cases where the number of years is quite unequivocally linked to the educational categories, as in the United States, will the credentials necessarily have a lesser explanatory power when entered into a linear regression. This is the more the case where the relationship is other than linear and is thus better captured by education in categories which allow for a non-linear relationship. Moreover, the more likely it is that attendance at different kinds of schools and success in different kinds of examinations will correspond to the same number of years in school, the less likely is "years in school" to turn out as a good predictor.

When comparing results across nations a caution must be exercised: education is measured with different detail in the various countries. In the most detailed measure available for the countries studied, there are different numbers of educational categories. It is then clear that inter-country differences in the (relative) explanatory power of the different measures of education could result from this fact. Such differences could result from educational categories corresponding more closely to the entire span of years in school in one country than in another. In the same vein, inter-country differences in the explanatory power of the CASMIN scale might be due to the fact that in some countries the full scale could not be constructed on the base of the national educational scales measured in the questionnaires. Moreover, for some of the countries under investigation, there has not been an explicit scale worked out by the CASMIN project. In this case, we tried to reconstruct such a scale according to the inherent logic of the CASMIN approach. With the Political-Action approach we proceeded in an analogous way, as there are countries in our sample for which an explicit scale has not been developed. Of course, under these circumstances neither the CASMIN nor the Political-Action researchers could be held responsible for the results which might be basically due to our regrouping of the original educational categories.

The information on education in the data sets that we could use is far from perfect. For instance, in countries in which educational systems have changed over time and differ for different cohorts of respondents, this is scarcely reflected the data. Information on the way education has been administered— whether the respondent attended a day-time or evening school or whether respondents have been in private or public school—are absent in nearly all of the data sets. This is, unfortunately, common practice and in no way an idiosyncrasy of the data we use here.

Data

We found it extremely difficult to find data sets which fit the purpose of our analyses. We needed data which included both accurate measures of educational categories *and* years of schooling. Many studies include the former, but contain no comparable measure of the latter. For example, the British Social Attitudes surveys use "age of school-leaving" as a proxy which cannot meaningfully be compared with the measures we have for other countries. In addition, we also needed data sets in which a considerable number of the dependent variables were measured in comparable ways across countries. This restricted the analysis to a small number of countries. But even for this small sample we do not have comparable data on all variables we would have liked to analyze.

For the *United States* we use the General Social Survey (GSS, see Davis and Smith 1991) series which has been conducted annually since 1972 (with the exception of 1979 and 1981). The highly constant use of questions in these surveys allows us to base the analysis on the entire time span. Therefore, for some variables, prestige, cultural capital or income, we could use a large database. This enables us to study effects of education in greater detail for this country, like particularly the effects of "rare events" such as very low and very high numbers of years of schooling. Unfortunately this is not the case for the other data sets because comparable information is available in most cases only for one survey. For *West and East Germany* we relied mostly on the 1992 survey of the biennial (since 1980) Allgemeine Bevölkerungsumfrage der Sozialwissenschaften (ALLBUS, see Braun and Mohler 1991; Zentralarchiv and ZUMA 1993) series, but for *West Germany* we also took information from the ALLBUS 1986 (see Zentralarchiv and ZUMA 1986). The data from *Poland* came exclusively from the first Polish General Social Survey (PGSS; see Cichomski and Sawinski 1992) which was conducted in 1992. Finally, the data from *Hungary* were collected in 1992 as part of the Mobility Survey (see Róbert 1992) and the Social Inequality module of the International Social Survey Program (see Kolosi and Róbert 1992).

In the following we present effects of education controlled for by age of respondent/the cohort the respondent belongs to, and in the American case—

where we use the entire cumulative GSS file—also net of the year when the survey was conducted. If this were not done, the effect of education would necessarily be confounded by age and/or cohort and, thus, likely to be overestimated in some cases (e.g., attitudes towards gender roles) and perhaps even underestimated in others (e.g., income), given the bivariate relationships of the control variables with education and the dependent variables. We restrict the analyses to those respondents for whom information on both the highest educational degree and years of schooling is available. Otherwise, the different regressions might not only have been based on different numbers of cases but perhaps also on data of different quality. For the regression of income, we introduce a further restriction by selecting only full-time employed white males over 30 years of age in order to construct a more homogeneous sample.

Results

Table 2 presents means, standard deviations and the number of cases for the dependent variables.

Table 3 shows the *correlations between years of schooling and different measures based on education in categories*. For Germany, we are able to distinguish between two measures of education in categories. The first is based on general education only, and the second includes in addition vocational training, measured in great detail by a variety of items. While vocational training virtually does not exist in the United States in similar form, the pertinent information is included in the Hungarian and Polish education measures, though with less detail than in the German case. Any comparison of the amount of correlation or variance explained between the different countries has to take this into account.

Several general results can be derived from this table. First, the Political-Action scale has the smallest correlation with years of schooling in all of the countries. All other (more refined) categorical measures of education correlate very highly with years of schooling. Even if the measures for East Germany, Poland and Hungary have to be considered with some reservation (because these countries were not included in the Political-Action study and, thus, the measures had to be constructed by the authors), it is clear that collapsing the available information on education into three broad categories results in a considerable loss of information. Interestingly, the smallest correlation between credentials and years of schooling is found for the United States, and the highest for the two former socialist countries East Germany and Poland.[11]

Table 4 displays the percentages of *variance of the dependent variables explained by all educational dummies* in the single countries. The amount of variance explained differs systematically by the domain under investigation and, in part, also by country. It is obvious that the highest variance explained is for prestige, a variable intrinsically related to the concept of education.

Table 2. Mean, Standard Deviation and N for Dependent Variables

	United States			West-Germany			East-Germany			Poland			Hungary		
	Mean	Std. dev.	N	Mean	Std. dev.	N	Mean	Std. dev.	N	Mean	Std. dev.	N	Mean	Std. dev.	N
Gender-role Ideology	2.6	0.8	8393	2.5	0.9	2076	2.8	0.8	1035	2.1	0.6	1622	—	—	—
Motivational function of inequality	2.4	0.8	1527	2.1	0.7	1981	2.2	0.7	990	2.0	0.8	1599	2.5	0.8	1226
Power explanation of inequality	2.7	0.9	1485	2.4	0.9	1923	2.2	0.8	983	2.3	0.9	1517	3.2	0.9	1199
Political interest	2.2	0.9	1797	3.1	1.0	2094	3.0	1.1	1055	2.5	1.0	1637	—	—	—
Prestige	40.9	14.2	14741	41.7	11.2	1023	41.1	12.2	578	42.2	12.6	810	40.3	13.9	1360
Personal income	34421	23908	3571	3591	1709	362	1913	1173	174	2634	2174	354	16810	9357	506
Cultural Capital	5.9	2.2	12853	0.9	0.9	3025	—	—	—	—	—	—	0.5	0.8	2998

183

Table 3.   Correlations Between Years of Schooling
and Different Measures Based on Education in Categories

Years of schooling and:	U.S.	West-Germany	East-Germany	Poland	Hungary
Education in Categories	.87	.92	.96	.98	.92
Education in Categories incl. vocational training	—	.93	.96	—	—
CASMIN-scale	—	.92	.96	.98	.92
Political-Action scale	.85	.82	.84	.42	.85

Table 4.   Variance Explained (net of cohort and year of survey)
in Regression of Various Variables on All Educational Dummies

	U.S.	West-Germany		East-Germany		Hungary	Poland
		without voc. tr.	with voc tr.	without voc. tr.	with voc. tr.		
Gender-role Ideology	3.7	5.6	6.4	4.4	5.4	—	7.7
Motivational function of inequality	5.4	2.4	3.2	1.5	2.6	1.8	1.4
Power explanation of inequality	3.6	4.7	5.9	0.7	1.8	0.6	7.1
Political interest	6.9	8.0	11.2	10.5	14.7	—	17.6
Prestige	31.0	39.7	41.6	32.2	37.7	45.9	49.2
Personal income	14.0	18.1	21.1	6.0	32.6	30.3	12.8
Cultural Capital	25.2	35.6	36.4	—	—	28.8	—

Similar values are obtained for the variables which can be regarded as indicators of cultural capital, WORDSUM in the United States and the number of foreign languages spoken in Germany and Hungary. Comparatively little is explained for the attitudinal variables, gender role ideology and attitudes towards inequality. The values for income are on an intermediate level and show a large degree of variability across nations. For political interest we find a closer association with education than for the attitudinal variables included, but in most cases it correlates less with education than income (except for Poland and East Germany, when vocational training is ignored). In the different countries there are only very few deviances from these general patterns.

The distinction made in both Germanys between measures that include vocational training and measures that do not, shows that taking vocational training into account may be crucial. In both Germanys the additional inclusion of vocational training contributes to an increase in variance explained for all variables. The increase is small for the attitudinal variables and for the measure of cultural capital used for West Germany (number of foreign languages spoken), but substantial otherwise. In the post-socialist society of East Germany the determination of income by general education is still lower than in West Germany. This is not true for the measurement where dummies for different types of vocational training are included. In East Germany the two measures of education produce an enormous difference in variance explained for personal income. We suspect that the reason lies in the interplay between features of the former socialist society of the GDR and effects of the transformation process in the year in which the data was collected.

Let us only briefly speculate on the underlying processes that might generate differential explanatory powers of some of the dependent variables. The variables which are best accounted for by education are those which are most directly related to the process of education in terms of knowledge and abilities. In all three countries for which measures are available we find a strong association between education and the respective indicators of cultural capital. Even stronger is the association of education with occupational prestige. However, the theoretical and causal interpretation of the correlation with the prestige component of occupations is not unambiguous. It could well be that occupations receive a high prestige rating precisely because obtaining them presupposes a high level of the highly valued good of education. If measured by income, the status-attainment consequences of education appear much less dominant. If we are ready to discount prestige as being related too intrinsically to education, we can consider the knowledge and cultural-capital correlates of education as being more important compared to personal income.

Table 5 shows the *ratio of variance explained by years of schooling compared to all educational dummies* (with and without vocational training in the two Germanys). Thus, numbers below unity indicate that years of schooling explain less than the educational dummies; numbers above unity that years of schooling provide a better account of the dependent variables. In most of the cases, years of schooling turns out as a less reliable predictor than the concept of credentials.[12] However, as predicted, the American case shows that there are exceptions where years of schooling are an even better predictor. In the case of prestige, in all countries years of schooling and credentials are the most similar in explanatory power. This, however, does not extend to income. Thus, one can conclude that a larger number of years of schooling per se is not honored by the labor market if not associated with higher credentials, with the exception of the United States. Here, any additional year of schooling seems to be more or less directly transformed into better earning opportunities, something which is not the case in Europe.

Table 5. Ratio of Variance Explained by
Years of Schooling/All Education Dummies
(for Germany with and without vocational training)

	U.S.	West-Germany		East-Germany		Hungary	Poland
		without voc. tr.	*with voc tr.*	*without voc. tr.*	*with voc. tr.*		
Gender-role Ideology	1.14	0.82	0.72	0.91	0.74	—	0.77
Motivational function of inequality	0.87	0.67	0.50	0.73	0.42	0.94	0.43
Power explanation of inequality	0.69	0.55	0.44	0.43	0.17	0.17	0.59
Political interest	1.26	0.86	0.62	0.99	0.71	—	0.89
Prestige	0.97	0.91	0.87	0.98	0.83	0.88	0.90
Personal income	1.02	0.78	0.67	0.57	0.10	0.64	0.45
Cultural Capital	1.14	—	—	—	—	0.74	—

Any *regrouping of the credentials* leads to some reduction in variance explained, but the *CASMIN scale* (see Table 6) fares quite well. In all cases in which comparisons can be made the CASMIN categories exhibit a smaller decline in variance explained (compared to all educational dummies) than the measures available for years of schooling. As the CASMIN categories use at least some information on vocational training, it is understandable that in Germany they explain even more than all educational dummies excluding information on vocational education. In Poland, where the original educational categories measured in the survey are already relatively similar to the CASMIN categories, the difference is, with the exception of income, very small. As there is no information on vocational training for the United States, a CASMIN measure could not be constructed. Finally, in Hungary, the original educational categories correspond almost completely to the CASMIN scale and the resulting correlations would be identical by definition.

The *Political-Action regrouping* (see Table 7) leads to markedly poorer results in most countries. This does not apply to the United States where even this 3-category measure is quite satisfactory. The predictive value of the Political-Action approach largely depends on how the cut-off points selected match the form of the relationship between education and the variables which are to be explained. Thus, the fact that the Political-Action regrouping produces very different marginal distributions in different countries (e.g., in West Germany nearly twice as many respondents are in the highest educational

Table 6.   Ratio of Variance Explained by
CASMIN Categories/All Education Dummies
(for Germany with and without vocational training)

	U.S.	West-Germany		East-Germany		Hungary	Poland
		without voc. tr.	with voc tr.	without voc. tr.	with voc. tr.		
Gender role Ideology		1.04	0.91	0.98	0.80		0.97
Motivational function of inequality		1.08	0.81	1.00	0.58		0.93
Power explanation of inequality		1.00	0.80	1.57	0.61		0.96
Political interest		1.28	0.91	1.17	0.84		0.97
Prestige		1.04	0.99	1.06	0.91		1.00
Personal income		1.07	0.92	1.17	0.21		0.56
Cultural Capital		0.99	0.97	—	—		—

Table 7.   Ratio of Variance Explained by
3-Category Political-Action Classification/All Education Dummies
(for Germany with and without vocational training)

	U.S.	West-Germany		East-Germany		Hungary	Poland
		without voc. tr.	with voc tr.	without voc. tr.	with voc. tr.		
Gender role Ideology	0.95	0.64	0.56	0.61	0.50	—	0.38
Motivational function of inequality	1.00	0.83	0.63	0.87	0.50	0.89	0.64
Power explanation of inequality	0.89	0.49	0.39	1.00	0.39	0.17	0.38
Political interest	0.99	0.73	0.52	0.81	0.58	—	0.19
Prestige	0.90	0.60	0.57	0.84	0.72	0.80	0.29
Personal income	0.89	0.65	0.55	0.47	0.09	0.47	0.04
Cultural Capital	0.95	0.67	0.65	—	—	0.73	—

category of the Political-Action measure as in the United States), might contribute to variations in the strength of association.

We now move to the third objective of the empirical analysis: the examination of the form of the relationships between educational measures and other variables. We are interested in the specific elements of the educational process that produce effects on the dependent variables: Do we find a continuous growth curve, or are effects specifically connected to passing particular examinations or obtaining particular credentials? Hereby we restrict ourselves to the United States and Germany and we study only those variables for which the correlations are relatively high. Figures 1 and 2 show, for the *United States*, the *means of the dependent variables for different credentials and years of schooling* (adjusted by cohort and year of survey), respectively.

From Figure 1 we can conclude that different parts of the educational process have different effects for different dependent variables in the United States. For gender-role ideology and political interest, most of the change occurs when a High School diploma has been obtained and thereafter the trend tends to flatten out. For prestige, however, change continues virtually unabated beyond this point. The indicator of cultural capital displays two marked up-turns: when a High School diploma and when a Bachelor's degree have been achieved. The relationship with prestige and income appears to be quite linear over the entire span of educational degrees.

However, using years of schooling as measure of education (Figure 2) we find elements of non-linearity for income and prestige as well. For all variables systematic differences in the dependent variables are found only beyond a minimum of 4 to 6 years education. Furthermore, for prestige and the indicator of cultural capital (due to a markedly lower number of cases, the results for income should be regarded with caution), more change occurs between the year prior to which a given educational certificate is generally attained and the year when it is actually awarded. For these variables we observe higher rates of change especially between years 11 and 12 (when the High School diploma is usually reached) and 15 and 16 (when the Bachelor's degree is usually reached), though there is also significant change during the non-transitional years. However, for the other variables as much or, at least nearly as much change takes place during the non-transitional years, suggesting that the effect of education is not so much due to the attainment of a given certificate as such, but to exposure to the process of education. It should be noted that there is an alternative to this explanation which cannot be ruled out with the present data base: any change could also be due to the selection of participants. To give an example, the rise in the number of words recognized in the WORDSUM test, which can be observed between, say, years 12 and 13 (that is for those respondents who, after passing High School diploma, continued their education by attending Junior College for one—and only one year), does not necessarily reflect that this amount of knowledge was conferred on them during the first year of Junior College. It is as likely that this group had a higher level of language knowledge than those who eventually finished High School and then immediately left the educational system already at the time of the High School diploma, or that they were more efficient in increasing their knowledge in the years which followed their Junior College episode, that is after having left the educational system. All in all, both figures show that even in the United

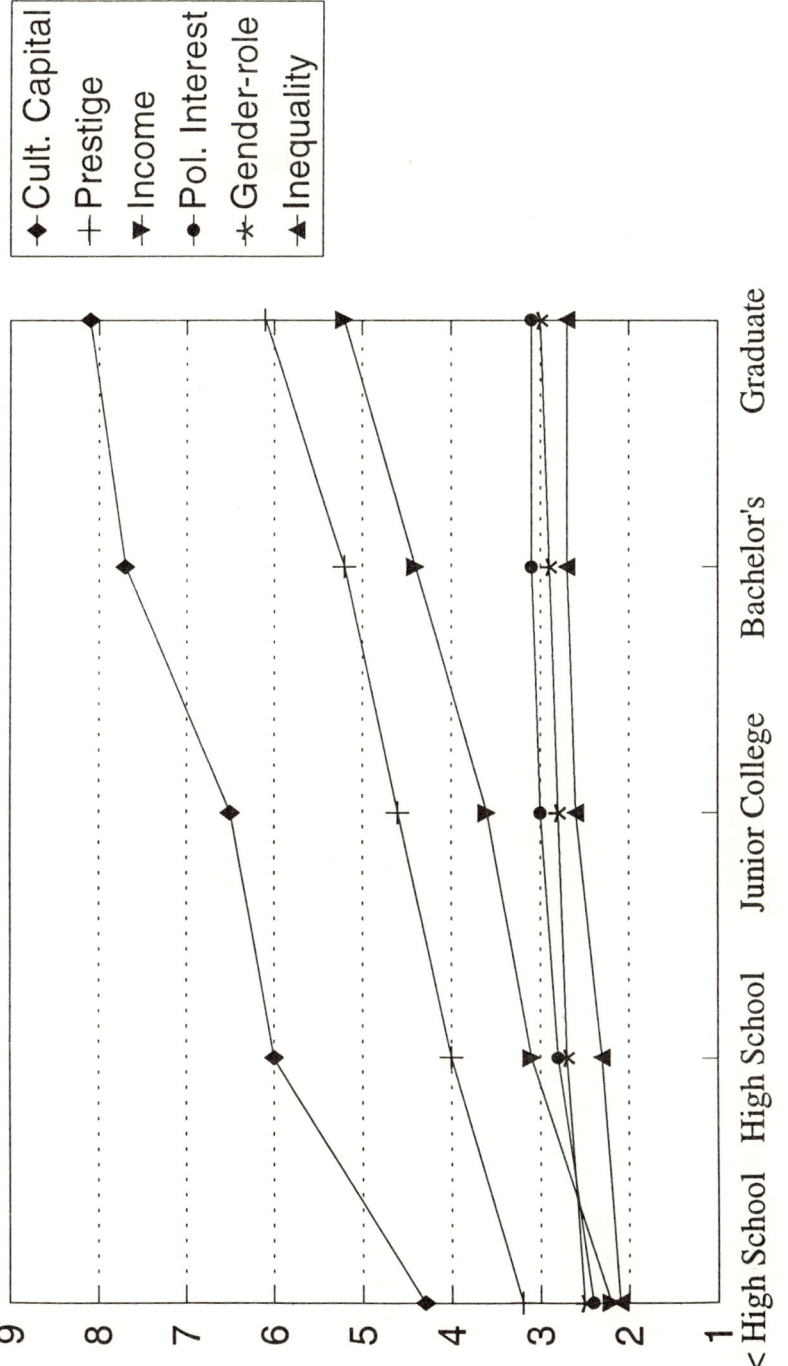

Legend (top right):
◆ Cult. Capital
+ Prestige
▼ Income
● Pol. Interest
✳ Gender-role
▲ Inequality

X-axis categories: < High School   High School   Junior College   Bachelor's   Graduate

Y-axis: 1 through 9

Figure 1. Adjusted Means for Various Variables Dependent on Highest Degree for the United States

189

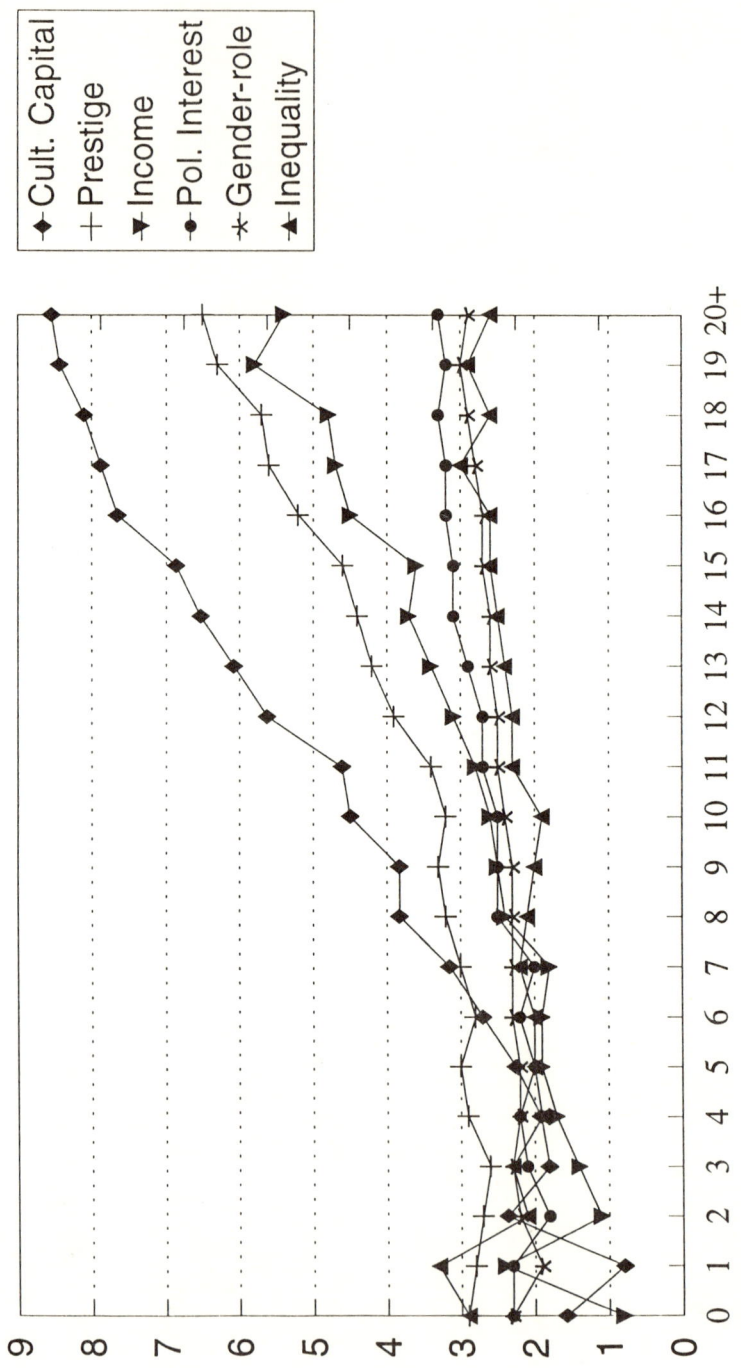

Legend:
♦ Cult. Capital
+ Prestige
▼ Income
● Pol. Interest
✳ Gender-role
▲ Inequality

Figure 2. Adjusted Means for Various Variables Dependent on Years of Schooling for the United States

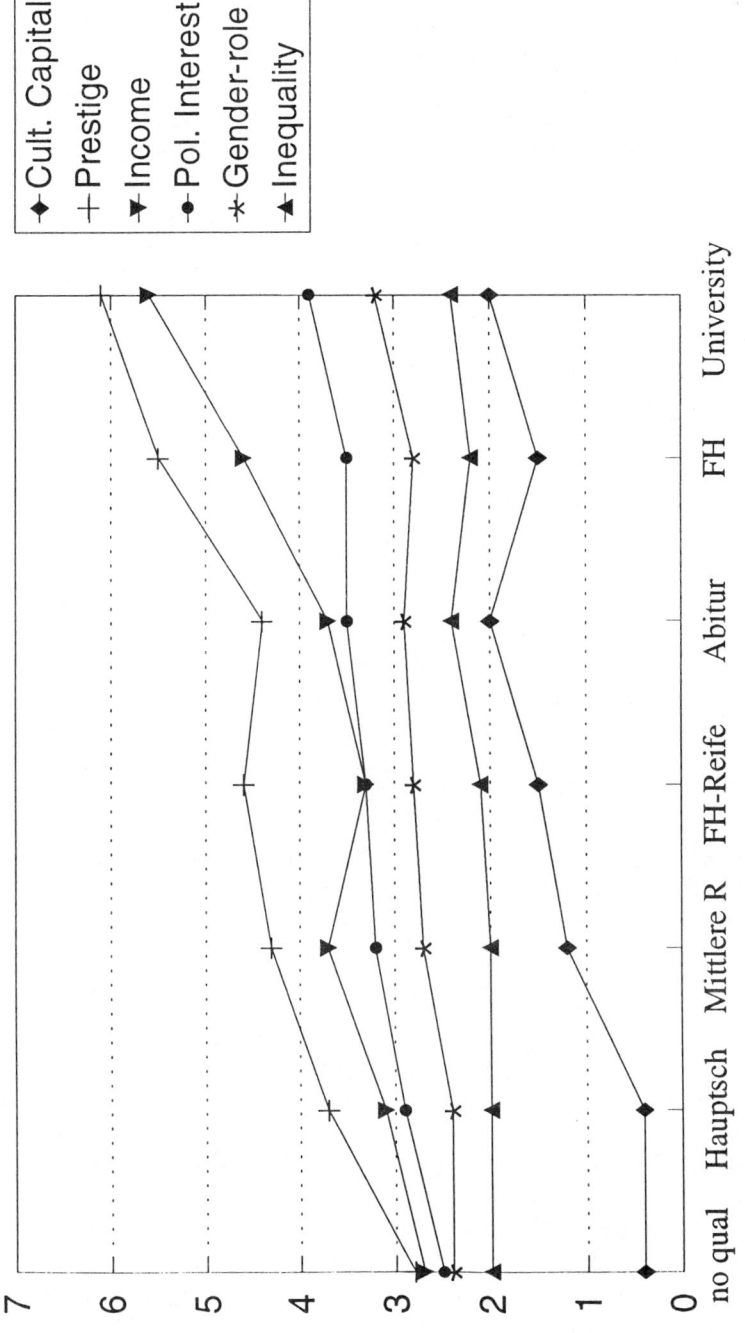

Figure 3. Adjusted Means for Various Variables Dependent on Highest Degree for West Germany

States elements of nonlinearity exist in the association between measures of educational attainment and those outcome variables with which the association is relatively strong (cultural capital and prestige). Reaching either the High School or the Bachelor's degree is associated with a higher change in the outcome variable than the average change found per year of schooling.

Due to the markedly smaller number of cases on which they are based, the corresponding figures for *West Germany* should be regarded with caution.

In clear contrast to the American case, we find that for West Germany the relationship between the indicator of cultural capital, prestige and income on the one hand, and educational categories on the other is much less linear (Figure 3). Income and prestige increase sharply through the *Mittlere Reife* level, and again for more than the *Abitur* level.

Knowledge of foreign languages is likely to reflect specifics of the curricula more strongly than the WORDSUM measure used in the United States such that two peculiarities of the German school system might be reflected in the data: The German "Gymnasium" has a special role in promoting the Humanities, and in the German universities only few students learn a new language (as a rule, they have already studied 2-3 foreign languages in the *Gymnasium*). For most of the cohorts studied here, foreign languages were not taught in the *Hauptschule*, but only in the courses that lead to the *Mittlere Reife*, the *Fachhochschulreife* and the *Abitur*. The growth curve for foreign languages spoken thus corresponds very closely to the emphasis given to learning foreign languages in different sections of the German educational system. Those having obtained a certificate from the *Fachhochschule* (special university) or the university have language scores equal to those of the educational levels required to enter the *Fachhochschule* (= *Fachhochschulreife*) and the university (= *Abitur*). While the irregularities in the growth curve make perfect sense, given the organization of learning experiences in the German educational system, the findings also assist in understanding why number of years of schooling has less predictive power in Germany than the United States for example.

CONCLUSIONS

In summary, education shows the highest impact on variables relating to various indicators of cultural capital, prestige and income. Correlations with ideological orientations are rather small while political interest shows an intermediate level of association with education. Although the size of the association varies across countries to some extent, the pattern described here is rather similar, at least in those countries investigated.

Switching from one measure of education to another proves to have consequences for the resulting *level* of association. Depending on the measurement of education the observed correlations between education and most other variables clearly vary in size. Generally, the *rank order in the level of association* between education and the various types of "consequences" of education investigated here (socialization effects, individual capacities, knowledge and returns in occupational prestige or income) remains rather similar for the different measurements of education, although the strength of association changes. The relative merits of the different measurements of education, however, clearly vary according to country. Since the pattern of association for the various types of variables is generally similar across countries, the consequences of using different measures of education seem to result from the different efficiencies of the various measures in capturing the essential elements that affect outcomes in various educational systems. In comparative research a measurement of education that is more congenial to the peculiarities of the educational system of one particular country than to those of other countries clearly privileges the potential explanatory power of education in the country whose educational system is more adequately grasped by the measure chosen. This is perhaps most clearly evident for years of schooling. While it seems to be the most powerful measure of education in the United States, it is a less reliable predictor of all dependent variables than earned degrees in all other countries studied.

All measurement devices which are based on collapsing the educational categories lead to some loss of predictive power. However, the CASMIN scale fares quite well. As exemplified by the German case, the inclusion of vocational qualifications in the CASMIN scale may be a crucial element for an adequate account of effects of education, in particular in countries in which vocational orientated study programs are an important segment of educational provisions. The three-category scale from the Political-Action project generally produced considerably lower correlations. The American case, however, shows that even a three-category scale may reflect a large extent of the potential association if the cutting-points happen to grasp the crucial differentiations in the various systems of education. Yet, for comparative purposes, on the basis of only a small number of categories it will be difficult to construct a theoretically sensible schema with maximum homogeneity within categories and heterogeneity between categories in a similar way for countries with different educational systems. The large variability of results across countries that we found for the three-category scales is an indication of this problem.

Our findings also indicate that we have a long way to go before a satisfactory multi-purpose measurement of education that is comparable for a large number of countries may be established. It may even be impossible to find such a measure. Since, particularly in Europe, educational systems have changed considerably in the postwar period and are still changing, measurement devices have to adapt to these changes. For the researcher doing secondary analysis it is therefore highly advisable to study carefully which measurement of education is the most viable given the specifics of his or her substantial problem and data. In many cases it may even be advisable not to rely on a comparable measurement in terms of strictly comparable procedures or a comparable set of categories. It may, indeed, be more sensible to use for each single country that measurement which explains most of the variance for the particular country in question. This strategy would be appropriate, for instance, if education is mainly used as a control variable and if the researcher's interest is to explain as much variance of a phenomenon by education before other variables are introduced into the model. For using education in a sensible way for comparative studies much could be gained, if knowledge on the crucial educational distinctions for various types of dependent variables were available for a large number of countries.

With regard to the collection of new data, it seems to be necessary to gather educational data in considerable detail, on general education as well as on vocational training, and where possible additional information such as type of curricula and obtained certificates, private vs. public school, and so forth, if available. The more information is available from the outset, the smaller is the chance that important distinctions will be overlooked, and the more likely it is that functionally equivalent measures necessary for comparative purposes can be derived. Years of schooling should not be used as an easily measurable substitute for more complex measures. On the contrary, it might make more sense to reconstruct years of schooling from the information given by education in categories. If years of schooling are collected in the surveys at all, every effort should be made regarding a careful and unambiguous measurement, as for instance by measuring the classes passed in various types of schools.

APPENDIX

Education in Categories

	United States	West Germany	East Germany	Poland	Hungary
(1)	Less than High School	No formal education certificate	No formal education certificate	Incomplete elementary	Less than 8 classes
(2)	High School	Lower secondary school certificate (Hauptschule)	8 or 9 classes of Polytechnic High School	Elementary	8 classes (for respondents born before 1940: 6 classes)
(3)	Associate/Junior College	Intermediate secondary school certificate (Mittlere Reife)	10 classes of Polytechnic High School	Basic vocational	Technical training school, vocational school

(continued)

Education in Categories (continued)

	United States	West Germany	East Germany	Poland	Hungary
(4)	Bachelor's	Specialized Abitur (Fachhochschul-reife)	Specialized Abitur (Fachhochschul-reife)	Incomplete secondary	Vocational/technical high school
(5)	Graduate	Abitur	12 classes of Extended High School	Secondary general	Finished gymnasium or other high school
(6)		Special university degree (Fachhochschul-abschluß)	Special university degree (Fachhochschul-abschluß)	Secondary vocational	College or technical college
(7)		University degree	University degree	Post secondary	University degree
(8)				Incomplete higher	
(9)				Complete higher	

Years of Schooling

While the German, Polish and Hungarian surveys simply include the number of years in the respective variables, the American survey distinguishes: No formal schooling, 1st through 12th grade of High School, 1 through 8 years of College.

CASMIN Classification*

	West Germany	East Germany	Poland	Hungary
(1)	No formal education certificate	No formal education certificate	Incomplete elementary	Less than 8 classes
(2)	Lower secondary certificate without apprenticeship	8 or 9 classes of Polytechnic High School	Elementary	8 classes (for respondents born before 1940: 6 classes)
(3)	Vocational schools with apprenticeship	Vocational schools with apprenticeship	Basic vocational	Technical training school, vocational school
(4)	Professional schools	Professional schools	Incomplete secondary	Vocational/technical high school
(5)	Intermediate secondary school certificate (Mittlere Reife)	10 classes of Polytechnic High School	Secondary general and secondary vocational	Finished gymnasium or other high school

(continued)

CASMIN Classification (continued)*

	West Germany	East Germany	Poland	Hungary
(6)	Abitur	12 classes of Extended High School	Post secondary and incomplete higher	College or technical college
(7)	Special university degree (Fachhochschul-abschluß)	Special university degree (Fachhochschul-abschluß)	Complete higher	University degree
(8)	University degree	University degree		

Note: * United States: not available.

Political-Action 3-Category Classification

	United States	West Germany	East Germany	Poland	Hungary
(1)	Less than High School	Primary School or less (Haupt-schule mit oder ohne Abschluß)	Primary School or less (less than 10 years of Poly-technic High School)	Incomplete or complete elementary	8 classes or less
(2)	High School	Occupational Training School (Berufsschule)	Occupational Training School (Berufsschule)	Basic vocational or incomplete secondary	Technical training school, vocational school
(3)	Post-High School education	Middle School or Occupational Training School completed (Mittlere Reife) or more	10 classes of Polytechnic High School or Occu-pational Training School or more	Secondary general or more	Vocational/tech-nical high school or more

THE DEPENDENT VARIABLES

Gender-Role Ideology

Was constructed as an average of the valid responses to the following:

"It is more important for a wife to help her husband's career than to have one herself."

"It is much better for everyone involved if the man is the achiever outside the home and the woman takes care of the home and the family."

Response categories were "strongly agree," "agree," "disagree" and "strongly disagree." High values indicate an egalitarian stance.

Motivational Function of Inequality

Was constructed as an average of the valid responses to the following:

"People would not want to take extra responsibility at work unless they were paid extra for it."

"Workers would not bother to get skills and qualifications unless they were paid extra for having them."

"No one would study for years to become a lawyer or doctor unless they expected to earn a lot more than ordinary workers."

Response categories were "strongly agree," "agree," "neither agree nor disagree," "disagree" and "strongly disagree." High values indicate a skeptical attitude with regard to a motivational function of inequality.

Power Explanation of Inequality

Was constructed as an average of the valid responses to the following:

"Inequality continues to exist because it benefits the rich and powerful."

"Inequality continues to exist because ordinary people don't join together to get rid of it."

Response categories were "strongly agree," "agree," "neither agree nor disagree," "disagree" and "strongly disagree." High values indicate a skeptical attitude with regard to a power explanation of inequality.

Political Interest

Was measured slightly differently in the single countries. It was recoded such that high values show high political interest.

Prestige

Treiman prestige scores were used for all countries.

Income

United States:	personal yearly gross income in constant Dollars (base = 1986).
Germany:	personal monthly net income in Deutschmarks.
Poland:	personal monthly income in 1.000 Zlotys (not specified whether net or gross income, respondents were assumed to refer to net income).
Hungary:	personal monthly net income in Forint.

Cultural Capital

United States
The WORDSUM measure we use consists of a multiple choice test of 10 rarely used English words. See also Alwin (1989).

West Germany
Number of foreign languages the respondent pretends to speak (maximum was set at 4 languages).

Hungary
Number of foreign languages the respondent claims to speak out of a list of 4 languages (English, German, French, Russian).

NOTES

1.   For instance, motivational factors or intelligence may at the same time affect school success and the acquisition of knowledge and other behavior outside schooling.

2.   See also Kerckhoff's argument concerning the differences among the various options within American High Schools, the effects of which are not discussed because nobody has really studied them.

3.   Consider also the fact that a high number of school years will not be interpreted primarily as a long duration of schooling. Rather the implication is that a person with many years of schooling has probably obtained university training and an academic degree.

4.   The more the labor force moves across the borders of different European countries the greater the need is felt for equating the educational attainments in different educational systems. As a point in case, the bureaucracies of the European Community need rules for deciding which educational credentials entitle employees from different nationalities to specific job levels in the bureaucratic hierarchy. The classification developed under these concerns may not only reflect differences in educational qualifications obtained but also the more or less successful struggle for occupational claims among certificate holders of different countries interested in a profitable rating of their qualification.

5.   The German case may be taken as an illustration. In the recent version of the ISCED scheme several different kinds of vocational education count as ISCED 3-type education. In this way persons who have obtained a manual apprenticeship after completion of the lowest stage of compulsory education are equated with persons who have obtained the *Abitur* and are entitled to enter university education. It is very unlikely that a researcher who understands the German context would equate these very different courses of education. But this is not a purely German idiosyncrasy; comparable differences between general and vocational education exist in many countries (for France, see e.g., Brauns 1996). Similar serious problems of equivalence occur at the tertiary level. ISCED, for instance, classifies courses for qualified technicians or for master-craftsmen as ISCED category 5, that is as qualifications beyond the *Abitur*-level. ISCED category 6 also appears to be a rather heterogeneous category. In Germany as well as in many other countries, there is a significant difference between degrees obtained from universities and those obtained from polytechnics, technical colleges or other institutions with a more practical rather than scientifically oriented training. Both types of qualifications, however, are grouped together in ISCED category 6.

6. Because of close links of this elementary level of education with the legal prescriptions of compulsory schooling we also call it *compulsory schooling.*

7. Whereas an intermediate exam alone suffices as a criterion, lengthened educational term and selective school type usually had to be present in combination in order to be classified as part of the intermediate level.

8. In the Federal Republic of Germany (and other German speaking countries), the existence of the apprenticeship system provides a clear separation between general education and vocational training. In other countries, these two types of education are more closely linked. In terms of historical development, a trend is found in most countries towards a greater degree of vocational training within schools and towards its linkage to elements of general education. The increasing number of technical schools, vocational technical schools, schools of commerce, technical colleges and so forth, is an indication of this development.

9. Unfortunately, the measures of cultural capital we could obtain are quite different in the different countries. For both West Germany and Hungary we have a subjective measure relating to the number of foreign languages a respondent pretends to speak, while for the United States we have an objective measure regarding proficiency in the English language. However, we find the knowledge component of education too important to leave out on the grounds of less than perfect comparability of the indicators. Moreover, as the empirical results reported below will show, the indicators in the three countries do not behave too differently to allow for meaningful comparisons.

10. It is an entirely different question whether it had not been more adequate to include vocational training as the measure of years of schooling in Germany in the first place. However, as years of schooling are actually measured, it captures something different in Germany compared to the other countries. And, of course, comparing the explanatory power of years of schooling with the educational categories including vocational training is thus more problematic in Germany.

11. It could be that the more centrally structured and controlled system of education in the socialist countries is responsible for the higher correlation between years of schooling and obtained certificates in these societies.

12. For both Germanys the more precisely interpretable figures are those in the columns without vocational training because the measurement of years of schooling in Germany does not include time spent in apprenticeships.

REFERENCES

Alwin, D.F. 1989. *Family Size and Cohort Differences in Vocabulary Knowledge in the United States Adult Population.* Chicago: NORC.

Archer, M.S. 1979. *Social Origins of Educational Systems.* London: Sage.

Arrow, K.J. 1973. "Higher Education as a Filter." *Journal of Public Economics* 2: 193-216.

Barnes, S.H., M. Kaase et al. (Eds.). 1979. *Political Action: Mass Participation in Five Western Democracies.* Beverly Hills, CA: Sage.

Blau, P.M., and O.D. Duncan. 1967. *The American Occupational Structure.* New York: Wiley.

Boli, J., F.O. Ramirez, and J. Meyer. 1985. "Explaining the Origins and Expansion of Mass Education." *Comparative Education Review* 29: 145-170.

Bourdieu, P., and J.C. Passeron. 1970. *La réproduction. Éléments pour une théorie du système d'enseignement* [The Reproduction. Elements for a Theory of the System of Teaching]. Paris: Minuit.

Bowles, S., and H. Gintis. 1976. *Schooling in Capitalist America: Educational Reform and the Contradictions of Economic Life.* New York: Basic Books.

Braun, M. 1994. "The International Social Survey Programme (ISSP)." In *Social Statistics and Social Reporting in and for Europe*, edited by Peter Flora et al. Bonn: Informationszentrum Sozialwissenschaften.

Braun, M., and P.P. Mohler. 1991. "Die allgemeine Bevölkerungsumfrage der Sozialwissen-schaften (ALLBUS): Rückblick und Ausblick in die neunziger Jahre [The German General Social Survey: History and Perspectives for the 90ies]." *ZUMA-Nachrichten* 29: 7-28.

Brauns, H. 1996. *Bildungsungleichheit in Frankreich. Eine empirische Untersuchung zum Wandel herkunfts- und geschlechtsspezifischen Bildungsverhaltens* [Educational Inequality in France. An Empirical Study on the Change of Origin- and Gender-based Educational Behavior]. Dissertation, Universität Mannheim, Fakultät für Sozialwissenschaften.

Cichomski, B., and Z. Sawinski. 1992. *Polish General Social Survey 1992, Codebook for 1992 Survey*. Warsaw: Institute for Social Studies, University of Warsaw.

Coleman, J.S., and T. Hoffer. 1987. *Public and Private High Schools*. New York: Basic Books.

Collins, R. 1979. *The Credential Society. An Historical Sociology of Education and Stratification*. New York: Academic Press.

Dahrendorf, R. 1956. "Industrielle Fertigkeiten und soziale Schichtung [Industrial Skills and Social Stratification]." *Kölner Zeitschrift für Soziologie und Sozialpsychologie* 8: 540-568.

Davis, J.A., and R. Jowell. 1990. "Measuring National Differences: An Introduction to the International Social Survey Programme (ISSP)." In *British Social Attitudes: Special International Report*, edited by Roger Jowell, Sharon Witherspoon and Lindsay Brook. Aldershot: Gower.

Davis, J.A., and T.W. Smith. 1991. *General Social Surveys, 1972-1991: Cumulative Codebook*. Chicago: National Opinion Research Center.

Fend, H., W. Knörzer, W. Nagl, W. Specht, and R. Váth-Szusdziara. 1976. *Sozialisationseffekte in der Schule* [Socialization Effects in Schools]. Weinheim und Basel: Beltz.

Haller, M., W. König, P. Krause, and K. Kurz. 1985. "Patterns of Career Mobility and Structural Positions in Advanced Capitalist Societies: A Comparison of Men in Austria, France and the United States." *American Sociological Review* 50: 579-603.

Hyman, H.H., C.R. Wright, and J.S. Reed. 1975. *The Enduring Effects of Education*. Chicago, London: University of Chicago Press.

Inglehart, R. 1979. "Political Action: The Impact of Values, Cognitive Level and Social Background." In *Political Action: Mass Participation in five Western Democracies*, edited by Samuel H. Barnes, Max Kaase et al. Beverly Hills, CA: Sage.

Kolosi, T., and P. Róbert. 1992. *TARKI-ISSP Social Inequality Survey*. Budapest: TARKI.

König, W., P. Lüttinger, and W. Müller. 1988. "Comparative Analysis of the Development and Structure of Educational Systems: Methodological Foundations and the Construction of a Comparative Educational Scale." Mannheim: CASMIN Working Paper Nr. 12, Institut für Sozialwissenschaften.

König, W., and W. Müller. 1986. "Educational Systems and Labour Markets as Determinants of Worklife Mobility in France and West Germany: A Comparison of Men's Career Mobility, 1965-1970." *European Sociological Review* 2: 73-96.

Müller, W., and W. Karle. 1993. "Social Selection in Educational Systems in Europe." *European Sociological Review* 9: 1-23.

Müller, W., P. Lüttinger, W. König and W. Karle. 1989. "Class and Education in Industrial Nations." *International Journal of Sociology* 19: 3-39.

Müller, W., Y. Shavit, and P. Ucem. 1996. "The Institutional Imbeddedness of the Stratification Process: A Comparative Study of Qualifications and Occupations in 13 Countries." Paper prepared for the thematic session on Curriculum and Inequality in a Cross-National Perspective, 1996 Meetings of the American Sociological Association. Ms. University of Mannheim and European University Institute, Florence.

OECD. 1995. *OECD Education Statistics 1985-1992*. Paris: Organization for Economic Co-operation and Development.

Peschar, J.L. 1984. "Neuere Entwicklungen in der vergleichenden Sozialstrukturforschung [New Developments in Comparative Social Structure Research]." In *International vergleichende Sozialstrukturforschung* [Internationally Comparative Social Structure Research], edited by Jules L. Peschar and Manfred Niessen. Frankfurt, New York: Campus.

Przeworski, A., and H. Teune. 1970. *The Logic of Comparative Social Inquiry.* New York: Wiley.

Ringer, F.K. 1979. *Education and Society in Modern Europe.* Bloomington: Indiana University Press.

Róbert, P. 1992. *TARKI-Mobility Survey.* Budapest: TARKI.

Rubinson, R. 1986. "Class Formation, Politics and Institutions: Schooling in the United States." *American Journal of Sociology* 92: 519-548.

Smith, H.L., and M. Garnier. 1986. "Association between Background and Educational Attainment in France." *Sociological Methods and Research* 14: 317-344.

Sorensen, A. 1983. "Processes of Allocation to Open and Closed Positions in Social Structure." *Zeitschrift für Soziologie* 3: 203-224.

Spilerman, S., and T. Lunde. 1991. "Features of Educational Attainment and Job Promotion Prospects." *American Journal of Sociology* 97: 689-720.

Thurow, L. 1976. *Generating Inequality. Mechanisms of Distribution in the U.S.* New York: Basic Books.

Treiman, D.J., and K. Terell. 1975. "Status Attainment in the United States and Great Britain." *American Journal of Sociology* 81: 563-583.

Wanner, R.A. 1986. "Educational Inequality: Trends in Twentieth-Century Canada and the United States." In *Comparative Social Research, Vol.9*, edited by R.F. Tomasson. London: JAI Press.

Weber, M. 1956. *Wirtschaft und Gesellschaft.* Tübingen: Mohr.

Zentralarchiv und ZUMA. 1986. *Allgemeine Bevölkerungsumfrage der Sozialwissenschaften, ALLBUS 1986, Codebook ZA-No. 1500* [German General Social Survey 1986 Codebook]. Köln: Zentralarchiv.

_____. 1993. *Allgemeine Bevölkerungsumfrage der Sozialwissenschaften, ALLBUS 1992, Codebook ZA-No. 2140* [German General Social Survey 1992 Codebook]. Köln: Zentralarchiv.

NOTES ON A COMPARATIVE POLITICAL ECONOMY OF LIFE COURSES

Karl Ulrich Mayer

ABSTRACT

This chapter addresses the problems arising in cross-national comparisons of life courses. The study of life courses is one of the most rapidly developing areas of research in the social sciences. Life courses are seen as important outcomes and indicators of current major changes in advanced capitalist societies. Whereas within-country modeling of single life transitions is by now well established, especially since the use of event-history-analysis, their embeddedness in institutional contexts is not well-understood. Cross-national comparisons of life courses are therefore an important research agenda. However, as the paper tries to argue, they also pose special difficulties. It is necessary to combine individual-level dynamic models with institutional explanations. The logic of both approaches and their possible linkages are being discussed.

INTRODUCTION

The study of life courses has become one of the most rapidly developing areas of research in the social sciences (Mayer 1990). The new opportunities created

Comparative Social Research, Volume 16, pages 203-226.
Copyright © 1997 by JAI Press Inc.
All rights of reproduction in any form reserved.
ISBN: 0-7623-0250-X

by the availability of data from longitudinal surveys, high-speed computers and of powerful statistical tools (Blossfeld, Hamerle, and Mayer 1989; Blossfeld and Rohwer 1995) may be one source of this development. More important, however, is the expectation that by means of life course studies generic current changes of modern societies can be depicted and understood most adequately. For instance, an increasing disorderliness in both family and working lives is seen as the outcome of educational expansion and economic restructuring (Buchmann 1989; Huinink 1995). Demographic aging is seen as both a cause and an opportunity to introduce more flexible life-time schedules (Mayer 1994; Riley, Kahn, and Foner 1994). Social policies are more and more conceived of as either effective premedial or unintentional interventions into the life course rather than as a means alleviating ills after they have occured (Allmendinger 1994). Also, the current attacks on the welfare state are feared to undermine the security and stability of work life trajectories and family lives. Some observers even claim that class politics are being replaced by "chrono-politics," that is politics which are articulated by or addressed to groups defined by their gender and stage in the life course rather than their class membership (Hernes 1987).

In many of these substantive areas a connection is being assumed between certain institutional conditions on the macrolevel of societies, that is their political economy, on the one hand and specific life course patterns on the other hand. To explicate and test such relationships obviously cross-national comparisons are called for. However, so far both grand and middle range theories have been almost exclusively couched in terms of general changes of modern societies as such rather than differences between varying political economies (Anderson 1985; Buchmann 1989; Mayer and Müller 1989). And even where exemplary empirical comparisons have been conducted (see e.g., Blossfeld 1995), little attention has been paid to which differences between societies should be expected to lead in which manner to life course outcomes. One reason for this kind of "misplaced universalism" might lie in the fact that sociological and economic life course analysis still has the old touch of "life cycle" and "human development" where the anthropological fundamentals and communalities of human lives are stressed in contrast to socio-historical variation.

The purpose of this paper is to explore the logic of cross-national research on life course patterns. The first question I should like to address is whether such comparisons which by nature would have to include both macro- and microfoundations are at all feasible and likely to be fruitful. The second question I would like to raise is that if and to the extent both feasibility and fecundity can be affirmed which theoretical and methodical assumptions must be fulfilled for such a research program to succeed. In this sense the paper has the character of "prologemona." The reader should therefore neither expect systematic and/or conclusive empirical findings nor an elaborated theory.

The title of this chapter suggests five assumptions: (1) that life course patterns vary systematically between societies of different types; (2) that life course patterns are influenced by "political economies," that is, by the specific relationships between capital, state and labor in given societies; (3) that there is a causal relationship between the institutional and systemic structure of a society as a whole and individual life courses; (4) that the macro-level is a rich source of explanations for observed life course patterns, (and probably vice versa); and finally, (5) that life courses as empirical variable clusters are amenable data for societal comparisons. Each of these five assumptions seems to me in need of scrutiny.

I will proceed in four steps. First (in the second section), using a particular life course transition, I would like to illustrate some problems and questions attendant in making cross-national comparisons. My example will be the transition into a nursing home in old age. This selection may at first be surprising to the reader, since most life course research so far has concentrated on transitions to adulthood. I have chosen this example primarily for didactic reasons. It is, on the one hand, less complex than, for example, schooling trajectories or employment histories. On the other hand, both good data on cross-national variation and good macrosociological theory-building are available. Second (in the third section), I would like to consider the problems of cross-national comparisons if we start from processes at the microlevel. In this context I will discuss how to conceptualize the dependent variable—life course patterns—and how explanatory factors close to the microlevel can be distinguished and how tractable they are for comparisons on the national level. Third (in the fourth section), I concentrate on problems which arise in cross-national comparisons of life courses if we start from the macrolevel. Here the most eminent issue is which conceptual tools are available in the literature to capture distinctions in the political economy of current-day societies and how suitable such distinctions are for explaining variations in life-course patterns. Although I conclude both the third and four sections with rather cautious and skeptical expectations in regard to the potential and feasibility of cross-national life-course comparisons, in the final section I will proceed in a more constructive manner. There, I will develop two contrasting ideal types as examples for showing how the explanatory linkages between macro-conditions and life course regimes might be construed.

MICRO-PROCESSES AND MACRO-CONFIGURATIONS: THE TRANSITION INTO A NURSING HOME

In this section one specific life course transition—the transition into a nursing home—will be used to illustrate how differential conditions at the microlevel and the macrolevel might account for variations in a fairly simple type of a

Table 1. Sources of Assistance and Care in Old Age

Sources	With Children in Berlin		Without Children in Berlin	
	All %	Only Private Households %	All %	Only Private Households %
Children	**7.5**	8.7	—	—
Other Kin	2.9	3.4	0.9	1.6
Informal Non-Kin	6.9	8.0	9.6	16.1
Professional Help	17.9	20.7	25.0	41.9
No Help, Living Alone	28.8	33.6	22.2	37.3
Nursing Home	**14.2**	—	**40.3**	—
Living with Kin in Household	**30.9**	33.2	**6.7**	11.6
Care or Assistance by Kin or Living with Kin in Household	37.6	41.0	7.7	13.5

Source: Berlin Aging Study—Mayer and Wagner (1996), Linden and Gilberg (1996), Gilberg (1997).

rate of transition, that is, a transition which usually consists of one single event and is non-reversible. It will become obvious that the explanatory factors which suggest themselves when we start from the processes at the microlevel are quite different from those which suggest themselves when we start at the macrolevel of national societies. It will further become apparent that a straightforward solution to the problem of the micro-macro linkage presents itself only if differences between societies are tantamount to differences in the aggregative features of microconditions. The didactic "catch-22" of our example of the nursing home transition might be seen in the fact that here this solution does not seem to work out.

Table 1, based on results from the Berlin Aging Study (Mayer and Baltes 1996), reports the proportion among the elderly in need of assistance and care that do not receive any type of care whatsoever and the proportion among the elderly living in nursing homes. For both fiscal and ideological reasons, the discussion in the Federal Republic has been focused on how much of care and assistance is provided by family members and what will happen when the proportion of the population with no children increases and when more daughters or daughters-in-law are gainfully employed.

Our numbers indicate that for the elderly living apart from other family members, children generally assume only a very small part of the everyday care responsibilities. It does not seem to make a difference where the children live. The proportion of those who do not receive care is approximately the same, irrespective of whether the children live in Berlin or not. These two groups differ, however, in the proportion of those who live in nursing homes (40% vs. 14%) and those who live with family members in the household. (7% vs. 31%) (Mayer and Wagner 1996).

When we look more carefully, we see that the deciding factor for whether one goes into a nursing home is not whether one has children or not, or if the children live close by, but rather whether one has a partner or spouse and if that partner is female. The transition into a home affects mainly women over 85 years old, who are single, divorced or widowed (Gilberg 1997).

In order to compare transition rates into a nursing home between countries, one would—on the basis of the above findings—be led to look for differences in rates of marriage, parenthood, and cohabitation or co-residence among older people. One would also want to know how the female employment rates and the age of children differ, in order to assess the informal provision potential. Ideally, one would like to also have information on the norms for the parent-child relationship, particulary those for the parent-daughter/daughter-in-law relationship, in order to assess the gaps between potential and probable care. Whether parents, as they get older, expect to be looked after by their children (more than the majority of parents in the Berlin Aging Study expect this, see Lang 1994), or whether, in the case of Japanese first-born sons, they are expected to move back into the parental home (Koyano 1995), appears to be crucial information for understanding differential transition rates to nursing homes.

Information about that what we really want to understand, namely nursing home transition rates as age-specific estimates of the likelihood of transitions given a variable population at risk, does not exist for either the Federal Republic or for other countries. What usually is available are only prevalence rates, that is, the proportion of the aging population and the relevant sub-groups who at a particular point in time find themselves in a home. In West Berlin, for example, the prevalence rate is approximately 6 percent of those over 70 years old.

It is only recently that internationally comparable data on the number of beds or places available in nursing homes in proportion to the size of the elderly population over 65 have been published (Table 2 taken from Alber 1995, p. 283). In the Netherlands, it is 12 percent, in Great Britain 11 percent, for West Germany, France and Ireland 5 percent, for Italy, Portugal and Spain 2 percent, and half a percent for Greece. We may ask ourselves, like Alber, how we can understand these differences.

The lower percentages for the southern European countries seem to confirm our expectations that number of children and family values, as well as size of the agrarian sector, all play a role. But how does Ireland fit in? The high quota for Great Britain leads us to assume that the female employment rate is significant. However, the higher values in the Netherlands (with a very low female employment rate) and the lower values for France (with a higher female employment rate but roughly the same nursing home quota as Germany) are contradictory. Alber measures care potential with an indicator which compares the number of women between the ages of 45 and 69 years old with persons

Table 2.   Places in Old Age Nursing
Care Homes per 100 Inhabitants,
Age 65 and Above

Netherlands	12.3
Denmark	10.6
United Kingdom	10.0
Luxemburg	7.8
Belgium	6.6
Federal Republic of Germany	5.4
France	5.1
Ireland	5.0
Italy	2.3
Portugal	2.0
Spain	2.0
Greece	0.5

Source: Alber (1995).

over 70, and size and intensity of the problem with the proportion of the elderly population. Variations in these indicators likewise do not account for the observed (country) rank ordering of the number of places available in nursing homes.

The supply of nursing home places thus can clearly not be explained as a function of pure demographic demand. The political test for the relative strength of the welfare state proves likewise negative. Neither the degree of unionization nor the proportion of social democratic votes between 1979 and 1989 correspond to the rank ordering of places available in nursing homes.

Alber concludes that institutional and organizational differences in the policies for the elderly are responsible for the variation in the number of places in nursing homes: the organizational base (the state/local communities/the church or independent associations), the form of financing (covered cost dependent vs. need dependent) and the form of regulation (central vs. federal). The available domestic help is no more helpful an explanation, since this care is more likely to function as an addition to nursing homes, not as a replacement or substitute. One has to conclude, therefore, that it is the historical reconstruction of the political functioning of various welfare states and of particular social policies which leads to relatively conclusive interpretations of the observed national differences.

In the case of the Netherlands, the construction of nursing homes was originally a reaction to the need for more housing. The subsequent growth was supported by independent welfare associations, and later by nursing insurance (Pflegeversicherung), by the rising responsibility and strength of the central state through the decline of the religious political parties and last but not least, by the revenues generated by the national gas resources. In the Federal

Republic, however, competition between independent associations and state based institutions as well as traditional forms of financing via the local community (Sozialhilfe) and statutory health insurance limited the expansion of nursing home places (Alber 1995, pp. 286-290).

Financial regulations can also influence transition rates into nursing homes not only by controlling availability but also by regulating demand for places in nursing homes. An essential factor in explaining national differences might also be whether or not home ownership and financial assets of older people can be enlisted to finance the costs of living in a nursing home. Children's tendency to have their parents or parents-in-law cared for and looked after in a nursing home will also thus be constrained by their concerns about having to renounce their inheritance of the house. This brings us back to the Berlin Aging Study. On the individual level, there are clear socioeconomic differences in the probability of transitioning into a nursing home. Elderly people with higher incomes are, in comparison, less frequently found in nursing homes. They remain in their own homes or apartments and are looked after by professional services. The proportion of semi-skilled and unskilled workers moving into nursing homes is also lower. They relatively more often live together with their children (Mayer and Wagner 1996; Linden et al. 1996; Gilberg 1997).

Our example of the transition to a nursing home illustrates, then, that for given life course transitions there are not only fairly complex explanatory stories to tell on the level of individuals, households and families, but partly additional explanatory stories on the level of local and national communities. For the purpose of our discussion here we might call the explanatory factors on the individual and group level "proximal" causes and the explanatory factors on the national level "distal" causes. To provide an adequate account of cross-national variations forces one to specify causal models not only on both levels, but also on the detailed interchanges between both levels. In some instances it might be feasible to translate micro-conditions into macro-variables by aggregation. In such a case it might possible to explain national differences by pure compositional effects. The example of the transition to a nursing home, however, demonstrates that one cannot simply expect this to be the case.

STARTING FROM THE BOTTOM: LIFE COURSE REGIMES AND THEIR DETERMINANTS ON THE MICROLEVEL

In this section I should like to address two problems. The first problem can be defined in the following manner: How can one design cross-national studies if the dependent variable is to be not a single transition in life, but what is commonly referred to as life course patterns or life course regimes, e.g as multitude of transitions across the whole life-span or a distribution of life time across spheres of activities. The second problem is whether we can specify in a general manner the proximal causes of life course transitions or patterns in order to get an idea of potential sources of cross-national variation.

Life course patterns are defined by the categorical and chronological structure of a multitude of transitions (events) and activities (states) (Mayer and Tuma 1990; Mayer 1990; Blossfeld and Rohwer 1995). The explananda for cross-national comparisons between life course regimes include such phenomena as age-specific enrollment rates in education and training, rates of moving out of the parental home, rates of youth unemployment, durations of life time spent in education, work, family roles and retirement, the duration between the end of education and training and employment, rates of non-marital cohabitation and the probability of such unions leading to marriage, indicators of women's employment histories (family-caused interruptions, re-entry, part-time work), and rates of transition into retirement. Usually when one speaks of life course patterns or life course regimes these terms are used in a fairly loose and often metaphorical and interpretative manner. For instance, if one wants to characterize life course patterns in a traditional, predominantly agrarian society such empirical indicators are enumerated as, for example, few and early years spent in school, early involvement in work, leaving home at an early age to work as a servant in a non-parental home or farm, late ages at marriage due to delayed succession of farm ownership and quite variable ages of gradual retirement connected with degrees of physical disability. For more rigorous cross-national comparisons one could then either resort to a series of empirical analyses where each of these indicators is taken as the dependent variable. Or one will have to define composite profiles as, for instance, the average of a number of median ages of various transitions or the number of life time months spent in dependent and independent labor as a proportion of the total life time after age 10.

For cross-national comparisons to make sense one would have to assume in either case, however, that at any given time there is a specific societal or state-wide logic which somehow structures all these life course "outputs" in a similar direction. For instance, in thinking about the peculiarities of life courses in "post-industrial" societies we might imagine that decreasing affluence and increasing economic insecurities would increase the variance of median ages at all major life transitions: leaving education, starting work, marrying, having a first child and retiring. The common force behind this unidirectionality might, for instance, the increasing inequality within a population and the lower dependability on resources provided by the welfare state. On reflection, however, this appears to be a very strong assumption which empirically is quite unlikely to hold. One can easily imagine a situation where the state supports and controls the school system with the result of a high degree of orderliness and uniformity whereas employment conditions of both younger and older workers are left to the volatile impacts of an unregulated labor market. We therefore are pushed toward the conclusion that the construction of an overall life course regime or life course pattern as a dependent variable which can be easily numerically expressed is not a very viable strategy for cross-national comparisons. We have pointed to two serious problems in this regard. The first problem is the one of devicing composite indicators for very complex phenomena. The second problem lies in the presumption that a common causal "regime" would regulate a number of different life course outcomes. This would leave two alternatives for the cross-national study of life courses. The first alternative is to give up the idea of national life course patterns alltogether and to fall back on detailed comparisons of single transitions or other aspects of the life course. The second alternative is to use a wide variety of life course indicators in an essentially descriptive manner and to leave cross-national comparisons to a much looser kind of interpretative exercise.

Let us now turn from the dependent to the independent variables. When we start off on the microlevel of individual behavior then a very rich source of both formal and conceptual tools are available for explaining life course processes: event history analysis (Blossfeld, Hamerle, and Mayer 1987; Mayer and Tuma 1990; Mayer and Huinink 1990; Blossfeld and Rohwer 1995). Within this framework individual transitions between discrete states or activities in continuous time are typically being explained by (a) the time duration or spell in the previous state, (b) other durations such as age, labor force experience or duration in marriage or on the labor market, (c) time-invariant properties of the individuals under consideration, such as social origin, (d) time-varying properties of individuals such as skills or family status, (e) constant or time-variant properties of collectivities of which the individual is a member such as employment status of the spouse or the size of the birth cohort and finally (f) attributes of the historical period relating to months, years or decades such as the introduction of laws, the business cycle, the unemployment rate and the like.

For instance, in our initial example of the transition to a nursing home (a) might be age, duration since diagnosed chronic illness or since death of the spouse, (b) might be time since retirement, (c) the normative expectation to be cared for by one's children, home-ownership, educational level or living in a city, (d) could be income or health status, (e) the employment status and occupation of daughters or daughthers-in-law, and (f) could be the number of available nursing home places, the level of welfare subsidies to private or stationary care and the like.

For any given numerical values of a transition rate outcome cross-national similarities or differences could then be, among else, the result of highly contingent differences in (i) individual dispositions like care norms or (ii) accumulated properties of the past like the higher disability rates of cohorts who were exposed to war and (iii) external opportunity structures like welfare budgets or nursing home places and iv) variations in the relative size of the populations at risk. It thus becomes apparent not only how numerous and varied the sources of variations between societies might be, but also that the comparison of outcome measures would hardly suffice to account for cross-national differences. Similar outcome measures might be due to very different causes and differences in outcome measures could be the result of quite different mixtures of influences. If one takes nations as proxies for causes one also faces the by now well elaborated problem that the number of main causes easily outnumbers the number of nations (Lieberson 1991). It follows from these considerations that a purely inductive approach to understanding national variations in aggreate life course outcomes will be most likely not fruitful. It also follows that the conventional methodology of cross-national indicators will probably be useless in the area of comparative life course studies. In contrast, fully specified complex models of the microprocesses using individual level data from longitudinal studies have to be employed for comparisons. One rare example of such a study is the one by Blossfeld and his collaborators on the role of education in family formation in various countries (Blossfeld 1995).

Another conclusion on comparative strategy we have to draw is that the task to be solved is one of a sequential double explanatory procedure. In a first step individual-level models of the kind outlined above would have to be carried through. Then, one would find, for example, that opportunity structures like the available nursing home places or their prize play indeed an important role for explaining the transition. Once such an explanandum has been established in a next step the target of explanation will have to be shifted to accounting for the variance between nations in these factors.

STARTING FROM ABOVE: MACRO-SOURCES
FOR DIFFERENCES IN LIFE COURSE REGIMES

Our illustration from Alber's study showed that within-country models for explaining life course transitions might not be sufficient to account—via adequate aggregation and the search for composition effects—for differences between countries. If that is more generally the case, then it is worthwhile to ask which distinctions between societies should be looked for as explanations on the macrolevel. In this section I would like to examine what the literature has to offer in this regard. In particular I shall discuss the concepts of "work society and the tripartite division of life" (Dahrendorf, Offe, and Kohli), of "life courses in the welfare state" (Mayer, Müller), the "Fordist Life Cycle" (Myles), the "Three Worlds of Welfare Capitalism" (Esping-Andersen) and concepts on the sources of national differences in education and training systems (Allemendinger, Müller).

Work Society and the Tripartite Life Course. The term work society was introduced to label industrial societies in which work and labor market experiences dominate and in which there can be observed a division of the life course into the three distinct parts of pre-work, employment and retirement (Dahrendorf 1983; Offe 1983; Kohli 1985). This concept derives from the pseudo-Marxist or functionalist notion that life course patterns are regulated by (macro)-economic imperatives. First people are educated and trained to develop skills which they can sell on the labor market, than in the active years their work is used for production and dsitribution and they have to leave employment when they either become unfit or when it is functional for firms to let them go. However plausible this formula may be, for comparative purposes of a cross-national rather than historical kind it appears to be of relatively little use, because current societies do not vary according to the criterion whether they fit the pattern of a tripartite life course or not. Rather, societies vary in great many details of the temporal organization of working lives—for example, in labor force participation rates, in the way the boundaries between dependent employment and nonpaid-work are drawn (on decommodification of work see Esping-Andersen 1990, 1993), in the relative constancy of life-long occupations and in employment security, in the availability of normal labor contracts, and in the relative replacement rate of retirement income. And just describing such differences leaves the question of explanation wide open. The theory of the work society is not an explanatory theory, but a tautology or—formulated more constructively—it can at best serve as a sensitizing concept.

But, nonetheless, working lives are a promising track for cross-national life course comparisons. For illustrative purposes, let me take up a comparison between Germany and the United States conducted by Tom DiPrete and Patricia McManus (1996). They ask how changes in technology and occupational structure have an impact on working lives in the two countries. DiPrete and McManus compare the period from 1985 to 1991 for the United States and West Germany for men using the data from the German Socio-Economic Panel Study (SOEP) and the American Panel of Income Dynamics Study (PSID). They confirm the very high degree of labor mobility in the United States—internally within companies as well as between companies themselves. As far as earned income is concerned, the degree of inequality in the United States was larger and became even larger during the period under consideration. Income gains and losses were more common and accentuated in the United States, particularly for those who were continually employed, while for those employed in West Germany, there was scarcely any loss of income. The German income distribution was altogether much more stable and the trajectories of the individual incomes were not only steady, but even showed rises. This indicates that structural change in West Germany had less of a negative influence on the career mobility and the income development of employed men than in the United States. However, the better employment prospects in Germany have their price: labor force particpation rates are quite lower and unmployment is higher. Thus, in oder to understand variations in national working life regimes one has to bring into the picture not only the employment histories, occupational careers and income trajectories of those actually working—the "insiders" of the labor market—but also the characteristics of those not working or not in the labor force, that is especially younger people in education and training, women with young children, and older workers who are phased out of work into retirement via unemployment or disability schemes.

Life Courses in the Welfare State. Mayer and Müller (1986, 1989) have developed a theory about how welfare states both in their historical development and in their modern practices influence life courses in the form of educational tracks, employment trajectories, occupational careers, family lives, retirement and old age as well as working lives in the public sector. First, they show how by controlling and expanding education, by regulating the labor market and legislating on family transitions the welfare state defines and brackets out activities, events and transitions much more sharply than before. In tendency it cuts up the life even further by, for example, tightly defining entry and exit from illness—for claims of health insurance benefits—by defining maternity, childleave and the like. It is argued then that the labor market and employers only in conjunction with the welfare state and its insurance systems have institutionalized and standardized the life course. Second, it is argued that the welfare state not only impacts on the life course by positive law, but in addition by using age as a criterion for entitlements, using age categories as targets for services and service occupations and by using monetary incentives such as stipends, maternity benefits, unemployment benefits and pensions. Third, the welfare state regulates life courses as an employer with labor contracts which generally contain more universal rules and more security than in the private sector (see also Mayer and Schoepflin 1989). Fourthly, as an aggregate result of these welfare-state-induced tendencies Mayer and Müller envisage not only greater stability and constancy of life courses in such societies, but alo speculate about the consequences for motivations and orientations of actors, for example, to behave according to state-provided incentive schemes or to avoid employment risks.

Although it might be claimed that this theory gives much more explicit causal linkages between intentional and unintentional actions of the welfare state on the one hand and life course patterns on the other hand, its practicability as a tool for comparative analysis is questionable. It can serve as a rough guide for deriving hypotheses on life courses in highly developed welfare states in comparison to nation-states with only rudimentary welfare state provisions. But for comparing a wide variety of nations with differential degrees of welfare state organization it will be of limited use, because many of the causal factors and tendencies discussed are not easily transformed into variables.

The Fordist and Post-Fordist Life Cycle. John Myles (1993) has more recently elaborated a comprehensive macro-theory of life course regimes: the theory of the Fordist Life Cycle. Myles starts with the pact between the automobile industry and the auto workers unions in the United States. This pact triggered occupational and wage agreements and reduced industrial conflicts in the production of bulk goods. Spreading to other industries the outcome was a mass middle class of male industrial workers with relatively steady incomes who were economically and socially integrated, who could afford their own homes, and who were able to send their children to college. Married women stayed only residually in the labor market if at all and were available to care for the children and elderly. The welfare state was oriented towards the entire household with a male breadwinner and concentrated on securing his income and covering for health risks in old age. There is, therefore, in this model, a fit between collective wage agreements and overall economic policy with male full employment, with a Keynesian steering of global economic demand and with welfare policies mainly for the not-employed-phase. There was furthermore a societal correspondence in the class structure and in complementary family sex roles and household division of labor.

What killed the Fordist life course? Endogenously, educational expansion, the skill differentaion tied to it and the women's movement. Exogenously, structural under-employment, the need for new skills which then do not last for a whole working life, the diversification of production and the expansion of the service sector undermine the security of male continuous employment. The welfare state is confronted with new demands in relation to the vocational training phase and the childcare of working women but above all in relation to the occupational and income risks during working life.

The major contribution of Myles should be seen in the fact that he not one-sidedly focuses either on the economy alone or the state alone, but rather elaborates the specifics of one type of political economy in a comprehensive manner and is therefore able to derive very convincingly determinate life course patterns.

For the purpose of comparative analysis, however, Myles' theory has also obvious weaknesses. It shares with the two approaches discussed above—work society and welfare state—the weakness that it captures a historical period better than national variants in a given period. One can also question how universal—geographically, according to class and ethnic group—the Fordist life course was in the fifties and sixties even within the confines of the United States. Moreover, the model of the white ethnic working class suburb of Detroit might have even been less widespread and of a shorter historical duration in Western Europe than in the United States. At any rate, the problem of supplanting this kind of theoretical concept across the Atlantic becomes even more formidable for Post-Fordism which is basically defined as the breakdown and absence of all the characteristics of the Fordist model of a life course regime.

Institutional Macro-Configurations (Müller, Esping-Andersen). A more decisive objection to Myles' attempt to construct historical socioeconomic macro-configurations and corresponding life course patterns for Western industrial societies in general rests on the claim that basic institutional setups varying between these countries should result in very different life course regimes. The idea of such basic institutions implies that societies developed specific institutional configurations in their reaction to the processes of their formation of nationhoood, their developement as a state and their manner of industrialization. These institutions, once established, can be assumed to show a high historical stability and with it to channel the way how societies deal with new challenges. The relationship of church and state, the development of party systems, the rise of regional administrative bodies and association structures count as some of these challenges. The question in our context then is whether there are such basic institutions which can account for societal differences in life course patterns. There are obviously three candidates for this function: the system of education and vocational training, industrial relations and the organization of labor markets, and the welfare state.

Three problem areas were essential for the emergence of national differences in the system of education and vocational training: the relationship between the state and the associations (in the age of Reformation), the creation of professions and state bureaucracies with the development of the public sector (in the seventeenth century), and the relationship between the state and markets in connection with the liberalization of the trade guilds (in the nineteenth century). The solution to the first problem was decided by either a centralized, standardized or a decentralized and unstandardized organization of the educational system and distinguishes, for example, Germany and France from England, Scotland and the United States (Allmendinger 1989, 1990; Blossfeld 1992; Müller 1994; Leschinsky and Mayer 1990). The solution to the second problem distinguishes England, with its very small amateur Civil Service, from France, with its Grand Ecoles and a very extensive state bureaucracy, but also distinguishes both from Germany with the integration of the civil servants' training within the universities (Müller 1994). The solution to the third problem differentiates the German-speaking countries, with their corporatist regulation of vocational training, from all other countries in which transition to the labor market is to take place immediately after general education (Schriewer 1986; Stratmann 1993).

These nationally differing institutional patterns do not only have consequences for class mentalities and class barriers but also for differing degrees of hierarchy in the work organization and variedly cut labor market segments (Lutz 1976; Maurice, Sellier, and Sylvestre 1986). They also result in differences in the patterns of age-specific unemployment, of career-entry phases (Allmendinger 1990; Blossfeld 1992; Büchtemann et al. 1994; Bynner and Heinz 1991; Bynner and Roberts n.d.; Mayer 1996), as well as in differences in firm-internal and between-firm mobility and the relative duration of job tenure (DiPrete and McManus 1996). Patterns of women's employment are also implicated because women in non-segemented labor markets more easily enter and re-enter employment (Mayer, Allmendinger, and Huinink 1991; Lauterbach 1994).

Educational and training systems thus suggest fairly clear hypotheses on the way life courses are structured before and after the start of the working life. However, they allow only few clear predictions for the later phases of occupational trajectories, for the probabilities of continuous employment of women and the patterns of transition into retirement, and, above all, for the way in which employment opportunities between groups and in the life course are distributed. If the state, however, privileges educational credentials, this tends to encourage estate-like privileges in income and job security for persons with higher occupational qualifications to the disadvantage of the unqualified and of those without the protection of stable work relationships.

Kohli and Rein (1993) have convincingly explained how the involvement of employers associations and trade unions as collective protagonists in decision making about social security influence different pathways, mean age variation and the extent of the transition into retirement. If employers and unions are involved in socio-political decisions, then the state tends to exert restraint from interventions in the labor market. And if there is a highly developed system of social security for unemployment and income security in old age, then there is a tendency to protect normal work relationships with high efficiency wages and good prospects of promotion to the the disadvantage of a growing number of people kept out of the labor market. That is the German case.

Intervention of the welfare state on the labor market with work place subsidies and, as a public employer, providing jobs for social services, opens up steady chances of employment and personal income resources especially for women—if only partly at a higher qualified level. The Scandinavian example of badly paid social services provided by women in the public sector is an exemplary case of a political economy because the coalition of the state and public sector unions had a high impact on the division of labor between men and women, the distribution of working hours and family relationships. France has, for another historical reason, namely the national fear of a decrease in population, child-care institutions which make a high standard of women's full-time employment possible.

If one were to add the residual case of societies in which the state engages itself neither in labor market policies nor by providing social services and no effective coordination of wage agreement parties takes place, as in the United States and Great Britain, then we have arrived at the construction of the recent past and rather gloomy visions for the future in Gösta Esping-Andersen's (1990) "Three Worlds of Welfare Capitalism." There the choice is offered between

KARL ULRICH MAYER

either a restricted male-dominated labor market or a female service proletariat in the private or public sector. Esping-Andersen's theoretical schema according to which nations differ in the extent to which they regulate the labor market, the extent to which they offer public employment jobs (especially for women) and the extent to which the welfare burden is being distributed between the family and the state are a good starting point for developing explanatory accounts for national variations in life course regimes.

If one were to ask then about the effects of national basic institutions on life course patterns, an assorted mixture of historical configurations turn up which affect different phases of the life course and have completely varying effects on men and women. One would, however, only expect a uniform correspondence relationship between macroinstitutions and life course patterns, if, for example, the main collective actors—state, employers and unions—would always be jointly involved in regulating the different life phases and various life transitions. For example, if these collective actors are involved in vocational training, in the regulation of retirement and social security and even nursing care insurance—as is the case in Germany—then one might indeed expect something like an overall logic of life courses. Otherwise, the effect of macroinstitutions on the one hand and life course patterns on the other hand may easily fall apart in disparate bits and pieces for which divergent explanations within and between countries have to be searched for.

Alber expressed an informed guess as to why it could have come to such diverging outcomes. He argues that where conflicts in the welfare state are over the size and sort of monetary transfer achievements, there is a tendency for these conflicts to be decided and institutionalized via the power relationships between state, capital and labor, as for instance, in regard to unemployment insurance, retirement benefits and health insurance and in regard to the definition of the working and earning population. Where these conflicts have to do with the provision of social services, they unfold as conflicts about the organisation, financing and regulation between regional and local administrative bodies and between states and associations (Alber 1995).

For the macrolevel, then, a number of theoretical constructs are available which could be useful for explaining cross-national variations in life course patterns. They tend to point to historically grounded institutional distinctions and, if so, generally offer little help for understanding current changes. To understand those more elaborate models of current day political economies are needed. Our discussion also made apparent that the observed life course patterns in a given country are not likely to be the consequence of one set of institutional developments. Thus the prerequisites in regard to institutional analysis might become quite complex, if we want to account for the life course from early schooling up to old age provisions.

LIFE COURSES IN DEREGULATED
AND FLEXIBLY COORDINATED SOCIETIES

Despite the skepticism articulated above let us assume that both of the tasks outlined could be satisfactorily resolved, namely, (a) the modeling on the micro-level of particular transitions and behavioral patterns across the life course, and (b) the clarification of historical institutional macroconfigurations, then still the question about the mechanisms which combine individual (micro) action with the macrolevel of general institutional conditions and opportunity structures remains open. How is the coordination of individual actions achieved through characteristics of the system, how do systems differ from each other in the way social action is coordinated, and how does this affect life course patterns?

I would now like to construct two complementary ideal types linking macro-systems and life course regimes. The purpose of this exercise is not so much to exhaust the potential national variation, but rather to exemplify how linkages between the institutional macrolevel and life course patterns could be construed explicitly instead of leaving their selective affinities to a black box. Since they are ideal types the question how well they fit actual societies must also be left open here.

For this exercise in theory-building I shall make use of a distinction which was introduced by, among others, Dore (1987), Streeck (1992) and Soscice (1993). Modern western industrial societies (including Japan) can roughly be categorized into two groups of overall societal organization: deregulated, open market systems, on the one hand, and flexibly coordinated corporate systems, on the other: "In recent work something like a pattern is beginning to emerge, pointing to similarities between Germanic, Scandinavian, Japanese, and even Italian economic systems. There are, of course, great differences between the organization of Scandinavian and Germanic economies, as they are, say the Swedish and Danish systems or between the Austrian, German and Swiss...Similarities are, however, concealed between these differences, in terms of incentive structures, institutions and relationships,..." (Soscice 1993, p. 4).

Using this distinction vocational training systems (Soscice 1993), financial markets and industrial relations (Streeck 1992) among others were analyzed. Fundamental to this economic behavior pattern is the degree of trust which the individual and collective participants invest in their mutual relationships. The permanence of these relationships is regarded as the immediate effect of the amount of trust invested.

(a) *Life courses in deregulated societies* are based on social relationships which are equipped with little advance of trust. They show a low mutual degree of obligation and tend to be temporary. The state stays to a large extent outside the contractual relations between employees and employers. It does not assume much responsibility in the area of occupational training. Individual and firm investments in training are therefore small. There is no quality standardization and there are no formal degrees and certificates which are accepted across firms. The transition between school and gainful employment leads to a series of partly marginal employment interrupted by phases of unemployment. Jobs are not so clearly defined and changes between jobs are common. Loyalty to one specific firm is also low. Intercompany job changes as well as internal moves within companies are more widespread. There are fewer career positions within companies and the career-ladders are shorter.

Downward mobility occurs more frequently during the working life, but so do bigger leaps up the ladder. The first jobs in the employment history are usually part of a search process and are, therefore, of a shorter duration. Income trajectories are more likely to be flat and irregular and reach the highest level ten to fifteen years after the start of the working life; they are closely attached to actual productivity. Being self-employed fits Schumpeter's image of the high risk entrepreneur, is often of short duration and interrupted by phases of dependent work.

The experience of unemployment and job interruptions is scattered among the entire working population and is less concentrated on specific segments of the working population. Unemployment insurance is relatively low and does not cover longer periods. Pensions and retirement payments make up less than half of earlier earned income. This is also the reason why some people over 65 years old are frequently forced to go on working or have to rely on accumulated assets. Organizational and technological restructuring are enacted by way of company closings and lay-offs. Health insurance is mostly private and segmented between high and low risk groups.

In such a context, all participants have to be keen to maximize their short-term profits. Employees maximize their incomes at the expense of job security and the quality of working conditions, while employers maximize their productivity yields and profits and minimize wages. Employees try to increase their incomes by hastily changing firms. Securing old age and safeguarding against risks of income loss through sickness or unemployment is done through shareholdings and real estate investments, and not by the confidence in a public social security system.

Similar orientations influence the family life. The income and employment uncertainty of the working life influence family commitments and stability. Because affluence is a more important life goal than security, decisions regarding marriage and divorce are more closely tied to income expectations. Since the risks of divorce are quite high, women have to invest in themselves, their work and their careers and can hardly depend on their investment into the family to pay off. Since families are less of a joint project, marriages are easier to enter and easier again to dissolve. Since the state does not bother to safeguard incomes in cases of divorce and children born out of wedlock, divorced women and single mothers often choose to marry or remarry to get themselves out of poverty.

(b) *Flexibly coordinated societies* in contrast have found a way out of the prisoners' dilemma of pure selfishness by strengthening the non-contractual elements in a contract on local and nationwide levels. This means, as a rule, stronger trade unions and a more active role of the state as an agent ensuring high trust relationships between union and employers' associations.

Life courses in flexibly coordinated societies are firmly structured in such a way that the individual job training investments are being rewarded by positions in the occupational hierarchy which in turn are based on differential qualification. Individual investments in training are possible because individuals can rely on ensuing employment and wage rewards. Conversely, companies are prepared to invest in training because they believe that those qualified employees whom they need will remain with the company after training. Employees accept lower training compensation and lower starting wages because they expect age or seniority based wage increases and because they know that their earning opportunities are greater when they remain in the firm (Schömann 1994).

The recruitment to firms or apprenticeships is often based on relationships of trust: children of employees or clients are preferred. The formal rights of participation of workers' councils and unions make lay-offs costly and expensive and they result in mutual expectations of longer time committment to a given company. Interfirm moves are predominantly voluntary and usually associated with promotions or gains in earnings. In order to make such long-time company affiliation productive, firms invest in job-oriented further training and offer internal careers which also frequently lead across the manual/non-manual boundary. Technological and organizational restructuring are not managed through lay-offs but rather through the natural turnover of workers. Technological and organizational changes in work roles are mediated through retiring and newly hired cohorts.

Even in the case of de-industrialization processes, the state tends to take over the responsibility for socially amicable solutions: shortened working hours retraining, or early retirement. Employees can accept moderate wage standards and moderate or even only nominal wage increases because a lot of risks are covered through the welfare state and no reserves have to be built up for the vocational training and education of children, for illness, unemployment, and old age. Moderate wage increases also become acceptable through rent subsidies and long-term mortgages.

A higher degree of trust, expectations for stability and continuity also regulate the family sphere. Although relationships between partners are increasingly entered into on the basis of equality, families are still joint projects and not the mere agglomerate of individual life designs. They are still symbolized through entry into matrimony when children are expected. Since families are joint projects, decisions about employment and family obligations are based on joint utility distributions, resulting in secondary female work employment, employment interruptions and part-time work. The state supports this family model with child allowances and tax benefits. Such life courses move in regional milieus of low or close-distance migration and the social advantages of regional immobility in comparison with the higher potential economic benefits of migration are appreciated.

There are, of course, also costs involved in the maintenance of life courses sustained by a high amount of confidence and stability in flexibly coordinated societies and specific conditions for their ability to function. One of these cost categories is to be found in a relatively short working life for a limited working population. Another pre-condition rests in the existence of a community of shared solidarity which is prepared to summon up the costs for the risks of others and to sustain a general insurance system.

In the these two ideal types of deregulated and flexibly coordinated societies the linkages between the macro-institutional structures and individual life courses are primarily construed as mutually reinforcing incentive systems. Initial historically given institutional differences shape the detailed regulations and policies pertaining to various areas, phase and transitions of the life course as well as the motives and orientations of the individual actors involved. Across the individual life course early influences shape and direct later trajectories in a cumulative manner. On such a basis one would expect stabilizing and homogenizing tendencies across the life course and across different segments of the population in flexibly coordinated societies whereas in deregulated societies one would expect diverging fortunes resulting in greater overall life time inequalities.

CONCLUDING REMARKS

In this chapter I addressed the question which conditions must hold for cross-national comparisons of life course patterns to be promising. In a first step I introduced the example of the transition to a nursing home to illustrate the distinction between an immanent way of modeling life course transitions and a way which would take national institutional and policy differences into account. As has been shown there is no simple connection between the two modes of explanation. In a second step I examined whether current ideas about life course regimes, like the one of the work society and the Fordist Life Cycle model, are suitable conceptual tools for international comparisons. In a third step I examined some of those national differences in institutional make-ups which might help to account for the structuration of life course regimes. As a result it became obvious that an individualizing strategy for comparisons—focusing on few specific nations—will be more fruitful than a universalizing strategy (Tilly 1984), that is specific historical institutional patterns must be assumed to be highly consequential for life course patterns. But even assuming that the satisfactory groundwork is done in regard to institutional preconditions, it still appears to be an almost impossible task to derive sufficiently specific hypotheses not only for single life course transitions, but for overall national life course regimes. Finally, in a last step, I elaborated one potential theoretical model which might prove suitable for achieving the latter task: the distinction between deregulated and flexibly coordinated societies.[1]

In sum, then, that is how a research program of cross-national comparison of life course patterns should be conducted, namely as a combination of the following ingredients: an explication of historical institutional macro-configurations, the laying out of current constellations of various collective actors, models of incentive systems, as well as modelling transitions on the individual level in family and household contexts. The realization of such a research program has still a long way to go.

ACKNOWLEDGMENT

An earlier version of this paper was presented at a Conference of the Sonderforschungs-bereich 186 "Statuspassagen und Risikolagen im Lebenslauf," Bremen, September 1995. I should like to thank Helena Maravilla for her translation from the original German text as well as Karen Aschaffenburg and Marion Binder for both linguistic and substantive suggestions. Special thanks are also due to an anonymous reviewer.

NOTE

1. It will have been obvious to the reader that the latter ideal type shares many affinities (West German society on the one hand and the United States and the United Kingdom on the other hand). However, whether this construct still applies to Germany and whether it will have a long continued existence is questionable (see, e.g., Mayer 1996; Streeck 1995). Of course, one can hardly imagine a tougher test for the "German model" than the consequences of unification for the East German population.

REFERENCES

Alber, J. 1995. "Soziale Dienstleistungen. Die vernachlässigte Dimension vergleichender Wohlfahrtsstaat-Forschung. Pp. 277-293 in *Die Reformfähigkeit von Industriegesell-schaften*, edited K. Bentele, B. Reissert, and Ronald Schettkatta. Fritz W. Scharpf—Festschrift zu seinem 60. Geburtstag. Frankfurt am Main, New York: Campus.

Allmendinger, J. 1989. "Educational Systems and Labor Market Outcomes." *European Sociological Review* 5(3): 231-250.

————. 1990. *Career Mobility Dynamics. A Comparative Analysis of the United States, Norway, and West Germany.* (Studien und Berichte Nr. 49). Berlin: Max-Planck-Institut für Bildungsforschung.

————. 1994. *Lebensverlauf und Sozialpolitik.* Frankfurt: Campus.

Anderson, M. 1985. "The Emergence of the Modern Life Cycle in Britain." *Social History* 10(1): 69-87.

Blossfeld, H.-P. 1992. "Is the German Dual System a Model for a Modern Vocational Training System? A Cross-national Comparison of How Different Systems of Vocational Training Deal with the Changing Occupational Structure." *International Journal of Comparative Sociology* 23: 168-181.

_____. (Ed.). 1995. *The New Role of Women: Family Formation in Modern Societies.* Boulder, CO: Westview Press.

Blossfeld, H.-P. and G. Rohwer. 1995. *Techniques of Event History Modeling: New Approaches to Causal Analysis.* Mahwah, NJ: Lawrence Erlbaum.

Buchmann, M. 1989. *The Script of Life in Modern Society: Entry Into Adulthood in a Changing World.* Chicago, IL: Chicago University Press.

Buechtemann, C., F. Schupp, Jürgen, and D.J. Soloff. 1994. "Challenges Facing Germany's 'Dual System' of Apprenticeship and Educational Reform Prospects in the United States: A Reply to David Marsden's Comment 'La genie du systeme allemand et la reforme du systeme americain'." In *Formation-Emploi* 1.

Bynner, J., and W. Heinz. 1991. "Matching Samples and Analysing their Differences in a Cross-national Study of Labour Market Entry in England and West Germany." *International Journal of Comparative Sociology* 32: 135-153.

Bynner, J., and K. Roberts (Eds.). n.d. *Transition to Employment in England and Germany.* London: Anglo-German Foundation.

Dahrendorf, R. 1983. "Wenn der Arbeitsgesellschaft die Arbeit ausgeht. Pp. 25-37 in *Krise der Arbeitsgesellschaft? Verhandlungen des 21. Deutschen Soziologentages in Bamberg 1982,* edited by Joachim Matthes. Frankfurt am Main: Campus Verlag.

DiPrete, T., and P. McManus. 1996. "Institutions, Technical Change and Diverging Life Chances: Earnings Mobility in the US and Germany." *American Journal of Sociology* 1(July): 34-79.

Dore, R. 1987. *Taking Japan Seriously: A Confucian Perspective on Leading Economic Issues.* London: The Athlone Press.

Esping-Andersen, G. 1990. *The Three Worlds of Welfare Capitalism.* Princeton, NJ: Princeton University Press.

_____. (Ed.). 1993. *Changing Classes: Stratification and Mobility in Post-Industrial Societies.* London: Sage Publications.

Gilberg, R. 1997. *Inanspruchnahme von Hilfe und Pflegeleistungen im höheren Lebensalter,* Dissertation. Berlin: Freie Universität.

Hernes, H. 1987. *Welfare State and Women Power: Essays in State Feminism.* Oslo: Norwegian University Press

Huinink, J. 1995. *Warum noch Familie? Zur Attraktivität von Partnerschaft und Elternschaft in unserer Gesellschaft.* Frankfurt: Campus.

Huinink, J., K.U. Mayer, M. Diewald, H. Solga, A. Sorensen, and H. Trappe. 1995. *Kollektiv und Eigensinn. Lebensverläufe in der DDR und danach.* Berlin: Akademie Verlag.

Kohli, M. 1985. "Die Institutionalisierung des Lebenslaufs: Historische Befunde und theoretische Argumente." *Kölner Zeitschrift für Soziologie und Sozialpsychologie* 37: 1-29.

Kohli, M., and M. Rein. 1991. "The Changing Balance of Work and Retirement." Pp. 1-35 in *Time for Retirement: Comparative Studies of Early Exit from the Labor Force,* edited by M. Kohli, M. Rein, A.-M. Guillemard, and H. van Gunsteren. Cambridge: Cambridge University Press.

Koyano, W. 1995. "Transition Into Old Age." Pp. 41-58 in *Japan ergraut.* Forum Demographie und Politik, October 5.

Lang, F.R. 1994. *Die Gestaltung informeller Hilfebeziehungen im hohen Alter–Die Rolle von Elternschaft und Kinderlosigkeit.* Eine empirische Studie zur sozialen Unterstützung und deren Effekt auf die erlebte soziale Einbindung. (Reihe: Studien und Berichte Nr. 59) Berlin: Max-Planck-Institut für Bildungsforschung.

Lauterbach, W. 1994. *Berufsverläufe von Frauen. Erwerbstätigkeit, Unterbrechung und Wiedereintritt.* Frankfurt am Main: Campus Verlag.

Lieberson, S. 1991. "Small N's and Big Conclusions: An Examination of the Reasoning in Comparative Studies Based on a Small Number of Cases." *Social Forces* 70(2): 307-320.

Leschinsky, A., and K.U. Mayer. (Eds.). 1990. *The Comprehensive School Experiment Revisited: Evidence from Western Europe.* Frankfurt am Main et al: Peter Lang Verlag.

Linden, M., G. Reiner, A. Horgas, and E. Steinhagen-Thiessen. 1996. "Die Inanspruchnahme medizinischer und pflegerischer Hilfe im hohen Alter." In *Die Berliner Altersstudie*, edited by Karl Ulrich Mayer and Paul B. Baltes. Berlin: Akademie Verlag.

Lutz, B. 1976. *Bildungssystem und Beschäftigungsstruktur in Deutschland und Frankreich. Zum Einfluß des Bildungssystems auf die Gestaltung betrieblicher Arbeitskräftestrukturen.* Pp. 83-151 in *Betriebs-Arbeitsmarkt-Organisation*, edited by H.-G. Mendius. Frankfurt am Main: Aspekte Verlag.

Maurice, M., F. Sellier, and J.-J. Silvestre. 1986. *The Social Foundations of Industrial Power.* Cambridge, MA: MIT Press.

Mayer, K.U. (Ed.). 1990. "Lebensverläufe und sozialer Wandel." *Kölner Zeitschrift für Soziologie und Sozialpsychologie* 31, special issue.

_____. 1994. "The Postponed Generation. Economic, Political, Social and Cultural Determinants of Changes in Life Course Regimes." In *Solidarity of Generations*, edited by H.A. Becker, and P.L.J. Hermkens. Amsterdam: Thesis Publishers

_____. 1996. "Ausbildungswege und Berufskarrieren." In *Forschung im Dienst von Praxis und Politik*, edited by Bundesinstitut für Berufsbildung. Berlin: Bundesinstitut für Berufsbildung.

Mayer, K.U., J. Allmendinger, and J. Huinink. 1991. *Vom Regen in die Traufe: Frauen zwischen Beruf und Familie.* Frankfurt am Main: Campus Verlag.

Mayer, K.U. and P.B. Baltes. (Eds.). 1996. *Die Berliner Altersstudie.* Berlin: Akademie Verlag.

Mayer, K.U., and J. Huinink. 1990. "Age, Period, and Cohort in the Study of the Life Course: A Comparison of Classical A-P-C-Analysis with Event History Analysis, or Farewell to Lexis?" In *Data Quality in Longitudinal Research*, edited by D. Magnusson, and L.R. Berman. Cambridge: Cambridge University Press.

Mayer, K.U. and W. Müller. 1986. *The State and the Structure of the Life Course.* In *Human Development and the Life Course: Multidisciplinary Perspectives*, edited by A.B. Sorensen, F.E. Weinert, and L.R. Sherrod. Hillsdale, NJ: Lawrence Erlbaum.

Mayer, K.U., and W. Müller. 1989. "Lebensverläufe im Wohlfahrtsstaat." In *Handlungs-Pielräume*, edited by A. Weymann. Stuttgart: Enke.

Mayer, K.U. and U. Schöpflin. 1989. "The State and the Life Course." *Annual Review of Sociology* 15: 187-209.

Mayer, K.U., and N.B. Tuma. (Eds.) 1990. *Event History Analysis in Life Course Research.* Madison, WI: University of Wisconsin Press.

Mayer, K.U. and M. Wagner. 1996. "Lebenslagen und soziale Ungleichheit im hohen Alter." In *Die Berliner Altersstudie*, edited by K.U. Mayer, and Paul B. Baltes. Berlin: Akademie Verlag.

Müller, W. 1994. "Bildung und soziale Plazierung in Deutschland, England und Frankreich." Pp. 115-134 in *Gesellschaft, Demokratie und Lebenschancen*, edited by H. Peisert and Wolfgang Zapf. Festschrift für Ralf Dahrendorf. Stuttgart: Deutsche Verlagsanstalt.

Myles, J. 1993. "Is There a Post-Fordist Life Course?" Pp. 171-185 in *Institutions and Gatekeeping in the Life Course.* Weinheim: Deutscher Studienverlag.

Offe, C. 1983. "Arbeit als soziologische Schlüsselkategorie." Pp. 38-65 in *Krise der Arbeitsgesellschaft?* Verhandlungen des 21, edited by Joachim Matthes. Deutschen Soziologentages in Bamberg 1982. Frankfurt am Main: Campus Verlag.

Riley, M.W., R.L. Kahn, and A. Foner. (Eds.). 1994. *Age and Structural Lag.* New York: Wiley.

Schömann, K. 1994. *The Dynamics of Labor Earnings Over the Life Course. A Comparative and Longitudinal Analysis of Germany and Poland.* (Reihe 'Studien und Berichte' Nr. 60). Berlin: Max-Planck-Institut für Bildungsforschung.

Schriewer, J. 1986. "Intermediäre Instanzen, Selbstverwaltung und berufliche Ausbildungsstrukturen im historischen Vergleich." *Zeitschrift für Pädagogik* 32(1): 69-90.

Soskice, D. 1993. "The Institutional Infrastructure for International Competitiveness: A Comparative Analysis of the UK and Germany." In *The Economics of the New Europe,* edited by A.B. Atkinson and R. Brunetta. London: MacMillan.

Stratmann, K. 1993. *Die gewerbliche Lehrlingserziehung in Deutschland. Modernisierungsgeschichte der betrieblichen Berufsbildung.* Bd. 1: *Berufserziehung in der ständischen Gesellschaft.* Frankfurt am Main: Verlag der Gesellschaft zur Förderung arbeitsorientierter Forschung und Bildung.

Streeck, W. 1992. *Social Institutions and Economic Performance. Studies in Industrial Relations in Advanced Capitalist Economies.* London: Sage

_____. 1995. "German Capitalism: Does it exist? Can it survive?" (Discussion paper 1995-5) Köln: Max-Planck-Institut für Gesellschaftsforschung.

Tilly, C. 1984. *Big Structures, Large Processes, Huge Comparisons.* New York: Sage Publications.

MAKING INSTITUTIONS DYNAMIC IN CROSS-NATIONAL RESEARCH:

TIME-SPACE DISTANCING IN EXPLAINING UNEMPLOYMENT

Thomas Janoski, Christa McGill, and Vanessa Tinsley

ABSTRACT

Explanations of economic performance have focused on purely economic variables or the impact of political parties. Researchers have rarely used labor market or firm institutions as explanations of unemployment, and in the few instances when they do, the analyses are cross-sectional and subject to the critique that the analyses do not capture the highly cyclical nature of unemployment. This chapter provides an approach to measuring institutions in a time-series format, and then puts institutions in 18 countries into a pooled "time-series and cross-sectional" analysis. Both private and public capital formation are controlled since these are important economic variables often used to explain economic growth and unemployment. Although capital formation has important effect, the results show that both labor market institutions and codetermination have independent and significant effects on unemployment. These results show how institutional theories can be advanced if institutional variables are measured in a more precise way over time, rather than being accepted as constants simply linked to political culture.

Comparative Social Research, Volume 16, pages 227-268.
Copyright © 1997 by JAI Press Inc.
All rights of reproduction in any form reserved.
ISBN: 0-7623-0250-X

Explanations of unemployment and other measures of economic performance in advanced industrialized countries have most often focused on economic or demographic variables (e.g., capital formation, economic growth, taxation levels or demographic shifts). Only a few have focused on political and economic institutions (Alvarez, Garrett, and Lange 1991; Hicks 1995b; Boreham and Compston 1992; Therborn 1986; Henley and Tsakalotos 1995; Freeman 1988), and fewer still provide an empirical analysis of unemployment. Institutions, which plan, implement, and affect policies in many ways, are frequently ignored because institutions are difficult to measure. Institutions seem to fluctuate little from year to year in their most important features, but in point of fact, they do change (Crouch 1992; Campbell, Hollingsworth, and Lindberg 1991; Janoski 1990, p. 249). In quantitative analyses of a number of countries, institutions tend to be cross-national constants that are measured on the basis of dummy variables. For instance, Huber, Ragin and Stephens (1993) measure institutions as constants in eighteen countries—federalism, legislative structure, proportional representation, bicameralism, and referendum elections—but in a pooled cross-national analysis the dynamic aspect of institutions drops out. In qualitative and historical analyses of a small number of cases, institutions are measured with much greater detail and the dynamic aspect of institutions is more readily apparent (Skocpol 1993; Orloff 1993). However, after being initially established, institutions are still often presented as constants (e.g., "weak state bureaucracies" or "the franchise being used as a trade union organizing issue").

Because institutions seem to inhabit the comparative world of space (i.e., comparisons seem more effective when made between two or more countries) rather than time (i.e., comparisons made with year to year changes), one of the central debates in the welfare state literature cannot be addressed—the debate between power-resources theory (Korpi 1989) and state-centric theory (Skocpol 1993; Orloff 1993). If institutions could be measured over time, they could be combined with political economy variables in a pooled time-series analysis, and we believe that the relative strengths of each theory could then be demonstrated. State-centric theory, which stresses the impacts of slowly changing state structures, would be strong in space because major differences in institutions stand out in cross-national comparisons, but this theory would still be influential in time at certain conjunctures. Power resources theory would be strong in time because of the cyclical flows of business conditions and political power, but it would also be somewhat influential in space on certain issues. These two theories are largely complementary but are separated by "time-space distancing"; that is, they largely operate in different dimensions of time and space.[1]

Substantively, our project focuses on this problem of measuring institutions as dynamic phenomena affecting one major type of economic performance— unemployment rates in 18 countries. With the ultimate aim of explaining economic performance—economic growth, unemployment, productivity, and inflation—we identify the strength and efficacy of employment service, works councils, codetermination and self-administration institutions over time. These are four different institutions that foster participation and cooperation among the social partners and the state. Participation by the social partners generally refers to tripartism of labor, management and government in the setting and implementing of social policy in many different venues. Measuring their strength in comparison to economic investment will help advance institutional theory (Janoski 1990, Chap. 4).

With regards to labor market policy, institutional strength most specifically resides in the employment service. Is a nation's employment service a strong organization with labor market power and resources, or is it a weak organization that is often overlooked concerning policy? Labor policy is also influenced by works councils, codetermination, and self-administration in the welfare state. The continued direction of employment and general welfare state policies by the social partners leads to greater cooperation and generalized exchange in the policy process (Marin 1990a, 1990b; Ekeh 1974). This is in contrast to the direction of policy by a bureaucracy directed by the executive branch of government, which often leads to resistance or lack of participation by either labor or management.

Although each one of these institutions does not change in large measure each year, they do change, and in combination, they make the institutional environment change even more. One could measure the size and budgets of these institutions, the number of cases handled, or other easily changing measures, but these measures do not really get at the strength of an institution. These size of personnel or budget variables are conveniently changing variables, but they often point to extraneous factors such as the size of tax revenues or the governmental hiring decisions of political parties. Resources are more the results of strong rules and norms regarding institutions, which often come in the form of power to constrain other actors with its main resource being the legitimation of the state. This power is much harder to measure because it may represent actions not taken, and inactions, in theory, are nearly infinite. Further, these institutions operate in a context or policy domain where similar institutions reinforce each other, and this magnifies the impact of each institution. This has the added benefit that they can be combined into larger contextual measures that exhibit more variation. In a cross-national study of seventeen countries, this paper will show how labor market and welfare institutions can be measured and analyzed in a dynamic way.

SEARCHING FOR THE DYNAMICS OF INSTITUTIONAL THEORY

Institutional theories themselves differ markedly in how they present change. With considerable generalization, four different strands can be discerned in the literature on institutional theory.[2] First, the old institutionalism involves the formal and informal networks of agencies, constituencies, and interest groups. Selznick's (1949) study of the Tennessee Valley Authority quashing its own participatory mandate is one of the best examples. An important part of this tradition is the formation of informal groups within organizations and networks that develop their own conceptions of what rights and obligations should be, just as the Hawthorne workers created their own norms for output restriction, sociability, and simple cooperation.[3] In political science, institutionalism involves the study of governmental agencies and institutions and how they operate. In economics, the views of institutional labor economists such as Commons (1934) and Veblen (1904) promote a view of structured economies rather than market-driven developments. In some ways change is ubiquitous in these theories, which often focus on a social constructionist approach to change—norms are in the process of being created and that is why the study was done in the first place. This institutional approach fell from favor in the 1960s and 1970s, but more because it failed to develop its own concepts than because it was superseded or proven wrong. Its concept of change, however, stayed at the case-study level.

Second, the new institutionalism in both sociology and political science tends to build on March and Olsen's (1984 and 1989) conceptions of organizational ambiguity, but also incorporates political science notions of institutions (Steinmo, Thelen, and Longstreth 1992). Social institutions are not structures of class, race, gender, or other social categories (Steimo et al. 1992, p. 11), but rather patterned interactions set up and controlled by formal and informal norms. These patterns refer to political institutions and voluntary associations with democratic or other forms of participation. In the welfare state literature, the policy domain and organizational network literature forms another facet of the organization of institutions (Burstein 1991; Knoke et al. 1996). The structuring of policy domains refers to how organizations, groups, and the public are tied together in specific networks, often with their own roles and ideologies. This work identifies important institutions, but does not develop a theory of dynamic institutions.

Third, economic institutionalism has developed in three directions: historical, transaction cost, and social choice institutionalism. The historical institutionalism focuses much more on how norms evolve over time. Institutions change because of organizational interaction in which actors invest in skills that shape their perceptions about opportunities and choices within institutions. These perceptions are mental constructs that lead to norms of often enduring qualities, such that even institutions that strongly deter economic growth may continue over long periods of time (North 1993, pp. 12, 17). The transaction cost approach focuses less on norms and more on the rationality of choosing between markets and hierarchy based on the costs associated with uncertainties of transacting in a market or compared to those of maintaining hierarchical control over suppliers and producers within an organization (Williamson 1975, 1985, 1986). In the transaction cost theory, change is external to the organizational environment since internal change is statically built on rationality in perceiving transaction costs. The social choice approach looks at the rational choosing of institutions with largely market-oriented principles. And again, change is externally driven. These three approaches range from the evolutionary and historical, which is least reliant on individual rationality and markets, to the social choice approach, which is most reliant on these mechanisms (Furubotn and Richter 1993, p. 3). Another way to view the difference is to see each theory differing on the degree to which institutions limit or constrict market principles. The combined effects of all three schools have tremendously increased the amount of research on economic institutions. Yet their contribution to measuring institutional change seems to mainly center on one side of the phenomena—decision makers.

Fourth, organizational institutionalism represents an approach to organizations centered around how organizations develop norms and an ethos or culture not directly connected to rationality (DiMaggio 1994; Dimaggio and Powell 1983; Zucker 1977, 1983, 1991; Fligstein 1990). Organizational theories differ somewhat from new institutionalism. They concentrate not only on what happens within the firm, but also on the interorganizational networks of firms, voluntary associations, and the state. More centered around economic institutions than political institutions, this approach is often involved in debates with organizational ecology and other sociological approaches to organizations. Some of its focus has been on change in failing organizations (Zucker and Meter 1989), but change is not clearly a focus. If change occurs, it is increasingly viewed as evolutionary change through adaptation (isomorphism) or selection (organizational death). These changes, while important, only focus on a small amount of the change that goes on within political and economic institutions.

However, two works on institutions have made dynamic institutions a feature of their work—Crouch (1992), and Campbell, Hollingsworth, and Lindberg (1991). Crouch provides a dynamic view of institutions over a panel of years looking at twelve countries at nine important periods of time in the last one hundred years.[4] He includes institutions on industrial relations (including qualitative measures of corporatism), trade union articulation (verging on most quantitative measures of corporatism), organization of capital, power of labor, political and economic development, and industrial conflict. Campbell and associates (1991) put institutional change in the center of their institutional theory of the growth of markets, networks, and hierarchies in the economy (see also Hollingsworth, Schmitter, and Streeck, 1994). They differentiate markets, networks, and hierarchies into bilateral and multilateral interaction. They both point toward a more complete theory of labor market policy that needs to bring the creation, evolution, and death of regimes into the forefront of institutional development for a variety of purposes.

Dynamically focusing on institutions to explain economic performance will entail the development of long run interests and cooperation. Methodologically, procedures need to be developed to identify and differentiate between restricted exchange involving self-interest, opportunism, and rationality, and generalized exchange involving group-interest, general welfare, and tradition/emotion. Tripartism in social policy is exactly the kind of mechanism that fills the theoretical categories of generalized exchange. We will use Crouch and Campbell and associates to focus on change or transformations of governance regimes as a primary point of research. Indeed, these changes create the most variation in institutions, but they resemble step functions with large increases or decreases at one point in time and then quiescence for the next few years. Not only does their dynamic approach provide a more accurate picture of institutions, but it often points to the underlying reasons or rationales for the existence of institutions in the first place. Welfare state regimes and exchange perspectives have some commonality in that much of this research has been static, and that new research needs to focus much more on the structures and logics of the formation, transformation, and replacement of institutions. This concept of the governance of the economy needs to be adapted to a theory of "regime transformations" in order to capture the dynamic aspects of regimes, but more importantly to further develop institutional theory.

In this brief review of the dynamics of institutional theories, we have shown that four different types of institutional theory have had little focus on institutional changes in political economy. The dynamics of institutions cannot help much in differentiating between these theories since these theories tend to be rather static. However, the two last studies mention focus on institutional dynamics and point us toward capturing the dynamics of labor market institutions.[5]

INSTITUTIONAL EXPLANATIONS
OF UNEMPLOYMENT RATES

Prior examinations of the impact of institutions on unemployment have focused on political parties, union density, and corporatism. Alvarez, Lange, and Lange (1991) focus on left party power as a determinant. Hicks (1995b) looks at a simple measure of corporatism and political party power. Boreham and Compston (1992) look at measures of party power and corporatism. However, none of these studies looks at institutions that have a direct impact on unemployment and what could be called societal corporatism rather than peak corporatism.[6] Typically, peak corporatism refers to national bargaining over wages. Societal corporatism refers to many different forms of bipartite and tripartite self-administration that exist at local, state, and firm councils and boards. Bargaining occurs among the social partners in formulating active labor market policies to reduce unemployment, set the payment of welfare state benefits, and formulate company plans for technological changes and downsizing.

In our approach, five types of institutions have an important impact on unemployment rates: (1) the structure and powers of the employment service, (2) the presence of shop floor institutions such as works councils, (3) the installation of labor representatives in the running of corporate boards through codetermination mechanisms, (4) the self-administration of national welfare state institutions through bipartite or tripartite boards, and (5) the long range and somewhat distant policies of corporatist institutions affecting wage and national economic bargaining. Societal corporatism with the formal cooperation of labor, management, and the state in tripartite arrangements at all levels of the state (items 1, 4 and 5) tend to produce more active labor market policies to reduce unemployment. At the firm level, cooperation between labor and management through bipartite councils at many different levels within the firm enhance training, personnel decisions, the implementation of technology, and ultimately higher productivity (items 2 and 3). With each institutional variable playing a different role, the end results are an institutional context that reduces unemployment.

First, the employment service has the most direct impact on unemployment since it plays a central role as a labor exchange and in many countries it implements most active labor market policies, which are direct state interventions in the labor market to prevent unemployment. The employment service may have monopoly power over job placement with requirements that firms report all vacancies to the service. Furthermore, after the oil crisis, many states further required that employers notify the employment service well in advance of large layoffs and plant closings. A strong employment service will be able to more successfully coordinate and/or implement a large number of active labor market policies when it has a strong presence in the labor market.

This presence will be reinforced by self-administration of the employment service by the social partners and various levels of the state. Tripartite policymaking brings labor, management, and the appropriate level of government together on a regular basis to discuss the labor market, and to cooperatively plan policies. It tends to bind groups together under a common fate and promotes more cooperation. When policy is set, the social partners have already agreed on the programs. This makes successful implementation much more likely. Countries with weak employment services will create new agencies that get in each other's way and perform poorly in the labor market. The lack of self-administration means that labor and management observe state policymaking as outsiders. After the state sets policy, labor and management may decide to fight the policies, ignore them, or be suspicious of them. And with suspicion, wary participants commit few resources and withdraw easily and early. A strong employment service that includes the social partners in the policy planning process will lead to much more successful policy and lower unemployment. In essence, the state can go a long way in shaping the labor market and the attitudes of the social partners through an agency with strong participation and intervention powers.

Second, one step removed from direct policy planning, works councils also have an impact on unemployment. When strong works councillors exist, they work on the shop floor with their workers, with company representatives, and with the employment service in formulating "social plans" that transfer workers within the plant, retrain them, and if need be, include important aspects of active labor market policies that ease laidoff workers back into the labor market with new jobs or into training programs to help create new career paths (Janoski 1990). Works councils facilitate cooperation within the firm with employers and with the employment service in reducing the incidence of unemployment.

Third, codetermination on corporate boards gives labor representatives the knowledge upon which to base important decisions, which include both deciding what the firm should do in the short and long-term, and what the union should do vis-à-vis the firm concerning bargaining demands, strikes, and other industrial actions.[7] The power to influence new technology and investment decisions enables labor representatives to take a responsible position on internal training and promotion policies. The end result is more emphasis on productivity and planning with union cooperation, rather than opposition to new machinery and re-organizations based on suspicion fed by the lack of information and rumors. The end result is greater productivity and less disruption in international markets, which leads to greater market share and higher employment.

Fourth, self-administration in other areas of the welfare state will produce results similar to self-administration in the employment service. Self-administration in pensions, health, disability, and unemployment insurance will further reinforce the context of generalized exchange among the social partners and the state. The impact of self-administration on unemployment is not direct. Nonetheless, the unemployed need continued benefit protections while seeking work. Further, self-administration in the welfare state has a spill-over effect on labor market policy. It can prevent the endless bickering among employers and trade unions about whether workers are avoiding work through disability, health, and other programs. It prevents a reactive approach based on unemployment compensation and welfare, and gives workers the security to pursue a pro-active approach through retraining and new production methods (Janoski 1994, 1996a; Esping-Andersen 1990). This is because the social partners are administering these same programs and are in part responsible for them.

Fifth, national institutions representing general cooperation throughout the economy will have a more distant but still important influence on unemployment. Corporatism with tripartite wage and social policy bargaining between labor, management, and the state will have beneficial impact on unemployment. If the tripartite logic and solidarity works at the employment service level, similar tripartite mechanisms in wage negotiations should have a similar impact.

PAST LIMITATIONS IN MEASURING INSTITUTIONS

One institutional variable that has been measured more often than most—neo-, labor, or democratic corporatism—may serve as an example of problems in measuring institutions. Neo-corporatism has been labeled a growth industry in the 1970s and a mainstay in the 1980s. Even in the 1990s, it provides much motive for analysis despite Crouch and Dore (1990, p. 1) asking "Whatever Happened to Corporatism?" and other critiques announcing yet another "death of corporatism." The long career of measuring corporatism over 20 years has, unfortunately, been mostly indirect by way of proxy variables measuring union centralization and even density, and very little of it has been dynamic.

An initial way of operationalizing corporatism has been to focus on "corporatist-technocratic linkages" connected to centralization of labor union federations and the appointment power of government. Wilensky's measure of the "new corporatism" combined the centralized appointment power at provincial, district and municipal levels of government, and the centralization of labor unions for collective bargaining (e.g., organizational centralization, control of strike funds, the standardized number of staff at headquarters, and percentage of dues collected by the federation). The central appointment power variable experiences little change over time, largely because it is a political structure variable. The labor union federation variable is the same for collective bargaining and strike funds, but central staff and percentage of dues collected most certainly varies every year. This variable has considerable potential for changing over time, but to my knowledge, it has rarely been collected in a dynamic fashion.

Schmitter's (1981 and 1982) corporatist variable was based on interest intermediation and regime governability. He uses Headey's measure of organizational centralization based on the centralization of collective bargaining, the percentage of strike funds controlled by confederations, the staff at headquarters, the standardized size of union confederation finances, the central control of strike funds, and the degree of control over member associations. What is distinctive is Schmitter's measure of associational monopoly, which combines the presence of a single national labor confederation, joint organization of manual and non-manual workers, and no disruptive factions within national confederations.

In Table 1, we survey the operationalization of corporatism variables from 1970 to 1993. After reviewing ten measures, it becomes apparent that most

Table 1. Operationalizing Corporatism: The Components of Various Indices (Y means the variable is operational, N means it was not)

	Union Centralization										
	(1) Collective Bargain (CB)	(2) Control Strike Funds	(3) Stdz. Hdqtrs. Staff	(4) % Dues going to Federation	(5) # of Feds. Organiz. Unity	(6) # of Labor Force in Unions	(7) Works Council	(8) Codeter-mination	(9) Shop Floor Power (low)	(10) Employer Federations	(11) Central Veto Power over Locals
Headey[a,b] (1970)	Y lmh[c] 0, 5, 10	Y lmh[c] 0, 5, 10	Y lmh[c] 0, 5, 10	Y lmh[c] 0, 5, 10	N	N	N	N	N	N	N
Wilensky (1976)	Y lmh 0, 5, 10	Y lmh 0, 5, 10	Y lmh 0, 5, 10	Y lmh 0, 5, 10		N	N	N	N	N	N
Schmitter[a] (1982)	Y lmhc 0, 5, 10	Y lmhc 0, 5, 10	Y lmhc 0, 5, 10	Y lmhc 0, 5, 10	Y 1, 2, 3	N	N	N	N	N	N
Cameron[b] (1984)	Y 0, 1	Y 0, 1	N	N	Y 0, 1	Y %	Y 0, 0.5	Y 0, 0.5	N	N	Y 0, 1
Bruno and Sachs (1985)	Y 0, 1	N	N	N	N	N	Y 0, 1	N	Y 0, 1	Y 0, 1	N
Calmfors and Driffl (1988)	Y nieo[d] 3, 2, 1	N	N	N	Y 1,2-5,0 3, 2, 1	N	N	N	N	N	N
Alvarez, Garrett, and Lange[b] (1991)	Y	Y	Y	Y	N	Y %	N	N	N	N	N
Lijphart and Crepaz (1991)	Y 7 catg 0-1	Y	Y	Y	Y	Y	Y	Y	Y	Y	Y
Western (1992-1993)	Y	Y 0-1	N	N	Y 0-1	N	N	N	Y	N	Y 0-1
Hicks and Swank[e]/Misra (1992-1993)	Y	N	N	N	Y #	Y %	N	N	N	N	N
Total # of Yeses	10	7	5	5	6	4	2	2	2	2	3

	(12) Manual and Non-manual Unions	(13) No Stable Faction in Union	(14) Scope and Range of CB Issues	Central Government Appointment Power			(18) Left Party Power % Cabinet Seats	(19) Left Party Power % Parliament	(20) Index of Class Voting	(21) Voter Turnout	(22) Cumulative Left Rule
				(15) Province	(16) District	(17) Municpal					
Headey[a,b] (1970)	N	N	N	N	N	N	N	N	N	N	N
Wilensky (1976)	N	N	N	Y 0 = local election, 1 = central	Y 0,1	Y 0,1	N	N	N	N	N
Schmitter[a] (1982)	Y 1, 2, 3	Y 1, 1.5	N	N	N	N	N	N	N	N	N
Cameron[b] (1984)	N	N	N	N	N	N	Y %*(19)	Y %*(18)	N	N	N
Bruno and Sachs (1985)	N	N	N	N	N	N	N	N	N	N	N
Calmfors and Drifl (1988)	N	N	N	N	N	N	N	N	N	N	N
Alvarez, Garrett, and Lange[b] (1991)	N	N	N	N	N	N	N	Y	Y	Y	Y
Lijphart and Crepaz (1991)	Y	Y	Y	Y	Y	Y	Y	Y	N	N	N
Western (1992-1993)	N	N	N	N	N	N	N	N	N	N	N
Hicks and Swank[g]/Misra (1992-1993)	N	N	N	N	N	N	N	N	N	N	N
Total # of Yeses	2	2	1	2	2	2	2	3	1	1	1

Notes: [a] The authors convert interval level data to ordinal.

[b] The authors do not label their index as "corporatist."

[c] l = low, m = medium, h = high.

[d] n = national, i = industry, e = enterprise, o = occupational.

[e] Corporatism = [(6)*[(13)+(1)+5)]/3] where numbers in parentheses represent column numbers above.

Class mobilization = [(19)+(20)]*(21).

237

corporatism indexes do not fall far from the tree of the initial attempts in the 1970s and early 1980s. Most of them focus on union centralization and density (columns 1 through 5). A few focus on government appointment power and indexes of left party power (Wilensky 1976; Lijphart and Crepaz 1991; Hicks and Swank 1992; Hicks and Misra 1993). What is amazing about these measures is that none of them actually measures the peak bargaining on a wide range of issues that corporatism is supposed to represent. The actual variables used are proxies, that is, the preconditions of corporatism, mainly union centralization and control. Further, none of these measurements are dynamic over time.

Also corporatism has focused almost exclusively on "peak corporatism" rather than the societal mechanisms whereby labor and management cooperate on a regular basis with the state. This more decentralized "societal corporatism" consists of bi- and tri-partite forms of self-administration of social and economic policies in welfare state and labor market organizations. In Regini's view, the "macro-concertation" of peak corporatism is now giving way to the various forms of "micro-concertation" involved with societal corporatism, which to him also involve the informal strategies of labor and management at the firm level (1995, pp. 79-84, 117-125). We will mainly focus on these less centralized forms of societal corporatism and also consider institutions at the firm level.

OPERATIONALIZING VARIABLES
TO EXPLAIN UNEMPLOYMENT

Five groups of institutional variables—employment service, works councils, codetermination, self-administration, and corporatism—are important to unemployment. Two economic investment variables—private sector capital formation and government capital formation—are also important determinants of economic growth and hence unemployment. They are put into a simple model in Figure 1. Each institutional variable has a two year lag since institutional variables take time before the full impact on unemployment is felt, but the capital expenditure variables are not lagged, which will be discussed below.[8]

The unemployment rate represents the standardized unemployment rates calculated by OECD (1995).[9] Some countries calculate unemployment rates from sample surveys, and other countries rely on employment service records that ignore workers who are not eligible for unemployment benefits. OECD standardizes unemployment rates to take into account these differences, and this makes it the most suitable variable to be used in time and space analyses. For Austria (all years), Denmark (all years), and New Zealand (only 2 years), OECD could not calculate standardized rates, so we used the government's

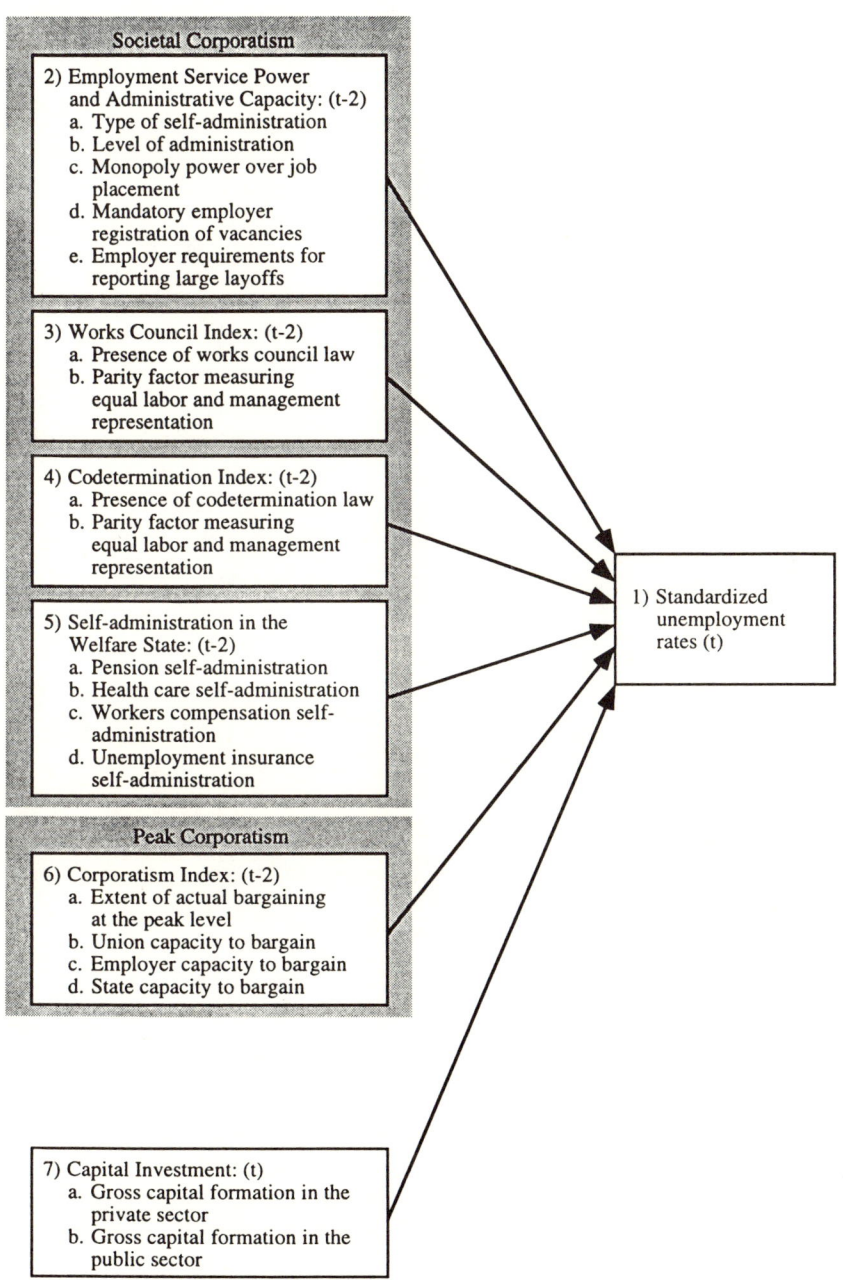

Figure 1. A Cross-sectional and Time Series Model Explaining Unemployment
Rates in Advanced Industrialized Countries

Table 2. Codetermination in Germany

Year	Montan Industry Codetermination Act of 1952: Applies to steel and mining firms.			Works Constitution Act of 1951 Act: Applies to firms with > 500 (and < 2,000 after 1976) employees.			Works Constitution Act of 1975: Applies to firms with > 2,000 employees.		
	X_{13} Law	Parity Factor$_4$	X_{14} % Ee's	X_{15} Law	Parity Factor$_5$	X_{16} Ee's	X_{17} Law	Parity Factor$_6$	X_{18} %Ee's
1955	1	1.0	.054	1	.50	.290	0	0	.097
1956	1	1.0	.054	1	.50	.291	0	0	.096
1957	1	1.0	.054	1	.50	.290	0	0	.096
1958	1	1.0	.054	1	.50	.291	0	0	.096
1959	1	1.0	.053	1	.50	.292	0	0	.095
1960	1	1.0	.053	1	.50	.293	0	0	.096
1961	1	1.0	.052	1	.50	.294	0	0	.095
1962	1	1.0	.052	1	.50	.295	0	0	.094
1963	1	1.0	.052	1	.50	.294	0	0	.094
1964	1	1.0	.051	1	.50	.295	0	0	.094
1965	1	1.0	.051	1	.50	.297	0	0	.095
1966	1	1.0	.050	1	.50	.296	0	0	.094
1967	1	1.0	.050	1	.50	.297	0	0	.093
1968	1	1.0	.050	1	.50	.297	0	0	.094
1969	1	1.0	.049	1	.50	.296	0	0	.093
1970	1	1.0	.049	1	.50	.296	0	0	.092
1971	1	1.0	.048	1	.50	.295	0	0	.092
1972	1	1.0	.048	1	.50	.296	0	0	.093
1973	1	1.0	.048	1	.50	.296	0	0	.091
1974	1	1.0	.048	1	.50	.295	0	0	.092

Year	X_{13}	Parity factor$_4$	X_{14}	X_{15}	Parity factor$_5$	X_{16}	X_{17}	Parity factor$_6$	X_{18}
1975	1	1.0	.048	1	.50	.299	0	0	.092
1976	1	1.0	.047	1	.50	.215	1	.71	.092
1977	1	1.0	.044	1	.50	.218	1	.71	.090
1978	1	1.0	.043	1	.50	.210	1	.71	.088
1979	1	1.0	.042	1	.50	.208	1	.71	.087
1980	1	1.0	.041	1	.50	.203	1	.71	.085
1981	1	1.0	.040	1	.50	.197	1	.71	.086
1982	1	1.0	.039	1	.50	.197	1	.71	.086
1983	1	1.0	.038	1	.50	.204	1	.71	.087
1984	1	1.0	.037	1	.50	.219	1	.71	.087
1985	1	1.0	.037	1	.50	.202	1	.71	.086
1986	1	1.0	.036	1	.50	.198	1	.71	.085
1987	1	1.0	.035	1	.50	.197	1	.71	.084
1988	1	1.0	.033	1	.50	.191	1	.71	.082
1989	1	1.0	.032	1	.50	.192	1	.71	.082

Notes:

X_{13}: The Codetermination Law for the coal and steel industries: 1 = effective law has been passed, 0 = no law.

Parity factor$_4$: Ratio of labor to management representatives on corporate boards. In this first law, there is full parity (i.e., 6 board members are labor representatives and 6 are management) so the score is 1.0 (6/6 = 1).

X_{14}: The percentage of employees covered by the first law.

X_{15}: The Codetermination Law for firms greater than 500 employees: 1 = effective law has been passed, 0 = no law.

Parity factor$_5$: Ratio of labor to management representatives on corporate boards. In the second law, there is partial parity (i.e., 4 board members are labor and 8 are employer representatives) so the score is 0.50 (4/8 = .50).

X^{16}: The percentage of employees covered by the second law.

X^{17}: The Codetermination Law for firms with more than 2,000 employees: 1 = effective law has been passed, 0 = no law.

Parity factor^6: Ratio of labor to management representatives on corporate boards. In the third law, there is nearly full parity (i.e., 5 board members are labor and 7 are worker representatives) so the score is 0.71 (5/7 = .71).

X_{18}: The percentage of employees covered by the third law.

241

reported rate of unemployment.[10] An inspection of differences between standardized and governmental rates shows they to be rather small and often the same after rounding to one decimal point. Consequently, we do not think this makes a major difference.

The method of constructing indexes representing institutions can vary. Lange, Golden and Wallerstein (1993) construct Guttman scale indexes ranked in ordinal fashion. We construct additive indexes since none of the variables really fits the strict ordering of a Guttman scale; that is, monopoly over job placement does not require self-administration and vice versa. Weighting the components of each index with precise coefficients is a problem. Our practice varies with each variable. In general we do not weigh components, but where we have multiple measures of institutional components, we combine them equally rather than let the number of sources rule (e.g., we use two measures of self administration and four measures of labor market power, but we balance the self-administration and labor market power equally rather than give labor market power a four to two edge in the final index). For example, see the time-series construction of codetermination based on three different laws for Germany in Table 2.

The sources for data on these institutional variables are highly varied and too numerous to list. We relied on the following works on a number of countries for much of the data: Bamber and Lansbury (1993), Bruno and Sachs (1985), Crouch (1992), Ferner and Hyman (1992), Flora (1987), Hartoog and Theeuwes (1993), Kennedy (1980), Lijphart and Crepaz (1991) Locke and associates (1995), OECD (1991, 1994), and Sisson (1987). Data on firm and sector size for the works council and codetermination variables came from national sources and Eurostat (1991, 1993).

With each variable we are careful not to measure economic or political resources. The aim is to find institutional rules that are represented by laws and norms rather than overall expenditures or personnel employed by an institution. The budget of the employment service is not included, because this is a result of overall society resources rather than institutional strength.[11] Instead, we tend to focus mainly on power embedded in rules established for the most part by legislation.

(1) *The Employment Service:* First, we look at a number of variables that reflect the strength of the employment service: self-administration, monopoly power over job placement, and employer reporting requirements. Self-administration of the employment service involves the amount of tripartite self-administration of labor, management, and the government in the administration of the employment service. The scores for the administrative style of employment service range from 3 for tripartite policy administration to 0 for no employment service at all.

Tripartite self-administration is measured on a range of levels as to whether it occurs in the federal, state and local government. The scores for self-administration at various levels of government range reflect self-administration at all three levels (federal, state or province, and local) in the employment service to no self-administration at any level of the employment service (see Table 3 for coding categories). The scores for the administrative style of employment service are: $3 =$ tripartite policy administration, $2 =$ bipartite policy administration, $1 =$ executive policy administration, and $0 =$ no employment service. Tripartite self-administration is also measured as to whether it occurs at the federal, state and local levels. The scores for self-administration at various levels of government are: $3 =$ all three levels (federal, state or province, and local) of employment services, $2 =$ two of three levels, $1 =$ one of three levels, and $0 =$ no self-administration. These two scores are put on a scale of 1.0 by dividing by the highest total score, which results in an index that ranges from zero—$0 = (0 + 0)/6$—to one—$1 = (3 + 3)/6$.

The employment service monopoly variable measures the extent of monopoly power over job placement (OECD 1991, p. 218). This is a key indicator of institutional strength that lays the foundation for employment service power. The scoring is: $2 =$ complete monopoly power with all private agencies being banned, $1 =$ partial monopoly with some temporary agencies being approved, $0 =$ no monopoly with all types of private agencies being permitted. A score of 0 means that there is widespread competition between the public employment service and a myriad of private services—temporary labor pools, college placement offices, and executive head hunters.

Employer reporting requirements to the employment service are measured in two ways. First, the reporting requirement for notifying vacancies to the public employment service generally refers to reporting external vacancies, that is, to the openings that a firm would advertise to the general public. A much more stringent requirement represents reporting both internal and external vacancies. Internal vacancies generally refer to promotions that would only be advertised within the firm for their internal labor markets. Reporting those vacancies is clearly much more significant than just reporting external vacancies. Employer reporting requirements were coded as follows: $2 =$ report internal and external vacancies, $1 =$ report external vacancies, $0 =$ no vacancy reporting requirements (OECD 1991, p. 218). Second, the reporting requirement also involves employer reporting large layoffs or plant closings to the employment service. In many countries since 1974, employers must report large layoffs to the employment service. These range from reporting layoffs as small as 50 persons, which we scored as a 2, to reporting much larger layoffs greater than a 100, which we scored as a 1. No layoff requirements were scored as 0.

These three variables are also added together and divided by their highest scores to produce a employment service power index that ranges from zero—$0 = (0 + 0 + 0)/6$—to 1 $(3 + 3 + 3)/6$.

Table 3.   The Formulas and Variables for Institutional Index Computations

1. Employment Service Index:

a. *Indexes:*

Employment service index:
  EMPSERVE = (ADM + ESP) * X_6
  (1) Employment service administrative capacity index:
  ADM = $(X_1 + X_2)/6$
  (2) *Employment service power index:*
  ESP = $(X_3 + X_4 + X_5)/6$

b. *Primary Variables:*

  X_1 Type of administration: 1 = executive bureaucracy, 2 = bipartite self-administration, or 3 = tripartite self administration.

  X_2 Level of self-administration at the federal, state, or local levels: 1 = one level, 2 = two levels, and 3 = three levels.

  X_3 Monopoly over job placement, especially with private employment agencies: 0 = private permitted, 1 = private temporary approved, or 2 = private agencies banned

  X_4 Employer vacancy reporting requirements: 0 = none, 1 = extermal but not internal vacancies, 2 = all vacancies.

  X_5 Employer layoff reporting requirements: 0 = none, 1 = more than 100 workers laid off, 2 = more than 50 persons laid off.

  X_6 Percentage of the labor force covered by the employment service, which for the purposes of this paper are private sector employees divided by the total labor force, except in the Scandinavian countries because the employment service also covers state employees.

2. Works Council Index:

a. *Works council index:*

  WORKSCO = $(X_7$ * parity factor$_1$ * $X_8) + (X_9$ * parity factor$_2$ * $X_{10}) + (X_{11}$ * parity factor$_3$ * $X_{12})$

b. *Primary Variables:*

  X_7 Works Council Law—1: The country has passed a works council law for the first sector (e.g., in Germany private firms greater than 5 employees) and the enforce it: 1 = effective law has been passed, 0 = no law.

  Parity factor$_1$: The parity factor is 1.0 because this first law had works council with equal representation by labor and manasgement.

  X_8 Percentage of employees in sector one.

  X_9 Works Council Law—2: The country has passed a works council law for a second sector and they enforce it (e.g., in Germany the federal government): 1 = effective law has been passed, 0 = no law.

  Parity factor$_2$: The parity factor is 1.0 when the works council is fully represented by labor nad has full codetermination rights based on the German system. When the council has management representatives, the percentage drops. When the council lacks any particular codetermination right, its percentage also drops.

  X_{10} Percentage of employees in sector two (e.g., federal government employment).

  X_{11} Works Council Law—3: The country has passed a works council law for as third sector and they enforce it (e.g., for state and local government employees in Germany): 1 = effective law has been passed, 0 = no law.

  Parity factor$_3$: The parity factor is 1.0 when the works council is fully represented by labor and has full codetermination rights based on the German system.

  X_{12} Percentage of employees in sector three (often state and local government employment).

(continued)

Table 3. (Continued)

3. Codetermination Index:

a. *Codetermination index:*

CODETERM = $(X_{13}$ * Parity Factor$_1$ * $X_{14})$ + $(X_{15}$ * Parity Factor$_2$ * $X_{16})$
+ $(X_{17}$ * Parity Factor$_3$ * $X_{18})$

b. *Primary Variables:*

X_{13} Codtermination Law—1: The country has passed a codetermination law for various sectors (i.e., coal and steel industries, firms greater than 500 employees, firms with greater
than 2,000 employees) that they enforce: 1 = effective law has been passed, 0 = no
law.

Parity factor$_1$: This represents the ratio of labor to management representatives in the first codetermination law. It is a ratio of labor to management representatives. For example, in
the first codtermination law in Germany, there is full parity (i.e., 6 of 12 board members
are labor representatives) so the score is 1.0

X_{14} The percentage of employees covered by the first law (e.g., in Germany these are
employees in steel and mining firms divided by the total work force).

X_{15} Codetermination Law—2: The country has passed a second codetermination law for a
second sector, and they enforce it: 1 = effective law has been passed, 0 = no law.

Parity factor$_2$: This represents whether there is equal representation between labor and manag-
sement in the second codetermination law. It is a ratio of labor to management representatives. For example, in the second codetermination law in Germany, there is partial
parity (i.e., 4 of 8 board members are labor representatives) so the score is 0.50.

X_{16} The percentae of employees covered by the second law, which is the percentage of
employees in firms with more than 500 employees.

X_{17} Codetermination Law—3: The country has passed a codetermination law for a third sector
and they enforce it: 1 = effective law has been passed, 0 = no law.

Parity factor^3: This represents whether there is equal representation between labor and management in the third codetermination law. It is a ratio of labor to management representatives. For example, in the third codetermination law in Germany, there is nearly full
parity (i.e., 5 labor to 7 management board members) so the score is 0.71.

X_{18} The percentage of employees covered by the third law, which is the percentage of
employees in firms with greater than 2,000 employees.

4. Self-administration Index:

a. *Self-administration index:*

SELFADM = $(X_{19} + X_{20} + X_{21} + X_{22})/12$

b. *Primary Variables:*

X_{19} Pension self-administration: 1 = executive control, 2 = bipartism, 3 = tripartism
X_{20} Health care system self-administration: 1 = executive control, 2 = bipartism, 3 =
tripartism
X_{21} Compensation sysltem administration: 1 = executive control, 2 = bipartism, 3 = tripartism
X_{22} Unemployment insurance system self-administration: 1 = executive control, 2 = bipar-
tism, 3 = tripartism

5. Corporatism index:

a. *Indexes:* (Stdz. = standardize by subtracting the mean and dividing by the standard deviation).
Corporatism index (Average of actual bargaining and capacity to bargain):

CORPORSM = Stdz. (AB) + Stdz. (SC + UC + SC)

(1) Extent of actual bargaining:

AB = Stdz. (X_{23}) + Stdz. (X_{24}) + Stdz. (X_{25}) + Stdz. (X_{26})

(continued)

Table 3.   (Continued)

5. **Corporatism index: (continued)**
    (2) Union capacity to bargain:
    $UC = (X_{27} + X_{28})/2 + (X_{29} + X_{30})/2$
    (3) Employer capacity to bargain:
    $EC = (1/X_{31}) + X_{32}$
    (4) State capacity to bargain:
    $SC = \text{Stdz. } (X_{33}) + \text{Stdz. } (X_{34}) + \text{Stdz. } (X_{35}) + (X_{36})$

b. *Primary Variables:*
    (1) Extent of actual bargaining:
    X_{23} Level of collective bargaining: 0.5 = company union with company, 1 = industrial or craft unions with company, 2 = regional federation bargaining, 3 = national federation in industry bargaining, 4 = national federations in national bargaining.
    X_{24} Range of collective bargaining: Extension of collective bargaining agreements tounionized and non-unionized industry, percentage.
    X_{25} Level of policy bargaining, range of issues: The number of following: incomes policies, welfare state policies, and other policies.
    X_{26} Formal Council: The presence of a formal corporatist council that meets on a regular basis.
    (2) Measures of trade union capacities:
    X_{27} Trade union staff: Trade union federation number of staff divided by the membership.
    X_{28} Trade union federation power to veto strikes: 1 = veto power, 0 = no veto power.
    X_{29} Trade union federation take of dues: Percent of total that goes to the federation.
    X_{30} Trade union frame bargaining in actual collective bargaining frame agreements: 1 = frame agreement participation, 0 = no frame agreement participation.
    (3) Measures of employer capacities:
    X_{31} Number of employer federations.
    X_{32} Employer federation disciplinary control over members: 1 = some disciplinary control over members; 0 = no disciplinary control over members.
    (4) Measures of state capacities:
    X_{33} Central state appointment power at state and local levels.
    X_{34} Party discipline: Percent of legislative votes decided on straight party line voting as an average of major parties.
    X_{35} Centralization of the federal government—parliamentary form: 1 = unicameral system, 0 = bicameral system.
    X_{36} Centralization of the federal government—leadership: 1 = cabinet or committee parliamentarianism, 0 = presidential system.

Finally, the total self-administration index sums the self-administration index score—$(ES_1 + ES_2/6$—and the labor market power index $(X_1 + X_2)/6$, $(X_3 + X_4 + X_5)/6$—and multiplies both by the percentage of the labor force (X_6) that is covered by the employment service. This produces an overall index that ranges from zero to 1.62 in practice. The average scores for 18 countries for each five year period between 1970 and 1989 can be seen in Table 4. Again, the budget of the employment service is not included, because this is part of the outcome and would also result in a partial tautology (OECD 1991, p. 218). Further, the index was not standardized statistically because each component

Table 4. Employment Service Index Scores,
Averaged for Four Five Year Periods from 1970 to 1989

Country:	Employment Service Index, Average of 5 Years:			
	1970-1974	*1975-1979*	*1980-1984*	*1985-1989*
Australia	0.1258	0.1262	0.1322	0.1326
Austria	—	0.6374	0.6265	0.6150
Belgium	0.9112	0.9211	0.8426	0.8243
Canada	0.1167	0.1667	0.1667	0.1667
Denmark	0.8103	0.9718	0.9270	0.9727
Finland	—	0.4131	0.4088	0.4644
France	0.4348	0.4221	0.7932	0.7935
Germany	0.9634	1.0873	1.0995	1.0993
Ireland	0.2082	0.3321	0.3321	0.5313
Italy	0.2875	0.2831	0.2701	0.3678
Japan	0.2146	0.2181	0.2284	0.2405
Netherlands	0.2401	0.3837	0.4740	0.4769
Norway	0.9872	1.0334	1.0022	1.0008
New Zealand	0.1667	0.1667	0.1667	0.1662
Sweden	1.1580	1.1120	1.0491	1.0545
Switzerland	0.1615	0.1612	0.1615	0.1618
U.K.	0.4825	0.4740	0.4601	0.3103
U.S.A.	0.1227	0.1238	0.1258	0.1274

Note: The maximum range of this index is 2.0 times the percentage of non-state employees, which vasries. A rough estimate of the range is 0 to 1.6.

variable has very similar units. This method of calculation weighs self-administration and powers over employers equally because these two aspects of employment service power naturally tend to cluster together. The subsequent index ranges from 0 to 2 (the maximum is the sum of 1 plus 1 times 100%). In many countries, there has been a trend toward increasing layoff reporting requirements in the 1970s due to the oil crisis, and a trend away from monopoly powers in the labor market due to the rise of market-oriented political regimes.

(2) Works Councils within Firms: Firm-based institutions are less directly connected to ALMP; however, they are involved in decisions about layoffs and various protections that the employment service offers. Workers councils tend to be enacted for different segments of the labor force, including state workers, at different points in time. Workers councils in each of the specific sectors of the economy (categories change from firm size in some countries to industrial sectors in other countries) were legislated and implemented.[12] We measure the law (as a dummy variable if the law is actually implemented), the percentage of the labor force that it covers, and then factor in a parity factor that measures the percentage of works councils issues and powers enabled by the law. The parity factor represents total employee control of the works council, since being an interest organization (i.e., representing employees) is

Table 5.   Works Council Index Scores,
Averaged for Four Five Year Periods from 1970 to 1989

Country:	Works Council Index, Average of 5 Years:			
	1970-1974	1975-1979	1980-1984	1985-1989
Australia	0.0000	0.0000	0.0000	0.0000
Austria	0.1474	0.7365	0.8422	0.3245
Belgium	0.2795	0.2795	0.2795	0.0104
Canada	0.0000	0.0000	0.0000	0.0000
Denmark	0.0684	0.0684	0.0684	0.0684
Finland	0.0367	0.0536	0.0786	0.0701
France	0.0000	0.0282	0.1320	0.1207
Germany	0.8150	0.8312	0.8471	0.8518
Ireland	0.0000	0.0000	0.0000	0.0000
Italy	0.0000	0.0000	0.0000	0.0000
Japan	0.0000	0.0000	0.0000	0.0000
Netherlands	0.1251	0.1509	0.3261	0.4251
Norway	0.1975	0.2281	0.4096	0.4195
New Zealand	0.0000	0.0000	0.0000	0.0000
Sweden	—	0.0666	0.0133	0.1144
Switzerland	0.0000	0.0000	0.0000	0.0000
U.K.	0.0000	0.0000	0.0000	0.0000
U.S.A.	0.0000	0.0000	0.0000	0.0000

Note: The range on this index is 0 to 1.0000.

its theoretical intent. Where managers are members of works councils, the parity factor is reduced in proportion to their presence. Since Germany has the strongest works councils, it is used as the standard for full works councils powers and abilities. The combined product of the law, the work force covered, and the parity factor results in the final works council measure in that sector. The same is done for the other sectors. The three sectors are then added to produce a variable that combines the percentage of the labor force covered by realistically enforced works councils. Scores for 18 countries are listed in Table 5.

(3) Codetermination on Corporate Boards: The codetermination measure operates in a similar way to the works councils. Since there are frequently different laws, a separate variable is computed for each sector (be it based on size, industry, or the private-state divide). A variable is developed for passage of a law and for the segment of the labor force covered. A codetermination parity factor measures the level of participation by labor representatives on corporate boards; it represents the equality between labor and management (i.e., it differs from the works council parity factor because boards represent all parties, while works councils only represent workers and employees).

For example, the Works Constitution Act of 1952 in Germany established codetermination requiring only two labor representatives on a six member

Table 6. Codetermination Index Scores,
Averaged for Four Five Year Periods from 1970 to 1989

	Codetermination Index, Average of 5 Years:			
Country:	*1970-1974*	*1975-1979*	*1980-1984*	*1985-1989*
Australia	0.0000	0.0000	0.0000	0.0000
Austria	0.0000	0.2697	0.3228	0.3245
Belgium	0.0000	0.0065	0.0111	0.0104
Canada	0.0000	0.0000	0.0000	0.0000
Denmark	0.0620	0.1240	0.1240	0.1240
Finland	0.0000	0.0000	0.0000	0.0000
France	0.0000	0.0000	0.0125	0.0238
Germany	0.2466	0.3052	0.3036	0.2955
Ireland	0.0000	0.0000	0.0000	0.0000
Italy	0.0000	0.0000	0.0000	0.0000
Japan	0.0000	0.0000	0.0000	0.0000
Netherlands	0.0000	0.0000	0.0000	0.0000
Norway	0.0219	0.0462	0.0466	0.0467
New Zealand	0.0000	0.0000	0.0000	0.0000
Sweden	—	0.0908	0.0868	0.0889
Switzerland	0.0000	0.0000	0.0000	0.0000
U.K.	0.0000	0.0000	0.0000	0.0000
U.S.A.	0.0000	0.0000	0.0000	0.0000

Note: The range is 0 to 1.0000.

board (see Table 2 for a time-series presentation). The result is 50 percent of full equality between labor and management on the board of directors; that is, the number of labor representatives is divided by the number of management representatives to obtain a measure of equality between the two ($2/4 = .50$, or the 50% parity factor is the worker's representation of 33% divided by the management representation of 67%). The 1952 Act for the Montan industries (coal, iron and steel companies) allowed an equal number of labor and management representatives ($5/5 = 1$ or 50% for labor divided by 50% for management). Consequently, the parity factor for this law was 1.0. The act of 1976 operates in a similar way on firms with more than 2,000 employees. It allowed six management and six labor representatives; however, one labor representative was elected by the leading employees (management and professional employees), so the parity score was .72 of full parity ($.7152 = 5/7$). The three variables—the dummy variable for the existence of a law, the parity factor for worker representation, and the percentage of the labor force covered by the law—are then multiplied together and then summed over the various laws to obtain the strength of codetermination in each country. See Table 6 for the codetermination scores in 18 countries.

Table 7. Self-administration Index Scores,
Averaged for Four Five Year Periods from 1970 to 1989

Country:	Self-administration Index, Average of 5 Years:			
	1970-1974	*1975-1979*	*1980-1984*	*1985-1989*
Australia	0.3333	0.3333	0.3333	0.3333
Austria	0.8333	0.8333	0.8333	0.8333
Belgium	0.5833	0.5833	0.5833	0.5833
Canada	0.6667	0.6667	0.6667	0.6667
Denmark	0.6667	0.6667	0.6667	0.6667
Finland	0.3333	0.3333	0.3333	0.3333
France	0.5833	0.5833	0.5833	0.5833
Germany	0.7500	0.7500	0.7500	0.7500
Ireland	0.6667	0.6667	0.6667	0.6667
Italy	0.6667	0.6667	0.6667	0.6667
Japan	0.3333	0.3333	0.03333	0.3333
Netherlands	0.4167	0.4167	0.4167	0.4167
Norway	0.3333	0.3333	0.3333	0.3333
New Zealand	0.3333	0.3333	0.3333	0.3333
Sweden	0.4167	0.4167	0.4167	0.4167
Switzerland	0.6667	0.6667	0.6667	0.6667
U.K.	0.6667	0.6667	0.6667	0.6667
U.S.A.	0.3333	0.3333	0.3333	0.3333

Note: The range is 0.3333 to 1.0000.

(4) *Self-Administrative Institutions in the Welfare State:* Welfare state institutions involve a number of measures that look at how much labor, management and the state set and implement policy in the four areas of pensions, health, disability and unemployment insurance. This measure looks at how much labor, management and the state set policy in these four areas. Self-administration is scored as follows: 3 = tripartite self-administration, 2 = bipartite self-administration of management and labor, 1.5 = bipartite self-administration of management and the state, 1 = executive bureaucracy (the state manages the whole program), and 0 = no policy organization at all (no country should fit this except health for the U.S.). The four areas are then summed and divided by twelve, which is the maximum score, to produce a percentage of total self-administration in the welfare state score that ranges from zero to one. See Table 7 for the self-administration scores in 18 countries.

(5) *Peak Corporatism:* Neo-corporatism looks at tripartism at a peak or elite level. These variables are not directly involved in labor market policy administration; nonetheless, they provide an institutional context of generalized exchange for other more directly involved institutions. Two NSF projects in political science have recently attempted to make corporatism dynamic. Miriam Golden, Peter Lange, and Michael Wallerstein attempt

dynamic measures of corporatism over the post-war period. In one project on union centralization (Lange, Wallerstein, and Golden 1991), they concentrate on processes and structures of union centralization, which if used as a measure of corporatism leads back to the same critique about focusing on capacities to act rather than real action. In a more recent project (Golden, Lange, and Wallerstein 1993), the authors focus more explicitly on corporatism. They measure the level at which bargaining occurs and the intensity of government involvement in wage setting. Their index of centralization of wage setting includes six levels of bargaining. Their index of government involvement in private wage setting ranges from no government involvement to parliament passing peak wage settlements. This is a major advance over prior attempts to measure corporatism because: (a) they directly measure corporatist bargaining rather than only presenting the preconditions of bargaining, and (b) their index of government involvement in private wage setting consists of disaggregating the analysis of union centralization to include component unions.[13] Nonetheless, it raises some issues. First of all, should corporatism be measured as a Guttman scale where score 2 requires score 1? Cannot a number of features of corporatism be combined in an additive fashion? After all, corporatism is a complex and not necessarily unidimensional phenomenon. We suggest measuring a range of issues covered in the bargaining. Also corporatism may be present in different policy domains, and the larger number of domains, the stronger the corporatism.

Our comprehensive measure of corporatism includes two basic components: direct measures of bargaining, and capacities of the social partners and the state to bargain. The direct measures include four variables focusing on the presence of a formal council for bargaining. The capacities for bargaining include a wide range of measures for unions, a few for employers, and a moderate number for the state.[14] A total corporatism measure combines and standardizes these direct bargaining and capacity to bargain variables. This measure would provide a comprehensive and complex measure of corporatism. However, we have too much missing data on direct bargaining phenomena to compute peak corporatism and will instead rely on societal corporatism for the analysis in this paper.

(*6*) *Capital Investment:* The second part of the model concerns standard economic explanations of unemployment that rely on capital investment (Boreham and Compston 1992). Investment in private sector machinery, plant facilities, and land creates new jobs by increasing production capacity. Similarly, capital investment in government activities leads to increases in infrastructure (roads, bridges, and expanding water and sewage treatment) that leads to new construction jobs and then an opening up of business expansion in new areas. Capital investment in buildings for service provision provides less job expansion for construction since the work is generally less technical than infrastructure, but these expenditures then lead to increasing numbers of jobs in the government service sector. While more complex models of job growth based on the corporate profits, money supply, taxation, inflation, deficits, and foreign trade are available (Hicks 1995b, p. 197), our purpose here is to provide both capital formation variables as control variables for institutional effects. The capital formation variables that we use are important components of job growth, which is largely the converse of unemployment, and putting them together with institutional variables provides an important check on the effectiveness of institutional theory.[15]

Total economy-wide and government capital expenditures were operationalized as a percentage of GNP. Private sector capital formation was calculated by subtracting government capital formation from total economic capital formation for each country. Capital formation variables were relatively easy to measure over time because they all came the OECD *National Accounts Statistics* (1995). However, they carried some limitations because many nations did not compile these measures before 1978, and New Zealand apparently has never met OECD data collection standards on this variable. The capital expenditure variables were not lagged because investment expenditures often produce an increase in jobs rather immediately compared to institutional variables. A case could be made for short lags, but we found that the effects for capital expenditures declined quickly with lags and would entirely disappear with lags over two years long.

METHODOLOGY

The data were put into a year by country case format for purposes of a pooled cross-sectional and time-series analysis using a generalized least squares procedure designed to correct for two types of error typical for such data (Hicks 1995a; Stimson 1985; Kmenta 1988). First, it corrects for auto-correlation due to the connection among years within countries, that is, unemployment in 1982 being related to unemployment in 1981. Second, it corrects for autocorrelation due to the connections between variables within a country itself, that is, unemployment in Sweden for any year will be lower than unemployment in the United States no matter what the year. This approach also allowed us to clearly divide the variance explained into time and country components. There are three popular models of pooled regression—Parks-Kmenta, Fuller-Battese (error or variance components), and DaSilva (variance-component moving average) models. We use the Parks-Kmenta model because it assumes first-order autoregressive correlation in time and contemporaneous correlation within countries in cross-sections (Hicks 1995a, pp. 173-176; SAS 1991, pp. 882-884). The Fuller-Battese model (Hicks 1995a, pp. 176-178; SAS 1991, pp. 879-881) assumes independently distributed errors, which does not describe the known structure of our data, and the Da Silva method (SAS 1991, pp. 884-

886) uses a moving average, which may be fine for seasonal (e.g., monthly data) but not yearly unemployment rates subject to a highly variable business cycle.

The data have 187 cases, which represent seventeen countries with eleven years of data (1978 to 1988). Because missing data violate the assumptions of the pooled statistical models, all data points must be present. The data constraints are due to the limitations on capital expenditures previously discussed—New Zealand not reporting this data, and many other countries are missing on many years from 1950 to 1977.

RESULTS

The average scores for the period of 1978 to 1988 in seventeen countries ranked according to their unemployment rates can be seen in Table 8, and the correlation coefficients are in Table 9. The employment service, works council, and codetermination variables are negatively correlated with unemployment, which means that they may prevent unemployment (see column 1 in Table 9), but only the last two are significant. Self-administration variable is positive and significantly correlated with unemployment, which means that it may increase rather than decrease unemployment. This result argues against the theory we presented on this variable. The results for capital formation are both strong and negative. Private capital formation is the strongest measure working against unemployment and government capital formation, even though it is at a much lower level of expenditure, is also quite strong.

Table 9 also indicates that there are some multicollinearity problems. All of the institutional variables are significantly correlated with each other (e.g., codetermination and works councils reach a coefficient of .72). The two capital formation variables are also highly correlated with themselves with a coefficient of .56. We will present a final equation in the analysis that will take only one institutional and one capital expenditure variable from each group to avoid these problems.

In the regression analysis, four pooled cross-sectional and time-series regression equations can be seen in Table 10. In equation 1, all four institutional variables are regressed on unemployment. The employment service strongly reduces unemployment with works councils in the right direction but not significantly. As one would expect from the correlation coefficients, self-administration is strong and significant but in the opposite direction from our original theory. Codetermination is not significant and close to zero, which may be a result of multicollinearity. In equation 2, the capital expenditure variables are both strongly negative, but only the private capital expenditure variable is significant. The institutional variables explain 26 percent of the variation in unemployment rates, while the two capital formation variables explain 18 percent.

Table 8. Average Scores for Unemployment and Its Causes

Country:	Unemployment 1978 to 1988: (1) UN	Institutional Variables, 1976 to 1986 (2) ES	(3) WC	(4) CD	(5) SLF	Capital Expenditure Variables from 1978 to 1988: (6) CPVT	(7) CPUB
Low unemployment:							
Switzerland	0.58	0.16	0.00	0.00	0.67	0.20	0.04
Norway	2.40	1.01	0.39	0.05	0.33	0.24	0.04
Japan	2.45	0.23	0.00	0.00	0.33	0.22	0.05
Sweden	2.50	1.06	0.10	0.09	0.42	0.15	0.03
Austria	3.10	0.62	0.83	0.32	0.83	0.20	0.04
New Zealand	3.79	0.17	0.00	0.00	0.33	—	—
Finland	5.29	0.43	0.08	0.00	0.33	0.22	0.04
Germany	6.14	1.10	0.85	0.30	0.75	0.18	0.03
Average:[a]	3.280	0.598	0.281	0.095	0.500	0.201	0.036
High unemployment:							
U.S.A.	7.08	0.13	0.00	0.00	0.33	0.18	0.02
Australia	7.15	0.13	0.00	0.00	0.33	0.22	0.03
Denmark	7.92	0.95	0.07	0.12	0.67	0.17	0.03
France	8.36	0.72	0.12	0.01	0.92	0.18	0.03
U.K.	8.98	0.43	0.00	0.00	0.67	0.15	0.02
Netherlands	9.11	0.48	0.33	0.00	0.42	0.19	0.03
Canada	9.17	0.17	0.00	0.00	0.67	0.20	0.03
Italy	9.29	0.29	0.00	0.00	0.67	0.19	0.03
Belgium	10.60	0.84	0.28	0.01	0.58	0.15	0.03
Ireland	12.96	0.38	0.00	0.00	0.67	0.21	0.04
Average:[a]	9.06	0.452	0.080	0.014	0.593	0.184	0.028
Ratio of high to low averages:	0.362	1.320	3.513	6.786	0.843	1.092	1.274

Variable Names: (1) *UN*: Unemployment rate from 1978 to 1988, standardized to common definitions for most countries (OECD 1995). Austria, Denmark and Ireland have national definitions. (2) *ES*: Employment service index. (3) *WC*: Works council index. (4) *CD*: Codetermination index. (5) *SLF*: Self-administration index. (6) *CPVT*: Private Sector capital formation. (7) *CPUB*: Government capital formation.

Note: [a] Averages are taken of the original data before rounding occurred for table presentation.

254

Table 9. Zero-Order Correlation Coefficients for 17 Countries from 1978-1988

	(1)	(2)	(3)	(4)	(5)	(6)	(7)
(1) Unemployment rate, no lag	1.00						
(2) Employment service, 2 yr. lag	-.11	1.00					
(3) Works councils, 2 yr. lag	-.20*	+.54*	1.00				
(4) Codetermination, 2 yr.lag	-.27*	+.54*	+.72*	1.00			
(5) Self-administration, 2 yr. lag	+.22*	+.18*	+.32*	+.33*	1.00		
(6) Government capital, no lag	-.30*	-.04	+.01	+.01	-.07	1.00	
(7) Private capital formation, no lag	-.38*	-.28*	-.01	-.01	-.25*	+.56*	1.00

Note: $*$ = significant at the $p < .05$ level.

255

Table 10. Pooled and Cross-sectional Regressions
Explaining Unemployment Rates from 1978-1988

	Equations in each column; scores are unstandardized Beta weights, standard errors, and probability values:			
Variables:	*(1)*	*(2)*	*(3)*	*(4)*
Institutions:				
Employment service, lagged 2 years	-4.477** (.6218) [.0001]	—	-4.231** (.5940) [.0001]	—
Works councils, lagged 2 years	-1.25 (1.260) [.3240]	—	-0.258 (1.020) [.8010]	—
Codetermination, lagged 2 years	0.42 (.7240) [.5660]	—	-0.090 (.8089) [.9120]	-2.403* (1.067) [.0240]
Self-administration, lagged 2 years	2.868** (.7465) [.001]	—	2.649** (.5290) [.0001]	—
Capital Formation:				
Private capital, unlagged	—	-14.574** (2.327) [.0001]	-18.524** (.5924) [.0001]	-14.283** (2.634) [.0001]
Public capital, unlagged	—	-23.472 (12.81) [.0609]	—	—
Constant	4.0331 (1.0331) [.0001]	9.5757 (.7061) [.0001]	5.9060 (1.114) [.0001]	8.1194 (.5995) [.0001]
Summary Statistics:				
R^2/R^2 Raw Moment[b]	.26/.69	.18/.67	.38/.87	.15/.67
n	187	187	187	187

Notes:　* Significant at the $p < .05$ level; ** significant at the $p < .01$ level.
　　　　[a] The Parks-Kmenta method is used for the pooled and cross-sectional regressions (SAS 1991; Shazam 1993).
　　　　[b] R^2s represent the Buse R^2 and nthe Buse Raw-Moment R^2 (see pooled program in SHAZAM 1993 and Buse 1973 and 1979). SAS TSCSREG does not calculate an R^2.

In equation 3, private capital expenditures and all four institutional variables are included in one equation. The results show that the employment service, self-administration, and private capital are strongly negative and significant, while self-administration is positive and significant. The employment service and private capital formation reduce unemployment, while self-administration

Table 11.   Time and Space Explanations of Unemployment
by Codetermination Laws and Private Capital Expenditures

Cross-sectional Analyses in 11 Different Years:		Time-series Analyses for 16 Countries:[1]		
	(1)		*(2)*	*(3)*
Year	R^2 each year	Country	R^2 1978-88	R^2 11 years or more
1978	.11	*Codetermination varies:*		
1979	.15	Austria	.32	.80 1973-88
1980	.26	Belgium	.87	.88 1965-89
1981	.25	France	.80	.91 1973-89
1982	.29	Germany	.45	.75 1973-88
1983	.26	Norway	.46	.61 1965-88
1984	.23	Sweden	.69	.44 1976-89
1985	.36			
1986	.49	*Codetermination is constant:*		
1987	.55	Australia	.47	.62 1973-88
1988	.30	Canada	.51	.76 1965-90
		Denmark	.40	.40 1973-89
		Finland	.52	.49 1965-90
		Ireland	.51	.84 1971-90
		Italy	.58	.83 1973-89
		Japan	.57	.80 1965-89
		Netherlands	.31	.78 1973-90
		Switzerland	.51	.58 1977-88
		U.K.	.61	.87 1965-90
		U.S.A.	.58	.60 1965-90

Note: [1] New Zealand is excluded due to missing data.

appears to increase it. These results are entirely consistent with the previous two equations.

In equation 4, codetermination is introduced into an equation with private capital formation. This might be surprising because it didn't work well before, but it has the highest correlation of all the institutional variables with unemployment.[16] This combination also has the virtue of having no multicollinearity problems since these two variables have nearly a zero correlation. The equation shows that both variables reduce unemployment, and are strong and significant.

The time-space distancing of institutions and capital expenditures can be separated in Table 11.[17] This table reports a breakdown of R^2's from the codetermination and private capital expenditure equation. In column 1 we show the R^2's for a cross-sectional analysis of seventeen countries in one year after another from 1978 to 1988. The R^2's tend to be stronger in the 1985 to 1988 period. Columns 2 and 3 show time-series equations for each country. These countries are divided into categories where codetermination varies or it is a constant over the period. Where codetermination is a constant, this institutional variable contributes absolutely nothing to the time-series explanation of unemployment. Two different sets of time-series equations are presented because an eleven year time-series is a little anemic and some equations were not rank order. Nonetheless, the R^2 in column 2 for eleven years estimates how much the time-series results in the various countries contributed to the overall pooled results. The equation shows that the institutional variable has a significant impact on unemployment in four of six countries. Column 3 shows the stronger impact of institutions where they are given more time to vary. These equations are not representative of the pooled analysis, but if more data were available on capital expenditures, these institutional variables would have even a greater chance of showing significance. In twelve of seventeen instances, the R^2s are higher, sometimes much higher. The problem being that while institutions change, some do not change frequently. Consequently, for institutions to have an impact in many countries, the length of each time-series most often needs to be extended.

In sum, the time-space comparison shows that institutions have a strong impact cross-sectionally, but also have some impact over time in the countries where the institutional variable actually varies. The capital expenditure variable has a strong impact in time-series, and it is one that has to be precisely tuned with no lag or very short lags. Its impact in space in the cross-sectional analysis is also moderately strong. Both results are important, because as Firebaugh (1980) demonstrates, the impact of variables in time and space may not only vary in strength but in direction. The institutional and capital expenditure variables in these equations are consistent in time and space (i.e., codetermination and private capital expenditures are negative and significant in both cross-sectional and time-series equations).

DISCUSSION

These results show the strength of institutional variables when controlling for the strong economic effects of capital investment. Certainly capital investment is primary in the sense of providing the actual plant and equipment that an employee needs in order to have a job. However, the institutional variables show that more efficient adjustments to technology brought about by management and labor cooperation in the employment service, works councils and codetermination also have an important effect in reducing unemployment. The one surprise is that self-administration is not effective in reducing unemployment in the 11 years of our study. This may be because the welfare state introduces a reactive rather than pro-active element into the labor market, and welfare programs actually tend to take workers out of jobs rather than guiding them into employment. This would be an example where the content of the policy explicitly works against the cooperative elements of a tri- or bi-partite institution in reducing unemployment.[18]

The nature of the relationships between institutional variables is methodologically problematic. These measures were conceived as part of an institutional complex that promotes cooperation, and were not intended to stand out of context. This is borne out by the high correlations between institutional variables. However, high correlations between independent variables brings up the question of multicollinearity in the first three equations. That is why the last equation in Table 10, a simple examination of one institutional and one capital variable, was used to show the strong effects of both capital and institutions with no multicollinearity problems. Regression analysis may not be the most appropriate method for examining this problem. However, whatever the complications arising from the correlations between institutional variables, one point is clear—institutional variables have an important effect on unemployment rates when controlling for one of the strongest economic variables affecting growth and employment.

In the final evaluation of these results, one must take into the account some of the difficulties in measuring institutions. In attempting to measure institutions dynamically, we faced three types of problems: First, institutions may differ widely between countries, and establishing the functional equivalence of institutions was sometimes very difficult. For example, some countries have tripartite courts that decide issues of union rights to organize, strike, and enforce contracts, and worker rights to social benefits and job security. Tripartite labor courts are summary measures that could provide a dummy variable on the existence of labor courts that is multiplied by a parity factor, but it would not be necessary to multiply by a labor force factor because most people are covered by this court. The U.S. National Labor Relations Board could be considered a tripartite court because of alternating political appointments, but it covers only a very small range of issues, and it does not guarantee labor and management participation at any one time.

However, we did not measured this variable because, if the differences between the NLRB in the United States and tripartite labor courts were not enough, we would need to consider a number of quasi-judicial bodies dealing with arbitration and mediation in Australia and New Zealand. These institutions were almost totally different in structure from labor courts. We initially measured them according to whatever small similarities that could be found by using German labor courts for the scope and range of labor court responsibilities. However, in the end, the resulting variable was too much of a composite variable of three different meanings and not really functionally equivalent.

Second, institutions appeared to be similar in some countries but on closer examination proved to be very different in their strength and impact. For instance, both Germany and Sweden have works council laws. However, on closer examination the powers of the Swedish works councils appeared to be very small and circumscribed. This difference required measurements of the number of issues covered by works councils and an estimate of the consultative or veto powers that each type of works council possessed. This resulted in a parity factor that deflated the value of the Swedish works councils by quite a bit. On the same issue, we decided not to consider the union presence in the Swedish firms to be the functional equivalent of a works council because unionization is not a uniform and legislated right to employee representation. It is an entirely different institution, which is based in civil society but its fluctuating power is not necessarily backed by the state. While unions in Sweden may be strong and influential, they are not universally legislated works councils.

Third, even after examining certain institutions in some countries in detail, variation simply could not be found. On the one hand, the Anglo-Saxon countries has no variation on works councils and codetermination, but this is to be understood. On the other hand, France and other countries sometimes had laws on the books with little or no implementation or sanctioning. The end result for the Anglo-Saxon countries was no variation on the variable in question.

Despite these difficulties, the time and space comparison of institutions has much more impact on cross-sectional than the time-series analysis. Institutional variables like the employment service index varies considerably over time and has a moderate impact in time-series. Codetermination has less variation over time. Clearly, institutions and capital formation in cross-sections have important variations that have definite effects. But over time, institutions only have an effect in those countries that had significant changes. This tended to include the Germanic and Scandinavian countries that increased their worker participation legislation. In the liberal countries, variation on these institutions was nil. Yet, changes over time in the northern European countries contributed to the overall pooled analysis in important ways.

CONCLUSION

Although finding the impact of institutions that constrain and cushion political and economic forces is a difficult task, this paper takes some initial and often successful steps in measuring the impact of labor market institutions on economic performance by focusing on unemployment rates. Some institutional variables changed every year (e.g., the employment service index), while others changed only at specified intervals with legal changes (e.g., codetermination). Nonetheless, each institutional variable contains important space and time variation. This paper pushes labor market institutions toward operationalization in a dynamic panel format. It also tries to measure the institutional context within which labor market institutions operate with five sets of variables.

Much, however, remains to be done. First, the institutional variables need to be further refined with labor force measures and complete analyses of changes from 1950 to the present. Some of these variables are in a rather crude state. Further, a peak corporatism variable needs to be constructed that reflects both capacity to bargain and actual bargaining. Second, the institutional and capital formation variables need to be brought together in a multiplicative rather than an additive index. This could be done by making indexes using canonical correlation to maximize each group of variables with unemployment rates. Third, economic growth and productivity need to be brought into the models with controls for inflation. This will require further intervening variables such as active labor market policies with unemployment rates (Janoski 1996), and industrial conflict mediation to prevent strikes for productivity improvements. Fourth, and a bit more distant, labor market regimes should be constructed from the characteristic features of the labor markets in these 18 countries. This may include some of the variables in the welfare state regime literature, but would also include unique aspects of labor market institutions.

Fifth, much more emphasis needs to be placed on the specifics and theory of labor market regime transformations. A number of transformations are clearly present in history. From 1900 to 1920, labor exchanges and unemployment insurance were introduced in many countries. From 1930 to 1940, many countries engaged in extensive job creation efforts. In the early 1960s and 1970s, job retraining and active labor market policy in general started to take off. And from the mid-1980s to the present, labor market institutions are transforming again in a way that makes the employment service a less and less central institution. Computer networking appears in the future of job exchange, and the state's role here is not entirely clear.

As these changes continue to occur, the institutional relationships discussed in this paper may not hold for the turn of the century. This may cause institutions to be major stumbling blocks in the future. OECD (1986) and Soltwedel (1988) contend that these works council and job security institutions inhibit flexibility and increase unemployment rates. Abraham and Houseman (1994, p. 88) find that works councils working with strong employment services in implementing extensive employment security measures are compatible with firm flexibility and that employers develop alternative strategies for work-place innovations. In any event, institutions can eventually become out of date over time, and the approach of Isaac and Griffin sensitizes us to detecting these changes (Isaac, Carlson, and Mathis 1994). When institutional change is required, institutional imprinting (Stinchcombe 1965) makes for a difficult transition because institutions are often like ocean liners that cannot make sharp and quick turns in a narrow harbor. One should expect that countries that have successful institutions in preventing unemployment may have to go through a difficult transition period of a number of years before new and more effective institutions are rebuilt. Whether this has occurred in Sweden, Germany and other countries is subject to empirical verification, as yet undone.

Developing the motivations and underlying logics of changing labor market regimes is a challenge for the next decade. We believe it needs to be met with the cooperation and planning of both in-depth case studies and cross-national comparisons, and research in a "synthetic analysis" tradition (Ragin 1987). This may require changing incentives for individual researchers about sharing data, and coordinating and improving the organizational forms for social research. Qualitative case studies form the backbone of making institutions dynamic, while quantitative studies of many countries allow statements about the breadth of institutional impact. For synthetic research to advance in this area, the building of institutional cooperation in academia is necessary.

The result of successfully building institutional variables and data sets in the area of the welfare state, we believe, will be the "time-space distancing" of institutional variables into space, and political economy variables into time. Time in advanced industrialized countries is clearly linear and consistent— "time marches on." Space in advanced industrialized countries is a bit more uneven, inconsistent, and particular, whether it is the spaces between individual bodies or the spaces between nation-states—oceans, plains, or mountains. In a sense, space will remain particular despite the advent of E-mail and cellular telephones. Consequently, we believe that we will always live in the interstices of time-generating regularities of generalization, and the space-generating particularities of individual countries. The end result will be a recognition of this time-space sharing of sociological theories of the welfare state rather than "time-space distancing" of past practice, and an increased effort to develop institutional theories about the development of economic performance.

ACKNOWLEDGMENT

A version of this paper was presented at the second session of the Comparative/Historical Sociology Miniconference on Methodology at the American Sociological Association Convention in Washington, D.C. in August, 1995

Günther Schmid, Bernd Reissert, Hugh Mosley, and Jan Johannssen were particularly helpful in the data collection phase of this project. Elizabeth Glennie, Haven White, Rahmah Abdulaleem, and Edward Freyfogel provided research assistance. And we thank Frederik Engelstad, Charles Ragin, and two anonymous reviewers for helpful comments. This project was funded for research assistance by NSF grant SES-92-11542, and funded for travel visits by the Wissenschaftszentrum-Berlin, the Swedish Bicentennial Fund, the Canadian Embassy Grant, and the Duke Center for International Studies.

NOTES

1.   Our concept of "time-space distancing" is used to demonstrate how state-centric and power-resources theories work in their own spheres of cross-sectional and time-series analysis. This term draws from Giddens' "time-space distanciation" term (Giddens 1979, pp. 198-233; and 1981, pp. 4-5, 26-48, 90-97). Giddens defines time-space distanciation as "The stretching of social systems across time-space, on the basis of mechanisms of social and system integration" (1984, p. 377). He further states that it refers to "the modes in which such 'stretching' takes place" or "how social systems are 'embedded' in time and space" (1981, pp. 4-5). His use is attempting to compare very different societies. In advanced industrialized societies, time is hegemonically imposed by the demands of global capitalism and international communications technologies. The availability of yearbooks and economic information attest to this fact. In the end, we refer to the distancing of theories and methods rather than the distanciation of social systems.

2.   For more general and detailed reviews of institutional theories, see Dugger (1992), Eggertsson (1990), Hodgson (1989), Knight (1992), and Powell and DiMaggio (1991).

3.   This approach to institutions can be seen in the works of Selznick (1949, 1957), Gouldner (1954), and the early Homans (1950).

4.   The twelve countries are Austria, Belgium, France, Finland, Germany, Italy, Netherlands, Portugal, Spain, Switzerland, Sweden and the United Kingdom, and the nine time periods are 1870, 1900, 1914, 1925, 1938, 1950, 1963, 1975, and 1990.

5.   Campbell and associates' categories will also require considerable adjustment in comparative social policy, especially with the integration of voluntary associations (e.g., trade union and advocacy groups for the disadvantaged) into the theoretical framework. In each case, profit will cease to become a major consideration and the focus will shift to internal political motivation, public symbols, and budgets and fund-raising efforts for organizational and social movement survival

6.   Peak corporatism has gone by many different names including "neo-corporatism," "democratic-corporatism," and "societal corporatism" (see Wilensky 1976; Regini 1995) We are taking the term "societal corporatism" and giving it a more decentralized meaning.

7.   This knowledge is much larger than firms in countries without codetermination; however, in many European countries, firms can conceal assets. American accounting procedures require a much fuller disclosure of assets. When the Daimler-Benz corporation sought funds through the New York Stock Exchange, they had to use American accounting practices and this revealed that they had been covering up losses with secret asset accounts for a number of years. These secret asset accounts are not reported to the corporate boards and the labor representatives on them.

8.   The precise measurement of lags must be left to further work. It is entirely conceivable that the institutional variables operate with a distributed lag of five years (i.e., Almon lags). The investment variables tend to quickly decline over time (i.e., Koyck lags), but one would have to separate the effects of construction employment concerning new plants and equipment, and the subsequent effect of hiring new employees to operate an expanded business period (see Janoski 1990, pp. 234-249).

9.   Unemployment is often referred to as frictional, structural, and demand induced. The employment service is generally considered to be concerned with mismatches the labor market (i.e., frictional unemployment), but many employment services implement structural and demand oriented unemployment policies. Other institutions are mainly focused on labor demand (increasing the number of jobs), rather than labor supply (eliminating labor bottlenecks). Our data, however, do not lend themselves to testing these differences in unemployment rates.

10.   Austria had low unemployment rates, while New Zealand and Denmark fluctuate from low to moderate unemployment rates (OECDb 1995, pp. 44-45).

11.   Active labor market policy would also be an intervening variable in further analyses (i.e., strong institutions create strong social policy expenditures that then have an impact on unemployment). We will do this analysis in a more complicated paper at a latter date.

12.   Countries reported firm size in diverse ways. As a result, cross-national data from OECD or UN did not exist. The only reports were from Eurostat (1991, 1992), which only covered two years

13.   Further disaggregation may be needed in these measures to encompass the full range of OECD countries. For instance, the United States is not well captured by the "0" category of industry level bargaining without coordination. Also the ordering of items 1, 2 and 3 in the government involvement scale could well be questioned. However, these are small criticisms given the fact that the authors are well on the right track to greatly improve the measurement of corporatism over time.

14.   The extension of union collective bargaining agreements to the non-unionized sector is also very important (OECD 1994). In some countries, collective bargaining agreements are automatically applied to the non-unionized sector.

15.   Other institutional variables that focus on capital expenditures and investment can also be created. For instance, the structures of taxation in terms of using general revenues or insurance-type contributions have an important impact (Schmid, Reissert, and Bruche 1992). Keynesian policies pursued through government spending, especially on job creation policies and overall increases in government spending, are certainly increased by public capital expenditures. Many of these other variables are important because they increase capital formation (e.g., lower capital gains taxation and a higher money supply increase capital). Finally, institutional variables can be addressed in the structure of financial markets and the banking system.

16.   The same equation with the employment service index and private capital formation does not produce significant results for either variable. Thus, while the employment service index shows consistent change over time, simple variation does ensure a high correlation or regression coefficient.

17.   We do not present a complete separation of time and space because that would require showing the complete results for twenty-eight equations (17 countries in all 11 years).

18.   Current welfare reforms in the United States attempt to correct for this effect with a rigorous attempt to cut eligibility for welfare and force people into the labor market.

REFERENCES

Abraham, K., and S. Houseman. 1994. "Does Employment Protection Inhibit Labor Market Flexibility? Lessons from Germany, France, and Belgium." Pp. 58-93 in *Social Protection versus Economic Flexibility*, edited by Rebecca Blank. Chicago: University of Chicago Press.

Alvarez, R.M., G. Garrett, and P. Lange. 1991. "Government Partisanship, Labor Organization, and Macroeconomic Performance." *American Political Science Review* 85(2): 539-556.

Bamber, G., and R. Lansbury. 1993. *International and Comparative Industrial Relations*, 2nd Ed. London: Allen Unwin.

Boreham, P., and H. Compston. 1992. "Labour Movement Organization and Political Intervention: The Politics of Unemployment in the OECD Countries, 1974-86." *European Journal of Political Research* 22: 143-170.

Burstein, P. 1991. "Policy Domains: Organization, Culture, and Policy Outcomes." *Annual Review of Sociology* 17: 327-350.

Buse, A. 1973. "Goodness of Fit in Generalized Least Squares Estimation." *American Statistician* 27: 106-108.

_____. 1979. "Goodness of Fit in the Seemingly Unrelated Regressions Model." *Journal of Econometrics* 10: 109-113.

Bruno, M., and J. Sachs. 1985. *Economics of Worldwide Stagflation*. Cambridge: Harvard University Press.

Calmfors, L., and D.J. Driffill. 1988. "Bargaining Structure, Corporatism and Macro-Economic Performance." *Economic Policy* 6.

Cameron, D. 1984. "Social Democracy, Corporatism, Labour Quiescence and the Representation of Economic Interest in Advanced Capitalist Society." In *Order and Conflict in Contemporary Capitalism*, edited by John Goldthorpe. Oxford: Clarendon Press.

Campbell, J., J.R. Hollingsworth, and L. Lindberg. 1991. *Governance of the American Economy*. Cambridge: Cambridge University Press.

Commons, J.R. 1934. *Institutional Economics: Its Place in Political Economy*. New York: Macmillan.

Crouch, C. 1992. *Industrial Relations and European State Traditions*. Oxford: Clarendon Press.

―――――. 1990. "Generalized Political Exchange in Industrial Relations in Europe during the Twentieth Century." Pp. 69-116 in *Governance and Generalized Exchange: Self-Organizing Policy Networks in Action*, edited by Bernd Marin. Boulder, CO: Westview Press.

Crouch, C., and R. Dore. 1990. "Whatever Happened to Corporatism?" Pp. 1-44 in *Corporatism and Accountability*, edited by Colin Crouch and Ronald Dore. Oxford: Clarendon.

DiMaggio, P. 1988. "Interest and Agency in Institutional Theory." Pp. 3-22 in *Institutional Patterns and Organizations: Culture and Environment*. Cambridge: Ballinger.

―――――. 1994. "Culture and Economy." *Handbook of Economic Sociology*, edited by Neil Smelser and Richard Swedberg. New York: Russell Sage Foundation.

DiMaggio, P., and W. Powell. 1983. "The Iron Cage Revisited: Institutional Isomorphism and Collective Rationality in Organizational Fields." *American Sociological Review* 48: 147-160.

Dugger, W.M. 1992. *Underground Economics: A Decade of Institutionalist Dissent*. Armonk, NY: Sharpe.

Eggertsson, T. 1990. *Economic Behavior and Institutions*. Cambridge: Cambridge University Press.

Ekeh, P. 1974. *Social Exchange Theory: The Two Traditions*. Cambridge: Harvard University Press.

Esping-Andersen, G. 1990. *Three Worlds of Welfare Capitalism*. Princeton, NJ: Princeton University Press.

Etzioni, A. 1988. *The Moral Dimension: Towards a New Economics*. New York: Free Press.

―――――. 1986. "Mixed Scanning Revisited." *Public Administration Review* 46(1): 159-183.

EUROSTAT. 1991. *Enterprises in Europe*. Luxembourg: Commission of the European Communities, EUROSTAT.

―――――. 1992. *Enterprises in Europe, Second Report*. Luxembourg: Commission of the European Communities, EUROSTAT.

Ferner, A., and R. Hyman. 1992. *Industrial Relations in the New Europe*. Oxford: Blackwell.

Firebaugh, G. 1980. "Cross-national Versus Historical Regression Models: Conditions of Equivalence in Comparative Analysis." *Comparative Social Research* 3: 333-344.

Fligstein, N. 1990. *The Transformation of Corporate Control*. Cambridge: Harvard University Press.

Flora, P. 1987. *Growth to Limits, Volumes 1-4*. Berlin: De Gruyter.

Freeman, R. 1988. "Labour Market Institutions and Economic Performance." *Economic Policy* (April): 63-80.

Furubotn, E., and R. Richter. 1993. "The New Institutional Economics: Recent Progress; Expanding Frontiers." *Journal of Institutional and Theoretical Economics* 149(1): 1-10.

Giddens, A. 1981. *A Contemporary Critique of Historical Materialism*. Berkeley: University of California Press.

―――――. 1979. *Central Problems in Social Theory*. Berkeley: University of California Press.

―――――. 1984. *The Constitution of Society*. Berkeley: University of California Press.

Golden, M., P. Lange, and M. Wallerstein. 1993. "Trade Unions, Employers' Organizations and Collective Bargaining: Data Collection and Analysis for Nineteen Countries." NSF Proposal, January.

Gouldner, A. 1954. *Patterns of Industrial Bureaucracy*. New York: Free Press.

Hartog, J., and J. Theeuwes. 1993. *Labour Market Contracts and Institutions*. Amsterdam: North-Holland.

Heady, B. 1970. "Trade Unions and National Wage Policies." *Journal of Politics* 32: 407-439.

Henley, A., and E. Tsakalotos. 1995. "Unemployment Experience and the Institutional Preconditions for Full Employment." Pp. 176-201 in *The Political Economy of Full Employment*, edited by Philip Arestis and Mike Marshall. Aldershot: Edward Elgar.

Hicks, A. 1995a. "Introduction to Pooling." Pp. 169-188 in *The Comparative Political Economy of the Welfare State*, edited by Thomas Janoski and Alexander Hicks. Cambridge: Cambridge University Press.

_____. 1995b. "The Social Democratic Corporatist Model of Economic Peformance in Short- and Medium-run Perspective." Pp. 189-217 in *The Comparative Political Economy of the Welfare State*, edited by Thomas Janoski and Alexander Hicks. Cambridge: Cambridge University Press.

Hicks, A., and J. Misra. 1993. "Political Resources and the Expansion of Welfare Effort." *American Journal of Sociology* 99: 668-710.

Hicks, A., and D. Swank. 1992. "Politics, Institutions and Welfare Effort." *American Political Science Review* 86: 658-674.

Hodgson, G. 1989. *Economics and Institutions*. Cambridge: Polity Press.

Hollingsworth, J.R., P. Schmitter, and W. Streeck. 1994. *Governing Capitalist Economies*. New York: Oxford University Press.

Homans, G. 1950. *The Human Group*. New York: Harcourt Brace World.

Huber, E., C. Ragin, and J. Stephens. 1993. "Social Democracy, Christian Democracy, Constitutional Structure, and the Welfare State." *American Journal of Sociology* 99(3): 711-749.

Isaac, L., S. Carlson, and M. Mathis. 1994. "Quality of Quantity in Comparative/Historical Analysis." Pp. 93-135 in *The Comparative Political Economy of the Welfare State* edited by Thomas Janoski and Alexander Hicks. New York: Cambridge University Press.

Janoski, T. 1990. *The Political Economy of Unemployment*. Berkeley: University of California Press.

_____. 1994. "Direct State Intervention in the Labor Market." Pp. 54-92 in *The Comparative Political Economy of the Welfare State*. New York: Cambridge University Press.

_____. 1996. "Explaining State Intervention to Prevent Unemployment: The Impact of Institutions on Active Labor Market Policy Expenditures in Eighteen Countries." Pp. 697-724 in *The International Handbook of Labor Market Policy and Evaluation*, edited by G. Schmid, C. Büchtemann, J. O'Reilly and Klaus Schümann. Aldershot: Edward Elgar.

Judge, G.G., W.E. Griffiths, R.C. Hill, and T.C. Lee. 1980. *Theory and Practice of Econometrics*, 2nd Ed. New York: Wiley.

Kennedy, T. 1980. *European Labor Relations*. Lexington, MA: Lexington Books

Kenworthy, L. 1995. *In Search of National Eclonomic Success*. Thousand Oaks, CA: Sage.

Kmenta, J. 1988. *Elements of Econometrics*, 2nd Ed. New York: Macmillan.

Knight, J. 1992. *Institutions and Social Conflict*. New York: Cambridge University Press.

Knoke, D., F. Pappi, J. Broadbent, N. Kaufman, and Y. Tsujinaka. 1996. *Comparing Policy Networks: Labor Politics in the U.S., Germany and Japan*. Cambridge: Cambridge University Press.

Korpi, W. 1989. "Power, Politics and State Autonomy in the Development of Social Citizenship." *American Sociological Review* 54: 309-328.

Lange, P., M. Wallerstein, and M. Golden. 1991. "Union Centralization Among Advanced Industrial Societies: An Empirical Study." NSF Proposal, January.

Lijphart, A., and M. Crepaz. 1991. "Corporatism and Consensus Democracy in Eighteen Countries: Conceptual and Empirical Linkages." *British Journal of Political Science* 21:235-56.

Locke, R., T. Kocan, and M. Piore. 1996. *Employment Relations in a Changing World.* Cambridge: MIT

March, J., and J. Olsen. 1984. "The New Institutionalism: Organizational Factors in Political Life." *American Political Science Review* 78(3): 734-749.

_____. 1989. *Rediscovering Institutions: The Organizational Basis of Politics.* New York: Free Press.

Marin, B. 1990a. *Governance and Generalized Exchange: Self-Organizing Policy Networks in Action.* Boulder, CO: Westview Press.

_____. 1990b. *Generalized Political Exchange: Antagonistic Cooperation and Integrated Policy Circuits.* Boulder, CO: Westview Press.

North, D. 1990. *Institutions, Institutional Change and Economic Performance.* New York: Cambridge University Press.

OECD. 1986. *Flexibility in the Labour Market: The Current Debate.* Paris: OECD.

_____. 1991. "Unemployment Benefit Rules and Labour Market Policy." Pp. 199-231 in the *Employment Outlook.* Paris: OECD.

_____. 1994. "Collective Bargaining: Trends and Coverage." *Employment Outlook* (July): 167-194.

_____. 1995a. *National Accounts Statistics: Main Aggregates* Paris: OECD.

_____. 1995b. *December. OECD Economic Outlook.* Paris: OECD.

Orloff, A.S. 1993. *The Politics of Pensions.* Madison: University of Wisconsin.

Powell, W., and P. DiMaggio. 1991. *The New Institutionalism in Organizational Analysis.* Chicago: University of Chicago Press.

Ragin, C. 1987. *The Comparative Method.* Berkeley: University of California Press.

Regini, M. 1995. *Uncertain Boundaries: The Social and Political Construction of European Economies.* Cambridge: Cambridge University Press.

SAS. 1991. *The Econometric Statistics Manual.* Cary: SAS Institute.

Schmid, G., B. Reissert, and G. Bruche. 1992. *Unemployment Insurance and Active Labor Market Policy.* Detroit, Wayne State University Press.

Schmitter, P. 1982. "Reflections on Where the Theory of Neo-Corporatism has Gone and Where the Praxis of Neo-corporatism May be Going." In *Patterns of Corporatist Policy-Making*, edited by Gerhard Lehmbruch and Philippe Schmitter. London: Sage.

_____. 1981. "Interest Intermediation and Regime Governability in Contemporary Western Europe and North America." In *Organizing Interests in Western Europe*, edited by Suzanne Berger. Cambridge: Cambridge University Press.

Selznick, P. 1949. *The TVA and the Grassroots.* Berkeley: University of California Press.

_____. 1957. *Leadership in Administration.* New York: Harper and Row.

SHAZAM. 1993. *Shazam User's Reference Manual, Version 7.0.* New York: McGraw-Hill.

Sisson, K. 1987. *The Management of Collective Bargaining.* Oxford: Blackwell.

Skocpol, T. 1993. *Protecting Soldiers and Mothers.* Cambridge: Harvard University Press.

Soltwedel, R. 1988. "Employment Problems in West Germany: The Role of Institutions, Labor Law, and Government Intervention." *Carnegie-Rochester Conference Series on Public Policy* 28:153-220.

Steinmo, S., K. Thelen, F. Longstreth. 1992. *Structuring Politics: Historical Institutionalism in Comparative Analysis.* Cambridge: Cambridge University Press.

Stimson, J. 1985. "Regression in Space and Time: A Statistical Essay." *American Journal of Political Science* 29: 915-947.

Stinchcombe, A. 1965. "Social Structure and Organizations." Pp. 142-93 in *Handbook of Organizations*, edited by James March. Chicago: Rand-McNally.

Streeck, W. 1992. *Social Institutions and Economic Performance*. London: Sage.

Sugden, R. 1986. *The Economics of Rights, Co-Operation and Welfare*. Oxford: Basil Blackwell.

Thelen, K., and S. Steinmo. 1992. "Historical Institutionalism in Comparative Politics." Pp. 1-32 in *Structuring Politics*, edited by Sven Steinmo, Kathleen Thelen and Frank Longstreth. Cambridge: Cambridge University Press.

Therborn, G. 1986. *Why Some Peoples are More Unemployed than Others*. London: Verso.

Veblen, T. 1904. *The Theory of Business Enterprise*. New York: Scribner.

Western, B. 1991. "A Comparative Study of Corporatist Development." *American Sociological Review* 56: 283-294.

Wilensky, H. 1976. *The New Corporatism, Centralization and the Welfare State Professional Papers in Contemporary Political Sociology*, No. 06-020. Beverly Hills: Sage.

Williamson, O. 1975. *Markets and Hierarchies*. New York: Free Press.

———. 1985. *The Economic Institutions of Capitalism*. New York: Free Press.

———. 1986. *Economic Organization*. New York: New York University Press.

Zucker, L. 1977. "The Role of Institutionalization in Cultural Persistence." *American Sociological Review* 42: 726-743.

———. 1983. "Organizations as Institutions" Pp. 1-42 in *Research in the Sociology of Organizations*, edited by S B. Bacharach. Greenwich, CT: JAI Press.

———. 1991. "Institutional Theories of Organization." *Annual Review of Sociology* 13: 443-464.

Zucker, L., and M. Meyer. 1989. *Permanently Failing Organizations*. Newbury Park, CA: Sage.

Comparative Social Research

Edited by **Fredrik Engelstad,**
Institute for Social Research, Oslo, Norway

**Volume 15, Institutional Aspects of Work
and Wage Determination**
1996, 257 pp. $73.25
ISBN 1-55938-649-5

CONTENTS: Introduction, *Fredrik Engelstad and Lars Mjoset.*
The Vicious Circle of the Welfare State? Women's Labour
Market Situation in Norway and Great Britain, *Marianne Nordli
Hansen.* The Indispensable Role of Culture. Explaining Differ-
ent Understandings of Work Through a Comparison of Ger-
man and Norwegian Factories, *Karl Henrik Sivesind.* The
Segmentation of Transitions from School to Work in Postwar
Germany: A Dynamic Perspective, *Klaus Schömann, Hans-
Peter Blossfeld, and Michael T. Hanan.* Organizations and
Wage Determination in Norway: A Multi-Level Approach, *Arne
L. Kalleberg and Peter V. Marsden.* Wage Determination and
the Male-Female Wage Gap: The Case of Norway, *Geir
Hogsnes.* Wage and Income Inequality in Two Welfare States:
Australia and Sweden, *Johan Fritzell and Peter Saunders.*
Global Market Modernization and Institutional Change. Case
Studies From Family Firms in the Fishing Industry, *Age Mari-
ussen*

Also Available:
Volumes 1-14 (1978-1994)
  + Supplement 1 (1990) $73.25 each

FACULTY/PROFESSIONAL discounts are available in
the U.S. and Canada at a rate of 40% off the list price
when prepaid by personal check or credit card and
ordered directly from the publisher.

JAI PRESS INC.
55 Old Post Road No. 2 - P.O. Box 1678
Greenwich, Connecticut 06836-1678
Tel: (203) 661- 7602   Fax: (203) 661-0792

J
A
I

P
R
E
S
S

J A I   P R E S S

International Review of Comparative Public Policy

Edited by **Nicholas Mercuro,** *Department of Economics and Finance, University of New Orleans*

Volume 7, Social Costs of Economic Transformation in Central Europe
1996, 245 pp. $73.25
ISBN 0-7623-0153-8

Edited by **János Mátyás Kovács,**
Institute for Human Sciences, Vienna, Austria

Also Available:
Volumes 1-6 (1990-1996) $73.25 each